Macmillan Secondary Mathematics

Student's Book 2

Geoffrey Buckwell • Edith Karaimu • Felicita Njuguna
Robert Solomon • Frederick Songole

MACMILLAN
KENYA

First published 2000 by
MACMILLAN KENYA PUBLISHERS LTD
Kijabe Street
PO Box 30797
Nairobi

ISBN 9966-945-18-0

10   9   8   7   6   5   4   3   2   1
09 08 07 06 05 04 03 02 01 00

This book is printed on paper suitable for recycling and
made from fully managed and sustained forest sources.

Printed in Hong Kong

Illustrations by M. Buckwell

Contents

Introduction

This book is the second of a series written for Kenyan secondary schools. It covers the mathematics syllabus required for the Kenyan Certificate of Secondary Education. This book deals with the material for Form 2 of secondary school, and next two books will cover the next two years. The books are written to fit the society, economy and education of Kenya, and an expert team of consultants has ensured that the text is appropriate for pupils in Kenyan schools.

This book is divided into 21 units. Each unit contains the following features.

- **This unit uses**   This is a short list of material, which has been previously covered, which will be used in the unit.
- **Explanation**   The topics of the unit are defined and explained. Important points are indicated with blue notes.
- **Examples**   There are many worked examples to show you how to solve questions on the topics of the unit.
- **Exercises**   Plenty of exercises are provided, carefully graded, for you to gain skills in the topics of the unit.
- **Summary**   A summary near the end of each unit lists the topics that have been covered.
- **Activities**   These contain material for you to explore. Often there is no single correct answer to be found.
- **Progress exercises**   These are questions similar to those in the unit itself.
- **Puzzles**   These questions are different from those in the unit. Often they introduce later work, or investigate a different area of mathematics.

In addition there are four sets of Consolidation exercises, answers to the questions in the main parts of the chapters, and mathematical tables.

Mathematics is used in all parts of life. It is needed in business, science, engineering and many other careers. But mathematics is not just about being successful at work. It is a huge body of abstract knowledge which describes the world we live in. To understand the world you need to understand mathematics.

1 Straight line equations

This unit uses
- Coordinates of points
- Ratios

1.1 Gradients

The **gradient** or **slope** of a path tells us how steep it is.
Suppose a straight path joins two points on different levels.
The **rise** is the vertical distance between the two points.
The **run** is the horizontal difference between the points.
The gradient is the ratio of the rise to the run.

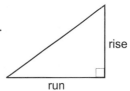

$$\text{gradient} = \frac{\text{vertical distance}}{\text{horizontal distance}} = \frac{\text{rise}}{\text{run}}$$

EXAMPLE 1

A straight path up a hill rises 4 m for a horizontal distance of 20 m.
(a) Find the gradient of the path.
(b) For this path, what is the rise for a horizontal distance of 45 m?

Solution
(a) Divide the rise by the run. $4 \div 20 = 0.2$.
   The gradient is 0.2.

(b) The run and the gradient are on the base
   of the triangle. To find the rise, multiply
   the run by the gradient.
   $0.2 \times 45 = 9$
   The rise is 9 m.

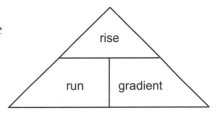

EXAMPLE 2

The distance along a straight path is 100 m, and it
rises 28 m. Find the gradient of the path.

Solution
The length along the path, the run and the rise
form a right-angled triangle. Use Pythagoras'
theorem to find the run.

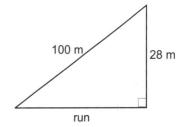

$$100^2 = 28^2 + \text{run}^2$$
$$\text{run}^2 = 100^2 - 28^2$$
$$= 10\,000 - 784 = 9216$$

So the run is $\sqrt{9216} = 96$ m.   Use square root tables
Divide this into the rise.

$$28 \div 96 = \tfrac{7}{24}$$

The gradient is $\tfrac{7}{24}$.

Exercise 1.1A

1   A straight road rises 2 m for 75 m horizontal distance. What is the gradient of the road?

2   Each stair of a staircase has a rise of 15 cm and a run of 20 cm. What is the gradient of the staircase?

3   The gradient of a road is $\tfrac{1}{20}$. What is the rise for a run of 200 m?

4   For the road of question **3**, what is the run for a rise of 2 m?

5   A ladder leans against a wall. The top of the ladder is 2 m off the ground, and the base of the ladder is 0.5 m from the base of the wall. Find the slope of the ladder.

Gradients using coordinates

The diagram shows two points A and B on a grid. The rise of the line AB is the y change between A and B, and the run is the x change. So the gradient of the line AB is the ratio of the y change to the x change.

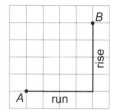

$$\text{gradient} = \frac{y \text{ change}}{x \text{ change}}$$

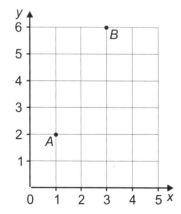

To find the y change, subtract the y coordinates. To find the x change, subtract the x coordinates. If A is at $(1, 2)$ and B is at $(3, 6)$, then the gradient is

$$\text{gradient} = \frac{y \text{ change}}{x \text{ change}} = \frac{6 - 2}{3 - 1} = \frac{4}{2} = 2$$

So the gradient of AB is 2.

Note Here we subtracted the coordinates of A from those of B. We would get the same result if we subtracted the coordinates of B from those of A.

$$\text{gradient} = \frac{y \text{ change}}{x \text{ change}} = \frac{2 - 6}{1 - 3} = \frac{-4}{-2} = 2 \qquad \text{Remember: } -4 \div -2 = +2$$

It doesn't matter whether you take the coordinates of B from the coordinates of A, or the coordinates of A from the coordinates of B. But you must be consistent. You *cannot* take A's y coordinate from B's y coordinate, then take B's x coordinate from A's x coordinate.

EXAMPLE 3

Find the gradient of the lines joining
(a) $(1, 3)$ and $(2, 7)$ (b) $(4, 1)$ and $(-1, 11)$

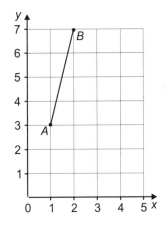

Solution
(a) Use the formula

$$\text{gradient} = \frac{y \text{ change}}{x \text{ change}} = \frac{7 - 3}{2 - 1} = \frac{4}{1} = 4$$

The gradient is 4.
The diagram shows the graph of the line joining the points. Notice that it is sloping *upwards*.

(b) Use the formula

$$\text{gradient} = \frac{y \text{ change}}{x \text{ change}} = \frac{11 - 1}{-1 - 4} = \frac{10}{-5} = -2$$

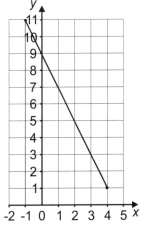

The gradient is -2.
The diagram shows the graph of the line joining the points. Notice that it is sloping *downwards*.

In general, if the gradient is positive, then the line slopes upwards going from left to right. If the gradient is negative, then the line slopes downwards going from left to right.

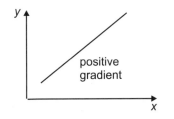

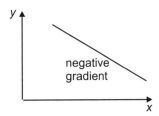

EXAMPLE 4

The gradient of the line joining (2, 3) and (4, k) is 2. Find k.

Solution

Use the formula for gradient. This gives an equation in k.

$$\frac{k-3}{4-2} = 2$$

$$\frac{k-3}{2} = 2$$

$$k - 3 = 4$$

$$k = 7.$$

Exercise 1.1B

1 Find the gradients of the lines joining these pairs of points.
  a (1, 1) and (2, 5) **b** (1, 2) and (4, 7) **c** (4, 4) and (3, 1)
  d (5, 1) and (2, –2) **e** (1.2, 2.4) and (1.3, 2.7) **f** $(0, \frac{1}{2})$ and $(\frac{1}{2}, \frac{3}{4})$
  g (–3, 4) and (3, –2) **h** (4, –2) and (–1, 0)
  i (–2, –3) and (–4, –7) **j** (3, 2) and (5, 2)

2 Try to find the gradient of the line joining (2, 5) and (2, 7). Explain with a diagram what has gone wrong.

3 The line joining (1, 1) and (3, k) has gradient 3. Find k.

4 The line joining (2, –3) and (k, 5) has gradient –2. Find k.

5 The line joining (0, 1) and (k, k) has gradient $\frac{1}{2}$. Find k.

6 The line joining (–2, 3) and (k, 7) has gradient 2. Find k.

7 The line joining (2, –4) and (1, k) has gradient –3. Find k.

8 The line joining (–5, –3) and (k, k) has gradient 3. Find k.

1.2

The diagram shows the graph of $y = 2x + 1$. Six points on the line are

$A(0, 1)$ $B(1, 3)$ $C(2, 5)$
$D(3, 7)$ $E(4, 9)$ $F(5, 11)$

The gradient of AB is

$$\text{gradient} = \frac{y \text{ change}}{x \text{ change}} = \frac{3-1}{1-0} = \frac{2}{1} = 2$$

The gradient of CF is

$$\text{gradient} = \frac{y \text{ change}}{x \text{ change}} = \frac{11-5}{5-2} = \frac{6}{3} = 2$$

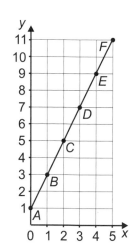

Exercise 1.2A

For the points A to F above, find the gradients of
a BC **b** DE **c** BE **d** AF

All your answers to the questions above should be 2. For any two points X and Y on the line $y = 2x + 1$, the gradient of XY is 2.
Now take the line $y = 3x - 2$ in the next exercise.

Exercise 1.2B

1 Fill in this table for the line $y = 3x - 2$.

Point	A	B	C	D	E	F
x-value	0	1	2	3	4	5
y-value	-2				10	

2 Find the gradients of the following.
   a BC **b** CF **c** BF **d** AB **e** AF

You should find that the gradient in all the questions above is 3. This is the gradient of the line $y = 3x - 2$.
Putting our results together:

the gradient of $y = 2x + 1$ is 2
the gradient of $y = 3x - 2$ is 3

In general, the gradient of $y = mx + c$ is m. (Here m and c are constant)
Note The equation must be in the form $y = mx + c$. If there is a number multiplying y, then divide by the number. The next example shows the method.

EXAMPLE 5

Find the gradient of the line $2y = 3x + 1$.

Solution
First get the equation in the form $y = mx + c$, by dividing both sides by 2.

$$y = 1\tfrac{1}{2}x + \tfrac{1}{2}$$

The gradient is $1\tfrac{1}{2}$.

Exercise 1.2C

1 Find the gradients of these lines.
   a $y = 4x - 5$ **b** $y = -3x + 4$ **c** $y = \tfrac{2}{3}x + \tfrac{1}{2}$
   d $2y = 5x + 1$ **e** $3y = 2x - 7$ **f** $3y = 5x + 2$
   g $x + y = 3$ **h** $2x + 3y = 5$ **i** $5y - x = 4$
   j $\tfrac{1}{2}y + \tfrac{1}{3}x = 9$ **k** $\tfrac{3}{8}y - \tfrac{1}{5}x = 7$ **l** $1\tfrac{2}{3}y + \tfrac{3}{4}x = 2$

2 Find the gradients of the lines in this diagram.

3 The gradient of the line $ky + x = 3$ is $-\frac{1}{6}$. Find k.

4 The gradient of the line $4y + kx = 3$ is 5. Find k.

5 The gradient of the line $ky = 3x + 2$ is 6. Find k.

6 The gradient of the line $y + kx = 6$ is $-\frac{1}{2}$. Find k.

7 The gradient of the line $ky = (k + 1)x + 7$ is 2. Find k.

8 The gradient of the line $ky + (2k + 3)x = 4$ is 5. Find k.

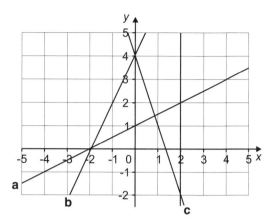

Intercepts

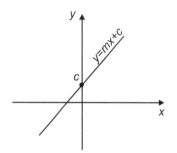

Consider again the equation $y = 2x + 1$. It crosses the y-axis when $x = 0$. The value of y is given by
$$y = 2 \times 0 + 1 = 1$$
Similarly the line $y = 3x - 2$ crosses the y-axis when
$$y = 3 \times 0 - 2 = -2$$
In general, the line $y = mx + c$ crosses the y-axis when $x = 0$, and the value of y is
$$y = m \times 0 + c = c$$

The value of c is the **y–intercept**.
Note The y-intercept is the value of y when the line crosses the y-axis.
Similarly, the x-intercept is the value of x when the line crosses the x-axis.

EXAMPLE 6

Find where the line $3y = 4x - 2$ crosses the y-axis.

Solution
First write in the form $y = mx + c$ by dividing both sides by 3.
$$y = \tfrac{4}{3}x - \tfrac{2}{3}$$
The line crosses the y-axis at $y = -\tfrac{2}{3}$.

Exercise 1.2D

1 Find the y-intercepts for the following lines.

   a $y = 3x + 5$ **b** $y = 2x - 3$ **c** $y = -\tfrac{1}{2}x + \tfrac{2}{3}$

   d $y = 3x - \tfrac{3}{8}$ **e** $2y = 4x + 3$ **f** $3y = 2x + 1$

g $y + 2x + 3 = 0$ **h** $2y - 4x - 5 = 0$ **i** $2x - 3y - 2 = 0$

j $\frac{1}{2}y + \frac{1}{4}x = 7$

2   The y-intercept of $y = 2x + k$ is 7. Find k.

3   The y-intercept of $ky + 3x = 4$ is 12. Find k.

4   The y-intercept of $ky = 2x + k + 1$ is 2. Find k.

5   The y-intercept of $(k + 3)y = 4x + 2k$ is 6. Find k.

6   For the equation $y = 4x + 12$, find the value of x when $y = 0$. (The x-intercept of the line, where it crosses the x-axis.)

7   Find the x-intercepts for the following lines.

a $y = 3x - 6$ **b** $y = -5x + 2$

c $y = -2x - 1$ **d** $3y + 2x = 12$

e $-3y + 4x = 7$ **f** $7y = 8 - 3x$

8   The line $y = kx + 10$ has x-intercept 5. Find k.

9   The line $2y = 3x + k$ has x-intercept -0.5. Find k.

10   The line $y = kx - k + 2$ has x-intercept 4. Find k.

1.3   Finding the equation of a straight line

The equation of a straight line is of the form $y = mx + c$, where m is the gradient and c is the y-intercept. You can find the equation if you know any of these:

- The gradient and the y–intercept
- The gradient and a point on the line
- Two points on the line

EXAMPLE 7

Find the equations of these lines.

   (a) Gradient 5 and y-intercept 3
   (b) Gradient 3 and through $(4, -1)$
   (c) Through $(3, 4)$ and $(5, 0)$

Solution

(a) In the equation $y = mx + c$ put $m = 5$ and $c = 3$.
   The equation is $y = 5x + 3$

(b) Put $m = 3$. The equation is $y = 3x + c$. The line goes through $(4, -1)$, so put $x = 4$ and $y = -1$.

$$-1 = 3 \times 4 + c$$
$$-1 = 12 + c$$
$$-13 = c$$

   The equation is $y = 3x - 13$

(c) Find the gradient of the line joining $(3, 4)$ and $(5, 0)$.

$$\text{gradient} = \frac{0 - 4}{5 - 3} = \frac{-4}{2} = -2$$

The equation is $y = -2x + c$. The line goes through (3, 4), so put $x = 3$ and $y = 4$

$$4 = -2 \times 3 + c$$
$$4 = -6 + c$$
$$10 = c$$

The equation of a straight line is $y = mx + c$, where m is the gradient. We have found that $m = -2$. Hence the equation is $y = -2x + 10$

Check We used the first point to find c. Use the second point, (5, 0), to check the result. Put $x = 5$.

$$y = -2 \times 5 + 10 = -10 + 10 = 0. \text{ This is correct.}$$

EXAMPLE 8

Sketch the graph of $y = 2x - 1$.

Solution
The y-intercept is -1, so mark $(0, -1)$ on the graph.
The gradient is 2, so the graph will rise by 2 from $x = 0$ to $x = 1$. Mark $(1, 1)$ on the graph.
Join up with a straight line as in the diagram.

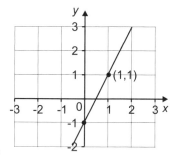

Note The graph can also be drawn using a table of values. For the line $y = 2x - 1$, the table is below.

x	-1	0	1	2	3
$2x$	-2	0	2	4	6
y	-3	-1	1	3	5

Exercise 1.3

1 Find the equations of these lines.
   a Gradient 2 and y-intercept -4.
   b Gradient $-\frac{3}{4}$ and y-intercept 2
   c Gradient 3, through the point (3, 2)
   d Gradient -2, through the point (4, -1)
2 Find the equations of the lines through the following pairs of points.
   a (1, 1) and (4, 7)   b (4, 1) and (2, 9)   c (2, 3) and (5, 9)
   d (5, 2) and (2, 5)   e (-1, 2) and (-5, -6)   f $(0, \frac{1}{2})$ and $(1, \frac{3}{4})$
   g (1.3, 2.8) and (1.5, 3.4)   h (101, 223) and (97, 199)
3 Find the equations of the lines in question **2** of Exercise 1.2C.
4 Sketch the graphs of these straight lines.
   a $y = 3x + 1$ b $y = -2x + 3$ c $y = \frac{1}{2}x + 1$
   d $y = -\frac{1}{3}x + 4$ e $y + x = 5$ f $2y + 3x = 6$

Many practical situations give rise to a straight line graph.

EXAMPLE 9

A publisher thinks that if a textbook is priced at sh 300, then it will sell 20 000 copies. If it is priced at sh 400, then it will sell 15 000 copies. Let the price be *p* and the sales be *s*. Assuming there is a straight line relationship between price and sales, find *s* in terms of *p*.

(a) What will be the sales if the book is priced at sh 350?
(b) At what price will the book sell 25 000 copies?

Solution

Suppose the relationship is $s = ap + b$, where *a* and *b* are constant. Put in the values given

$$20\ 000 = 300s + b \qquad [1]$$
$$15\ 000 = 400s + b \qquad [2]$$
$$-5000 = 100s \qquad \text{(subtracting [1] from [2])}$$
$$s = -50$$
$$20\ 000 = 300 \times -50 + b \qquad \text{(substituting in [1])}$$
$$b = 35\ 000$$

> **NOTE**
> Remember simultaneous equations from Unit 24 of Book 1. Number the equations.

The relationship is $s = -50p + 35\ 000$
The graph opposite shows the relationship between *s* and *p*.

(a) If $p = 350$, then

$$s = -50 \times 350 + 35\ 000$$
$$= -17\ 500 + 35\ 000 = 17\ 500$$

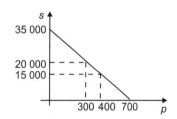

The book will sell 17 500 copies.

(b) If $s = 25\ 000$, then

$$25\ 000 = -50p + 35\ 000$$
$$-10\ 000 = -50p$$
$$200 = p$$

The book is priced at sh 200.

Exercise 1.4

1   In a certain country, a person earning 2000 dollars pays 100 dollars in tax, and a person earning 4000 dollars pays 300 dollars in tax. Assuming there is a straight line relationship between earnings and tax, find an expression giving tax *t* in terms of earnings *e*.

    a   How much tax does someone earning 3500 dollars pay?
    b   A woman pays 600 dollars in tax. How much does she earn?

2 When a mass of 5 kg is suspended from a spring, the length of the spring is 20 cm. When a mass of 10 kg is suspended, the length is 24 cm. Let the mass be w and the length be l, and find a straight line relationship between l and w.

   a What is the length of the spring if the mass is 12 kg?

   b What mass will give a length of 30 cm?

3 A telephone bill is sh 2000 if 300 units are used, and sh 1500 if 100 units are used. If the bill is sh b for u units, find a straight line relationship giving b in terms of u.

   a What is the bill if 350 units are used?

   b If the bill is 2500 units, how many units have been used?

4 A money changer will give sh 4500 for £50, and sh 9500 for £100. Let the number of shillings be s, and the number of £ be p. Find a straight line relationship between p and s.

   a How many shillings does the money changer give for £150?

   b How many £ are needed to obtain sh 8500?

5 A clothing firm makes T-shirts. Production costs consist of a fixed cost and a cost per T-shirt produced. If 1000 are made, the total cost is sh 150 000, and if 2000 are made the total cost is sh 180 000. Let the cost of making t shirts be sh C. Find an equation $C = mt + c$.

   a What is the total cost of making 1500 shirts?

   b How many can be made for a total cost of sh 210 000?

6 A clothing firm makes ties. If the ties cost sh 100 each, 1500 will be sold. If the ties cost sh 150 each, 800 will be sold. Let the price be sh p and the number sold be N. Find an equation $N = mp + c$.

   a Find the number sold if the price is sh 130.

   b Find the price if 1220 ties are sold.

- The gradient of a slope is the rise divided by the run.
- The gradient of the line between two points on a graph is the y change divided by the x change.
- The equation of a straight line is $y = mx + c$. The gradient is m and the y-intercept is c.
- The equation of a straight line can be found from two points on it.

This is a game for two players. Mark out a grid. The first player chooses a square on the grid (without telling the second player which square it is). The second player 'shoots' at the square, by giving the equation of a straight line.

If the line goes through the square, the round ends. If the line misses the square, the first player says whether it is above or below the square.

In the diagram the chosen square is bounded by $x = 6$, $x = 7$, $y = 3$ and $y = 4$. The line is $y = 2x - 1$, which has gone above the square.

Play continues until the square has been hit. Then the players change round. The winner is the player who takes fewer shots to hit the square.

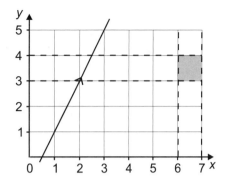

1 Find the gradient of the line joining (2, 3) and (4, 11).
2 Write down the gradient, y-intercept and x-intercept of these lines.
   a $y = 5x - 2$ **b** $5y + 4x = 20$
3 Find the equations of these lines.
   a Gradient 4 and y-intercept -2
   b Through (4, 7) and (-2, 10)
4 Sketch the graph of the equation $y = \frac{3}{4}x - \frac{1}{4}$.
5 A crop is being harvested. After 1 hour there is 8000 m² left, and after 2 hours there is 5000 m² left. Let the crop left be c m², and the time be h hours. Find a straight line relationship between c and h.
   a How much crop was there originally?
   b When will all the crop be harvested?

1 Consider the line $\frac{x}{a} + \frac{y}{b} = 1$, where a and b are constant.
   a Where does this line cross the axes?
   b What is the gradient of the line?
   c What happens if $a = 0$, or if $b = 0$?
2 ABCD is a square, with A at (1, 1) and B at (5, 6). Give the possible coordinates of C and D.
3 In Example 9 above, a relationship was found between the price p of a book and its sales s. For what values of p could the relationship hold?

2

Lines and coordinates

This unit uses

- Coordinates
- The gradients of straight lines
- The equations of straight lines
- Pythagoras' theorem

2.1

This diagram shows the graphs of $y = 2x$, $y = 2x - 2$, $y = 2x - 1$, $y = 2x + 1$ and $y = 2x + 2$. Notice that

the lines have the same gradient, 2

the lines are parallel.

Two lines are parallel if they have the same gradient.

$y = mx + c$ and $y = m'x + c'$ are parallel if $m = m'$.

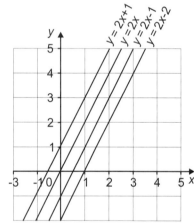

EXAMPLE 1

Find the equation of the line which is parallel to $y = 3x - 7$ which goes through (4, 2).

Solution

The line must have the same gradient as $y = 3x - 7$, which is 3. The equation is $y = 3x + c$. We need to find c. The line goes through (4, 2), so put $x = 4$ and $y = 2$.

$$2 = 3 \times 4 + c$$
$$-10 = c$$

The equation is $y = 3x - 10$.

EXAMPLE 2

Let A, B and C be at (1, 1), (3, 5) and (7, 13). Show that A, B and C are **collinear** (lie in a straight line).

Solution

Find the gradients of AB and of BC.

$$\text{gradient of } AB = \frac{5-1}{3-1} = \frac{4}{2} = 2$$

$$\text{gradient of } BC = \frac{13-5}{7-3} = \frac{8}{4} = 2$$

Hence AB and BC are parallel. Because they pass through the same point B, it follows that ABC is a straight line.

Exercise 2.1A

1 Which of the lines below are parallel?
   a $y = 2x + 7$ **b** $y = 3x - 4$ **c** $2y = 3x$ **d** $y + 2x = 4$
   e $2y = 6y + 1$ **f** $y - 2x = 1$ **g** $\frac{1}{4}y = \frac{1}{2}x + 3$ **h** $\frac{1}{3}y + x = 8$

2 Find k so that $ky + 3x = 2$ is parallel to $y = \frac{1}{2}x - 4$.

3 A quadrilateral $ABCD$ has vertices at $(1, 1)$, $(4, 7)$, $(9, 5)$ and $(6, -1)$. Show that $ABCD$ is a parallelogram.

4 A quadrilateral $PQRS$ has vertices at $(2, 4)$, $(5, 7)$, $(10, 6)$ and $(6, 2)$. Show that $PQRS$ is a trapezium but not a parallelogram.

5 Show that the points $(1, 6)$, $(2, 4)$ and $(4, 0)$ are collinear.

6 For each of the following sets of points, find whether they are collinear.
   a $(0, -1)$, $(2, 0)$, $(8, 3)$ **b** $(-2, 6)$, $(-1, 3)$, $(0, -1)$
   c $(-2, -2)$, $(4, -1)$, $(6, 0)$ **d** $(2, 6)$, $(6, 4)$, $(8, 3)$

7 The points $(1, 1)$, $(3, 6)$ and $(7, k)$ are collinear. Find k.

8 A, B, C and D are at $(2, 1)$, $(4, 7)$, $(3, 2)$ and $(5, k)$. If AB and CD are parallel, find k.

9 The points $(-1, 2)$, $(3, 7)$ and $(m, 2m)$ are collinear. Find m.

10 P, Q, R and S are at $(-2, 4)$, $(3, -1)$, $(5, 1)$ and (m, m). If PQ and RS are parallel, find m.

Perpendicular lines

Look at this diagram, showing several pairs of lines.

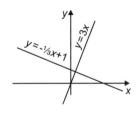 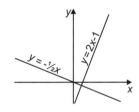 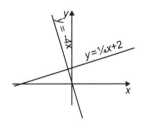 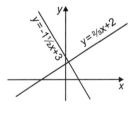

$y = 3x$ and $y = -\frac{1}{3}x + 1$ $y = 2x - 1$ and $y = -\frac{1}{2}x$
$y = -4x$ and $y = \frac{1}{4}x + 2$ $y = -1\frac{1}{2}x + 3$ and $y = \frac{2}{3}x + 2$

Notice that for each pair

- the lines are perpendicular
- the product of the gradients is -1.

Two lines are perpendicular if the product of the gradients is –1.

$y = mx + c$ and $y = m'x + c$ are perpendicular if $mm' = -1$

Justification

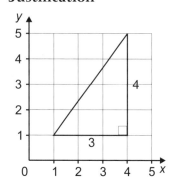

Look at this triangle. The vertical side is 4, and the horizontal side is 3. So the gradient of the hypotenuse is $\frac{4}{3}$.

Now turn the triangle through 90°. The horizontal side is 4, and the vertical side is –3. The value is –3 because it is going downwards. Hence the gradient of the hypotenuse is $-\frac{3}{4}$.

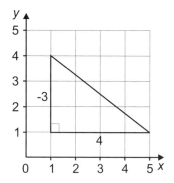

The two hypotenuses are perpendicular.
The product of the gradients is $\frac{4}{3} \times -\frac{3}{4} = -1$.

EXAMPLE 3

Find the equation of the line through (1, 4) which is perpendicular to $y = 3x + 2$.

Solution

Suppose the line is $y = mx + c$. The product of the gradients is –1.

$$-3 \times m = -1$$
$$m = -1 \div -3 = \tfrac{1}{3}$$

Now put $x = 1$ and $y = 4$

$$4 = \tfrac{1}{3} \times 1 + c$$
$$c = 4 - \tfrac{1}{3} = 3\tfrac{2}{3}$$

The equation is $y = \tfrac{1}{3}x + 3\tfrac{2}{3}$.

Exercise 2.1B

1   Which pairs of the lines below are perpendicular?

a $y = 3x + 5$ b $y = -3x$ c $3y + x = 4$

d $y = \tfrac{1}{3}x + 2$ e $y - 3x = 10$ f $\tfrac{1}{3}y + x = 3$

g $6y + 2x = 1$ h $3y - 9x = 2$

2 Find the equations of the lines which are
  a perpendicular to $y = 2x$ and through $(4, 7)$
  b perpendicular to $y = 3x - 4$ and through $(1, 1)$
  c perpendicular to $y = \frac{1}{2}x + 2$ and through $(4, 7)$
  d perpendicular to $4y + 3x = 1$ and through $(0, 5)$.
3 The lines $y = 3x + 2$ and $ky + x = 7$ are perpendicular. Find k.
4 The lines $3y + mx = 4$ and $2y + x = 1$ are perpendicular. Find m.
5 The lines $ky + 2x = 1$ and $y = (k + 2)x + 7$ are perpendicular. Find k.
6 A, B, C and D are at $(6, 8)$, $(2, -4)$, $(2, 3)$ and $(k, 1)$. If AB and CD are perpendicular find k.
7 P, Q, R and S are at $(3, 1)$, $(4, 8)$, $(2, 10)$ and (m, m). If PQ and RS are perpendicular find m.
8 Let A be at $(2, 7)$. Find the equation of the line through A which is perpendicular to the line $y = x + 1$. Find where the two lines meet.
9 Show that $(3, -2)$ lies on the line $y = 2x - 8$. Find the equation of the line through $(3, -2)$ which is perpendicular to the line $y = 2x - 8$.
10 Let A be at $(1, 7)$. Find the point B on the line $y = 3x + 1$ such that AB is perpendicular to the line.

2.2

Suppose we are given the coordinates
of two points. We can use
Pythagoras' theorem to find
the distance between the points.
In the diagram point A is at $(1, 2)$
and point B is at $(13, 7)$.
The horizontal distance between
A and B is 12 units.
The vertical distance between
A and B is 5 units.

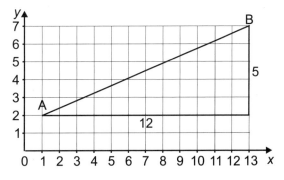

Hence the distance between
A and B is $\sqrt{12^2 + 5^2}$, which is
13 units.

Remember Pythagoras' theorem,
that $c = \sqrt{a^2 + b^2}$

In general, the distance between (x_1, y_1) and
(x_2, y_2) is

$$\sqrt{(x_2 - x_1)^2 + (y_2 - y_1)^2}$$

Note It does not matter whether we take
$(x_2 - x_1)^2$ or $(x_1 - x_2)^2$. The square of any number
is positive.

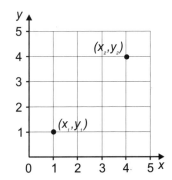

Exercise 2.2

1 Find the distances between these pairs of points. If the distance is not a whole number, leave it in $\sqrt{}$ form.

  a (1, 1) and (4, 5)   **b** (4, 1) and (10, –7)
  c (–3, 1) and (4, 3)   **d** (2, –3) and (4, 8)

2 A quadrilateral has vertices at (1, 1), (4, 5), (9, 5) and (6, 1). Find the lengths of the sides of the quadrilateral, and show that it is a rhombus.

3 Find the gradients of the diagonals of the rhombus of question **2**. Check that they are perpendicular.

4 A triangle has vertices at (2, 3), (7, –3) and (8, 8). Show that the triangle is right angled

  a by showing that two of the sides are perpendicular
  b by showing that the lengths of the sides obey Pythagoras' theorem.

5 Which of the following represents the distance between the points (a, b) and (c, d)?

  a $\sqrt{(a - b)^2 + (c - d)^2}$ **b** $\sqrt{(a - d)^2 + (b - c)^2}$
  c $\sqrt{(c - s)^2 + (d - b)^2}$ **d** $\sqrt{(a - c)^2 - (b - d)^2}$

6 A circle has centre (2, 5) and radius 25 units. Which of these points lie on the circle?

  (22, 20)   (20, 30)   (9, –19)   (2, –20)   (8, –15)

7 The vertices of a triangle are at (1, 2), (6, 2) and (5, 5). Show that the triangle is isosceles. Is it equilateral?

8 The vertices of a triangle are at (–3, –1), (2, –6) and (1, 1). Show that the triangle is isosceles. Is it equilateral?

9 The distance between (1, 5) and $(k + 5, k + 1)$ is 8. Find k, given that it is positive.

10 The distance between $(m + 2, 1)$ and $(5, m + 4)$ is 10. Find m, given that it is positive.

2.3

Suppose you are given the coordinates of two points A and B. The **midpoint** is halfway along AB. The coordinates of the midpoint are found by averaging the coordinates of A and B.

So if A is at (x_1, y_1) and B is at (x_2, y_2), the midpoint is at

$$\left(\frac{x_1 + x_2}{2}, \frac{y_1 + y_2}{2} \right)$$

EXAMPLE 4

(a) Find the midpoint of the line between $A(1, 1)$ and $B(3, 5)$.
(b) Find the perpendicular bisector of this line.

Solution

(a) The midpoint of AB is $\left(\dfrac{1+3}{2}, \dfrac{1+5}{2}\right)$, which is (2, 3).

The midpoint of AB is (2, 3).

(b) The perpendicular bisector of AB goes through the midpoint of AB, and is perpendicular to it.

The gradient of AB is $\frac{4}{2}$, giving 2. Hence the gradient of the perpendicular bisector is $-\frac{1}{2}$.

The equation of the perpendicular bisector is $y = -\frac{1}{2}x + c$. Put $x = 2$ and $y = 3$.

$$3 = -\frac{1}{2} \times 2 + c. \text{ Hence } c = 4.$$

The perpendicular bisector is $y = -\frac{1}{2}x + 4$.

Exercise 2.3

1 Find the midpoints of the following pairs of points.
   a (1, 2) and (7, 8)   b (0, 4) and (6, 0)
   c (2, 3) and (5, 8)   d (−3, 4) and (5, −6)
   e (−1, −4) and (−4, 1)   f (1, 3) and (−3, −1)

2 Find the equations of the perpendicular bisectors of the lines through the following pairs of points.
   a (1, 5) and (6, 0)   b (−1, 3) and (5, 5)
   c (2, −3) and (−4, 7)   d (−1, −4) and (5, 0)

3 A triangle has vertices at $A(1,1)$, $B(1, 6)$ and $C(5, 4)$.
   a Show that the triangle is isosceles.

   b Find the perpendicular bisector of BC. Verify that it goes through A.

4 A quadrilateral has vertices at (2, 3), (7, 3), (10, 7) and (5, 7).
   a Show that the quadrilateral is a rhombus.

   b By finding the midpoints of the diagonals, show that the diagonals bisect each other.

- Two lines are parallel if they have the same gradient. $y = mx + c$ and $y = m'x + c'$ are parallel if $m = m'$.
- Two lines are perpendicular if the product of their gradients is −1. $y = mx + c$ and $y = m'x + c'$ are perpendicular if $m \times m' = -1$.
- You can use Pythagoras' theorem to find the distance between points.
- The midpoint between two points is found by averaging the coordinates of the two points. The midpoint of the line joining (x_1, y_1) and (x_2, y_2) is at $\left(\dfrac{x_1 + x_2}{2}, \dfrac{y_1 + y_2}{2}\right)$.

If you are given three points on a circle, you can *construct* its centre by finding the perpendicular bisectors of two sides of the triangle that joins the three points. Now you can *calculate* the coordinates of the centre.

Suppose the three points are $A(1, 1)$, $B(7, 7)$ and $C(7, -3)$.
a Find the perpendicular bisectors of AB and AC.

b Find the coordinates of the intersection X of the bisectors.
c Find AX, BX and CX. Are they equal?

1 Find the equation of the line which is parallel to $y = 4x + 7$ and through $(1, 6)$.
2 Find the equation of the line which is perpendicular to $y = 4x + 7$ and through $(8, 3)$.
3 Find the distance between the points $(2, 5)$ and $(7, -7)$.
4 Find the midpoint of the points $(3, -6)$ and $(4, 12)$.
5 The coordinates of the vertices of a quadrilateral are $(1, 1)$, $(16, 21)$, $(23, -3)$ and $(8, -23)$.
    a Show that the quadrilateral is a rhombus.
    b Show that the diagonals of the quadrilateral bisect each other perpendicularly.
6 Let A be at $(2, 5)$ and B at $(k, 4)$.
    a If AB is parallel to $y = 3x + 1$, find k.
    b If AB is perpendicular to $y = \frac{1}{2}x - 7$, find k.

1 Find the coordinates of the vertices of a quadrilateral such that
    ● the quadrilateral is a rhombus
    ● none of the sides are vertical or horizontal
    ● neither of the diagonals are vertical or horizontal.
2 Find the equations of the bisectors of the *angles* between the lines $x = 3$ and $y = 4$.
3 If the lines $y = kx$ and $ky = 4x$ are parallel, find the possible values of k.
4 If the lines $2y + mx = 1$ and $18y - mx = 5$ are perpendicular, find the possible values of m.

3 Statistics

This unit uses
- Percentages
- Ratios

3.1

In the world we are surrounded by numerical facts.
    Our weight, our height.
    The populations of towns and cities.
    The temperature at different times of the year and so on.

The numerical facts have to be collected to be of use. They are called **statistical data**. The subject of **statistics** is concerned with analysing data and making conclusions based on them.

In order to do this, the data must be *collected*, *organised* and *presented* in some way. It is important that the data is collected in the correct way otherwise incorrect conclusions may be made.

Sometimes, *all* of the data needed is available to be collected. On other occasions, you have to collect a **sample** of the data. For example, if you wanted to find the average distance travelled to school by the pupils in your class, you could easily ask all of them individually how far they had travelled. However, if you were looking at the proportion of different makes of cars travelling on the roads in Kenya, you would have to look at a sample of the traffic. Where you chose this sample would be very important. You would have to take data from country roads, town roads and city streets.

You can collect data for yourself by using a **questionnaire**. The following example of a questionnaire is suitable if you want to look at the sporting activities of pupils in your school. You can then ask a sample of pupils to fill it in. Once the data has been collected, you can try to interpret it.

SPORTS QUESTIONNAIRE

Put a tick in the correct box.

1. **Age**
     Under 11   ☐
     11–15   ☐
     16 and over   ☐

2. **Sex**
     Male   ☐
     Female   ☐

3. What is your favourite sport?

Football ☐
Basketball ☐
Hockey ☐
Swimming ☐
Athletics ☐
Golf ☐
Other (specify) ....

4. How many hours a week do you normally spend on sport?

0–2 hours ☐
3–4 hours ☐
5–6 hours ☐
7 hours and over ☐

In a good questionnaire, the questions must be clear and easy to answer. It should produce useful information and not contain biased questions.

Exercise 3.1

1 Think of a topic you would like to find out about. Design a questionnaire and ask your friends and people you know to fill it in. Tabulate your results and see what conclusions you come to.
2 Suppose you want to survey the diets of the pupils in your class. Write down three questions that would be good to ask. Write down three questions that would be bad to ask, and give reasons why.
3 Write down facts about yourself, such as your height, weight, shoe size, number of brothers and sisters and so on. Put together the results of the whole class.

3.2

Once the data has been collected, it has to be presented in a concise way so that trends and patterns can be seen quickly. Before it is tabulated the data is called **raw data**. The process of putting data in a table is called **tabulation**. The simplest type of table is called a **frequency** table. The data is recorded by using tally marks. Study the following example.

EXAMPLE 1

Ndinda asked the students in her class how many times they practised at sport in the evening during the previous week. The results are as follows:

```
0  0  7  2  6  3  0  3  0  5
1  3  2  3  5  2  0  1  0  5
5  1  0  3  4  0  0  0  1  4
1  0  1  1  4  1  1  2  4  1
0  6  2  6  4  2  2  3  3  0
```

Enter this data into a frequency table by means of a tally. What pattern can you see in the results?

Solution
The tally table is completed as follows:

Evenings practising	Tally	Frequency
0	1111 1111 111	13
1	1111 1111	10
2	1111 11	7
3	1111 11	7
4	1111	5
5	1111	4
6	111	3
7	1	1
	Total	50

Note that 5 is represented by 1111

You can see clearly from the table, that most students only practised once or did not practise at all during the week.

Data that can only take clearly defined values (in this case 0, 1, 2, 3, ...) is called **discrete** or **listed**.

The next example shows a slightly different way of **grouping** the data. This is needed when the data can take a great number of values.

EXAMPLE 2

In order to see whether a firm needed an extra secretary to answer the phone, the number of calls received per day were recorded as follows. Put this data into a frequency table. What pattern can you see in the results?

```
19   4  23  16   8  28  21  33  26  30
 7  32  22  31   3  26  25  17  19  11
24  21  36  24  37  18  19  16  18  19
17  18   2  27  31  17  12   7  20  24
 8  22  11  19  29  20  14  12  15  14
```

Solution
In the previous example, there were only 7 possible values. The range of the discrete data here is from 2 to 37. This would need a table with 36 rows. We can solve the problem by putting the data into **groups** or **classes**. Try not to make the range of values in the group too small or too large. Here we shall use 0–5; 6–10; 11–15; 16–20; 21–25; 26–30; 31–35; and 36–40.

The table is as follows:

Number of calls	Tally	Frequency
0–5	111	3
6–10	1111	4
11–15	1111 11	7
16–20	1111 1111 1111	15
21–25	1111 1111	9
26–30	1111 1	6
31–35	1111	4
36–40	11	2
	Total	50

It appears that on most days between 11 and 25 calls were received.

Exercise 3.2

1 A class of students took a mental arithmetic test. The total possible mark was 10. The results were as follows:

```
4  8  5  2  3
8  7  6  6  4
2  5  8  7  6
6  6  4  4  3
8  5  7  6  5
```

Enter these results into a suitable frequency table.

How well do you think the class did ?

2 Kariuki carried out an experiment rolling a die numbered 1 to 6. The results he obtained were as follows:

```
4  2  3  3  1  6  2  5  1  2
6  3  4  2  1  3  5  3  4  1
2  5  1  3  3  4  2  3  6  1
5  1  3  3  1  2  5  4  3  6
3  2  1  3  4  5  4  3  5  3
```

Put these results into a frequency table. Do they tell you anything about this die?

3 Wanjiru kept a record of the number of matatu passing a point on the road. The results for 30 one-minute periods are below. Enter the results into a frequency table.

```
0  1  1  0  2  3  2  0  1  5
3  0  1  4  1  0  1  1  0  0
0  2  4  1  1  2  2  0  0  1
```

4 The ages of 40 people at a meeting were as follows. Enter the results into a frequency table, using classes 10–19, 20–29 and so on.

$$
\begin{array}{cccccccccc}
18 & 22 & 16 & 39 & 44 & 42 & 40 & 31 & 27 & 38 \\
26 & 20 & 39 & 16 & 44 & 52 & 41 & 25 & 49 & 56 \\
37 & 42 & 30 & 60 & 22 & 45 & 18 & 33 & 29 & 44 \\
33 & 37 & 31 & 21 & 22 & 17 & 22 & 53 & 28 & 51
\end{array}
$$

5 Aida was doing a biology experiment classifying worms. Worms less than 3 cm are small. Worms between 3 cm and 6 cm inclusive are medium. Worms more than 6 cm are large. Her results were as follows (in cm):

$$
\begin{array}{cccccccc}
1.8 & 2.5 & 4.7 & 3.6 & 7.1 & 2.2 & 8.4 & 3.1 \\
1.9 & 5.9 & 6.2 & 5.3 & 4.7 & 5.1 & 6.2 & 5.5 \\
0.9 & 3.7 & 5.8 & 4.3 & 6.6 & 8.1 & 4.4 & 2.2
\end{array}
$$

Group these results into a suitable frequency table.

6 The results of some students in a mathematics test were as follows (as %):

$$
\begin{array}{cccccccc}
33 & 36 & 85 & 44 & 37 & 58 & 33 & 12 \\
90 & 71 & 65 & 40 & 23 & 62 & 51 & 36 \\
63 & 58 & 63 & 50 & 93 & 51 & 27 & 55 \\
72 & 49 & 78 & 42 & 61 & 40 & 18 & 63 \\
66 & 37 & 89 & 18 & 56 & 31 & 23 & 39
\end{array}
$$

Using classes 10–19, 20–29, and so on, put this data into a grouped frequency table.

7 In Exercise 3.1 you were asked to collect information about you and your fellow students. For one of the topics, put the data into a frequency table.

3.3

A good way of illustrating data is by a pictogram. This method requires you to use a shape or symbol to represent a chosen frequency. The shape is then repeated or divided to represent other frequencies.

EXAMPLE 3

A group of students were asked to choose their favourite colour. The results of this are given below. Draw a pictogram to illustrate these results.

Colour	red	green	blue	yellow	purple	other
Frequency	5	20	22	15	16	9

Solution

When choosing your shape or symbol, make sure it is easy to divide up. In this case, we have ♀ = 4, ♀ = 3, ♀ = 2, and ○ = 1. The result is shown below.

FAVOURITE COLOURS

RED ☺ ○   ☺ = 4 people

GREEN ☺ ☺ ☺ ☺ ☺

BLUE ☺ ☺ ☺ ☺ ☺ ♀

YELLOW ☺ ☺ ☺ ♀

PURPLE ☺ ☺ ☺ ☺

OTHER ☺ ☺ ○

A pictogram is used to show discrete or listed data.

Exercise 3.3

1 A local wholesaler sold oranges to five shops A, B, C, D and E. They were sold in boxes. The amount sold to the shops is illustrated in the following pictogram.

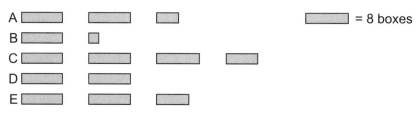

 ⬜ = 8 boxes

 a How many boxes did shop B buy?
 b How many boxes did the wholesaler sell in total?

2 A stall sells cassettes. The pictogram below shows how many cassettes were sold on five days of the week.

CASSETTE SALES

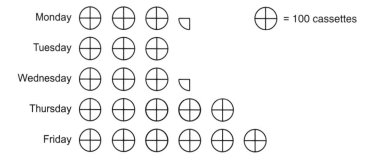

⊕ = 100 cassettes

 a How many cassettes were sold on Tuesday?
 b How many cassettes were sold over the five days?

3 The pictogram below shows the numbers of mangoes sold in a market over a week.

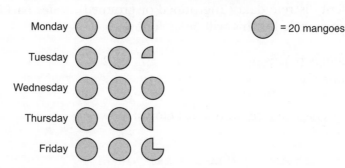

SALES OF MANGOES

= 20 mangoes

Monday
Tuesday
Wednesday
Thursday
Friday

a How many mangoes were sold on Friday?
b How many mangoes were sold over the week?

4 The pictogram below shows the ages of the people at a meeting. It uses the same symbol as Example 3.

PEOPLES AGES

= 4 people

10-19
20-29
30-39
40-49
50-60

a How many people were between 20 and 29?
b How many people were there in total?

5 A group of 30 pupils were asked how they had come to school. The results are below. Using the same symbols as for Example 3 construct a pictogram for the data.

Walk	Bus	Cycle	Car
13	7	8	2

6 The daily sales of oranges from a stall are given below. Using a round symbol to represent 100 oranges, construct a pictogram for the data.

Monday	Tuesday	Wednesday	Thursday	Friday
150	225	200	250	275

7 Illustrate the results given in question **2** of Exercise 3.2 by means of a pictogram. State clearly the value of the symbol you use.

A bar chart (sometimes called a bar graph, or block graph) is a convenient way to represent discrete data (ungrouped or grouped). Refer back to Example 1. The frequency table for this will be as follows.

Evenings practising	0	1	2	3	4	5	6	7
Frequency	13	10	7	7	5	4	3	1

The bar chart can be drawn as below

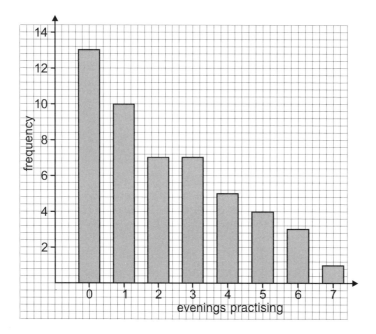

The frequency axis is usually vertical, but sometimes a bar graph is drawn with the bars horizontal. Data can also be compared by using two or more graphs on the same diagram. This is called a **multiple bar graph**. See the next example.

EXAMPLE 4

Four groups of students were given a physics test. The average marks for the boys and girls were calculated separately, and are given in the following table.

	Group 1	Group 2	Group 3	Group 4
Girls	50	53	60	68
Boys	52	56	58	70

Draw a comparative bar chart to illustrate these results.

Solution

Shade the blocks differently for the boys and the girls. The result can be seen in the diagram below.

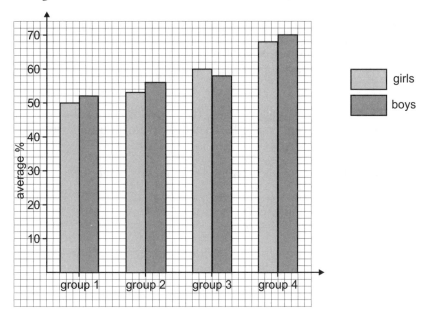

You can see how easy it is to compare the results.

Another type of bar chart is a **compound** bar chart where a single bar is used. They are particularly useful when percentages are used.

EXAMPLE 5

The areas of the major land masses expressed as percentages are given in this table.

Land mass	Africa	Asia	Europe	America	Rest
%	20	28	7	28	17

Represent this data in a compound bar graph.

Solution

Because the numbers add up to 100, try to draw the block a suitable length. Here the length = 10 cm = 100 mm.

Exercise 3.4

1 A selection of cars was examined for major defects. The results are shown in this table.

Defects	0	1	2	3	more than 3
No. of cars	5	2	8	3	15

Show this information in a bar chart.

2 The number of goals scored by Muite's football team each match last season are given in the following table:

Goals	0	1	2	3	4	5
Frequency	2	8	12	4	1	1

Represent this information in a bar chart.

3 Using the data of question **6** Exercise 3.2, draw a bar chart to represent the results.

4 The age distribution of pupils in three forms are given in the following table. Draw a multiple bar graph with the bars drawn horizontally, to represent this information.

Age	13–14	15–16	17–18	over 18
Class 1	6	12	7	1
Class 2	7	20	3	0
Class 3	5	8	10	1

5 Jane did a survey on the types of buildings in her local town centre, to see how many floors they had. Here are the results.

No. of floors	1	2	3	4	more than 4
% of buildings	40	30	15	10	5

Show these results using
a a bar graph
b a composite bar graph.
Which do you think is better and why?

3.5

Another useful way of displaying the results of a frequency table is by a **frequency polygon** or **line graph**. They are good for comparing data or showing **trends**.

EXAMPLE 6

The data in the following table shows how many times per month Wanza and Wayua were late in the last two years.

Days late/month	0	1	2	3	4	5	6
Wanza	3	5	2	6	4	1	3
Wayua	9	3	2	4	3	2	1

Plot these results on the same frequency diagram. What does the diagram show?

Solution

After plotting the points, join with straight lines as shown below.

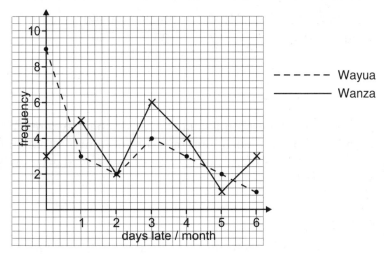

The line for Wayua is nearly always below that for Wanza, except for 0 days. This shows that she is more reliable.

Exercise 3.5

1   Illustrate the results of question **2** Exercise 3.4 by means of a frequency polygon.
2   Show the results of question **4** Exercise 3.4 using a multiple frequency diagram. Do you think this is clearer than the bar graph?
3   The profits of a firm selling electrical goods are shown in the following table, for the year 1999.

Month	Jan	Feb	Mar	Apr	May	Jun	Jul	Aug	Sep	Oct	Nov	Dec
Profit	20	15	20	22	18	24	23	28	28	27	30	31

The profits are in thousands of shillings.
Draw a line graph to represent the figures. What trend can you see?

4   50 pupils were asked how many brothers or sisters they had. The results are below. Draw a frequency polygon for the data.

Number	0	1	2	3	4	5	6
Frequency	9	17	13	4	5	1	1

5   A group of people were asked how many films they had seen at the cinema over the past month. The results are below. Draw a frequency polygon for the data.

Number	0	1	2	3	4	5	6
Frequency	13	9	8	4	7	3	1

6   The frequency table below shows the marks in a maths exam. Draw a frequency polygon for the data.

Mark	0–19	20–39	40–59	60–79	80–100
Frequency	12	38	78	110	54

7   The frequency table below gives the number of letters received each day by a business, over a period of 50 days. Draw a frequency polygon for the data.

Number	0–9	10–19	20–29	30–40
Frequency	5	17	25	3

3.6

A popular way of representing data is in a pie chart, where a circle is divided up into sectors to represent each item or group of items. Although the result is very effective, a pie chart is often not easy to draw or read accurately. Look at the following example.

EXAMPLE 7

An athletics team is chosen from five local schools to represent a region. The number of pupils selected from each school is given in the following table.

School	A	B	C	D	E
No. of pupils	8	12	6	15	7

Show this information in a pie chart.

Solution

(a) Find the total frequency. $8 + 12 + 6 + 15 + 7 = 48$

(b) Remember that there are $360°$ in a circle, and these will represent 48 people. We can now find the angle for each sector as follows:

$$\text{For A} \qquad \frac{8}{48} \times 360° = \frac{1}{6} \times 360° = 60°$$

$$\text{For B} \qquad \frac{12}{48} \times 360° = \frac{1}{4} \times 360° = 90°$$

$$\text{For C} \qquad \frac{6}{48} \times 360° = \frac{1}{8} \times 360° = 45°$$

$$\text{For D} \qquad \frac{15}{48} \times 360° = \frac{5}{16} \times 360° = 112.5°$$

$$\text{For E} \qquad \frac{7}{48} \times 360° = \frac{7 \times 15°}{2} = 52.5°$$

Check that the angles add up to $360°$

$$60 + 90 + 45 + 112.5 + 52.5 = 360$$

The diagram can now be drawn. Make sure that the sectors are clearly labelled. You do *not* have to write the angles on the diagram.

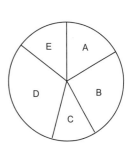

A pie chart looks good and gives a quick idea about how the data divided up. However, you must take care to read accurately as the following example shows.

EXAMPLE 8

The total amount earned by three sales people P, Q and R in a week was sh 40 000. Their individual amounts are illustrated in the diagram. How much did P earn?

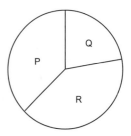

Solution
The angle for P is about $135°$

The amount earned by $P = \frac{135}{360} \times 40\ 000 = 15\ 000$ sh.

This will almost certainly not be the *exact* answer.

Exercise 3.6

1 The number of hours homework done each week by a group of 24 students is as follows:

No. of hours	5	6	7	8	9
No. of students	2	7	9	4	2

Show these results in a pie chart.

2 Katana spends 8 hours a day asleep, 6 hours at school, 2 hours travelling and the rest at home. Draw a pie chart to show how his day is divided.

3 The vehicles passing a check point are as follows. Draw a pie chart to show the data.

Cars	Buses	Lorries	Motorcycles
55	27	37	45

4 The books in a school library are classified as below. Construct a pie chart to show the data.

Fiction	Reference	Biography	Other
240	160	50	150

5 The animals on a farm are as follows. Construct a pie chart to show the data.

Sheep	Goats	Cows	Pigs
21	6	12	15

6 Wambua drew a pie chart to show the favourite subjects of 72 pupils. The angles in the pie chart are given.

Maths	Science	Ki-Swahili	English	Other
$70°$	$60°$	$100°$	$40°$	$90°$

  a How many pupils liked Ki-Swahili best?

  b How many pupils liked Maths best?

7 A farmer divides his farm into four areas. He uses three for growing maize, beans and coffee. The other he uses for grazing. The total area of the farm is 60 hectares. A pie chart to represent this would have the following size sectors:

Area	maize	beans	coffee	grazing
Angle	90°	84°	120°	66°

Find the area used for each item.

8 Akinyi noted the colours of the cars in a car park. She drew a pie chart to show the results. The angles of the sectors are below.

White	Black	Red	Blue	Other
120°	48°	72°	42°	78°

a There were 100 white cars. How many cars were there in total?
b How many blue cars were there?

3.7

If you measure accurately the weights of a group of people, the values will not be whole numbers of kilograms. Each value could be at any point on the continuous scale between the lightest and the heaviest. This is **continuous data**. The value you record for each person is only restricted by how accurate you can make the measurements. For peoples' weights this would be to the nearest 0.1 kg. This means that a weight of 63.4 kg could be anywhere between 63.35 kg and 63.45 kg. The following case shows you how to deal with continuous data.

The heights of pupils in Kimanzi's class were measured to the nearest cm. The results are as follows:

```
166  169  143  185  171  169  181  158
178  159  164  177  173  149  130  141
170  155  183  170  162  160  155  148
132  136  161  163  182  141  158  144
141  178  159  137  185  180  160  164
```

The frequency table for this data is shown in the table below. We have used groups of 130–139, 140–149 and so on.

Group	Tally	Frequency
130–139	1111	4
140–149	1111 11	7
150–159	1111 1	6
160–169	1111 1111	10
170–179	1111 11	7
180–189	1111 1	6
	Total	40

Choose the width of the groups (classes) such that it is
- **not too large, giving only a few groups**
- **not too small, giving too many groups, some of which may have zero frequency.**

About 6 classes is usually a suitable number.

When you draw a bar chart for grouped continuous data, it is called a **histogram**. The first group is labelled 130–139. However you must remember that it actually is 129.5–139.5. The width of this group is $139.5 - 129.5 = 10$. When you draw the histogram, there must not be any gaps between the blocks. 129.5 is called the **lower class boundary**, and 139.5 is the **upper class boundary**. The histogram is shown below.

The frequency is proportional to the *area* of the blocks. At this level, we shall assume all blocks are the same width and then we can use the height to measure the frequency.

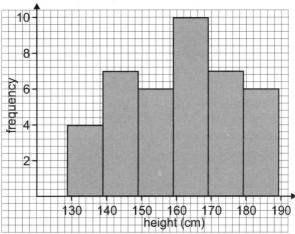

It is also possible to illustrate data in a grouped frequency table by means of a frequency polygon. You must remember to plot the points at the *midpoint* of the classes. If we use the data again from the table above, the graph will be the one drawn here.

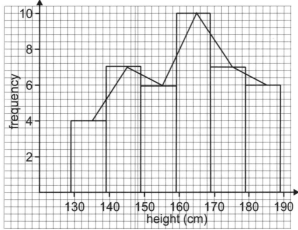

Exercise 3.7

1 The time spent on homework by 30 pupils is summarised in this table.

Time (hours)	0–4	5–8	9–12	13–16	17–20
No. of pupils	5	18	4	2	1

Show these figures
a in a histogram   **b** in a frequency polygon.

2 The wages earned each week by employees at a small factory are summarised in the following table.

Wages (K£)	30–39	40–49	50–59	60–69	70–79
Frequency	8	20	35	16	9

Show these figures
a in a histogram   **b** in a frequency polygon.

3 40 pupils were asked how far they had to travel to school each day. The results are below.

Distance (km)	0–2	3–4	5–6	7–8	9–10
Frequency	13	11	7	6	3

Show these figures
a in a histogram   **b** in a frequency polygon.

4 The midday temperature was measured each day for 60 days. The results are below.

Temperature (°C)	60–65	65–70	70–75	75–80	80–85	85–90
Frequency	3	7	13	18	11	8

Show these figures
a in a histogram   **b** in a frequency polygon.

5 The weights of 50 young goats are given in the table below.

Weight (kg)	15–20	20–25	25–30	30–35	35–40
Frequency	18	12	9	8	3

Show these figures
a in a histogram   **b** in a frequency polygon.

6 The times for 80 people to run 200 metres are given below.

Times (seconds)	30–32	32–34	34–36	36–38	38–40
Frequency	3	13	27	21	16

Show these figures
a in a histogram   **b** in a frequency polygon.

- Statistics is concerned with the collection and analysis of data.
- Data can be collected in a variety of ways, including questionnaires, sampling and reference books.
- Data can be discrete or continuous.
- Data can be illustrated using a pictogram, a pie chart, a bar chart, a frequency polygon, or a histogram (continuous data).

Activity 3

Conduct your own survey to collect data. You might investigate:

1. The average number of children in a family.
2. The distances travelled to school by your teachers.
3. The type of books people read.

Remember, you cannot ask everyone, and so your methods must ensure that all possibilities are fairly represented. It would be better to work with a friend.

1 Devise three different questions to put on a questionnaire for a survey about what type of music people like.
2 An experiment on growing maize was carried out by taking batches of 10 seeds under different conditions. The numbers of seeds that grew in each batch are as follows:

```
8   7   9   5   6   8   5   10
6   9   10  8   5   8   7   9
7   7   8   9   7   6   8   9
5   7   8   7   9   8   9   10
6   8   7   9   9   8   7   5
```

Make a tally chart and from your results, draw a clearly labelled bar graph to represent the data.
3 The diagram shows the make up of a special paint called Covapaint, using three chemicals A, B and C.

A	B	C

a How much of chemical B would there be in a 5 litre can?
b How much of chemical A would there be in a 25 litre drum?
4 A tour to the Masai Mara game park contained 30 people from abroad. The table below shows where they came from. Construct a pie chart to show the data.

America	Europe	Japan	Other
8	11	5	6

5 The fruits in a basket are illustrated by a pie chart. The angles are given below.

oranges	bananas	pineapple	mangoes
100°	90°	100°	70°

There are 14 mangoes.
a How many fruits are there in total?
b How many bananas are there?

6 A class of 30 pupils attempts the high jump. Their best results are given in the table below. Construct a frequency polygon and a histogram to show the data.

Height (cm)	80–100	100–120	120–140	140–160
Frequency	7	12	10	1

7 A football team has five players who have scored over the season. Their results are below. Construct a pictogram to show the data, using a round shape to represent four goals.

Kinala	Bosire	Momanyi	Obege	Maina
10	7	1	12	5

1 The angles in a pie chart with four sectors A, B, C and D are as follows:

A	B	C	D
110	x	y	80

Find x and y, if it is known that y is three times the value of x.

2 If you draw comparative pie charts, the radii of the circles must be different if the total quantities represented by the circles are different. If the grades obtained by 40 pupils in one class are represented on a circle of radius 4 cm, the grades of a different group of 30 pupils will be represented on another circle with area proportional to the area of the first circle.
So, the area of circle 1 : area of circle 2 = 40 : 30. What will the radius of the second circle be?

3 A pie chart shows the favourite colours of a group of people. The angle in the red sector is 70°. How many people could there be in this sector, given that it is less than 30?

Reflections and symmetry

This unit uses
- Coordinates
- The equations of lines
- The special types of triangle, quadrilateral and polygon

4.1 Line symmetry

Exercise 4.1A

Cut out a copy of this rectangle *ABCD*. Mark *E* and *F* at the midpoints of *AB* and *CD*. Fold the rectangle along *EF*. What do you notice?

In this exercise, you should find that the two halves of *ABCD* lie exactly on top of each other. The shape *AEFD* is exactly equal to the shape *BEFC*.

For the rectangle *ABCD*, when it is folded over along the dotted line *EF*, *A* moves to *B* and *D* moves to *C*. When unfolded the shape *ABCD* is identical on either side of *EF*. The dotted line *EF* is a **line of symmetry** of the rectangle.

In general, a line is a line of symmetry if the shape is identical on both sides of the line.

Exercise 4.1B

Many objects in real life have lines of symmetry.
For example, many leaves have a line of symmetry.
Make a list of five common objects which have lines of symmetry.

EXAMPLE 1

The diagram shows a square. Draw all its lines of symmetry.

Solution
The square is identical on both sides of a vertical line through its centre, and also on both sides of a horizontal line through its centre. The square is also identical on both sides of the diagonal lines.
The four lines of symmetry are shown.

EXAMPLE 2

An isosceles triangle has vertices at $(1,1)$, $(4,-2)$ and $(4,4)$.
Plot the triangle and find the equation of its line of symmetry.

Solution
The points are plotted as shown. Notice that the triangle is symmetrical about the horizontal line through $y = 1$. The line of symmetry is $y = 1$.

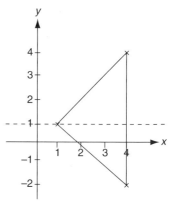

Exercise 4.1C

1 Draw a rectangle, and show all its lines of symmetry.
2 Draw a rhombus, and show all its lines of symmetry.
3 How many lines of symmetry does a parallelogram have?
4 The diagrams below show intersecting circles. How many lines of symmetry are there if
    a the circles are equal   **b** the circles are unequal.

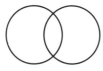   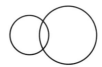

5 How many lines of symmetry are there for
    a a regular pentagon   **b** a regular hexagon.
6 Draw four quadrilaterals, **a**, **b**, **c** and **d**, which have
    a no lines of symmetry
    b exactly one line of symmetry
    c exactly two lines of symmetry
    d exactly four lines of symmetry.
7 Copy these shapes, and draw their lines of symmetry.
    a   **b**   **c**   **d**

8 An isosceles triangle has vertices at (5, 6), (3, 2) and (7, 2). Draw the triangle on graph paper. Find the equation of the line of symmetry of the triangle.

Remember: finding equations of lines, from Unit 1

9 A square has vertices at (3, 2), (3, 5), (6, 5) and (6, 2). Find the equations of its lines of symmetry.

10 A rhombus has vertices at (1, 1), (4, 5), (4, 10) and (1, 6). Find the equations of its lines of symmetry.

11 For each of the following, plot the points and then join them up in the order given. Join the last point to the first point. For each shape, state the number of lines of symmetry, and give the equations of the lines of symmetry.

    a (1, 0), (1, 2), (−1, 2)

    b (1, 1), (2, 2), (3, 1), (2, −1)

    c (4, 0), (6, −4), (2, −6), (0, −2)

    d (−1, 3), (0, 0), (2, 3)

38 Reflection

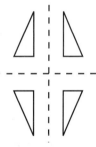

Look at this shape. It does not have any symmetry.
But when we add a copy of the shape, reversed, then the dotted line is now a line of symmetry.

Similarly, if we add two more copies, as shown opposite, then both dotted lines are lines of symmetry.

We say that the original shape has been **reflected** in the dotted lines.
When you look at yourself in a mirror, you see a copy of yourself, on the other side of the mirror. You see a **reflection** of yourself.

In a reflection, every point is taken to the other side of a mirror. In two dimensions, the mirror is a line. Take each point to the same distance on the other side of the line.

Look at the rectangle *ABCD* of Exercise 4.1A. The line *EF* was a line of symmetry of the rectangle. If *EF* is a mirror line, then *A* is reflected to *B* and *D* is reflected to *C*. *AEFD* is reflected to *BEFC*.

We call the original shape the **object**, and the reflected shape the **image**.

EXAMPLE 3

Reflect the line AB in the dotted mirror line.

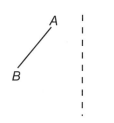

Solution

Each point must go to a point at the same distance from and on the other side of the mirror line. Drop a perpendicular from A to X on the line. Continue this perpendicular an equal distance to A', so that $AX = XA'$. Repeat with B. Join up $A'B'$ as shown.

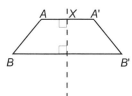

Reflections are easier if you use graph paper or squared paper.

EXAMPLE 4

Reflect the triangle ABC in the dotted line.

Solution

Point A is 2 units to the left of the line. So reflect it to A', 2 units to the right of the line.
Point B is 3 unit to the left of the line. So reflect it to B', 3 units to the right of the line.
Point C is 1 unit to the left of the line.
So reflect it to C', 1 unit to the right of the line.
The reflected triangle $A'B'C'$ is shown here.

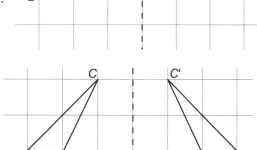

Exercise 4.2A

1   Reflect the line AB in the dotted line.

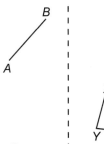

2   Reflect the triangle XYZ in the dotted line.

3   Reflect the kite $PQRS$ in the dotted line.

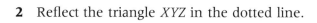

4 Reflect the triangle *ABC* in the dotted line.

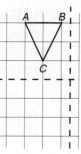

5 Reflect the arrowhead in the dotted line.

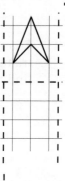

6 Reflect the rectangle *WXYZ* in the dotted line.

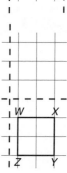

7 Complete the shapes below so that the dotted line is a mirror line.

a

b

c

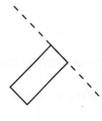

8 Complete the shape so that both dotted lines are mirror lines.

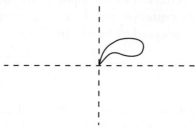

9 In this diagram, *A* has been reflected to *B*. Copy the diagram. By finding the perpendicular bisector of *AB*, find the mirror line of the reflection.

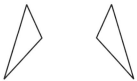

10 These triangles are reflections of each other. Copy the diagram and find the mirror line of the reflection.

11 Triangle *ABC* has been reflected to triangle *DEF*. Copy the diagram and find the mirror line of the reflection.

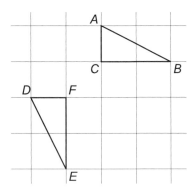

12 The diagram shows three pairs of shapes which are reflections of each other. Copy the diagram, and for each pair find the mirror line of the reflection.

a    b   c

Reflections using coordinates

If the coordinates of a point are given, then the coordinates of its reflection can be calculated.

A vertical line has equation $x = c$, for c a constant. If any point is to the left of the line, then it will be reflected to the right of the line.
A horizontal line has equation $y = k$, for k a constant. If any point is above the line, then it will be reflected to below the line.

EXAMPLE 5

Find the reflection of the point (1, 2) after reflection
(a) in the line $x = 3$ (b) in the line $y = -1$

Solution

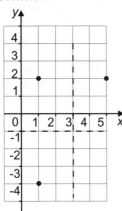

(a) The point is 2 to the left of the line $x = 3$. Reflect it to 2 to the right of the line.
The point is reflected to (5, 2).

(b) The point is 3 above the line $y = -1$. Reflect it to 3 below the line.
The point is reflected to (1, –4).

Exercise 4.2B

In questions **1** to **8**, find the reflections of the points in the line given.
1. (2, 2) in the line $x = 3$
2. (4, 7) in the line $x = 1$
3. (–3, –1) in the line $x = 2$
4. (2, 3) in the line $y = 1$
5. (5, –3) in the line $y = -1$
6. (2, 4) in the line $y = -2$
7. (4, 2) in the x-axis
8. (2, –1) in the y-axis
9. The point (3, 4) is reflected to (7, 4). Find the equation of the mirror line.
10. The point (5, 2) is reflected to (–1, 2). Find the equation of the mirror line.
11. The point (–1, 3) is reflected to (–1, –7). Find the equation of the mirror line.
12. The point (–2, 5) is reflected to (–2, –3). Find the equation of the mirror line.

Reflection in $y = \pm x$

The two diagonal lines through the origin have equations $y = x$ and $y = -x$. There are simple ways to reflect points in these lines.

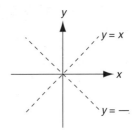

Exercise 4.2C

1. Draw x- and y-axes on graph paper. Draw the line $y = x$. Reflect the following points in the line, and write down the new coordinates.

   (3, 2)   (4, 1)   (2, 5)   (1, 6)   (0, 3)   (2, 0)

   Find a rule for reflecting points in this line. What is the reflection of (a, b)?

2 Draw the line $y = -x$. Reflect the following points in the line, and write down the new coordinates.

$$(2, 0) \qquad (0, 3) \qquad (2, -1) \qquad (3, 2) \qquad (-3, 2) \qquad (-2, -1)$$

Find a rule for reflecting points in this line. What is the reflection of (a, b)?

3 The point $(4, 7)$ is reflected to $(7, 4)$. What is the equation of the mirror line?

4 The point $(-2, 1)$ is reflected to $(-1, 2)$. What is the equation of the mirror line?

5 The x-axis is reflected on to the y-axis. Show that there are two possible mirror lines, and give their equations.

6 The line $y = x$ is reflected on to the line $y = -x$. Show that there are two possible mirror lines, and give their equations.

After doing this exercise, you have found that

> To reflect in the line $y = x$, exchange the x- and y-coordinates. So $(2, 4)$ is reflected to $(4, 2)$.
> To reflect in the line $y = -x$, exchange the x- and y-coordinates and multiply both by -1. So $(-2, 4)$ is reflected to $(-4, 2)$.

4.3

You can prove theorems in geometry by using symmetry and reflection.

EXAMPLE 6

ABC is an isosceles triangle, with $AB = AC$. Show that the base angles $\angle B$ and $\angle C$ are equal.

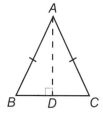

Solution

Drop a perpendicular from A to D on BC. Then AD is a line of symmetry of the triangle. It follows that $\angle B = \angle C$.

EXAMPLE 7

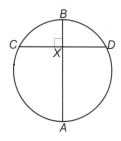

In the circle shown, AB is a diameter. CD is a chord, cutting AB at X, at $90°$. Show that $CX = DX$.

Solution

Reflect the left hand side of the diagram on to the right hand side. Because $\angle CXA = \angle DXA = 90°$, it follows that CX is reflected to DX.
Hence $CX = DX$.

Exercise 4.3

Answer these questions using reflection or symmetry.

1 The figure on the following page shows two lines AB and CD crossing at X. Show that $\angle AXC = \angle BXD$.

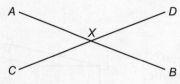

2 The figure shows a kite *ABCD*, with *AB* = *AD* and *CB* = *CD*. Show that ∠*B* = ∠*D*.

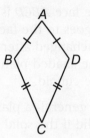

3 This figure shows a circle, centre *O*. *AB* is a diameter, and *CD* and *EF* are equal chords crossing *AB* at 90°. Show that *CD* and *EF* are equal distances from *O*.

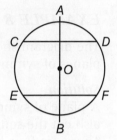

4 In the figure, *AB* and *PQ* are equal chords of the circle. Show that *AP* is parallel to *BQ*.

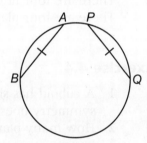

5 The diagram shows an isosceles triangle at one end of a rectangle. The perpendicular bisectors of *AB* and *AC* meet at *X*, and the perpendicular bisectors of *BD* and *CE* meet at *Y*. Show that *A*, *X* and *Y* lie on a straight line.

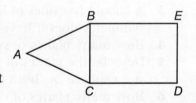

6 This diagram shows a square *ABCD*, with equilateral triangles *BCE* and *DCF*. Show that *AC*, *DE* and *BF* meet at a point.

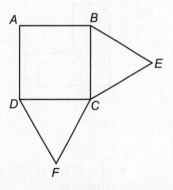

In the diagram, the shaded plane cuts the cuboid *ABCDEFGH* into equal halves. When the face *ABCD* is reflected in the shaded plane, it goes to the face *EFGH*. The cuboid is unchanged after reflection in the shaded plane. The shaded plane is a **plane of symmetry** of the cuboid.

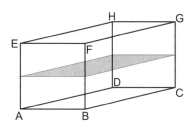

In general, a plane is a plane of symmetry of a solid if the solid is unchanged after reflection in the plane.

EXAMPLE 8

The diagram shows a square-based pyramid. How many planes of symmetry does it have?

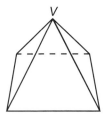

Solution
A plane of symmetry must go through the vertex *V*. It must also cut the square base in a line of symmetry of the square. There are four lines of symmetry of the square. There are four planes of symmetry.

Exercise 4.4

1　A cuboid has sides of length 4 cm, 5 cm and 6 cm. How many planes of symmetry does it have?

2　How many planes of symmetry does a regular tetrahedron (four-sided solid) have?

3　A cuboid has sides of length 3 cm, 3 cm and 4 cm. How many planes of symmetry does it have?

4　How many planes of symmetry does a cube have?

5　Describe the planes of symmetry of
　　a a sphere　　**b** a cylinder　　**c** a cone.

6　How many planes of symmetry are there for the objects shown below?

a 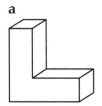　　　**b** 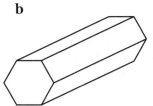　　　**c**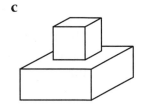

● If a shape is identical on both sides of a line, the line is a line of symmetry of the shape.

- A reflection takes points to the other side of a mirror line.
- Reflections can be done using coordinates.
- If a plane shape is unchanged after a reflection, the mirror line is a line of symmetry of the shape.
- If a solid shape is unchanged after a reflection, the mirror plane is a plane of symmetry of the shape.

1 Any shape can be extended so that it is symmetrical. Draw any shape on paper, and fold it over while the ink is still wet. The fold line is a line of symmetry.
These shapes are sometimes called Rorschach blots. A Swiss psychiatrist called Rorschach made ink blots, and asked his patients what the blots showed. Make some Rorschach blots and say what they represent.
By making two folds, make Rorschach blots with two lines of symmetry.
2 Fold a sheet of paper twice, and cut out a piece as shown. What can you say about the symmetry of the hole?

1 Draw the lines of symmetry of this shape.

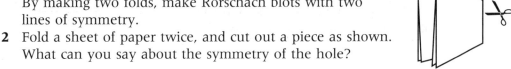

2 How many lines of symmetry does a regular octagon have?
3 Draw a pentagon with exactly one line of symmetry.
4 Draw quadrilaterals **a** and **b** which have
    a exactly one line of symmetry which is a diagonal
    b exactly one line of symmetry which is not a diagonal.
5 Plot these points, and join them up in the order given. Join the last point to the first. Find the equations of the lines of symmetry of the shape.
    (0, 1), (4, 4), (−1, 4), (−5, 1)
6 Make a copy of this diagram and reflect the shapes in the dotted line.

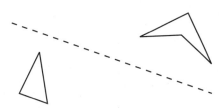

7 Find the coordinates of the point (1, 3) after it has been reflected
    a in $x = -1$ **b** in $y = 5$ **c** in $y = x$.

8 Complete the shape so that both dotted lines are lines of symmetry.

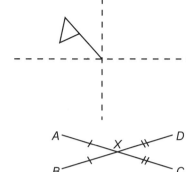

9 In the diagram $AX = BX$ and $CX = DX$. Show that AB is parallel to CD.

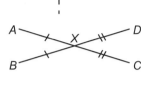

10 In the diagram triangle ABC is isosceles, and $ABDE$ and $ACFG$ are squares. Show that $EC = GB$.

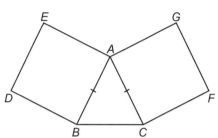

11 A prism has a cross-section which is an equilateral triangle. How many planes of symmetry does the prism have?

1 The year 1881 was the last year which had a line of symmetry. When will be the next such year?

2 The diagram shows a wall and two balls. In a game, you need to hit the ball A so that it hits the wall, then strikes ball B. What path must ball A follow?

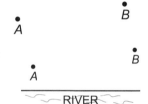

3 A farmer wants to take his cow from A to the river to drink, and then to the shed at B. What is the shortest route? Make a copy of the diagram, and find the shortest route.

4 A rope passes over a smooth rod as shown. Two people pull with equal strength at each end. Make a copy of the diagram, include the positions of the people, and show where the rope will cross the rod.

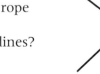

5 What are the coordinates of (a, b) after reflection in these lines?
   a $x = k$ **b** $y = k$

6 Draw the next shape in the sequence below.

 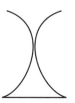 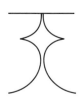

5

Vectors and translations

This unit uses
- Coordinates
- Pythagoras' theorem

5.1 Definition of column vectors

Look at the grid opposite. Suppose it is part of a map. If an aeroplane flies in a straight line from A to B, how can you state its direction? One way is by its bearing, the angle of $56.3°$ from the North.

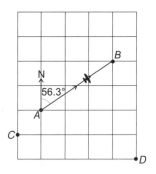

Instead, we can use a **vector** to indicate the direction. To move from A to B you move $+3$ units horizontally (the x-direction), and then $+2$ units vertically (the y-direction). This is written in the following way as a **column vector**.

$$\overrightarrow{AB} = \begin{pmatrix} +3 \\ +2 \end{pmatrix}$$

The arrow $\rightarrow$ above $\overrightarrow{AB}$ indicates the direction of movement. The vector $\overrightarrow{BA}$ means move from B to A. Because $\overrightarrow{AB}$ and $\overrightarrow{BA}$ are equal but in opposite directions, we write

$$\overrightarrow{AB} = -\overrightarrow{BA}.$$

Sometimes the vector is written in bold type without an arrow, as **AB**. This means move from A to B and **BA** means move from B to A. As above, we write

AB $= -$**BA**

Note When writing by hand, $\overrightarrow{AB}$ is easier than **AB**. When printing, **AB** is easier.

Now look at the movement from D to C on the grid above. This requires a move of -5 (5 back) parallel to the x-axis, and then $+1$ parallel to the y-axis.

Hence   **DC** $= \begin{pmatrix} -5 \\ +1 \end{pmatrix}$

In general, when we write a vector **AB** $= \begin{pmatrix} x \\ y \end{pmatrix}$, the top number x is called the

x-**component**, and the bottom number y is called the y-**component**. A vector written in this way is called a **column vector**.

As well as having direction, the arrow is drawn to scale and so a vector has a length (or **magnitude**). If you want to write the magnitude of the vector **PQ**, use this notation :

$$\text{magnitude} = |\mathbf{PQ}|.$$

Notice the difference between a vector $\overrightarrow{AB}$ and a line segment of the same length AB. For the vector, the direction matters. For the line segment, the direction does not matter. Its length is just written AB.

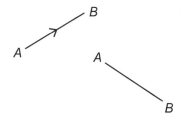

A quantity that has size and no direction, is called a **scalar**. Compare these:

> The distance from Nairobi to Mombasa is 500 km.
> The displacement from Nairobi to Mombasa is 500 km on a bearing of 120°.

The distance is just the length of the journey. It is a scalar.
The displacement is the length and the direction of the journey. It is a vector.

> RULE
>
> **A quantity that has size and direction is a vector quantity.**
> **A quantity with size only is a scalar quantity.**

The following table gives some examples of vectors and scalars used in everyday life.

Scalar	Vector
mass	force (direction needed)
speed (direction not needed)	velocity (speed and direction)
length	acceleration (rate of change of velocity)

Now look at the following example.

EXAMPLE 1

The path of a race is marked out on a square grid. The start of the race is at the point $S(1, 2)$. The first stage **SA** is $\begin{pmatrix} +4 \\ -1 \end{pmatrix}$. The second stage **AB** is $\begin{pmatrix} -6 \\ -1 \end{pmatrix}$, and the third stage to the finish F is **BF**, $\begin{pmatrix} -4 \\ +5 \end{pmatrix}$. Draw a diagram to show the path of the race. Where does the race finish?

Solution

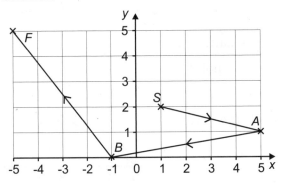

SA must go +4 parallel to the x-axis and 1 down (−1) parallel to the y-axis. Hence A is the point (5, 1).

Then from A it is back 6 parallel to the x-axis, and down 1 parallel to the y-axis to give B as (−1, 0).

Finally back 4 in the x-direction and up 5 in the y-direction we reach the finish F at the point (−5, 5). The path is shown in the diagram.

Exercise 5.1

1 Which of the following are scalars and which vectors?
  (i) temperature   (ii) magnetic attraction   (iii) time
  (iv) income   (v) electrical current
2 Write the following displacements as column vectors.
  (i) 2 along the x-direction and 3 up the y-direction
  (ii) 4 to the left along the x-direction and 5 down the y-direction
3 Construct the following path on a square grid.
  Start at $A(1, 3)$.

  Then find B if $\mathbf{AB} = \begin{pmatrix} 2 \\ -4 \end{pmatrix}$. Join AB.

  Find C if $\mathbf{BC} = \begin{pmatrix} -4 \\ 3 \end{pmatrix}$. Join BC.

  Find D if $\mathbf{CD} = \begin{pmatrix} 7 \\ 1 \end{pmatrix}$. Join CD. What is $\mathbf{DA}$?

4 Find the following vectors from the diagram on the right.
  (i) **BA**   (ii) **BC**   (iii) **DC**
5 On a grid mark the points $A(1, 1)$, $B(3, 4)$ and $C(8, 1)$. Find the vectors
  (i) **AB**   (ii) **BC**   (iii) **CA**
6 The point A is at (3, 4). The points B, C, D and E are such that
  $$\mathbf{AB} = \begin{pmatrix} 2 \\ 7 \end{pmatrix} \qquad \mathbf{AC} = \begin{pmatrix} 4 \\ -7 \end{pmatrix} \qquad \mathbf{BD} = \begin{pmatrix} -3 \\ 6 \end{pmatrix} \qquad \mathbf{EA} = \begin{pmatrix} 7 \\ -3 \end{pmatrix}$$
  Find the coordinates of B, C, D and E.

5.2 The arithmetic of vectors

(i) Addition

We will introduce here another notation for vectors, a single letter in bold type such as **a** or, if handwritten, a.

For example $\mathbf{a} = \begin{pmatrix} 2 \\ 3 \end{pmatrix}$ and $\mathbf{b} = \begin{pmatrix} 4 \\ 1 \end{pmatrix}$ are two different vectors. If we want to find $\mathbf{a} + \mathbf{b}$ this means $\mathbf{a}$ *followed* by $\mathbf{b}$.

The diagram shows a displacement starting at O, moving $\begin{pmatrix} 2 \\ 3 \end{pmatrix}$ then $\begin{pmatrix} 4 \\ 1 \end{pmatrix}$ to reach the point $(6, 4)$. This point could be reached in one move using the vector $\begin{pmatrix} 6 \\ 4 \end{pmatrix}$. This is the vector $\mathbf{a} + \mathbf{b}$.

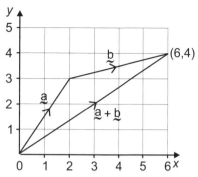

$$\text{So} \begin{pmatrix} 2 \\ 3 \end{pmatrix} + \begin{pmatrix} 4 \\ 1 \end{pmatrix} = \begin{pmatrix} 6 \\ 4 \end{pmatrix}.$$

> **R U L E**
>
> **To add two or more vectors, you add the x-components, and add the y-components.**

Suppose you want to add two vectors without the help of a grid. Take vectors $\mathbf{a}$ and $\mathbf{b}$ such as those shown opposite. Draw a triangle where the beginning of vector $\mathbf{b}$ is joined to the end of vector $\mathbf{a}$. The result is shown here.

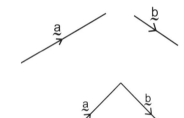

The vector going from the beginning of $\mathbf{a}$ to the end of $\mathbf{b}$ is the vector $\mathbf{a} + \mathbf{b}$. This is called the **triangle addition rule**. You can also see that $\mathbf{b}$ followed by $\mathbf{a}$ gives $\mathbf{b} + \mathbf{a}$ and this is exactly the same as $\mathbf{a} + \mathbf{b}$.

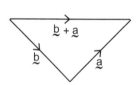

> **F A C T**
>
> $\mathbf{a} + \mathbf{b} = \mathbf{b} + \mathbf{a}$

(ii) Multiplication by a scalar

If $\mathbf{a} = \begin{pmatrix} 4 \\ 2 \end{pmatrix}$, then to find $3\mathbf{a}$

$$3\mathbf{a} = \mathbf{a} + \mathbf{a} + \mathbf{a} = \begin{pmatrix} 4 \\ 2 \end{pmatrix} + \begin{pmatrix} 4 \\ 2 \end{pmatrix} + \begin{pmatrix} 4 \\ 2 \end{pmatrix} = \begin{pmatrix} 12 \\ 6 \end{pmatrix} = \begin{pmatrix} 3 \times 4 \\ 3 \times 2 \end{pmatrix}$$

To multiply a vector by a scalar, you multiply each component by that scalar.
If you look at the diagram, you can see that $3\mathbf{a}$ is parallel to $\mathbf{a}$. This leads to the following important rule.

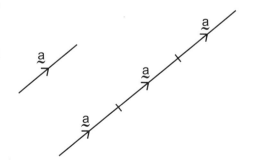

(iii) Subtraction

If $\mathbf{a} = \begin{pmatrix} 5 \\ 8 \end{pmatrix}$ and $\mathbf{b} = \begin{pmatrix} 7 \\ 3 \end{pmatrix}$, then to find $\mathbf{a} - \mathbf{b}$ you proceed as follows :

$$\mathbf{a} - \mathbf{b} = \mathbf{a} + -1 \times \mathbf{b} = \begin{pmatrix} 5 \\ 8 \end{pmatrix} + \begin{pmatrix} -7 \\ -3 \end{pmatrix} = \begin{pmatrix} -2 \\ 5 \end{pmatrix}$$

$$= \begin{pmatrix} 5 \\ 8 \end{pmatrix} - \begin{pmatrix} 7 \\ 3 \end{pmatrix}$$

You can see we have the rule for subtraction.

You can illustrate subtraction by using the triangle addition rule. To find $\mathbf{a} - \mathbf{b}$, you add $\mathbf{a}$ and $-\mathbf{b}$. This is seen in the diagram.

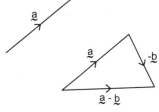

EXAMPLE 2

If $\mathbf{a} = \begin{pmatrix} 1 \\ 3 \end{pmatrix}$, $\mathbf{b} = \begin{pmatrix} 4 \\ 2 \end{pmatrix}$ and $\mathbf{c} = \begin{pmatrix} 1 \\ -2 \end{pmatrix}$, find

(a) $\mathbf{a} + \mathbf{b} + 2\mathbf{c}$ (b) $\mathbf{a} - 2\mathbf{b}$ (c) $3\mathbf{a} - 4\mathbf{b} + 5\mathbf{c}$

Solution

(a) $\quad \mathbf{a} + \mathbf{b} + 2\mathbf{c} = \begin{pmatrix} 1 \\ 3 \end{pmatrix} + \begin{pmatrix} 4 \\ 2 \end{pmatrix} + 2\begin{pmatrix} 1 \\ -2 \end{pmatrix}$

$$= \begin{pmatrix} 1 \\ 3 \end{pmatrix} + \begin{pmatrix} 4 \\ 2 \end{pmatrix} + \begin{pmatrix} 2 \\ -4 \end{pmatrix} = \begin{pmatrix} 7 \\ 1 \end{pmatrix}$$

(b) $\quad \mathbf{a} - 2\mathbf{b} = \begin{pmatrix} 1 \\ 3 \end{pmatrix} - 2\begin{pmatrix} 4 \\ 2 \end{pmatrix} = \begin{pmatrix} 1 \\ 3 \end{pmatrix} - \begin{pmatrix} 8 \\ 4 \end{pmatrix}$

$$= \begin{pmatrix} -7 \\ -1 \end{pmatrix}$$

(c) $\quad 3\mathbf{a} - 4\mathbf{b} + 5\mathbf{c} = \begin{pmatrix} 3 \\ 9 \end{pmatrix} - \begin{pmatrix} 16 \\ 8 \end{pmatrix} + \begin{pmatrix} 5 \\ -10 \end{pmatrix} = \begin{pmatrix} -8 \\ -9 \end{pmatrix}$

EXAMPLE 3

The grid shows the two vectors $\mathbf{a}$ and $\mathbf{b}$.
Draw a diagram to show (a) $2\mathbf{a} - \mathbf{b}$
(b) $2\mathbf{a} + \frac{1}{2}\mathbf{b}$

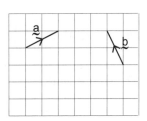

Solution

Remember that $2\mathbf{a} - \mathbf{b}$ means $2\mathbf{a}$ followed by $-\mathbf{b}$ and $2\mathbf{a} + \frac{1}{2}\mathbf{b}$ means $2\mathbf{a}$ followed by $\frac{1}{2}\mathbf{b}$.

The answers are shown in the diagram.

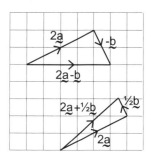

Exercise 5.2

1   In this question take $\mathbf{a} = \begin{pmatrix} 2 \\ 1 \end{pmatrix}$ and $\mathbf{b} = \begin{pmatrix} 3 \\ -2 \end{pmatrix}$. Find

   (i) $2\mathbf{a}$ (ii) $\mathbf{a} + \mathbf{b}$ (iii) $\mathbf{a} - \mathbf{b}$ (iv) $2\mathbf{a} - 3\mathbf{b}$

2   Let $\mathbf{u} = \begin{pmatrix} 3 \\ 4 \end{pmatrix}$ and $\mathbf{v} = \begin{pmatrix} -2 \\ 3 \end{pmatrix}$. Find

   (i) $\mathbf{u} + \mathbf{v}$ (ii) $\mathbf{v} - \mathbf{u}$ (iii) $-3\mathbf{v}$ (iv) $5\mathbf{u} + 3\mathbf{v}$

3   In the following question, take $\mathbf{a} = \begin{pmatrix} -2 \\ \frac{1}{2} \end{pmatrix}$, $\mathbf{b} = \begin{pmatrix} 3 \\ \frac{1}{4} \end{pmatrix}$, $\mathbf{c} = \begin{pmatrix} -\frac{1}{2} \\ -2 \end{pmatrix}$. Find

   (i) $2\mathbf{b} - 3\mathbf{a}$ (ii) $\mathbf{a} - 2\mathbf{b} - 3\mathbf{c}$ (iii) $\frac{1}{2}\mathbf{a} - \frac{1}{4}\mathbf{c}$

4   The diagram shows a grid with three vectors $\mathbf{a}$, $\mathbf{b}$, and $\mathbf{c}$ drawn. Draw a similar grid and draw vector triangles to show
   (i) $-2\mathbf{b}$ (ii) $\mathbf{b} - \mathbf{c}$
   (iii) $\mathbf{a} + 2\mathbf{b}$.

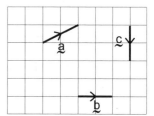

5   Using the grid opposite, write down in terms of $\mathbf{a}$ and $\mathbf{b}$ only, the vectors
   (i) $\mathbf{AC}$
   (ii) $\mathbf{BC}$
   (iii) $\mathbf{DA}$
   (iv) $\mathbf{EA} + \mathbf{BC}$
   (v) $\mathbf{DB} - \mathbf{AE}$
   (vi) $2\mathbf{AB} - 3\mathbf{AC}$

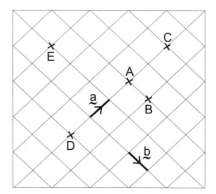

6   Given that $\begin{pmatrix} k \\ 3 \end{pmatrix} + \begin{pmatrix} 2 \\ 7 \end{pmatrix} = \begin{pmatrix} 5 \\ m \end{pmatrix}$, find k and m.

7   Given that $\begin{pmatrix} x \\ y \end{pmatrix} + \begin{pmatrix} 2x \\ 5 \end{pmatrix} = \begin{pmatrix} 9 \\ 2y \end{pmatrix}$, find x and y.

Two vectors are equal (equivalent) if they are

    (i)   in the same direction, *and*

    (ii) they have the same magnitude (length).

In this diagram **AB** = **CD**. This also means that *ABDC* is a parallelogram.

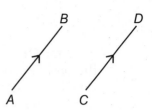

EXAMPLE 4

The diagram shows a cube, *ABCDEFGH*. Write down two other vectors equal to

(a) **EH**   and   (b) **DC**

Solution

(a) *FG* and *AD* are parallel to *EH* and of the same length because it is a cube. The direction must be the same as *EH*, because opposite edges of a cube are parallel. Hence two possible vectors would be **FG** and **AD**.

(b) Similarly, two possible answers here would be **AB** and **HG**.

Null vector

If you subtract a vector from itself, then the result is zero displacement. This is denoted by **O**, and is the **null** or **zero** vector.

    So **a** − **a** = **O**

As a column vector, the zero vector is $\begin{pmatrix} 0 \\ 0 \end{pmatrix}$. It has zero size and no direction. But it is a vector, not a scalar.

Exercise 5.3

1 In the diagram, identify pairs of (i) equal vectors (ii) parallel vectors.

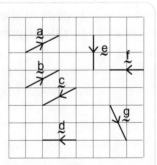

2 *B* is the midpoint of *AC* and *E* is the midpoint of *FD*. Write down vectors that are equal to

    (i) **AF**   (ii) **ED**   (iii) **BF**

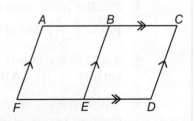

5.4

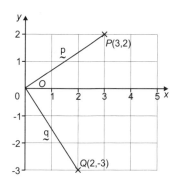

A vector **OP** which starts from the origin will locate the position coordinates of the point P, and so is called a **position vector**.

In the diagram you can see that

OP $= \begin{pmatrix} 3 \\ 2 \end{pmatrix}$ leads to the position $P(3, 2)$.

Also **OQ** $= \begin{pmatrix} 2 \\ -3 \end{pmatrix}$ leads to the position $Q(2, -3)$.

Position vectors are usually denoted by a single letter – the same as the letter for the point, but in lower case. Hence, for example, **h** would be used for the position vector of H.

For the above diagram, $\quad \mathbf{p} = \begin{pmatrix} 3 \\ 2 \end{pmatrix}$ and $\mathbf{q} = \begin{pmatrix} 2 \\ -3 \end{pmatrix}$

You can see that **QP** $= \begin{pmatrix} 1 \\ 5 \end{pmatrix} = \begin{pmatrix} 3-2 \\ 2--3 \end{pmatrix} = \begin{pmatrix} 3 \\ 2 \end{pmatrix} - \begin{pmatrix} 2 \\ -3 \end{pmatrix}$

So **QP** $= \mathbf{p} - \mathbf{q}$

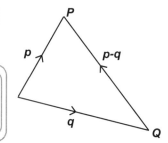

> **R U L E**
>
> **The vector joining two points, Q to P, is the difference between the position vectors, that is p – q.**

Exercise 5.4

1 Draw a diagram to show the points A, B and C with position vectors given by $\mathbf{a} = \begin{pmatrix} 3 \\ -1 \end{pmatrix}$, $\mathbf{b} = \begin{pmatrix} 2 \\ 2 \end{pmatrix}$ and $\mathbf{c} = \begin{pmatrix} 4 \\ 3 \end{pmatrix}$.

2 Write down the position vectors of the points shown in this diagram.

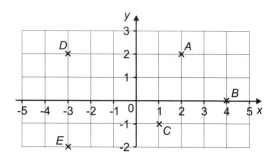

3 P is the point with position vector $\mathbf{p} = \begin{pmatrix} 4 \\ -1 \end{pmatrix}$ and Q is a point such that **PQ** $= \begin{pmatrix} 2 \\ -3 \end{pmatrix}$. What is the position vector of Q?

4 A and B are points with position vectors $\mathbf{a} = \begin{pmatrix} 5 \\ 7 \end{pmatrix}$ and $\mathbf{b} = \begin{pmatrix} 2 \\ -3 \end{pmatrix}$. Find the vectors (i) **AB** (ii) **BA**.

5 A has position vector $\begin{pmatrix} 4 \\ -5 \end{pmatrix}$ and B is a point for which **AB** $= \begin{pmatrix} -2 \\ 5 \end{pmatrix}$. Find the position vector of B.

6 C has position vector $\begin{pmatrix} 3 \\ 2 \end{pmatrix}$ and D is a point for which $\mathbf{DC} = \begin{pmatrix} -4 \\ -8 \end{pmatrix}$. Find the position vector of D.

5.5 Magnitude of a vector

In the diagram $\mathbf{OP} = \begin{pmatrix} 3 \\ 4 \end{pmatrix}$ and so $|\mathbf{OP}| = \sqrt{3^2 + 4^2}$

(using Pythagoras' theorem).

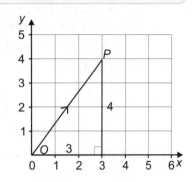

> **RULE**
> **The magnitude of a vector** $\begin{pmatrix} x \\ y \end{pmatrix}$ **is** $\sqrt{x^2 + y^2}$.

EXAMPLE 5

Find the magnitude of the vector $\begin{pmatrix} 6 \\ -7 \end{pmatrix}$.

Solution
Use the formula, with $x = 6$ and $y = -7$. Remember that the square of -7 is $+49$.

$$\sqrt{6^2 + (-7)^2} = \sqrt{36 + 49} = \sqrt{85}.$$

The magnitude of $\begin{pmatrix} 6 \\ -7 \end{pmatrix}$ is $\sqrt{85}$.

Exercise 5.5

Find the magnitude of the following vectors.

1 $\begin{pmatrix} 5 \\ 12 \end{pmatrix}$ **2** $\begin{pmatrix} 3 \\ -4 \end{pmatrix}$ **3** $\begin{pmatrix} 5 \\ 8 \end{pmatrix}$ **4** $\begin{pmatrix} 8 \\ -6 \end{pmatrix}$ **5** $\begin{pmatrix} 8 \\ 11 \end{pmatrix}$

6 The magnitude of the vector $\begin{pmatrix} x \\ 10 \end{pmatrix}$ is 26. Find x, given that it is positive.

7 The magnitude of the vector $\begin{pmatrix} k \\ 3k \end{pmatrix}$ is 160. Find k, given that it is positive.

8 Points A and B have position vectors $\begin{pmatrix} 4 \\ 3 \end{pmatrix}$ and $\begin{pmatrix} 2 \\ -5 \end{pmatrix}$. Find the magnitude of **AB**.

9 Points X and Y have position vectors $\begin{pmatrix} 5 \\ 2 \end{pmatrix}$ and $\begin{pmatrix} 7 \\ 8 \end{pmatrix}$. Find the magnitude of **YX**.

If three or more points lie on a straight line, we say that they are **collinear**. If you look at the diagram,

then $\mathbf{AB} = \mathbf{b} - \mathbf{a} = \begin{pmatrix} 3 \\ 2 \end{pmatrix}$.

Also, $\mathbf{BC} = \mathbf{c} - \mathbf{b} = \begin{pmatrix} 6 \\ 4 \end{pmatrix}$

$= 2 \times \begin{pmatrix} 3 \\ 2 \end{pmatrix} = 2 \times \mathbf{AB}$.

So **BC** is twice the vector **AB**, which means it is in

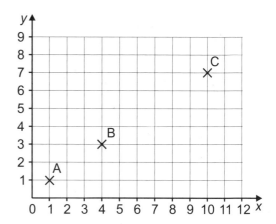

the same direction as **AB** and twice its length. This is only possible if ABC is a straight line, and so A, B and C are collinear.

The ratio of the lengths of the line segments $AB : BC$ is 1 : 2.

NOTE
In Unit 2 we showed that points were collinear by using gradients. Here we use vectors.

EXAMPLE 6

Points $A(2, 3)$, $B(k, 7)$ and $C(7, 13)$ are collinear. Find k.

Solution

$\mathbf{AB} = \begin{pmatrix} k - 2 \\ 4 \end{pmatrix}$ and $\mathbf{AC} = \begin{pmatrix} 5 \\ 10 \end{pmatrix}$. If these vectors are parallel, then

$$\frac{k - 2}{4} = \frac{5}{10} = \frac{1}{2}$$

Hence $k - 2 = 4 \times \frac{1}{2} = 2$.

$k = 4$

Exercise 5.6

1 Show that the points $P(1, 2)$, $Q(3, 3)$ and $R(9, 6)$ are collinear. What is the ratio $PQ : QR$?

2 Show that the points $A(3, 7)$, $B(4, 10)$ and $C(6, 16)$ are collineat. Find the ratio $AB:BC$

3 The points $(4, 3)$, $(6, x)$ and $(10, 6)$ are collinear. Find x.

4 The points $M(2, 3)$, $N(3, 4)$ and $Q(7, q)$ lie in a straight line. Find the value of q.

5 Let points A, B and C be at $(1, 1)$, $(4, 5)$ and $(10, 13)$ respectively.
   (i)   Show that the points are collinear.
   (ii) Find the magnitudes of **AB**, **BC** and **AC**.
   (iii) Show that the sum of the magnitudes of **AB** and **BC** is equal to the magnitude of **AC**. Show on a diagram why this happens.

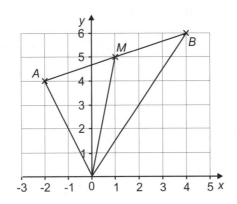

In the diagram A is the point $(-2, 4)$, B is at $(4, 6)$ and M is the midpoint of AB. The

vector $\mathbf{AB}$ is $\begin{pmatrix} 6 \\ 2 \end{pmatrix}$.

Since $\mathbf{AM} = \frac{1}{2} \mathbf{AB}$, $\mathbf{AM} = \begin{pmatrix} 3 \\ 1 \end{pmatrix}$.

Also, since A is $(-2, 4)$ then M is $(-2 + 3, 4 + 1) = (1, 5)$

M's coordinates are the *average* of A's and B's.

So M is $\left(\dfrac{-2 + 4}{2}, \dfrac{4 + 6}{2} \right) = (1, 5)$

> **RULE**
> **The mid point of $A(x_1, y_1)$ and $B(x_2, y_2)$ is M at $\left(\dfrac{x_1 + x_2}{2}, \dfrac{y_1 + y_2}{2} \right)$.**

EXAMPLE 7

If $A(2, 3)$, $B(h, 5)$ and $C(6, k)$ are in a straight line with B as the midpoint, find the values of h and k.

Solution

Since B is the midpoint, its coordinates are given by the midpoint formula.

So $h = \dfrac{2 + 6}{2} = 4$

And $5 = \dfrac{3 + k}{2}$ so $10 = 3 + k$, giving $k = 7$.

Exercise 5.7

1 Find the midpoints of the line segment joining the following pairs of points:
   (i) $(3, 5)$ and $(6, 8)$ (ii) $(4, -3)$ and $(12, 0)$

2 The midpoint of $\begin{pmatrix} m \\ 3 \end{pmatrix}$ and $\begin{pmatrix} 6 \\ n \end{pmatrix}$ is $\begin{pmatrix} 7 \\ -2 \end{pmatrix}$. Find m and n.

3 The line joining the points $D(-1, 3)$ and $E(3, 5)$ is extended to a point F so that E is the midpoint of DF. Find the coordinates of F.

4 $ABCD$ is a rectangle, M is the midpoint of BC, and N is on AB extended so that $AB = BN$.

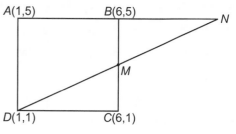

   (i)   Find the coordinates of M and N.

   (ii) Prove that DMN is a straight line.

5.8

When a shape moves so that all points of the shape move the same distance in the same direction, it is said to have undergone a translation.

The translation can be represented by the vector for moving each point. Here the vector $\mathbf{AA'} = \begin{pmatrix} 5 \\ -4 \end{pmatrix}$

We can write the translation as

$$\mathbf{T} = \begin{pmatrix} 5 \\ -4 \end{pmatrix}.$$

The image of a point P under a translation $\mathbf{T}$ will be written $\mathbf{T}(P)$.

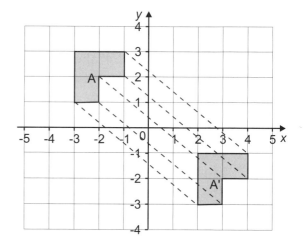

EXAMPLE 8

Find the image of the point $Q(3, -2)$ under the translation $\mathbf{T} = \begin{pmatrix} 2 \\ 3 \end{pmatrix}$.

Solution

The image of Q will be $(3 + 2, -2 + 3) = (5, 1)$

EXAMPLE 9

If $M(6, 8)$ is the image of N under the translation $\mathbf{T} = \begin{pmatrix} 5 \\ -4 \end{pmatrix}$, find the coordinates of N.

Solution

Use the translation $-\mathbf{T}$ to reverse the translation.

So N is $(6 - 5, 8 - -4) = (1, 12)$.

Exercise 5.8

1   Make a copy of this diagram. Draw the image of the shape after a translation

$$\mathbf{T} = \begin{pmatrix} 4 \\ -3 \end{pmatrix}.$$

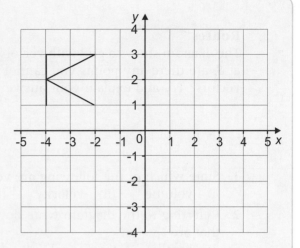

2   Find the image of the points $A(1, -3)$ and $B(7, -2)$ under the translation

$$\mathbf{T} = \begin{pmatrix} 3 \\ -2 \end{pmatrix}.$$

3   Find the images of the points $(3, 7)$, $(-1, -5)$ and $(-2, 3)$ under the translation $\begin{pmatrix} 3 \\ -2 \end{pmatrix}$

4   Find the translations which take
   (i) $(1, 2)$ to $(4, 7)$ (ii) $(7, -3)$ to $(2, 8)$ (iii) $(1, 5)$ to $(-1, -2)$

5   $V(7, 3)$ is the image of the point G under the translation $\mathbf{T} = \begin{pmatrix} 2 \\ 5 \end{pmatrix}$. Find the coordinates of G.

6   The translation $\begin{pmatrix} 4 \\ 3 \end{pmatrix}$ takes a point A to $(-2, 7)$. Find the coordinates of A.

7   A translation $\mathbf{T}$ takes $A(x, y)$ to the point A' $(x + 3, y - 5)$. Find $\mathbf{T}$.
8   Find the translation which takes (a, b) to $(a - 1, b + 5)$.

9   The translation $\begin{pmatrix} -2 \\ -3 \end{pmatrix}$ takes P to $P'(-8, 3)$. Find the midpoint of PP'.

Summary

- A vector has magnitude and direction.
- A quantity that has magnitude but not direction is a scalar.
- Addition of vectors follows the triangle rule.
- Vectors are added or subtracted by adding or subtracting the components (or elements).
- The length of a vector can be found using Pythagoras' theorem.
- The midpoint position vector is the average of the position vectors at the ends of the line segment.
- A vector can be used to represent a translation.

Activity 5

Routes

The diagram shows a grid with vectors **a**, **b**, **c** and **d**. Starting at S, are there any points you cannot reach using just these vectors? Try and explain your answers.

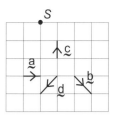

1 State which of the following are vector quantities.
   (i)   volume   (ii)   velocity   (iii)   force   (iv)   energy

2 Referring to the diagram write down two vectors that are
   (i)   parallel   (ii)   equal.

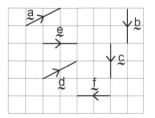

3 Complete the statement below about the vectors shown in this diagram.
   PQ+ QR =

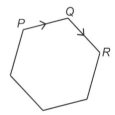

4 If $\mathbf{a} = \begin{pmatrix} 2 \\ -2 \end{pmatrix}$, $\mathbf{b} = \begin{pmatrix} 1 \\ 1 \end{pmatrix}$ and $\mathbf{c} = \begin{pmatrix} 0 \\ 2 \end{pmatrix}$, find
   (i) $\mathbf{a} + 2\mathbf{b}$ (ii) $\mathbf{a} + 2\mathbf{b} - \mathbf{c}$ (iii) $3\mathbf{a} - \mathbf{b} + 2\mathbf{c}$

5 Using a grid similar to that opposite, draw on it the vectors
   (i) $\mathbf{a} + 2\mathbf{b}$ (ii) $2\mathbf{a} - \mathbf{b}$.

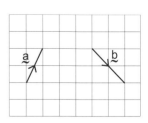

6 Simplify: (i) $4(\mathbf{a} + 3\mathbf{b}) - 3(2\mathbf{a} + \mathbf{b})$
   (ii) $\frac{1}{2}(3\mathbf{a} - \mathbf{b}) + \frac{1}{4}(2\mathbf{b} + \mathbf{a})$

7 *ABCDEF* is a regular hexagon.
   (i)   Show that **AB** = **a** + **b**.
   (ii)   Find **FC** and **AD** in terms of **a** and **b**.

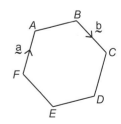

Puzzles 5

1 Show how to arrange 16 pieces on a chess board (8 × 8 squares) so that no three of them are in a straight line.

2 If the points $A(a, b)$, $B(c, d)$ and $C(e, f)$ lie on a straight line, prove that $de + bc + dc + af = fc + ad + dc + be$.

3 If $\mathbf{i} = \begin{pmatrix} 1 \\ 0 \end{pmatrix}$ and $\mathbf{j} = \begin{pmatrix} 0 \\ 1 \end{pmatrix}$ then any vector can be written as $x\mathbf{i} + y\mathbf{j}$.
Find h and k if $(h - 2)\mathbf{i} + (3 + k)\mathbf{j} = \begin{pmatrix} 4 \\ 3 \end{pmatrix}$.

6

Averages

6.1

Once you have collected the data, organised it and illustrated it by means of diagrams, you need to calculate certain statistical measures to describe the data more precisely. There are various types of **averages** – the **arithmetic mean** (or simply the **mean**), the **median**, and the **mode**. Once the averages are found, it is easier to compare two or more sets of data. These averages are called **measures of central tendency**.

6.2

When people are asked to find the average of some numbers, they usually find the total of the numbers, and then divide this total by however many numbers there are. This type of average is the **arithmetic mean**.

EXAMPLE 1

The masses of some parcels are 5 kg, 8 kg, 20 kg and 15 kg. Find the mean mass of the parcels.

Solution

> Total mass = 5 + 8 + 20 + 15 = 48 kg
>
> The number of parcels = 4
>
> The mean mass = 48 ÷ 4 = 12 kg

The arithmetic mean used as an average can be misleading, as you can see in the following example.

EXAMPLE 2

Niraj and Onyango played for the local cricket team. In the last six batting innings, they scored the following number of runs.

> Niraj   : 64, 0, 1, 2, 4, 1
>
> Onyango : 15, 20, 13, 11, 10, 3

Find the average score of each player. Which player would you rather have in your team? Give a reason.

Solution

$$\text{Niraj's mean} = (64 + 0 + 1 + 2 + 4 + 1) \div 6 = 12$$

$$\text{Onyango's mean} = (15 + 20 + 13 + 11 + 10 + 3) \div 6 = 12$$

Each player has the *same* mean score. However if you look at the individual scores, it would suggest they were different types of player. If you were looking for a steady reliable player, you would probably choose Onyango.

Often it is possible to use the mean of one set of numbers to find the mean of another set of related numbers. Study the next example.

EXAMPLE 3

(a) Find the mean of the numbers 4, 9, 15, 12 and 8.
(b) Use your answer to part (a) to find the mean of
   (i)   604, 609, 615, 612 and 608
   (ii) 103, 108, 114, 111 and 107

Solution

(a) The mean $= (4 + 9 + 15 + 12 + 8) \div 5 = 9.6$
(b) (i) Each number is 600 more than the five numbers in part (a), hence the mean of these numbers is $600 + 9.6 = 609.6$
    (ii) This is not so easy to see, but each of these five numbers is 99 more than the numbers in part (a), hence the mean is $99 + 9.6 = 108.6$

Exercise 6.2

1 Find the mean for each of the following sets of numbers.
   a 5, 11, 20, 31, 6, 8, 7, 15
   b 9, 13, 95, 63, 87, 23, 0, 12
   c 2.1, 3.2, 4.8, 5.6, 7.5, 8.2, 3.1, 4.9
   d −5, −8, −3, 2, 8, 11, 4
   e $x, 2x, 3x, 5x, 7x$
   f $(w + 4)$, $(3w + 3)$, $(2w + 1)$, $(2w + 16)$. Simplify your answer.

2 Find the mean of the numbers 8, 11, 12, 32, 40, 50. Hence, find the means of the following numbers and explain carefully how you got your answers.
   a 208, 211, 212, 232, 240, 250
   b 16, 22, 24, 64, 80, 100
   c 92, 89, 88, 68, 60, 50

3 Over six hours, the temperature of a patient in a hospital was as below. Find the mean temperature as quickly as you can. Explain how you got your result.

     38.1°   38.9°   38.7°   38.6°   38.9°   39.0°

4 Ten athletes run a 100 m race. Their times, in seconds, are below. Find, as quickly as you can, their mean time.

11.1   11.5   11.6   11.4   11.2   11.6   11.3   11.5   11.1   11.4

5 The average age of a class of 20 pupils is 14 years. The average age of a different class of 30 pupils is 16 years. What is the average age of all 50 pupils?

6 A car travels at an average speed of 30 km/h for 2 hours and 40 km/h for a further 3 hours. What is the average speed over the 5 hours?

6.3 the median

Mr Muita owns a small factory. He earns about sh 400 000 from it each year. He employs 4 people. They earn sh 55 000, sh 50 000, sh 45 000 and sh 40 000.

If you work out the mean income, it is

$$(400\ 000 + 55\ 000 + 50\ 000 + 45\ 000 + 40\ 000) \div 5 = \text{sh } 118\ 000$$

If you said to one of the employees that they earned about sh 118 000 each year they would disagree with you. In this type of situation when one of the values is different from the others (as we saw in Example 2), the mean is not the best average to use.

If we arrange the incomes in increasing order of size, we get:

40 000   45 000   50 000   55 000   400 000

median

The value that is in the *middle* is called the **median**. In this case the value of sh 50 000 is a much better idea of the average wage earned by the employees. The median is not affected by isolated values (sometimes called **rogue** values) that are much larger or smaller than the rest of the data.

If the data consists of an even number of values, you find the mean of the two middle values as shown in the next example.

EXAMPLE 4

Find the median of the numbers: 12, 23, 10, 8, 22, 14, 30, 18.

Solution
Arranging in increasing order of size, we get

8   10   12   14   18   22   23   30

$$\text{median} = (14 + 18) \div 2 = 16$$

Exercise 6.3

1 Find the median of the following sets of numbers.
    a 3, 4, 6, 8, 10   **b** 3, 4, 7, 8, 10, 12
    c 12, 50, 34, 25, 15, 23, 67, 12, 13

2 The times of five athletes in the 100m were : 12.5 s, 12.9 s, 14.8 s, 15.0 s, 25.2 s. Find the median time. Why is this a better average to use than the mean?

3 An office has an air-conditioning machine. The midday temperature on five days is given below. Find the median temperature. Explain why the median is a better average to use than the mean.

     23.2°   24.1°   23.8°   23.6°   31.5°

4 Baraza has 6 maths tests during a school term. His marks are below. Find the median mark. Explain why the median is a better average than the mean.

     73   78   82   0   75   86

6.4 The mode

The value that occurs most often in a set of data is called the **mode** of the data. This is another type of average. It is possible for data to have more than one mode. Data with two modes are said to be **bi-modal**.

The mode is often important to know. For example:

(a) If you were running a shoe shop you would want to know the most popular size.

(b) If you ran a restaurant you would want to know what type of food is ordered most.

EXAMPLE 5

State the mode for the following sets of numbers:

(a) 0, 0, 1, 1, 1, 2, 2, 3, 4, 5, 5

(b) 58, 57, 60, 59, 50, 56, 62

(c) 5, 10, 10, 10, 15, 15, 20, 20, 20, 25

Solution

(a) 1 occurs most (3 times):   The mode = 1

(b) All the numbers appear once: There is no mode

(c) there are three 10s and three 20s: Mode = 10 and 20

Exercise 6.4

1 Find the mode of these sets of numbers.

  a 0, 1, 1, 3, 4, 5, 5, 5, 6, 7, 8

  b 3, 8, 4, 3, 8, 4, 3, 8, 8, 3, 3, 4

  c 5, 12, 6, 5, 11, 12, 5, 5, 8, 12, 7, 12

2 Ten pupils were asked how many brothers or sisters they had. The results are below. Find the mode number.

     0   1   1   2   5   0   1   3   1   4

3 Eight motorists were asked how many times they had taken the driving test before they passed. The results are below. Find the mode number.

     1   4   2   1   3   1   4   1

4 Give examples of where the mode is a better measure of central tendency than either the mean or the median.

6.5 Averages from frequency tables

If the data has already been put into a frequency table, the calculation of the averages is slightly easier.

EXAMPLE 6

Imbuga rolled a six-sided die 50 times. The scores he obtained are summarised in the following table.

Score (x)	1	2	3	4	5	6
Frequency (f)	8	10	7	5	12	8

Calculate (a) the mode score (b) the median score (c) the mean score.

Solution
(a) The value that occurs most often is 5 with a frequency of 12.
The mode = 5
(b) There are 50 items of data, so if you arrange them in order of size, the positions are 1.........25 and 26............50. The median will be the average of the 25th and 26th number.

In the table there are 8 scores of 1, followed by 10 scores of 2. This gives you 8 + 10 = 18 numbers. These are then followed by 7 scores of 3. This gives 18 + 7 = 25 numbers. It follows that the 25th number is a 3. The 26th number must be the first number in the next group, which is a 4.
The median = $(3 + 4) \div 2 = 3.5$
(c) 8 scores of 1 gives a total $8 \times 1 = 8$
10 scores of 2 gives a total $10 \times 2 = 20$
and so on to give a total score of
$$8 \times 1 + 10 \times 2 + 7 \times 3 + 5 \times 4 + 12 \times 5 + 8 \times 6 = 177$$
The total frequency $= 8 + 10 + 7 + 5 + 12 + 8 = 50$
The mean score $= 177 \div 50 = 3.54$

RULE

$$\text{The mean using a frequency table} = \frac{\text{total of (value} \times \text{frequency)}}{\text{total frequency}}$$

There is a very useful symbol for total (or sum) which is $\sum$.

$$\text{Hence the mean} = \frac{\sum fx}{\sum f}$$

Exercise 6.5

1 The numbers of aircraft landing at a small airport each week during part of 1999 are summarised in the table. Find the median number of aircraft landing each week. How many weeks did the number landing exceed the median?

Number of aircraft	20	21	22	23	24	25
Frequency	5	6	12	7	2	1

2 For the following frequency table, find **a** the mode **b** the median and **c** the mean.

x	5	6	7	8	9	10	11
Frequency	3	8	9	7	5	4	4

3 In an experiment on counting beans in pods, the results were

No. of beans	5	6	7	8	9	10
Frequency	10	12	20	12	8	6

For the number of beans in a pod, find
   a the mean   **b** the median   **c** the mode.

4 Hadija asked a sample of children at her school how many brothers and sisters they had. The results are shown below.

No. of brothers or sisters	1	2	3	4	5	6
Frequency	2	15	8	5	3	1

Find the mean number of brothers and sisters. Does this give a good representation of the numbers shown in the table? Justify your answer.

5 100 letters were posted. The number of days they took to reach their destination is shown in the table below. Find the mean number of days.

Number of days	1	2	3	4	5
Frequency	43	29	17	8	3

6 80 students were asked how many books they had read in the last month. The results are below. Find the mean number of books.

Number	0	1	2	3	4	5	6	7
Frequency	4	25	11	10	13	8	4	5

If data has been grouped together in classes, then unless you have a list of all the individual values, you only know approximately what each value is. For this reason, you can only *estimate* the mean and the median. Also you do not have a single value as the mode. Instead you have a **modal class**.

EXAMPLE 7

The examination results (rounded to the nearest whole number %) are given for a group of students.

Mark (%)	30–39	40–49	50–59	60–69	70–79
Frequency	5	3	20	2	10

(a) State the modal class (b) estimate the mean score (c) estimate the median score.

Solution

(a) The highest frequency is 20. This is the frequency of the modal class, which is 50–59.

(b) To estimate the mean and median, you have to assume that all the data in a class is equal to the **mid value** of that class. The mid value is the average of the upper and lower class boundaries. For the 30–39 class, this would be $(30 + 39) \div 2 = 34.5$

> **NOTE**
> This works for discrete or continuous data.

The table of values is now done again with the mid class values:

Class	Mid class value m	Frequency f	$f \times m$
30–39	34.5	5	172.5
40–49	44.5	3	133.5
50–59	54.5	20	1090.0
60–69	64.5	2	129.0
70–79	74.5	10	745.0
	Total	40	2270.0

The last column is found by multiplying together the value of the midpoint m, and the frequency f.

$$\text{The estimated mean} = \frac{\sum f \times m}{\sum f} = \frac{2270}{40} = 56.75$$

> **RULE**
> **The estimated mean from a grouped frequency table is** $\dfrac{\sum fm}{\sum f}$

(b) To estimate the median is more complicated. Follow the steps given below.

Step 1: Find the *position* of the middle value:
There are 40 values, so the middle is between the 20th and 21st (20.5th position).

Step 2: Find which class contains the median:
The first 2 classes contain 8 values, the first 3 classes contain 28 values, and so the median is in the 50–59 class.

Step 3: Find the position within the class.
20.5 − 8 = 12.5. We want the 12.5th position in the class of 20.

Step 4: The top and bottom limits of the class are 59.5 and 49.5.
Width of the class = 59.5 − 49.5 = 10.
Find $(12.5 \div 20) \times 10 = 6.25$

Step 5: Add 6.25 on to the lower class boundary of 49.5
49.5 + 6.25 = 55.75
The estimate for the median = 55.75

Exercise 6.6

1 For the following frequency table, find estimates for the mean and the median.

x	5–9	10–14	15–19	20–24
Frequency	5	8	6	1

2 The heights of a selection of plants are given in the table.

Height (cm)	0–4	5–9	10–14	15–19
Frequency	12	15	20	3

State the modal class. Also find estimates for

a the mean height **b** the median height.

3 The average scores in a test of reaction times are given in the table.

React. times (sec)	0–0.1	0.2–0.3	0.4–0.5	0.6–0.7
Frequency	2	6	5	8

a State the modal class. **b** Estimate the mean.
c Estimate the median.

4 The midday temperatures over 80 days were as follows.

Temperature (°)	60–69	70–79	80–89	90–99
Frequency	9	29	24	18

a State the modal class. **b** Estimate the mean.
c Estimate the median.

5 The times that 100 athletes took to run 1000 m are given below.

Time (seconds)	200–209	210–219	220–229	230–239
Frequency	17	34	38	11

   a State the modal class.   **b** Estimate the mean.
   c Estimate the median.

6 The weights of 60 people are given below.

Weight (kg)	50–59	60–69	70–79	80–89
Frequency	3	23	27	7

   a State the modal class.   **b** Estimate the mean.
   c Estimate the median.

Summary

- The mean, median and mode are averages that measure central tendency.
- To find the mean of n numbers, add them and divide by n. To find the median, arrange the numbers in order and find the middle. To find the mode, look for the most common number.
- The mean is badly affected by rogue values.
- The median is best when there are rogue values in the data.
- For grouped frequency, you can only *estimate* the median and the mean.

Activity 6

Writing styles
You can compare the styles of two or more authors, types of book, newspapers or magazines by analysing the lengths of sentences used, or the lengths of words used.

Firstly collect together two things to compare. You might find it easier to work with a friend. Then proceed as follows:

    1 Select a page from each.
    2 Count the length of the sentences (or words) and record your results.
    3 Find the mean sentence (or word) for each.
    4 Compare the results. What do they tell you? Are the results what you expected?

Progress exercise 6

1 For the set of numbers 0, 1, 3, 5, 5, 7, 8, 10, 12, find
   a the mode   **b** the median   **c** the mean.

2 Give an example of where the median and not the mean would be the best average to use. Justify your answer.

3 Find the mean of the set of numbers 4, 5, 8, 11, 15, 23, 30. Hence find the mean of the following sets of numbers explaining how you obtained your answers
   a 304, 305, 308, 311, 315, 323, 330
   b 8, 10, 16, 22, 30, 46, 60
   c 96, 95, 92, 89, 85, 77, 70

4 The average weight of 4 parcels is 2 kg. The average weight of another 6 parcels is 4 kg. Find the average weight of all 10 parcels.

5 A single die numbered 1 to 6 was rolled 40 times, and the results were recorded as follows:

Score	1	2	3	4	5	6
Frequency	7	5	5	6	x	8

   a Find x.   **b** Find the mean score.

6 The areas of a selection of tobacco plant leaves were found and the results given in a table.

Area (cm)^2	2–3	4–5	6–7	8–9	10–11
Frequency	12	34	15	11	8

   Estimate   **a** the mean area   **b** the median area.

Puzzles 6

1 Find a set of four positive integers containing the number 8 which have a mean of 10 and a median of 9. How many different sets can you find?

2 The numbers 2, 3, 5, x, 8, 12, y are in order of increasing size. They have a median of 7, and a mean of 8. Find x and y.

3 A group of 30 children were asked how many brothers or sisters they had. The results are below. Unfortunately two results were lost. Find the missing numbers, given that the mean number of brothers or sisters was 1.4.

Number	0	1	2	3	4
Frequency	7		7	3	

7

Indices

This unit uses
- The square of a number x, written x^2.
- The square root of a number y, written $\sqrt{y}$. If $x^2 = y$, then $x = \sqrt{y}$.
- The cube and cube root of numbers, written x^3 and $\sqrt[3]{y}$.

7.1 Powers

Two xs multiplied together give the square of x. If a square field has side x m, the area of the field is x^2 m^2.

Three xs multiplied together give the cube of x. If a solid cube has side x cm, the volume of the cube is x^3 cm^3.

If four xs are multiplied together, the result is written x^4.

$$x \times x \times x \times x = x^4$$

In general, if n xs are multiplied together, the result is written x^n.

$$\underbrace{x \times x \times x \times ... \times x}_{n \text{ factors}} = x^n$$

In the expression x^n, the number n is the **index** and the number x is the **base**. The expression x^n is a **power**.
So for 7^6, the index is 6 and the base is 7.
The plural of index is **indices**.

> **NOTE**
> Don't confuse x^n (x raised to the power n) with xn (x multiplied by n).
> $3^5 = 3 \times 3 \times 3 \times 3 \times 3$
> (*not* 3×5)

EXAMPLE 1

Find 5^4.

Solution
This is four 5s, multiplied together.

$$5 \times 5 \times 5 \times 5 = 5 \times 5 \times 25$$
$$= 5 \times 125$$
$$= 625$$

$5^4 = 625$

Exercise 7.1

Evaluate these expressions.

1 2^3 **2** 4^3 **3** 7^2 **4** 2^5

Write these expressions as powers.

5 $3 \times 3 \times 3$ **6** $9 \times 9 \times 9 \times 9$ **7** $8 \times 8 \times 8 \times 8 \times 8 \times 8 \times 8$

Write out these expressions in full.

8 15^3 **9** x^4 **10** y^5

11 A *googol* is 1 followed by a hundred 0s. Write a googol as a power of 10.

12 Evaluate these, leaving your answers as fractions.

   a $\left(\frac{1}{2}\right)^3$ **b** $\left(\frac{1}{3}\right)^2$ **c** $\left(\frac{3}{4}\right)^3$ **d** $\left(\frac{2}{3}\right)^2$

13 Write as powers of 10.

   a a hundred   **b** a thousand   **c** a million

14 *Lakh* and *crore* are Hindi words meaning a hundred thousand and ten million respectively. Write both of these as powers of 10.

7.2 Arithmetic of powers

Multiplying powers

Here two powers are multiplied together.

$$5^3 \times 5^4 = 5 \times 5 \times 5 \quad \times \quad 5 \times 5 \times 5 \times 5$$
$$= 5^7$$

5^3 has three 5s multiplied together. 5^4 has four 5s multiplied together. When 5^3 and 5^4 are multiplied, the result is seven 5s multiplied together. The indices, 3 and 4, are added.

$$5^3 \times 5^4 = 5^{3+4} = 5^7$$

In general, suppose x^n and x^m are multiplied.

$$x^n \times x^m = \underbrace{x \times x \times x \times \ldots \times x}_{n \text{ factors}} \quad \times \quad \underbrace{x \times x \times x \times \ldots \times x}_{m \text{ factors}}$$
$$= x^{n+m}$$

> **RULE**
> **When powers of the same base are multiplied, the indices are added.**
> $x^n \times x^m = x^{n+m}$

> **NOTE**
> When you multiply powers, add the indices. Don't multiply.
> $3^5 \times 3^4 = 3^9$ (*not* 3^{20})

EXAMPLE 2

Simplify $x^3 \times x^5 \times x^7$.

Solution
These are powers of the same base, x. Add the indices.

$$x^3 \times x^5 \times x^7 = x^{3+5+7} = x^{15}$$

Exercise 7.2A

Simplify these expressions.

1 $3^8 \times 3^5$	**2** $4^7 \times 4^2$	**3** $x^3 \times x^8$	**4** $y^6 \times y^5$
5 $2^x \times 2^y$	**6** $3^n \times 3^m$	**7** $2^4 \times 2^5 \times 2^7$	**8** $x^3 \times x^4 \times x^5$
9 $3^5 \times 3$	**10** $x^5 \times x$	**11** $2^{3x} \times 2^{4x}$	**12** $5^{3y} \times 5^y \times 5$
13 $2^{x+1} \times 2^{2x-3}$	**14** $3^{2x+1} \times 3^{4-x}$	**15** $x^a \times x^b$	**16** $y^{2k+3} \times y^{2-3k}$

17 Write the product of a *lakh* and a *crore* as a power of 10. (See the previous exercise.)

Dividing powers

Here one power is divided by another.

$$\frac{5^5}{5^3} = \frac{5 \times 5 \times 5 \times 5 \times 5}{5 \times 5 \times 5}$$

Cancel three 5s from top and bottom.

$$\frac{5^5}{5^3} = \frac{5 \times 5 \times 5 \times 5 \times 5}{5 \times 5 \times 5}$$
$$= 5 \times 5 = 5^2$$

When we cancelled three 5s from the top of the fraction, we subtracted 3 from the index.

$$\frac{5^5}{5^3} = 5^{5-3} = 5^2$$

In general, suppose x^n is divided by x^m.

$$x^n \div x^m = \frac{x \times x \times x \times x \times x \times x \times x \times x \ldots \times x \times x \times x \times x}{x \times x \times x \times x \times x \times x \ldots \times x \times x \times x \times x \times x}$$

Cancel m xs from top and bottom.

$$x^n \div x^m = x^{n-m}$$

> **RULE**
> **When a power is divided by another power of the same base, subtract the indices.**
> $$x^n \div x^m = x^{n-m}$$

> **NOTE**
> When you divide powers, subtract the indices. Don't divide.
> $2^8 \div 2^2 = 2^6$ (*not* 2^4)

EXAMPLE 3

Simplify this expression.

$$\frac{x^3 \times x^5}{x^2}$$

Solution

The top of the fraction is x^8, by the rule for multiplying powers. Now subtract 2, to obtain x^6, by the rule for dividing powers.

$$\frac{x^3 \times x^5}{x^2} = x^6$$

Exercise 7.2B

Simplify these expressions.

1 $5^{10} \div 5^3$ **2** $2^8 \div 2^3$ **3** $7^{11} \div 7^4$ **4** $8^9 \div 8^5$

5 $2^x \div 2^y$ **6** $3^n \div 3^m$ **7** $x^6 \div x^2$ **8** $y^9 \div y^2$

9 $6^{3x} \div 6^x$ **10** $7^{5n} \div 7^{2n}$ **11** $x^{6n} \div x^{3n}$ **12** $z^{5m} \div z^{2m}$

13 $\dfrac{y^7 \times y^5}{y^2}$ **14** $\dfrac{x^{13}}{x^4 \times x^5}$ **15** $\dfrac{2^y \times 2^x}{2^z}$ **16** $\dfrac{z^8 \times z^9}{z^3 \times z^4}$

17 $2^{2x+3} \div 2^{x+1}$ **18** $3^{x-2} \div x^{3-x}$ **19** $5^{2x-3} \div 5^{3x-7}$

20 $\dfrac{7^{x+3} \times 7^{x-1}}{7^{5x-5}}$ **21** $\dfrac{3^{2a+1}}{3^{3a-4} \times 3^{6-7a}}$

Powers of powers

Here a power is raised to a power.

$$
\begin{aligned}
(5^4)^3 &= (5 \times 5 \times 5 \times 5)^3 \\
&= (5 \times 5 \times 5 \times 5) \times (5 \times 5 \times 5 \times 5) \times (5 \times 5 \times 5 \times 5) \\
&= 5 \times 5 \times 5 \times 5 \times 5 \times 5 \times 5 \times 5 \times 5 \times 5 \times 5 \times 5 \\
&= 5^{12}
\end{aligned}
$$

So three lots of four 5s are multiplied together. The result is 4×3, giving 12, 5s multiplied together.

$$(5^4)^3 = 5^{4 \times 3} = 5^{12}$$

In general, take x^n to the power m.

$$n \text{ } xs$$

$$
\begin{aligned}
(x^n)^m &= (x \times x \times \ldots \times x)^m \\
&= (x \times x \times \ldots \times x) \times (x \times x \times \ldots \times x) \times \ldots \times (x \times x \times \ldots \times x) \\
&= x^{nm}
\end{aligned}
$$

> **RULE**
>
> **When you take a power of a power, remove the brackets and multiply the indices.**
> $(x^n)^m = x^{n \times m}$

EXAMPLE 4

Simplify $(x^4)^5$.

Solution
Multiply the indices.
$$(x^4)^5 = x^{4\times5} = x^{20}$$

EXAMPLE 5

(a) Write 4^2 as a power of 2.

(b) Write $2^3 \times 4^2$ as a power of a single number.

Solution
(a) Note that $4 = 2^2$.

Hence $4^2 = (2^2)^2 = 2^{2\times2}$
$4^2 = 2^4$

(b) Use part (a).
$2^3 \times 4^2 = 2^3 \times 2^4$
$2^3 \times 4^2 = 2^7$

Exercise 7.2C

In questions **1** to **12**, simplify the expressions.

1 $(2^3)^5$	**2** $(5^3)^3$	**3** $(10^4)^2$	**4** $(x^3)^6$
5 $(y^3)^8$	**6** $(2^x)^y$	**7** $(3^m)^n$	**8** $(5^x)^3$
9 $(2^3 \times 2^4)^2$	**10** $(3^7 \div 3^2)^6$	**11** $(2^3)^5 \times 2^4$	**12** $(3^6)^2 \div 3^5$

In questions **13** to **24**, write the expressions as a power of a single number.

13 $2^5 \times 4^3$	**14** $3^2 \times 9^2$	**15** $8^2 \times 4^5$	**16** $3^5 \times 9^3 \times 27^2$
17 $4^7 \div 8^2$	**18** $25^3 \div 5^4$	**19** $49^4 \div 7^3$	**20** $2^8 \times 16^3 \div 8^2$
21 $\dfrac{2^3 \times 4^8}{8^3}$	**22** $\dfrac{10^9 \times 100^4}{1000^3}$	**23** $\dfrac{3^{15}}{9^2 \times 27^2}$	**24** $\dfrac{2^8 \times 16^3}{4^3 \times 8}$

7.3 Zero and negative indices

Zero index

Here 5^3 is divided by itself. Use the law for division of powers.

$$\frac{5^3}{5^3} = 5^{3-3} = 5^0$$

We know that $5^3 = 125$. Any number divided by itself is 1.

$$\frac{5^3}{5^3} = \frac{125}{125} = 1 \qquad \text{i.e.} \quad \frac{5 \times 5 \times 5}{5 \times 5 \times 5} = \frac{1}{1} = 1$$

Hence $5^0 = 1$.

In general, suppose x is not zero, and n is any number.

$$\frac{x^n}{x^n} = x^{n-n} = x^0$$

Any non-zero number divided by itself is 1.

$$x^0 = 1$$

> **RULE**
> For any non-zero x, $x^0 = 1$.

> **NOTE**
> x^0 is 1, it is *not* 0.

Negative indices

Consider 1 divided by 5^3. Use the rule for division of powers, and the fact that $5^0 = 1$.

$$\frac{1}{5^3} = \frac{5^0}{5^3} = 5^{0-3} = 5^{-3}$$

So 1 divided by a power with the index $+3$ gives a power with the index -3.

In general, consider 1 divided by x^n, where x is not zero.

$$\frac{1}{x^n} = \frac{x^0}{x^n} = x^{0-n} = x^{-n}$$

So 1 divided by a power with a positive index gives a power with the same, but negative, index.

> **RULE**
> For any non-zero x, $\dfrac{1}{x^n} = x^{-n}$

> **NOTE**
> Taking a negative power is *not* the same as multiplying by -1.
> $3^{-2} = \frac{1}{3^2} = \frac{1}{9}$ (*not* -3^2)

EXAMPLE 6

Find 4^{-3}.

Solution
Use the rule. $4^{-3} = \frac{1}{4^3} = \frac{1}{64}$.
$4^{-3} = \frac{1}{64}$.

EXAMPLE 7

Find $\left(\frac{1}{2}\right)^{-3}$.

Solution
Use the rule. $\left(\frac{1}{2}\right)^{-3} = \frac{1}{\left(\frac{1}{2}\right)^3} = \frac{1}{\frac{1}{8}}$

Multiply top and bottom of this fraction by 8. $\frac{1}{\frac{1}{8}} = 8$.

$\left(\frac{1}{2}\right)^{-3} = 8$

EXAMPLE 8

Write $2^3 \div 8^2$ as a power of a single number.

Solution
Note that $8^2 = (2^3)^2 = 2^{3 \times 2} = 2^6$.

$2^3 \div 2^6 = 2^{-3}$

$2^3 \div 8^2 = 2^{-3}$

Exercise 7.3

In questions **1** to **12**, evaluate the expressions.

1 3^0 **2** 15^0 **3** $k^0 \ (k \neq 0)$ **4** 5^{-1}

5 2^{-2} **6** 4^{-2} **7** $\left(\frac{1}{3}\right)^{-2}$ **8** $\left(\frac{1}{4}\right)^{-3}$

9 $\left(\frac{2}{3}\right)^{-2}$ **10** $\left(\frac{3}{4}\right)^{-3}$ **11** $\left(1\frac{1}{4}\right)^{-1}$ **12** $\left(1\frac{1}{3}\right)^{-1}$

In questions **13** to **20**, write the expression as a power of a single number.

13 $2^4 \div 4^3$ **14** $9^2 \div 27^4$ **15** $3^2 \times 9^{-5}$ **16** $4^{-3} \times 8^{-2}$

17 $2^3 \times 4^{-2} \times 8$ **18** $9^4 \times 3^3 \div 27^5$ **19** $2^x \div 4^{2x}$ **20** $9^a \times 3^{-3a}$

7.4 Fractional indices

We have found that $2^0 = 1$ and that $2^{-1} = \frac{1}{2}$. What does $2^{\frac{1}{2}}$ mean? Use the law for powers of powers.

$$\left(2^{\frac{1}{2}}\right)^2 = 2^{\frac{1}{2} \times 2} = 2^1 = 2$$

So when $2^{\frac{1}{2}}$ is squared, the result is 2. Hence $2^{\frac{1}{2}}$ is the square root of 2.

$$\left(2^{\frac{1}{2}}\right)^2 = 2$$

Hence $2^{\frac{1}{2}} = \sqrt{2}$

Similarly, $\left(2^{\frac{1}{3}}\right)^3 = 2^{\frac{1}{3} \times 3} = 2^1 = 2$

$$\left(2^{\frac{1}{3}}\right)^3 = 2$$

Hence $2^{\frac{1}{3}} = \sqrt[3]{2}$

In general, let x be a positive number and let n be a whole number. Then
$$(x^{\frac{1}{n}})^n = x^{\frac{1}{n} \times n} = x^1 = x$$
Hence $x^{\frac{1}{n}} = \sqrt[n]{x}$, the nth root of x.

> **RULE**
> If x is positive, $x^{\frac{1}{n}} = \sqrt[n]{x}$

> **NOTE**
> Taking a fractional power is *not* the same as multiplying by the fraction. It is taking the root equal to the denominator of the fraction.
> $9^{\frac{1}{2}} = \sqrt{9} = 3$ (*not* $9 \times \frac{1}{2}$)

EXAMPLE 9

Find $36^{\frac{1}{2}}$.

Solution
This is $\sqrt{36}$, the square root of 36. This is 6.
$36^{\frac{1}{2}} = 6$

EXAMPLE 10

Find $\left(\frac{1}{8}\right)^{\frac{1}{3}}$.

Solution
This is $\sqrt[3]{\frac{1}{8}}$, the cube root of $\frac{1}{8}$. Take the cube root of top and bottom of the fraction.
The cube root of 1 is 1, and the cube root of 8 is 2.
$\left(\frac{1}{8}\right)^{\frac{1}{3}} = \left(\frac{1}{2}\right)$

Exercise 7.4

Find the following

1 $49^{\frac{1}{2}}$	2 $27^{\frac{1}{3}}$	3 $100^{\frac{1}{2}}$	4 $1000^{\frac{1}{3}}$
5 $\left(\frac{1}{4}\right)^{\frac{1}{2}}$	6 $\left(\frac{1}{9}\right)^{\frac{1}{2}}$	7 $0.01^{\frac{1}{2}}$	8 $0.25^{\frac{1}{2}}$
9 $\left(\frac{4}{9}\right)^{\frac{1}{2}}$	10 $16^{\frac{1}{4}}$	11 $81^{\frac{1}{4}}$	12 $32^{\frac{1}{5}}$

13 Write the following as powers.
    a $\sqrt{7}$ b $\sqrt{\frac{1}{3}}$ c $\sqrt[3]{2}$ d $\sqrt[5]{8}$

7.5 Practice in powers

All powers obey the same rules of arithmetic, whether the index is positive, negative or fractional.

EXAMPLE 11

Find   (a) $8^{\frac{2}{3}}$ (b) $3^{-4} \times 3^{-8}$ (c) $5^{-4} \div 5^{-8}$

Solution

(a) Write $\frac{2}{3}$ as $\frac{1}{3} \times 2$.
$$8^{\frac{2}{3}} = (8^{\frac{1}{3}})^2 = 2^2 = 4$$
$$8^{\frac{2}{3}} = 4$$

(b) Add the indices. $-4 + -8 = -12$.
$$3^{-4} \times 3^{-8} = 3^{-12}$$

(c) Subtract the indices. Be careful when subtracting a negative number.
$$(-4) - (-8) = -4 + 8 = 4$$
$$5^4 \div 5^{-8} = 5^4$$

EXAMPLE 12

Simplify the expression $\sqrt[3]{\frac{x}{x^7}}$.

Solution

The expression inside the root sign is $x \div x^7$, which is x^{-6}.
$$\sqrt[3]{x^{-6}} = x^{\frac{1}{3} \times (-6)} = x^{-2}$$

$$\sqrt[3]{\frac{x}{x^7}} = x^{-2}$$

Exercise 7.5

Evaluate these.

1 $4^{1\frac{1}{2}}$ **2** $16^{\frac{3}{4}}$ **3** $9^{2\frac{1}{2}}$ **4** $125^{\frac{2}{3}}$

Write these expressions as single powers.

5 $4^3 \times 4^{-7}$ **6** $7^8 \div 7^{16}$ **7** $12^{-8} \times 12^{-2}$ **8** $3^{-2} \div 3^8$

9 $x^{\frac{1}{2}} \times x^{1\frac{1}{2}}$ **10** $\sqrt{x^4}$ **11** $\sqrt[3]{x^6}$ **12** $(x^{\frac{3}{4}})^8$

13 $4^3 \times 2^5$ **14** $9 \times 27^2 \times 3^4$ **15** $y^{\frac{1}{2}} \times y^{-\frac{1}{2}}$ $(y \neq 0)$

Simplify these expressions. All the variables are non-zero.

16 $(3ab)^3$ **17** $(2x^3)^4$ **18** $(3x^3y^2)^{-3}$ **19** $\sqrt{4x^{-4}}$

20 $\sqrt[3]{8y^6}$ **21** $\sqrt{\frac{x^6}{9}} \times \sqrt{\frac{x^2}{4}}$ **22** $\dfrac{a^3b^4c^5}{a^{-2}b^{-3}c^{-4}}$ **23** $(a^{\frac{1}{2}}b^{\frac{1}{3}})^6$

24 $\dfrac{x^{\frac{1}{2}}y^{\frac{1}{4}}}{x^{\frac{1}{3}}y^{\frac{1}{2}}}$ **25** $\sqrt{\left(\dfrac{1}{x}\right)^{-4}}$ **26** $\left(\dfrac{x^3y^5}{xy^7}\right)^{\frac{1}{2}}$ **27** $\sqrt[3]{\left(\dfrac{16a^4}{2a^7}\right)}$

28 $\sqrt{x} \times \sqrt[3]{x}$ **29** $\dfrac{\sqrt{a} \times a^3}{\sqrt[4]{a}}$ **30** $\sqrt{(\sqrt[3]{x})}$

31 Show that $\sqrt[m]{(\sqrt[n]{x})} = \sqrt[n]{(\sqrt[m]{x})}$

- When n xs are multiplied together, the product is written x^n. This is a power of x. The base is x and the index is n.
- When two powers of the same base are multiplied, the indices are added.
$$x^n \times x^m = x^{n+m}$$

- When two powers of the same base are divided, the indices are subtracted.

  $x^n \div x^m = x^{n-m}$
- When a power is raised to another power, the indices are multiplied.

  $(x^n)^m = x^{n \times m}$
- If x is not zero, then $x^0 = 1$.
- If x is not zero, then $x^{-n} = \frac{1}{x^n}$.
- If x is positive, then $x^{\frac{1}{n}} = \sqrt[n]{x}$.

Activity 7

The memory of a computer is measured in **bytes**. Each byte can hold one letter or one digit. A larger unit is the **kilobyte**. 1 kilobyte $= 2^{10}$ bytes.

1 Work out 2^{10}. Why is the prefix *kilo* used?
2 1 **megabyte** $= 2^{10}$ kilobytes. How many bytes are there in 1 megabyte?
3 1 **gigabyte** $= 2^{10}$ megabytes. How many bytes are there in 1 gigabyte?
4 If you used a computer to write a book, about how many bytes of memory would it need to hold the words?
5 If you have a computer at your school, find how much memory it has.

Progress exercise 7

1 Find the value of
   a 3^4 **b** 5^{-2} **c** 7^0 **d** $125^{\frac{1}{3}}$.
2 Write these expressions as powers of a single number.
   a $5^3 \times 25^2$ **b** $3^{12} \div 8^2$ **c** $25^{-3} \times 5^2$
3 Simplify these expressions.
   a $2^x \times 2^{3x}$ **b** $3^{a+2} \div 3^{a+1}$ **c** $5^{3-x} \times 5^{2x}$
   d $2^x \times 4^x$ **e** $9^a \div 3^b$ **f** $125^{\frac{1}{2}x} \times 25^{\frac{1}{3}x}$

   g $\dfrac{4p^2q^3}{2p^{-3}q^4}$ **h** $\sqrt{100a^4b^{-6}}$ **i** $\dfrac{\sqrt{64x}}{\sqrt[3]{64x}}$

Puzzles 7

1 What is wrong with this argument?

   We know that $\dfrac{1}{-1} = \dfrac{-1}{1}$. Take the square root of both sides.

$\dfrac{\sqrt{1}}{\sqrt{-1}} = \dfrac{\sqrt{-1}}{\sqrt{1}}$. Now multiply across.

$\sqrt{1} \times \sqrt{1} = \sqrt{(-1)} \times \sqrt{(-1)}$
Hence $1 = -1$

2 Which of the following equations are always true? For the false ones, correct the right hand side.

a $(2xy)^2 = 2x^2y^2$ **b** $(x^4)^3 = x^{12}$ **c** $a^2 \times a^3 = a^6$

d $(b^2)^3 = b^5$ **e** $\sqrt{16x^2} = 8x$ **f** $\left(\frac{1}{2}\right)^{-3} = 8$

3 Solve these equations.

a $2^x = 4^{x-3}$ **b** $9^x \times 27^{x-1} = 1$

8

Standard form

This unit uses
- Indices
- Laws of indices
- Negative indices

8.1 Large numbers

Betelgeuse is a very bright star. Its distance from Earth is about

2 000 000 000 000 000 000 m

It is difficult to understand a large number like this. Notice that it consists of 2, followed by eighteen 0s. So it is 2, multiplied by 10^{18}. Write it as

2×10^{18}

Write the large number as a number between 1 and 10, multiplied by a power of 10. The number is in **standard form**.

In many parts of science we have to deal with very large numbers and very small numbers. We use standard form to deal with them.

With two numbers in standard form, it is easy to tell which is larger. If they have different powers of 10, then the number with the larger power is larger. If they have the same powers of 10, the number with the larger value in front is larger.

So 4×10^8 is larger than 9×10^7 (as $8 > 7$)

4×10^8 is less than 9×10^8 (as $4 < 9$)

EXAMPLE 1

Write 530 000 000 000 in standard form.

Solution

From the right, move the decimal point until it is between the 5 and the 3. Note that 5.3 is between 1 and 10. We moved the decimal point 11 times, so we have divided by 10^{11}.

5 . 3 0 0 0 0 0 0 0 0 0 0

11 places

So we must multiply 5.3 by 10^{11}.

$530\ 000\ 000\ 000 = 5.3 \times 10^{11}$

Exercise 8.1

1 Write these numbers in standard form.
  a 800 000   **b** 4 000 000   **c** 50 000 000
  d 120 000   **e** 43 500 000   **f** 123 460 000 000
  g five million   **h** six hundred and thirty thousand

2 Write out these numbers in ordinary notation.
  a 3×10^5 **b** 4.7×10^7 **c** 1.27×10^6

3 The area of Kenya is about 580 000 000 000 square metres. Write this in standard form.

4 The population of the world is about 6 000 000 000. Write this in standard form.

5 The area of the Indian Ocean is about 73 000 000 km^2. Write this in standard form.

6 The speed of light is about 300 000 000 metres per second. Write this in standard form.

7 A kilogram is 1000 grams. A megagram is 1000 kilograms. A gigagram is 1000 megagrams. A teragram is 1000 gigagrams. How many grams are there in 1 teragram? Give your answer in standard form.

8 Of these pairs of numbers, write down which is greater.
  a 5×10^8 and 7×10^7 **b** 4.23×10^{12} and 5.01×10^{14}
  c 4.73×10^6 and 4.09×10^6

9 The distances of the stars Betelgeuse and Canopus are about 2×10^{18} m and 1×10^{18} m respectively. Which star is further away?

10 The areas of the Atlantic and Pacific oceans are about 8.22×10^7 km^2 and 1.65×10^8 km^2 respectively. Which is larger?

11 The diameter of the planet Jupiter is 1.43×10^5 km, and the diameter of Saturn is 1.20×10^5 km. Which is larger?

8.2 small numbers

The mass of a hydrogen atom is 0.000 000 000 000 000 000 000 000 2 grams. It is difficult to understand a number as small as this. The first significant digit is 2, and there are 25 0s in front of it (including the 0 before the decimal point). This number is 2 divided by 10, 25 times. The decimal point is moved 25 places to the right to make the number 2.

$$0.000\ 000\ 000\ 000\ 000\ 000\ 000\ 000\ 2 = 2 \div 10^{25}.$$

Recall that $\frac{1}{10^{25}}$ can be written as 10^{-25}. So   Remember from Unit 7, $\frac{1}{x} = x^{-n}$

$$0.000\ 000\ 000\ 000\ 000\ 000\ 000\ 000\ 2 = 2 \times 10^{-25}$$

This number is in standard form. It consists of a number which is between 1 and 10, and a negative power of 10.

Be careful when comparing small numbers in standard form.

4×10^{-8} is greater than 5×10^{-9} (as $-8 > -9$)

EXAMPLE 2

Put 0.000 000 005 32 in standard form.

Solution

Move the decimal point until it is between the 5 and the 3. The number 5.32 is between 1 and 10. We move the decimal point 9 times, so multiply by 10^{-9}.

$$0.00000000532$$
$$0.000\ 000\ 005\ 32 = 5.32 \times 10^{-9}$$

> **N O T E**
> The negative power of 10 is the number of 0s (including the 0 before the decimal point).

Exercise 8.2

1 Write these numbers in standard form.
   a 0.000 000 7   b 0.000 000 04   c 0.000 9
   d 0.000 032   e 0.001 532   f 0.000 000 043
   g one thousandth   h five millionths   i seven billionths
2 Write these numbers in ordinary notation.
   a 4×10^{-4} b 3.6×10^{-5} c 1.29×10^{-6}
3 The width of a certain virus is 0.000 000 028 m. Write this in standard form.
4 The width of a certain atom is 0.000 000 000 000 000 000 3 m. Write this in standard form.
5 A gram is 1000 milligrams. A milligram is 1000 micrograms. A microgram is 1000 nanograms. A nanogram is 1000 picograms. Write 1 picogram as a fraction of a gram, giving your answer in standard form.
6 Of these pairs of numbers, write down which is greater.
   a 5×10^{-7} and 8×10^{-9} b 5.2×10^{-3} and 5.08×10^{-3}
   c 4.3×10^{-7} and 2.5×10^{-10} d 7.03×10^{-5} and 7.19×10^{-6}
7 The masses of a carbon atom and a hydrogen atom are about 2×10^{-24} grams and 2×10^{-25} grams respectively. Which is larger?

8.3 Arithmetic of numbers in standard form

Consider the product of these two numbers in standard form.
$$(3 \times 10^6) \times (2 \times 10^5)$$
Rearrange as $(3 \times 2) \times (10^6 \times 10^5)$
$3 \times 2 = 6$ and $10^6 \times 10^5 = 10^{11}$

Remember, when you multiply two powers, you add the indices.

So $(3 \times 10^6) \times (2 \times 10^5) = 6 \times 10^{11}$.

In general, when you multiply two numbers in standard form, you multiply the numbers between 1 and 10, and you *add* the indices.

$$(x \times 10^n) \times (y \times 10^m) = xy \times 10^{n+m}$$

Consider the division of two numbers in standard form.

$$(8 \times 10^7) \div (4 \times 10^3)$$

Rearrange as $\quad (8 \div 4) \times (10^7 \div 10^3)$

$8 \div 4 = 2$ and $10^7 \div 10^3 = 10^4$

Remember, when you divide two powers, you subtract the indices.

So $(8 \times 10^7) \div (4 \times 10^3) = 2 \times 10^4$.

In general, when you divide two numbers in standard form, you divide the numbers between 1 and 10, and you *subtract* the indices.

$$(x \times 10^n) \div (y \times 10^m) = \frac{x}{y} \times 10^{n-m}$$

EXAMPLE 3

Evaluate:
(a) $(2.1 \times 10^5) \times (2 \times 10^8)$ (b) $(7.2 \times 10^{12}) \div (3 \times 10^4)$
(c) $(4.3 \times 10^{-5}) \times (2 \times 10^{-7})$ (d) $(8.4 \times 10^{-5}) \div (4 \times 10^{-14})$

Solution
(a) Multiply the numbers between 1 and 10, and add the indices.

$2.1 \times 2 = 4.2$ and $5 + 8 = 13$

$(2.1 \times 10^5) \times (2 \times 10^8) = 4.2 \times 10^{13}$

(b) Divide the numbers between 1 and 10, and subtract the indices.

$7.2 \div 3 = 2.4$ and $12 - 4 = 8$

$(7.2 \times 10^{12}) \div (3 \times 10^4) = 2.4 \times 10^8$

(c) When we add the negative powers of 10, the result is negative.

$4.3 \times 2 = 8.6$ and $-5 + -7 = -12$

$(4.3 \times 10^{-5}) \times (2 \times 10^{-7}) = 8.6 \times 10^{-12}$

(d) When we subtract -14, the result is the same as adding $+14$.

$8.4 \div 4 = 2.1$ and $5 - (-14) = -5 + 14 = 9$

$(8.4 \times 10^{-5}) \div (4 \times 10^{-14}) = 2.1 \times 10^9$

Exercise 8.3

Evaluate these expressions. Give your answers in standard form.

1   $(1.4 \times 10^5) \times (2 \times 10^3)$ 2 $(2.3 \times 10^9) \times (3 \times 10^4)$
3   $(5 \times 10^6) \times (1.5 \times 10^8)$ 4 $(1.6 \times 10^{13}) \times (2 \times 10^5)$
5   $(3.6 \times 10^{14}) \div (3 \times 10^4)$ 6 $(7.2 \times 10^8) \div (2 \times 10^5)$
7   $(4.8 \times 10^7) \div (1.2 \times 10^4)$ 8 $(4.2 \times 10^{17}) \div (2.1 \times 10^{11})$
9   $(3.1 \times 10^{-6}) \times (2 \times 10^{-8})$ 10 $(3.2 \times 10^5) \times (3 \times 10^{-7})$
11   $(6 \times 10^5) \div (5 \times 10^{11})$ 12 $(1.6 \times 10^{-7}) \times (4 \times 10^{14})$

13 $(2.8 \times 10^5) \div (1.4 \times 10^{-8})$ **14** $(5.5 \times 10^{-6}) \div (5 \times 10^{-3})$

15 $(7.5 \times 10^{-3}) \div (1.5 \times 10^{-8})$ **16** $(9.3 \times 10^{-7}) \div (3 \times 10^{13})$

17 $14\,000 \times 20\,000$ **18** $0.000\,22 \times 0.000\,004$

19 $660\,000 \div 11\,000$ **20** $0.000\,000\,72 \div 0.000\,003$

21 A spaceship flies at 4.2×10^{12} metres per second. How far does it travel in 2×10^8 seconds?

22 The density of a metal is 1.7×10^4 kg per m³. What is the mass of 3×10^4 m³ of the metal? (Remember: density is mass divided by volume.)

23 A firm has 3×10^3 employees, who each earns 1.5×10^4 sh. What is the total wage bill?

24 The mass of the Earth is about 5×10^{15} kg. The mass of the planet Neptune is about 1.7 times the mass of the Earth. What is the mass of Neptune?

25 The mass of the Moon is about 1.2×10^{-2} times the mass of the Earth. What is the mass of the Moon?

8.4 Changing to standard form

Consider $(3 \times 10^8) \times (5 \times 10^9)$. Using our rules, the result is

$$3 \times 5 \times 10^{8+9} = 15 \times 10^{17}.$$

This answer is correct, but it is not in standard form. Convert 15 to 1.5, and increase the index by 1.

$(3 \times 10^8) \times (5 \times 10^9) = 1.5 \times 10^{18}.$

> **N O T E**
> This is very similar to 'carrying' when we do addition.

Similarly, consider $(3.5 \times 10^7) \div (5 \times 10^3)$.
Using our rules, the result is

$$3.5 \div 5 \times 10^{7-3} = 0.7 \times 10^4.$$

This answer is correct, but it is not in standard form. Convert 0.7 to 7, and decrease the index by 1.

$(3.5 \times 10^7) \div (5 \times 10^3) = 7 \times 10^3$

> **N O T E**
> This is very similar to 'borrowing' when we do subtraction.

EXAMPLE 4

Convert these numbers to standard form.

(a) 350×10^7 (b) 0.003×10^{12} (c) 73×10^{-7} (d) 0.63×10^{-5}

Solution

(a) Note that $350 = 3.5 \times 10^2$. So add 2 to 7.
   $350 \times 10^7 = 3.5 \times 10^9$

(b) Note that $0.003 = 3 \times 10^{-3}$. So subtract 3 from 12.
   $0.003 \times 10^{12} = 3 \times 10^9$

(c) Note that $73 = 7.3 \times 10^1$. When we add 1 to -7, the result is -6.
   $73 \times 10^{-7} = 7.3 \times 10^{-6}$

(d) Note that $0.63 = 6.3 \times 10^{-1}$. When we subtract 1 from -5, the result is -6.
$$0.63 \times 10^{-5} = 6.3 \times 10^{-6}$$

Exercise 8.4

In questions **1** to **15**, convert the numbers to standard form.

> **NOTE**
> If the number part is greater than 10, increase the power of 10. If the number part is less than 1, decrease the power of 10.

1 47×10^8 **2** 73×10^6 **3** 11×10^{12}
4 126×10^8 **5** 1081×10^4 **6** 99×10^{-8}
7 28×10^{-6} **8** 174×10^{-8} **9** 0.23×10^{11}
10 0.66×10^{41} **11** 0.034×10^{16} **12** 0.34×10^{-5}
13 0.18×10^{-8} **14** 0.022×10^{-10} **15** $0.001\,72 \times 10^{-7}$

Evaluate these, giving your answers in standard form.

16 $(8 \times 10^5) \times (3 \times 10^7)$ **17** $(6 \times 10^6) \times (2 \times 10^5)$
18 $(6 \times 10^6) \times (8 \times 10^9)$ **19** $(7.2 \times 10^9) \times (2 \times 10^{10})$
20 $(2 \times 10^6) \div (5 \times 10^2)$ **21** $(6 \times 10^{11}) \div (8 \times 10^5)$
22 $(4.2 \times 10^8) \div (7 \times 10^{12})$ **23** $(6.3 \times 10^4) \div (9 \times 10^{16})$
24 $(6 \times 10^{-3}) \times (7 \times 10^{-4})$ **25** $(3.5 \times 10^{-9}) \times (8 \times 10^{-4})$
26 $(7 \times 10^{-4}) \div (8 \times 10^{12})$ **27** $(1.5 \times 10^{-13}) \div (5 \times 10^{-3})$
28 $54\,000 \times 2000$ **29** $0.000\,62 \times 0.003$ **30** $60\,000 \div 0.000\,008$

31   A spaceship flies at 2.8×10^8 km per second. How far does it travel in 5×10^5 seconds?

32   About three-quarters of the mass of the Sun is hydrogen. The mass of a hydrogen atom is about 2×10^{-28} kg. The mass of the Sun is about 1.8×10^{21} kg. How many hydrogen atoms are there in the Sun?

33   A medicine of mass 3.6×10^{-7} kg is divided into 60 equal doses. What is the mass of each dose?

8.5   Addition and subtraction of numbers in standard form

When you add or subtract distances, the units must be the same. Similarly, when you add or subtract numbers in standard form, the indices must be the same.

EXAMPLE 5

Evaluate:
(a) $(4 \times 10^6) + (2 \times 10^6)$ (b) $(7 \times 10^8) + (9 \times 10^8)$
(c) $(4.2 \times 10^5) - (3.9 \times 10^5)$ (d) $(6 \times 10^{-7}) + (8 \times 10^{-7})$

Solution
(a) Add the numbers. The result is 6.
$$(4 \times 10^6) + (2 \times 10^6) = 6 \times 10^6$$

(b) Add the numbers. The result is 16, which is greater than 10.

$(7 \times 10^8) + (9 \times 10^8) = 16 \times 10^8$

Convert to standard form by the method of the previous section.

$(7 \times 10^8) + (9 \times 10^8) = 1.6 \times 10^9$

(c) Subtract the numbers. The result is 0.3, which is less than 1.

$(4.2 \times 10^5) - (3.9 \times 10^5) = 0.3 \times 10^5$

Convert to standard form by the method of the previous section.

$(4.2 \times 10^5) - (3.9 \times 10^5) = 3 \times 10^4$

(d) Add the numbers. The result is 14, which is greater than 1.

$(6 \times 10^{-7}) + (8 \times 10^{-7}) = 14 \times 10^{-7}$

Convert to standard form by the methods of the previous section.

$(6 \times 10^{-7}) + (8 \times 10^{-7}) = 1.4 \times 10^{-6}$

Exercise 8.5A

Evaluate these, giving your answers in standard form.

1 $(2 \times 10^7) + (5 \times 10^7)$ 2 $(5 \times 10^5) + (3 \times 10^5)$

3 $(7 \times 10^7) + (6 \times 10^7)$ 4 $(2.6 \times 10^8) + (9.1 \times 10^8)$

5 $(8 \times 10^{-3}) + (6 \times 10^{-3})$ 6 $(7.5 \times 10^{-9}) + (3.2 \times 10^{-9})$

7 $(6 \times 10^8) - (5.8 \times 10^8)$ 8 $(6.3 \times 10^{10}) - (6.2 \times 10^{10})$

9 $(4 \times 10^{-8}) - (3.5 \times 10^{-8})$ 10 $(7.8 \times 10^{-5}) - (7.6 \times 10^{-5})$

11 When empty, a ship weighs 4.4×10^7 kg. What is the weight if the ship carries 1.1×10^7 kg of cargo?

12 The Earth is about 1.5×10^8 km from the Sun. The planet Venus is about 1.1×10^8 km from the Sun. What is the distance between the Earth and Venus

  a when they are on directly opposite sides of the Sun

  b when they are on exactly the same side of the Sun?

13 In a certain country, there are 8.3×10^6 people over 25 years old and 7.6×10^6 people who are at most 25 years old.

  a What is the total population of the country?

  b How many more people are there over 25 than 25 and under?

Suppose a distance of 750 metres is added to a distance of 1.2 kilometres. We cannot add metres and kilometres directly. Either convert the metres to kilometres or convert the kilometres to metres.

0.750 km + 1.2 km = 1.95 km

750 m + 1200 m = 1950 m

When we find $(5 \times 10^9) + (3 \times 10^8)$, we must convert one of the numbers so that the indices are the same. Convert the number with the smaller index.

$$(5 \times 10^9) + (3 \times 10^8) \quad = (5 \times 10^9) + (0.3 \times 10^9)$$
$$= 5.3 \times 10^9$$

EXAMPLE 6

Evaluate $(7 \times 10^8) - (9 \times 10^7)$.

Solution
Convert the second number so that it has the same index as the first number.
$(7 \times 10^8) - (9 \times 10^7) = (7 \times 10^8) - (0.9 \times 10^8)$
Now subtract $7 - 0.9 = 6.1$
$(7 \times 10^8) - (9 \times 10^7) = 6.1 \times 10^8$

Exercise 8.5B

Evaluate these, giving your answers in standard form.

1   $(5 \times 10^9) + (4 \times 10^8)$ 2 $(6 \times 10^7) + (8 \times 10^6)$
3   $(3.2 \times 10^9) + (6 \times 10^8)$ 4 $(7.23 \times 10^7) + (9 \times 10^5)$
5   $(6 \times 10^{-7}) + (9 \times 10^{-8})$ 6 $(4.2 \times 10^{-10}) + (8 \times 10^{-11})$
7   $(5 \times 10^8) - (6 \times 10^7)$ 8 $(2 \times 10^{-3}) - (8 \times 10^{-5})$
9   $(1 \times 10^9) - (9.5 \times 10^8)$ 10 $(1 \times 10^{-6}) - (9.95 \times 10^{-7})$

11   The area of Africa is about 3×10^7 km², and the area of Australasia is about 8.9×10^6 km².
   a   What is the combined area of Africa and Australasia?
   b   What is the difference between these areas?

12   The Earth is about 1.5×10^8 km from the Sun. The planet Mercury is about 5.8×10^7 km from the Sun. What is the distance between the Earth and Mercury
   a   when they are on directly opposite sides of the Sun
   b   when they are on exactly the same side of the Sun?

13   The mass of a hydrogen atom is about 2×10^{-28} kg. The mass of an oxygen atom is about 3.2×10^{-27} kg.
   a   What is the difference in mass between a hydrogen atom and an oxygen atom?
   b   A water molecule consists of two hydrogen atoms and one oxygen atom. What is the mass of a water molecule?

- In standard form, a number consists of a number part between 1 and 10, and a power of 10.
- A large number in standard form has a positive index of 10. A small number in standard form has a negative index of 10.
- To multiply numbers in standard form, multiply the number parts and add the indices.
- To divide numbers in standard form, divide the number parts and subtract the indices.
- The result of a multiplication or a division may not be in standard form.
- To add or subtract numbers in standard form, ensure that the index is the same.

We use standard form for very large numbers, such as the distance or the mass of a star. Find details about a star, and compare it to the Earth. You might find:
- How much larger is it than the Earth?
- How much heavier is it than the Earth?
- How long would it take to reach the star?

1 Put these numbers in standard form.
   a 490 000   b 34 000 000   c 0.000 004 561
2 Write these numbers in full.
   a 6.5×10^6 b 5.06×10^{-5}
3 Evaluate these expressions, giving your answers in standard form.
   a $(2.3 \times 10^7) \times (2 \times 10^4)$ b $(2.1 \times 10^{-3}) \times (3 \times 10^{-6})$
   c $(4.6 \times 10^8) \div (2 \times 10^3)$ d $(8.4 \times 10^{-10}) \div (4.2 \times 10^{-3})$
   e $(3.2 \times 10^6) \times (4 \times 10^8)$ f $(7 \times 10^{-5}) \times (8 \times 10^{-7})$
   g $(1.2 \times 10^9) \div (4 \times 10^5)$ h $(8.1 \times 10^{-8}) \div (9 \times 10^7)$
   i $(4.2 \times 10^3) + (6.8 \times 10^3)$ j $(3.7 \times 10^{-6}) + (9.2 \times 10^{-6})$
   k $(8 \times 10^{12}) + (8 \times 10^{13})$ l $(7 \times 10^{-5}) + (6.2 \times 10^{-4})$
   m $(5 \times 10^6) - (6 \times 10^5)$ n $(1.45 \times 10^{-6}) - (6.8 \times 10^{-7})$
4 A country has a population of 6×10^7 people, and the average wealth is 3×10^3 US dollars. What is the total wealth of this country?
5 The electrical charge on an electron is about 1.6×10^{-19} coulombs. What is the total charge on 7×10^{21} electrons?
6 The population of China is about 1.1×10^9, and the population of Japan is about 1.2×10^8.
   a What is the difference between these populations?
   b What is the sum of these populations?

1 Evaluate these, giving the answers in standard form.
   a $(4 \times 10^6) - (3.95 \times 10^6)$
   b $(x \times 10^6) \times (y \times 10^7)$, where x and y are digits less than 3.
   c $(x \times 10^6) + (y \times 10^6)$, where x and y are digits less than 5.
   d $(x \times 10^6) + (y \times 10^7)$, where x and y are digits less than 5.
   e $(x \times 10^8) - (y \times 10^7)$, where x and y are digits less than 5.
2 This is another way of adding numbers in standard form. Consider $8 \times 10^8 + 7 \times 10^7$.
   a Factorise by 10^7.
   b Simplify your answer and convert to standard form.
   c Is your answer the same as that obtained by the methods of section 8.5?

Logarithms

This unit uses
- Indices
- The laws of indices
- Tables to find logarithms and antilogarithms

9.1 Definition of logarithms

In the expression $3^4 = 81$, the number 3 is the **base** and the number 81 is the **power**. We say that 81 is the 4th power of 3. To go in the other direction, we say that 4 is the **logarithm** of 81 to the base 3. This is written $4 = \log_3 81$.

$$3^4 = 81 \qquad 4 = \log_3 81$$

Similarly, since $2^5 = 32$, the logarithm of 32 to the base 2 is 5.

$$2^5 = 32 \qquad 5 = \log_2 32$$

In general, if $a^n = x$, then $n = \log_a x$. We say that n is the 'log of x to the base a'. Learn these special cases:
- Since $a^1 = a$, it follows that $\log_a a = 1$.
- Since $a^0 = 1$, it follows that $\log_a 1 = 0$.

Note that taking logarithms is the reverse operation to taking powers. If you take a power of x and then take the logarithm, you return to x.

$$\log_a(a^x) = x$$

Similarly, if you take the logarithm of y and then take the power, you return to y.

$$a^{\log y} = y$$

EXAMPLE 1

Find (a) $\log_{10} 1000$ (b) $\log_2 \frac{1}{8}$ (c) $\log_9 3$.

Solution

(a) We know that $1000 = 10^3$. This gives the logarithm of 1000, to base 10.
$$\log_{10} 1000 = 3$$
(b) We know that $\frac{1}{8} = \frac{1}{2^3} = 2^{-3}$. Remember that $a^{-n} = 1/a^n$
$$\log_2 \frac{1}{8} = -3$$
(c) We know that $3 = \sqrt{9} = 9^{\frac{1}{2}}$. Remember that $a^{1/n} = \sqrt[n]{a}$
$$\log_9 3 = \frac{1}{2}$$

Exercise 9.1

Find these logarithms.

1 $\log_{10}100$	**2** $\log_{10}10\,000$	**3** $\log_{10}10$	**4** $\log_{10}1$
5 $\log_2 4$	**6** $\log_2 16$	**7** $\log_3 27$	**8** $\log_4 64$
9 $\log_2 \frac{1}{2}$	**10** $\log_3 \frac{1}{9}$	**11** $\log_{10}0.1$	**12** $\log_{10}0.001$
13 $\log_4 2$	**14** $\log_8 2$	**15** $\log_{1000}10$	**16** $\log_{64}8$
17 $\log_{10}\sqrt{10}$	**18** $\log_4 \frac{1}{2}$	**19** $\log_{10}10^{2.5}$	**20** $\log_2 2^{1.7}$

9.2 Laws of logarithms

When powers of the same base are multiplied, the indices are added.

$$a^n \times a^m = a^{n+m}$$

The numbers n and m are the logarithms of a^n and a^m. The logarithm of a^{n+m} is $n + m$. So the logarithm of $a^n \times a^m$ is $n + m$.

It follows that the logarithm of a product is the *sum* of the logarithms.

$$\log_a xy = \log_a x + \log_a y$$

When powers of the same base are divided, the indices are subtracted.

$$a^n \div a^m = a^{n-m}$$

It follows that the logarithm of a quotient is the *difference* of the logarithms.

$$\log_a x/y = \log_a x - \log_a y$$

Consider $\log_a x^n$. By the result above, this is

$$\log_a x^n = \log_a x + \log_a x + \log_a x + \ldots + \log_a x = n \times \log_a x$$

> **R U L E S**
> **There are three rules of logarithms**
> **[1]** $\log_a xy = \log_a x + \log_a y$
> **[2]** $\log_a x/y = \log_a x - \log_a y$
> **[3]** $\log_a x^n = n \log_a x$

EXAMPLE 2

Correct to 3 significant figures, $\log_{10}2 = 0.301$ and $\log_{10}3 = 0.477$. Find
(a) $\log_{10}6$ (b) $\log_{10}\frac{1}{4}$ (c) $\log_{10}\sqrt{\frac{2}{3}}$

Solution

(a) $\log_{10}6 = \log_{10}(2\times3) = \log_{10}2 + \log_{10}3$ Using rule [1]
$$= 0.301 + 0.477$$
$$= 0.778$$

$\log_{10}6 = 0.778$

(b) Note that $\frac{1}{4} = 2^{-2}$. Hence $\log_{10}\frac{1}{4} = \log_{10}2^{-2}$
$$= -2 \times \log_{10}2 \qquad \text{Using rule [3]}$$
$$= -2 \times 0.301$$

$\log_{10}\frac{1}{4} = -0.602$

(c) Write $\sqrt{\frac{2}{3}}$ as $\left(\frac{2}{3}\right)^{\frac{1}{2}}$.

$$\log_{10}\sqrt{\tfrac{2}{3}} = \log_{10}\left(\tfrac{2}{3}\right)^{\frac{1}{2}} = \tfrac{1}{2} \times \log_{10}\tfrac{2}{3} \qquad \text{Using rule [3]}$$
$$= \tfrac{1}{2} \times (\log_{10}2 - \log_{10}3) \qquad \text{Using rule [2]}$$
$$= \tfrac{1}{2} \times (0.301 - 0.477)$$
$$= \tfrac{1}{2} \times -0.176 = -0.088$$

$$\log_{10}\sqrt{\tfrac{2}{3}} = -0.088$$

Exercise 9.2

1 Using the values of $\log_{10}2$ and $\log_{10}3$ above, find
   a $\log_{10}9$ **b** $\log_{10}1.5$ **c** $\log_{10}5$
2 To 3 significant figures, $\log_{10}7 = 0.845$ and $\log_{10}8 = 0.903$. Find
   a $\log_{10}56$ **b** $\log_{10}0.875$ **c** $\log_{10}14$
3 Simplify these expressions.
   a $\log_{10}50 + \log_{10}2$ **b** $\log_{10}25 \div \log_{10}5$
   c $\log_{10}\tfrac{1}{8} \div \log_{10}2$ **d** $\log_{10}2^k \div \log_{10}2$

9.3

The logarithm of a product is the sum of two logarithms. The logarithm of a quotient is the difference of two logarithms. Addition and subtraction are easier than multiplication and division. So we use logarithms to make multiplication and division easier. In this section, we shall see how to multiply and divide using logarithms.

From now on all logarithms are to base 10. We omit the 10.

$$\log x = \log_{10}x$$

The word 'logarithm' is often shortened to 'log'. There are tables of logarithms at the back of this book. There are also tables of antilogarithms, which go from the logarithm to the original number. These tables are used in the same way as the tables of squares and square roots.

The log tables are for numbers between 1 and 10. The values given are between 0 and 1. Similarly, the antilog tables are for logs between 0 and 1. The values given are between 1 and 10.

EXAMPLE 3

Use logs to find
(a) 3.253×2.742 (b) $9.462 \div 5.662$ (c) $\sqrt[5]{8.035}$

Solution
(a) An extract from the logarithm tables is shown. Next to 32 is 5051. This is log 3.2. Go across to the 5 column, to find 5119. So log 3.25 = 0.5119. Finally find the 3 column in the differences, and add 4 to 5119, obtaining 5123. So log 3.253 = 0.5123. Similarly, log 2.742 = 0.4381.

	0	1	2	3	4	5	6	7	8	9	1 2 3	4 5 6	7 8 9
27	4314	4330	4346	4362	4378	4393	4409	4425	4440	4456	2 3 5	6 8 9	11 13 14
28	4472	4487	4502	4518	4533	4548	4564	4579	4594	4609	2 3 5	6 8 9	11 12 14
29	4624	4639	4654	4669	4683	4698	4713	4728	4742	4757	1 3 4	6 7 9	10 12 13
30	4771	4786	4800	4814	4829	4843	4857	4871	4886	4900	1 3 4	6 7 9	10 11 13
31	4914	4928	4942	4955	4969	4983	4997	5011	5024	5038	1 3 4	6 7 8	10 11 12
32	5051	5065	5079	5092	5105	5119	5132	5145	5159	5172	1 3 4	5 7 8	9 11 12

Add these two values obtaining 0.9504. Now use the antilogarithm tables, to obtain 8.921. An extract from the antilogarithm tables is shown.

	0	1	2	3	4	5	6	7	8	9	1 2 3	4 5 6	7 8 9
.94	8710	8730	8750	8770	8790	8810	8831	8851	8872	8892	2 4 6	8 10 12	14 16 18
.95	8913	8933	8954	8974	8995	9016	9036	9057	9078	9099	2 4 6	8 10 12	15 17 19
.96	9120	9141	9162	9183	9204	9226	9247	9268	9290	9311	2 4 6	8 11 13	15 17 19

Set out the calculation like this

	Number	Log	
	3.253	0.5123	
×	2.742	0.4381	
	8.921	0.9504	(add the logs)

$$3.253 \times 2.742 = 8.921$$

(b) Follow the same procedure, but subtract the logarithms instead of adding.

	Number	Log	
	9.462	0.9760	
÷	5.662	0.7530	(subtract the logo)
	1.671	0.2230	

$$9.462 \div 5.662 = 1.671$$

(c) Write $\sqrt[5]{8.035}$ as $8.035^{\frac{1}{5}}$, and use the rule $\log x^n = n \log x$. Find the logarithm of 8.035, then multiply by $\frac{1}{5}$, that is, divide by 5.

Number	Log	
8.035	0.9050	(divide log by 5)
1.517	0.1810	

$$\sqrt[5]{8.035} = 1.517$$

Exercise 9.3

Use logarithms to evaluate the expressions in questions 1 to 18.

1 1.663×4.550 2 2.403×3.112 3 4.034×2.019

4 1.833×3.055 5 4.223×2.055 6 2.537×2.994

7 5.377×2.438 8 $7.563 \div 5.032$ 9 $3.644 \div 1.534$

10 $8.441 \div 3.299$ 11 $6.394 \div 1.046$ 12 $7.535 \div 5.046$

13 $\sqrt[5]{7.375}$ 14 $\sqrt[10]{9.376}$ 15 $1.34^{1.5}$

16 1.07^8 17 $2.452^{2.5}$ 18 $9.132^{0.8}$

19 Evaluate $\sqrt{4.295}$

    a using the square root table

    b using logarithms.

Are your answers the same?

In section 9.3, all the numbers were between 1 and 10. Their logarithms were between 0 and 1. We can use logarithms for numbers greater than 10 or less than 1. Standard form (Unit 8) is very useful for this.

For example

$$123.4 = 1.234 \times 10^2$$

Hence
$$\begin{aligned} \log 123.4 &= \log (1.234 \times 10^2) \\ &= \log 1.234 + \log 10^2 \\ &= 0.0913 + 2 \\ &= 2.0913 \end{aligned}$$

The whole number part, 2, is the **characteristic** of the logarithm. It is the log of the power of 10, in this case 10^2.

The decimal part, 0.0913, is the **mantissa** of the logarithm. It is the log of the digits, in this case 1.234.

Numbers greater than 10

With a number greater than 10, express it as a number between 1 and 10 multiplied by a power of 10. The power of 10 is the characteristic. Look up the number between 1 and 10 in the tables. This gives the mantissa.

When using the antilogarithm table, the characteristic of the logarithm gives the power of 10.

EXAMPLE 4

Find 42.33×842.8.

Solution

Find the logarithms of these numbers, using $42.33 = 4.233 \times 10$ and $842.8 = 8.428 \times 10^2$. So log 42.33 is log 4.233 + 1, and log 842.8 is log 8.428 + 2.

The sum of the logarithms is 4.5523. The characteristic is 4, and the mantissa is 0.5523.

Look up the antilogarithm of 0.5523. Then multiply by 10^4, that is, by 10 000. The working is shown below.

Number	Log
42.33	1.6266
$\times$ 842.8	2.9257
35 670	4.5523

$42.33 \times 842.8 = 35\ 670$

Exercise 9.4A

1   Find the logarithms of the following.
   a   52.66   **b**   125.3   **c**   6385

2   Find the antilogarithms of the following.
   a   1.4435   **b**   2.4483   **c**   5.3647

3 Evaluate the following.

a 46.22 × 18.33	**b** 234.6 × 12.43	**c** 5399 × 4329
d 3882 × 39.25	**e** 2044 × 1993	**f** 45 020 × 61.57
g 66.39 ÷ 2.763	**h** 4492 ÷ 27.95	**i** 5503 ÷ 1946
j 674.2 ÷ 3.225	**k** 37 590 ÷ 3341	**l** 543.2 ÷ 1.329
m 34.55^5	**n** $\sqrt[5]{4536}$	**o** 1.13^{100}

Numbers less than 1

With a number less than 1, express it as a number between 1 and 10, multiplied by a *negative* power of 10. This is the number in standard form.

For example

$$0.0034 = 3.4 \times 10^{-3}$$

Hence $\log 0.0034 = \log (3.4 \times 10^{-3})$

$$= \log 3.4 + \log 10^{-3}$$
$$= 0.5315 + -3$$

So the characteristic is –3, and the mantissa is 0.5315. Write this as $\bar{3}.5315$. In this expression, only the $\bar{3}$ is negative. The .5315 is positive.

EXAMPLE 5

Evaluate 3.465 ÷ 74.35.

Solution
Find the logs of these numbers, as 0.5397 and 1.8713. Subtract, to obtain –1.3316.
The mantissa must be positive. Subtract 0.3316 from 1, obtaining 0.6684.
Hence we can write –0.3316 as –1 + 0.6688. Hence –1.3316 = –2 + 0.6684, which we write as $\bar{2}.6684$.
The characteristic is –2, and the mantissa is 0.6684. Look up 0.6684 in the antilogarithm table, then multiply by 10^{-2}, that is, divide by 100. The working is shown below.

	Number	Log
	3.465	0.5397
÷	74.35	1.8713
	0.0466	$\bar{2}.6684$

3.465 ÷ 74.35 = 0.0466

EXAMPLE 6

Evaluate 0.04524 ÷ 0.000 0027

Solution

Find the logs of these numbers, as $\bar{2}.6555$ and $\bar{6}.4314$. Subtract, being careful with the negative numbers. $\bar{2} - \bar{6} = \bar{2} + 6 = 4$.

Number	Log
0.04524	$\bar{2}.6555$
$\div$ 0.000 0027	$\bar{6}.4314$
16 750	4.2241

$0.04524 \div 0.000\ 0027 = 16\ 750$

FACT

The characteristic of the log of a number less than 1 is negative. The mantissa is always positive.

Exercise 9.4B

1 Find the logs of these numbers.
   a 0.0481 **b** 0.1533 **c** 0.000 3744

2 Find the antilogs of these expressions
   a $\bar{2}.5538$ **b** $\bar{1}.4662$ **c** $\bar{3}.5522$

3 Evaluate these expressions.
   a $3.655 \div 2784$ **b** $1.443 \div 45.32$ **c** $123 \div 138$
   d $0.032\ 55 \times 0.756\ 6$ **e** $0.003\ 31 \times 0.008\ 321$ **f** 23.44×0.4822
   g $0.334 \div 0.1431$ **h** $0.00346 \div 0.7842$ **i** $2.443 \div 0.023\ 1$
   j $43.58 \div 0.006\ 32$ **k** $0.003\ 412 \div 0.000\ 23$ **l** $\sqrt[5]{0.3744}$
   m 0.4473^{10} **n** $0.002^{0.1}$ **o** $0.3572^{1.5}$

4 The area of a circle is given by πr^2. Find the area if $r = 1.463$ cm. (The log of π is 0.4971.)

5 The volume of a sphere is given by $\frac{4}{3}\pi r^3$. Find the volume if $r = 0.3621$ m.

6 The volume of a cylinder is given by $\pi r^2 h$. Find the volume if $r = 5.453$ cm and $h = 11.34$ cm.

7 The time of swing of a pendulum is given by $2\pi\sqrt{\dfrac{l}{g}}$. Find the time if $l = 1.021$ m and $g = 9.81$ m/sec^2.

8 The gravitational attraction between two bodies is given by $\dfrac{mMG}{r^2}$. Find this force if $m = 6834$ kg, $M = 98\ 540$ kg, $r = 21.33$ and $G = 6.672 \times 10^{-11}$.

- The logarithm of a number is the index of a certain base which will give that number. If $a^n = x$, then $n = \log_a x$.
- Logarithms obey these rules:
  $$\log_a xy = \log_a x + \log_a y \qquad \log_a x/y = \log_a x - \log_a y \qquad \log_a x^n = n \log_a x$$
- Use logarithms to base 10 to multiply, divide and find powers.

- The integer part of a logarithm is the characteristic. The decimal part of a logarithm is the mantissa. The logarithm of a number greater than 10 has a positive characteristic. The logarithm of a number less than 1 has a negative characteristic. The mantissa is always positive.

Activity 9

A **slide rule** is a tool for calculating. It is based on logarithms. You can make a simple slide rule using cardboard.

Take two pieces of cardboard, a bit over 10 cm in length. For each piece, mark 1 at one end and 10 at 10 cm away, near the other end. For each number between 1 and 10, find its log and multiply by 10. Mark the number at that distance from 1. For example, log 2 = 0.301. So mark 2 at 3.01 cm from 1. Each piece of cardboard should look roughly like this.

| 1 | 2 | 3 | 4 | 5 | 6 | 7 | 8 | 9 | 10 |

Suppose you want to multiply 2 by 3. Place the 1 on the lower strip next to the 2 on the upper strip. The 3 on the lower strip will be on 6 on the upper strip. Hence $2 \times 3 = 6$.

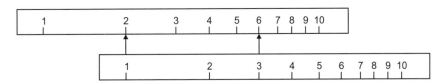

1 Try some other multiplications.
2 How do you use the slide rule for division?
3 How do you use the slide rule for numbers greater than 10 or less than 1?

Progress exercise 9

1 Find these.
   a $\log_3 81$ b $\log_5 0.2$ c $\log_{125} 5$
2 To three significant figures, $\log_2 3 = 1.585$ and $\log_2 5 = 2.322$. Find
   a $\log_2 15$ b $\log_2 10$ c $\log_2 0.6$
3 Use logarithms to evaluate these.
   a 4.384×2.446 b $76.44 \div 23.1$ c $0.022\,1 \times 0.583$
   d $\sqrt[3]{34.11}$ e $53.33^{1.6}$ f 1.08^{20}
4 The volume of a cone is given by $\frac{1}{3}\pi r^2 h$. Find the volume if $r = 8.332$ cm and $h = 6.184$ cm.
5 Find the value of the expression PV^n when $P = 17.17$, $V = 32.11$ and $n = 4$.

1 Solve the equation $2^x = 3$.
2 Find $\log_2 5$.
3 Suppose $\log_a b = x$. Express $\log_b a$ in terms of x.
4 Solve the equation $\log (x + 27) - \log x = 1$.
5 A population is increasing at 4%. (So every year the population is multiplied by 1.04.) How long does the population take to double?

10

Quadratics

This unit uses
- Letters to stand for numbers
- Brackets
- Solving equations

10.1 Expanding brackets

This expression consists of two pairs of brackets multiplied together.

$$(x + 3)(x + 7)$$

When we remove the brackets, we **expand** it. Both terms in the first pair of brackets multiply both terms in the second pair.

$$(x + 3) \times (x + 7) = x \times x + x \times 7 + 3 \times x + 3 \times 7$$

$x \times x$ is written x^2. $x \times 7$ and $3 \times x$ are written $7x$ and $3x$. $3 \times 7 = 21$.

$$(x + 3)(x + 7) = x^2 + 7x + 3x + 21$$

Recall that $7x$ and $3x$ are like terms, and can be combined to $10x$.

$$(x + 3)(x + 7) = x^2 + 10x + 21$$

This last step, of collecting like terms, is **simplifying**.

EXAMPLE 1

Expand $(a + b)(c + d)$

Solution
Both terms in the first brackets multiply both terms in the second brackets. So a multiplies c and d, and b multiplies c and d.

$$(a + b)(c + d) = a \times c + a \times d + b \times c + b \times d$$

$$(a + b)(c + d) = ac + ad + bc + bd$$

Note We can check the expansion by putting in numbers for the letters.
Suppose $a = 5$, $b = 3$, $c = 4$ and $d = 7$. The expansion becomes

$$(5 + 3)(4 + 7) = 5 \times 4 + 5 \times 7 + 3 \times 4 + 3 \times 7$$

$$8 \times 11 = 20 + 35 + 12 + 21$$

$$88 = 88$$

So the expansion is correct in this case.

Exercise 10.1

1 Expand and simplify these expressions.
   a $(x + 2)(x + 3)$ b $(x + 5)(x + 4)$ c $(x + 6)(x + 7)$
   d $(y - 3)(y + 4)$ e $(a + 4)(a - 6)$ f $(b + 8)(b - 3)$
   g $(x - 4)(x - 9)$ h $(x - 8)(x - 4)$ i $(x - 6)(x - 3)$

2 Expand these expressions.
   a $(p + q)(m + n)$ b $(a + b)(c - d)$ c $(w + x)(y - z)$
   d $(j - k)(m - n)$ e $(a + 3)(b - 2)$ f $(x - 7)(y - 3)$
   g $(a - 7)(b - 9)$ h $(w + 5)(z + 3)$ i $(m - 4)(n + 6)$

3 Expand and simplify these expressions.
   a $(2x + 3)(3x + 2)$ b $(3y + 4)(y + 5)$ c $(5z - 2)(2z + 3)$
   d $(3a - 2)(2a - 5)$ e $(7b - 2)(b - 7)$ f $(3x - 5)(4x - 1)$
   g $(4x - 5)(2x + 3)$ h $(5a + 3)(2a + 4)$ i $(3k - 1)(2k - 7)$

10.2

The expression $(a + b)^2$ means $(a + b)(a + b)$. Expand and simplify.
$$(a + b)^2 = (a + b)(a + b)$$
$$= a^2 + ab + ba + b^2$$
$$= a^2 + 2ab + b^2$$

This is an **identity**. It is true for all values of a and b.

Similarly, the expression $(a - b)^2$ means $(a - b)(a - b)$. Expand and simplify.
$$(a - b)^2 = (a - b)(a - b)$$
$$= a^2 - ab - ba + b^2$$
$$= a^2 - 2ab + b^2$$

Expand the expression $(a + b)(a - b)$.
$$(a + b)(a - b) = a^2 - ab + ba - b^2$$
$$= a^2 - b^2$$

This expression consists of the square of b subtracted from the square of a. It is called the **difference of two squares**.

The expansion of $(a + b)^2$ is shown by this diagram. The square has side $(a + b)$. Its area is $(a + b)^2$.

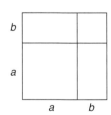

The square is built up from four smaller squares and rectangles. These have areas a^2, ab, ba and b^2.
$$(a + b)^2 = a^2 + ab + ba + b^2 = a^2 + 2ab + b^2.$$

RULES

These three identities should be learnt by heart.
$(a + b)^2 = a^2 + 2ab + b^2$
$(a - b)^2 = a^2 - 2ab + b^2$
$(a + b)(a - b) = a^2 - b^2$

EXAMPLE 2

Expand the expression $(x - 3)^2$.

Solution
This is like the second identity above, with $a = x$ and $b = 3$.
So $2ab = 2x3 = 6x$ and $b^2 = 9$.
$(x - 3)^2 = x^2 - 6x + 9$

EXAMPLE 3

Expand the expression $(n - 7)(n + 7)$.

Solution
This is like the third identity above. It is the difference of two squares, with $a = n$ and $b = 7$. So $b^2 = 49$.
$(n - 7)(n + 7) = n^2 - 49$

Exercise 10.2

1 Expand and simplify these expressions.
    a $(x + y)^2$ **b** $(m + n)^2$ **c** $(a + 4)^2$
    d $(b + 3)^2$ **e** $(c + 9)^2$ **f** $(w + \frac{1}{2})^2$
    g $(3x + 2)^2$ **h** $(5y + 3)^2$ **i** $(2a + 3b)^2$
    j $(3x + 5y)^2$ **k** $(2m + 7n)^2$ **l** $(5z + 4w)^2$

2 Expand and simplify these expressions.
    a $(x - y)^2$ **b** $(m - n)^2$ **c** $(x - 5)^2$
    d $(k - 3)^2$ **e** $(a - 7)^2$ **f** $(b - \frac{1}{3})^2$
    g $(2x - 5)^2$ **h** $(3a - 4)^2$ **i** $(7y - 2)^2$
    j $(2a - 3b)^2$ **k** $(4x - 5y)^2$ **l** $(2r - 7t)^2$

3 Expand and simplify these expressions.
    a $(x + y)(x - y)$ **b** $(m - n)(m + n)$ **c** $(x - 5)(x + 5)$
    d $(k - 4)(k + 4)$ **e** $(y + \frac{1}{2})(y - \frac{1}{2})$ **f** $(2a - 3b)(2a + 3b)$
    g $(5m + 3n)(5m - 3n)$ **h** $(2x - 4)(x + 2)$
    i $(b + 5)(3b - 15)$ **j** $(4k + \frac{1}{2})(4k - \frac{1}{2})$

10.3 Factorising

Factorising is the opposite of expanding. When you factorise an expression, you write it as a product of its factors. Put in brackets where needed.

You have already factorised expressions like these.

    $6x - 2y = 2(3x - y)$ The factors are 2 and $(3x - y)$
    $15x^2 + 9xy = 3x(5x + 3y)$ The factors are 3, x and $(5x + 3y)$

In these examples each term has a common factor. In this section we factorise expressions which do not have a common factor.

Consider the expansion of $(x + 4)(x + 5)$.

$$(x + 4)(x + 5) = x^2 + 4x + 5x + 20$$
$$= x^2 + 9x + 20.$$

Suppose we want to go in the other direction, that is, to find the factors of $x^2 + 9x + 20$. We look at the numbers 9 and 20.

The number multiplying x, 9, is the **coefficient** of x. The number term, 20, is the **constant**. Notice that:

The coefficient of x is the sum of 4 and 5

The constant is the product of 4 and 5

Suppose you want to factorise an expression like $x^2 + bx + c$. Look for numbers whose sum is b and whose product is c. It is easiest to find the factors of c, and find the pair which add up to b.

EXAMPLE 4

Factorise the expression $x^2 + 8x + 12$.

Solution
The constant term is 12. The factors of 12 are (in pairs):

1 and 12   2 and 6   3 and 4

The sum of 1 and 12 is 13
The sum of 2 and 6 is 8
The sum of 3 and 4 is 7
We want 2 and 6, as their sum is 8.
$x^2 + 8x + 12 = (x + 2)(x + 6)$

Exercise 10.3A

1 Find whole numbers with
   a sum 6 and product 8   b sum 5 and product 6
   c sum 7 and product 10   d sum 19 and product 60

Factorise these expressions.
2 $x^2 + 5x + 6$ 3 $x^2 + 7x + 12$ 4 $x^2 + 6x + 8$
5 $x^2 + 10x + 24$ 6 $x^2 + 4x + 3$ 7 $x^2 + 8x + 7$
8 $x^2 + 7x + 10$ 9 $x^2 + 8x + 15$ 10 $x^2 + 19x + 60$
11 $x^2 + 11x + 10$ 12 $x^2 + 16x + 28$ 13 $x^2 + 17x + 42$

Use the identity $(a + b)^2 = a^2 + 2ab + b^2$ to factorise these expressions.
14 $x^2 + 4x + 4$ 15 $x^2 + 6x + 9$ 16 $x^2 + 14x + 49$
17 $x^2 + 20x + 100$ 18 $x^2 + 16x + 64$ 19 $x^2 + x + \frac{1}{4}$

Consider this expansion.

$$(x - 4)(x - 5) = x^2 - 4x - 5x + 20$$
$$= x^2 - 9x + 20$$

Again, notice that the sum of –4 and –5 is –9, and the product of –4 and –5 is 20. To factorise $x^2 + bx + c$, find factors of c whose sum is b. If b is negative, then these factors are negative.

EXAMPLE 5

Factorise $x^2 - 8x + 15$

Solution
The factors of 15 are (in pairs):

  1 and 15   3 and 5

The sum of 3 and 5 is 8. Because the coefficient of x is –8, we want –3 and –5.
$x^2 - 8x + 15 = (x - 3)(x - 5)$

Exercise 10.3B

Factorise these expressions.
1 $x^2 - 7x + 12$ 2 $x^2 - 9x + 20$ 3 $x^2 - 5x + 4$
4 $x^2 - 10x + 21$ 5 $x^2 - 10x + 24$ 6 $x^2 - 17x + 60$
7 $x^2 - 10x + 16$ 8 $x^2 - 15x + 26$ 9 $x^2 - 13x + 36$
Use the identity $(a - b)^2 = a^2 - 2ab + b^2$ to factorise these expressions.
10 $x^2 - 2x + 1$ 11 $x^2 - 8x + 16$ 12 $x^2 - 10x + 25$
13 $x^2 - 14x + 49$ 14 $x^2 - 12x + 36$ 15 $x^2 - \frac{2}{3}x + \frac{1}{9}$

Consider this expansion.
$$(x - 4)(x + 5) = x^2 - 4x + 5x - 20 \qquad \text{Remember: } -4 \times 5 = -20$$
$$= x^2 + x - 20$$

Notice that the sum of –4 and 5 is 1, and that the product of –4 and 5 is –20. So we want numbers whose sum is 1 and whose product is –20. So we find factors of 20 whose *difference* is 1. As the coefficient of x is positive, take the larger factor to be positive and the smaller factor negative.

EXAMPLE 6

Factorise   (a) $x^2 + 3x - 18$ (b) $x^2 - 2x - 8$

Solution
(a) The factors of 18 are: 1 and 18, 2 and 9, 3 and 6. Of these, the difference of 3 and 6 is 3. Because the coefficient of x is +3, take +6 and –3.
     $x^2 + 3x - 18 = (x + 6)(x - 3)$
(b) The factors of 8 are: 1 and 8, 2 and 4. Of these, the difference of 2 and 4 is 2. Because the coefficient of x is –2, take –4 and + 2.
     $x^2 - 2x - 8 = (x - 4)(x + 2)$

Exercise 10.3C

Factorise these expressions.

1 $x^2 + 4x - 5$ **2** $x^2 - x - 20$ **3** $x^2 - 4x - 12$

4 $x^2 + 2x - 24$ **5** $x^2 - x - 42$ **6** $x^2 - 6x - 7$

7 $x^2 + x - 12$ **8** $x^2 - 2x - 3$ **9** $x^2 + 4x - 60$

Use the identity $(a + b)(a - b) = a^2 - b^2$ to factorise these expressions.

10 $4x^2 - y^2$ **11** $9a^2 - 16b^2$ **12** $49x^2 - 1$

Suppose you are given any expression of the form $x^2 + bx + c$. Follow this flow diagram to factorise it.

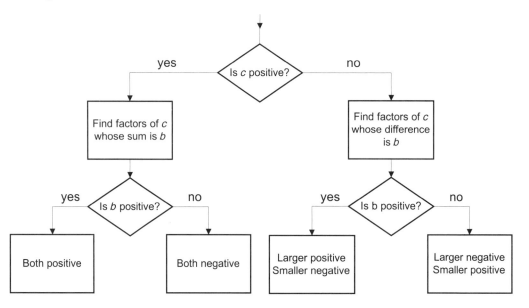

Exercise 10.3D

Factorise these expressions.

1 $x^2 - 7x + 10$ **2** $x^2 + 5x - 36$ **3** $x^2 + 11x + 30$

4 $x^2 - x - 56$ **5** $x^2 + 24x - 25$ **6** $x^2 - 28x - 60$

7 $x^2 - 24x + 63$ **8** $x^2 + 12x - 45$ **9** $x^2 + 18x + 32$

10 $x^2 - 3x - 28$ **11** $x^2 - 5x - 36$ **12** $x^2 + 11x - 26$

10.4 The general quadratic $ax^2 + bx + c$

The general quadratic expression is of the form $ax^2 + bx + c$. In the examples above, a was always equal to 1. To factorise a general quadratic expression, follow these steps:

1. Form the product ac.

2. Find pairs of factors of *ac*.

> If *ac* is positive, find a pair whose sum is *b*.
> If *ac* is negative, find a pair whose difference is *b*.

3. Write *b* in terms of the pair, and then factorise again.

EXAMPLE 7

Factorise (a) $3x^2 - 8x + 5$ (b) $5x^2 + 8x - 4$

Solution

(a) The product *ac* is 15. The factors of 15 are 1 and 15, and 3 and 5. The sum of 3 and 5 is 8. Because the coefficient is –8, take –3 and –5.

$$3x^2 - 8x + 5 = 3x^2 - 3x - 5x + 5$$
$$= 3x(x - 1) - 5(x - 1) \qquad \text{Note that } -5x - 1 = +5$$
$$= (x - 1)(3x - 5)$$
$$3x^2 - 8x + 5 = (x - 1)(3x - 5)$$

(b) The product *ac* is –20. The factors of 20 are 1 and 20, 2 and 10, and 4 and 5. The difference of 2 and 10 is 8. The coefficient of *x* is +8, so take +10 and –2.

$$5x^2 + 8x - 4 = 5x^2 + 10x - 2x - 4$$
$$= 5x(x + 2) - 2(x + 2) \qquad \text{Note that } -2 \times 2 = -4$$
$$= (x + 2)(5x - 2)$$
$$5x^2 + 8x - 4 = (x + 2)(5x - 2)$$

Exercise 10.4

Factorise these expressions.

1 $2x^2 + 5x + 2$	2 $6x^2 - x - 2$	3 $2x^2 + 5x - 3$
4 $5x^2 + 9x + 4$	5 $6x^2 + 11x + 5$	6 $6x^2 + 35x - 6$
7 $3x^2 - 10x - 8$	8 $3x^2 - 7x - 6$	9 $4x^2 - 4x + 1$
10 $5x^2 + 13x - 6$	11 $8x^2 - 2x - 3$	12 $7x^2 - 16x + 4$

10.5   Quadratic equations

An expression of the form $ax^2 + bx + c$ is a quadratic expression. When it is put equal to 0, it is a **quadratic equation**. So $ax^2 + bx + c = 0$ is a quadratic equation.

If the quadratic expression factorises, then the equation can be solved.
Suppose $x^2 + bx + c = (x + k)(x + l)$. The equation is

$$(x + k)(x + l) = 0$$

Now, when two non-zero numbers are multiplied, the result is also non-zero. Hence if a product is zero, then one of the factors must be zero.

> **FACT**
> If $ab = 0$, then either $a = 0$ or $b = 0$

So if $(x + k)(x + l) = 0$, that is, the product of $(x + k)$ and $(x + l)$ is 0, then either $(x + k)$ or $(x + l)$ is 0.

Either $(x + k) = 0$ or $(x + l) = 0$.

It follows that either $x = -k$ or $x = -l$.

EXAMPLE 8

Solve the equation $x^2 - 4x - 12 = 0$

Solution

The quadratic expression factorises, to $(x - 6)(x + 2)$. The equation becomes

$$(x - 6)(x + 2) = 0$$

Either $x - 6 = 0$ or $x + 2 = 0$

If $x - 6 = 0$ then $x = 6$ (adding 6 to both sides)

If $x + 2 = 0$ then $x = -2$ (subtracting 2 from both sides)

Either $x = 6$ or $x = -2$

Check Put $x = 6$ and $x = -2$ into the original equation.

$$6^2 - 4 \times 6 - 12 = 36 - 24 - 12 = 0 \qquad \text{So } x = 6 \text{ is correct}$$
$$(-2)^2 - 4 \times (-2) - 12 = 4 + 8 - 12 = 0 \qquad \text{So } x = -2 \text{ is correct}$$

Exercise 10.5A

Solve these equations. Check your answers.

1	$x^2 - 7x + 12 = 0$	**2**	$x^2 - 5x + 6 = 0$	**3**	$x^2 - 19x + 60 = 0$
4	$x^2 + 6x + 5 = 0$	**5**	$x^2 + 11x + 30 = 0$	**6**	$x^2 + 2x - 15 = 0$
7	$x^2 - 5x - 6 = 0$	**8**	$x^2 - 3x - 40 = 0$	**9**	$x^2 + 4x - 12 = 0$
10	$x^2 - 15x + 50 = 0$	**11**	$x^2 + 6x - 55 = 0$	**12**	$x^2 - 3x - 130 = 0$

EXAMPLE 9

Solve the equation $2x^2 - 7x - 4 = 0$

Solution

The left hand side factorises, to $(2x + 1)(x - 4)$. The equation is

$$(2x + 1)(x - 4) = 0$$

So $2x + 1 = 0$ or $x - 4 = 0$

If $2x + 1 = 0$ then $x = -\frac{1}{2}$ (subtracting 1, then dividing by 2)

If $x - 4 = 0$ then $x = 4$ (adding 4)

$x = -\frac{1}{2}$ or $x = 4$

Exercise 10.5B

Solve these equations.

1 $3x^2 - 5x + 2 = 0$	**2** $4x^2 - 4x - 3 = 0$	**3** $3x^2 - 5x - 12 = 0$
4 $6x^2 - 13x + 6 = 0$	**5** $2x^2 - x - 15 = 0$	**6** $6x^2 - 7x + 2 = 0$
7 $12x^2 + 11x + 2 = 0$	**8** $7x^2 - 19x - 6 = 0$	**9** $12x^2 + 7x - 10 = 0$
10 $5x^2 - 17x + 6 = 0$	**11** $10x^2 + 11x - 6 = 0$	**12** $9x^2 + 20x + 4 = 0$

Sometimes you must rearrange the equation before solving.

EXAMPLE 10

Solve these equations.

(a) $x^2 + 3x = 10$ (b) $x + \frac{1}{x-5} = 7$

Solution

(a) Take the 10 to the left

$$x^2 + 3x - 10 = 0$$

This can now be factorised as above.

$$(x + 5)(x - 2) = 0$$
$$x = -5 \text{ or } x = 2$$

(b) Multiply both sides by $(x - 5)$.

$$x(x - 5) + 1 = 7(x - 5)$$
$$x^2 - 5x + 1 = 7x - 35$$
$$x^2 - 12x + 36 = 0$$
$$(x - 6)(x - 6) = 0$$
$$x = 6$$

Exercise 10.5C

Solve these equations.

1 $x^2 - 5x = 14$	**2** $x^2 = 6x - 8$	**3** $x^2 + 20 = 9x$
4 $2x^2 + 3x = 27$	**5** $25x - 3x^2 = 38$	**6** $x = 6x^2 - 57$
7 $(x + 3)(x + 4) = 72$	**8** $x(x - 7) = 18$	**9** $(x + 1)(2x + 1) = 15$
10 $(x + 1)(x + 3) = 8x$	**11** $x(3x - 5) = x + 24$	

12 $(x - 3)(x - 4) = 2x^2 - 48$

13 $\dfrac{3}{x} + \dfrac{4}{x+1} = 2$ **14** $\dfrac{6}{x} - \dfrac{5}{x+2} = 1$ **15** $\dfrac{x+2}{x} = \dfrac{2x+4}{x+3}$

16 $x - \dfrac{6}{x-2} = 7$ **17** $\dfrac{24}{x+3} + \dfrac{24}{x-3} = 15$ **18** $\dfrac{x}{4} + \dfrac{3}{x} = 3\dfrac{1}{4}$

Problems that lead to quadratic equations

Some problems can be solved by forming a quadratic equation.

EXAMPLE 11

A rectangular hall is 2 m longer than it is wide. The area is 63 m². Find its width.

Solution

Let the width be x m. Then the length is $(x + 2)$m. The area is the product of these.

$$x(x + 2) = 63$$
$$x^2 + 2x - 63 = 0$$
$$(x + 9)(x - 7) = 0$$

So $x = -9$ or $x = 7$. Ignore the negative answer.
The width is 7 m.

Exercise 10.5D

1 The length of a rectangular sheet of paper is 3 cm greater than the width. If the area is 70 cm², find the length.

2 The area of a circle is 35π greater than its perimeter. Find the radius.

3 Two numbers differ by 7. Their product is 60. Find the numbers.

4 The difference of two numbers is 5. The sum of their squares is 73. Let smaller number be x. Find a quadratic equation in x and solve it.

5 The sum of two numbers is 12. The sum of their squares is 74. Let one of the numbers be x. Find a quadratic equation in x and solve it.

6 The perimeter of a rectangle is 40 cm. Its area is 96cm². Let the breadth be x cm. Find a quadratic equation in x and solve it.

7 The two shorter sides of a right-angled triangle are x cm and $(x + 5)$ cm. The area of the triangle is 18 cm². Find x.

8 The sides of a right-angled triangle are $(2x + 1)$ cm, $2x$ cm and $(x - 1)$ cm. Find x.

9 A ball is thrown up in the air, and after t seconds its height h metres is given by $h = 30t - 5t^2$. Find the time when the ball is 40 m high.

10 Mutua buys x pencils at $(x + 6)$ sh each. He spends 55 sh. Find x.

11 x ties at $(20x + 10)$ sh each cost the same as $(x - 2)$ ties at $(30x + 15)$ sh each. Find x.

12 Atieno has 180 sh to spend on cakes. If the price of each cake decreases by 2 sh, then she can buy 3 more of them. Find the original price of each cake.

13 The total age of group of parents is 342. A new parent aged 48 joins the group and the average rises by 1. What was the original average?

14 A man can swim at x m/sec. He swims in a river where the current is 2 m/sec. He swims against the current for 600 m, and then with the current for 600 m. The total time is 225 seconds. Find x.

15 A plane can fly at x km/hour. There is a wind of 20 km/hour. A journey of 960 km against the wind takes 2 hours longer than the same journey with the wind. Find x.

The **roots** of an equation are its solutions.
Suppose a quadratic equation has roots 3 and 6. Then the equation can be written as $(x - 3)(x - 6) = 0$. Expand out:

$$x^2 - 3x - 6x + (-3) \times (-6) = 0$$
$$x^2 - (3 + 6)x + 3 \times 6 = 0$$

So the coefficient of x is minus the sum of 3 and 6, and the constant term is the product of 3 and 6. If you are given the roots of a quadratic equation, you can write down the original equation. The coefficient of x is minus the sum of the roots, and the constant term is the product of the roots.

EXAMPLE 12

Find the equation with roots $2\frac{1}{2}$ and $1\frac{1}{2}$.

Solution
The sum of the roots is 4, and the product of the roots is $3\frac{3}{4}$.
The equation can be written as

$$x^2 - 4x + 3\frac{3}{4} = 0$$

Multiply by 4 to eliminate the fraction
The equation is $4x^2 - 16x + 15 = 0$

Exercise 10.6

Form the equations with these pairs of numbers as roots.

1 3 and 4	**2** 2 and 5	**3** −1 and −7
4 −5 and −6	**5** −6 and 3	**6** 5 and −4
7 4 and −4	**8** $\frac{1}{2}$ and $\frac{1}{4}$	**9** 0.1 and 10
10 $\frac{1}{3}$ and −2$\frac{1}{3}$	**11** −$\frac{1}{4}$ and −$\frac{3}{4}$	**12** 2$\frac{1}{8}$ and 3$\frac{3}{8}$

Summary

- To factorise $x^2 + bx + c$, find factors of c whose sum is b. If c is positive and b is negative, both these factors are negative. If c is negative, one factor is positive and the other negative.
- To factorise $ax^2 + bx + c$, find factors of ac whose sum is b. Write bx in terms of these factors, then factorise again.
- A quadratic equation is of the form $ax^2 + bx + c = 0$. If the left hand side can be factorised, then the equation can be solved.
- Sometimes you need to rearrange an equation before it can be solved.
- Some practical problems give rise to quadratic equations.
- From the roots of an equation you can write down the equation.

Some quadratics do not factorise. For example, $x^2 - 6x + 3$ does not factorise. So some quadratic equations cannot be solved exactly. Here is a geometric way to solve $x^2 - 6x + 3 = 0$

Plot A at $(0, 1)$ and B at $(6, 3)$. Construct the circle with diameter AB. The points where the circle cuts the x-axis are the solutions of the equation.

Solve $x^2 - 6x + 2 = 0$ by this method, taking A at $(0, 1)$ and B at $(6, 2)$.

1   Expand   **a** $(x + 7)(x - 3)$ **b** $(2a + 3)(3b - 1)$
2   Expand   **a** $(v + 7)^2$ **b** $(2v + u)(2v - u)$
3   Factorise   **a** $x^2 - 18x + 81$ **b** $x^2 + 7x - 18$
4   Factorise $6x^2 - 11x - 7$
5   Solve these equations.
    a $x^2 + 8x - 20 = 0$ **b** $(2x + 3)(x - 2) = 39$ **c** $\dfrac{12}{1 + x} = x$
6   The sum of the perimeter of a square in cm and its area in cm^2 is 45. Find the side of the square.
7   A man can row a boat at 5 km/hour. A journey of 24 km takes 9 hours longer against a current than with the current. How fast is the current?
8   Find the equation with roots $-\frac{2}{3}$ and $-4\frac{1}{3}$.

1   The quadratic expressions $x^2 + 5x + 6$ and $x^2 + 5x - 6$ both factorise. Can you find another example? Can you find integers m and n such that both $x^2 + mx + n$ and $x^2 + mx - n$ factorise?
2   Solve the equation $x^4 - 13x^2 + 36 = 0$.
3   Solve the equation $4^x - 6 \times 2^x + 8 = 0$.
4   Find a quick way to evaluate $2114^2 - 2113^2$.
5   If p is a prime number, and $x^2 + qx + p$ factorises, what can q be?
6   Suppose the roots of the equation $x^2 + bx + c = 0$ are m and n. We know that $m + n = -b$ and that $mn = c$. Find expressions in terms of b and c for
    a $m^2 + n^2$ **b** $\frac{1}{m} + \frac{1}{n}$ **c** $m^2n + mn^2$
7   Suppose the roots of the cubic equation $x^3 + bx^2 + cx + d = 0$ are l, m and n. Find in terms of b, c and d
    a $l + m + n$ **b** lmn **c** $lm + mn + nl$
8   On page 104 there is a diagram to illustrate the expansion of $(a + b)^2$. Find similar diagrams to illustrate the expansions of
    a $(a - b)^2$ **b** $(a + b)(a - b)$.

11

Rotation

This unit uses
- The coordinates of points
- The names of different types of triangle, quadrilateral and polygon

11.1 Rotation

A **rotation** is an operation which turns an object. The angle of turn can be either clockwise or anticlockwise. (This is the **sense** or **direction** of the turn). If no sense is given, the sense is anticlockwise.

Rotations of 90° or 180° are easiest. In a rotation of 90°, horizontal lines become vertical and vertical lines become horizontal. In a rotation of 180° horizontal lines remain horizontal and vertical lines remain vertical.

EXAMPLE 1

Rotate the F shape through 90°.

Solution

As no sense is given, assume it is anticlockwise. Imagine picking the letter up, turning it and putting it back on the page. The vertical part of the F becomes horizontal, and the two horizontal parts become vertical, pointing upwards. The diagram shows the result.

Exercise 11.1

1 Rotate the E shape through 90° clockwise.

2 Rotate the P shape through 180°.

3 Rotate this shape through 60°.

4 In this figure triangle A has been rotated to triangle B. Find the angle of rotation.

5 A letter M is rotated through 180°. What letter is it now?
6 A letter p is rotated through 180°. What letter is it now?

11.2

In a rotation, one point remains fixed. This is the **centre of rotation**. If the centre of rotation is X, we say that the rotation is **about X**.

EXAMPLE 2

Turn the P shape through 60° clockwise, about the point X.

Solution
Think of a pin fixing point X to the desk. Rotate the shape though 60° clockwise about X. The result is shown in the diagram.

Note The rotation can be done accurately using tracing paper. Trace the P shape on the paper, turn the paper through 60°. Then copy the P back on to the original paper.

Exercise 11.2A

1 Make a copy of these diagrams, and rotate the shapes about the point given by the angle given.

a 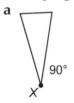 **b** 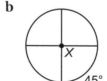 **c**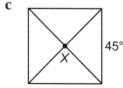

2 On a clock, the hour hand is pointing at 12 o'clock. The hand is rotated 150° about the centre of the clock. What time is it pointing at now?
3 What angle does the hour hand of a clock rotate through, between 6 o'clock and 3 o'clock?
4 It is 3 o'clock. The minute hand of the clock rotates through 270°. What time is it now?
5 Between 3 o'clock and 3.35 what has been the angle of rotation of
   a the minute hand of a clock   **b** the hour hand of the clock

6 What angle does the line between the Earth and the Sun rotate through between 1st January and 31st March?

7 How many days have passed when the line between the Earth and the Sun has rotated through 130°?

Rotation using coordinates

If a shape is given by coordinates, then rotation can be done more accurately, especially when the angle of rotation is 90° or 180°.

EXAMPLE 3

Rotate the triangle shown through 90°, about (1, 2).

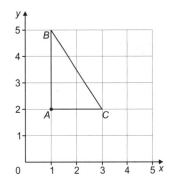

Solution

The vertices of the triangle are $A(1, 2)$, $B(1, 5)$ and $C(3, 2)$.

> A is the centre of rotation, and so it remains fixed.
> B is 3 units above A. After rotation B is 3 units left of A, at (−2, 2).
> C is 2 units right of A. After rotation C is 2 units above A, at (1, 4)

The rotated triangle is shown in the diagram.

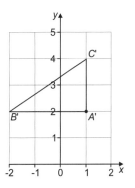

EXAMPLE 4

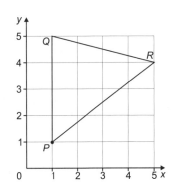

Rotate the triangle shown through 180°, about (1, 1).

Solution

The vertices of the triangle are $P(1, 1)$, $Q(1, 5)$ and $R(5, 4)$.

> P is the centre of rotation, and so it remains fixed.
> Q is 4 units above P. After rotation Q is 4 units below P, at (1, −3).
> R is 4 units right of P and 3 units above P. After rotation R is 4 units left of P and 3 units below P, at (−3, −2).

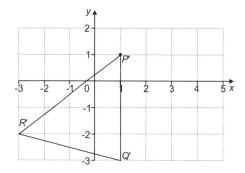

The rotated triangle is shown in the diagram.

Exercise 11.2B

1 Copy this diagram, and rotate the triangle through 90° anticlockwise about (2, 2). Write down the coordinates of the new vertices.

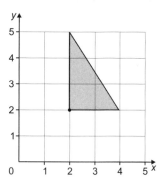

2 Copy this diagram, and rotate the triangle through 180° about (−1, 1). Write down the coordinates of the new vertices.

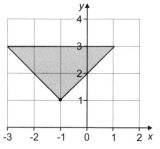

3 A triangle has vertices at (0, 3), (4, 3) and (4, 5). Plot the triangle, and then rotate it through 90° clockwise about (0, 3). Write down the coordinates of the new vertices.

4 A rectangle has vertices at (1, 2), (1, 5), (5, 5) and (5, 2). Plot the rectangle, and then rotate it through 180° about (1, 2). Write down the coordinates of the new vertices.

5 Plot the points (1, 1), (1, 3), (1, 5), (4, 5) and (4, 3). Join them up to make an F shape. Rotate the shape through 90° about (1, 5). Write down the coordinates of the new vertices.

6 Plot points at (1, 1), (3, 4) and (5, 0). Join them up to make a triangle. Rotate the triangle through 70° anticlockwise about (1, 1). Write down the coordinates of the new vertices.

7 Plot the triangle with vertices at (−2, 3), (0, 1) and (4, 4). Rotate the triangle through 60° clockwise about (0, 1). Write down the coordinates of the new vertices.

When the centre is not in the shape

Rotations are harder to do when the centre of rotation is not in the shape. It may help to imagine a 'bent wire' joining the centre of rotation to the shape. The wire is bent so that part is horizontal and part vertical.

For example, suppose (3, 4) is rotated through 90° about (0, 0). The bent wire has horizontal part 3 and vertical part 4. After rotation, the wire has vertical part 3 and horizontal part –4, as shown in the diagram. The point is rotated to (–4, 3).

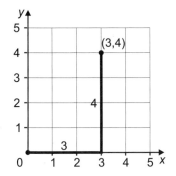 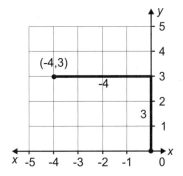

EXAMPLE 5

Rotate the triangle shown about the point (0, 1) through 90° clockwise.

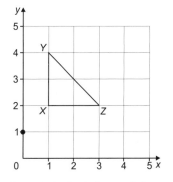

Solution
Imagine a 'bent wire' joining the centre of rotation and the triangle. Imagine the wire turning through 90° clockwise.
The vertices of the triangle are X(1, 2), Y(1, 4) and Z(3, 2).

X is 1 right and 1 up from the centre. After rotation, it is 1 right and 1 down.

Y is 1 right and 3 up from the centre. After rotation, it is 3 right and 1 down.

Z is 3 right and 1 up from the centre. After rotation, it is 1 right and 3 down.

The rotated triangle is shown in the diagram.

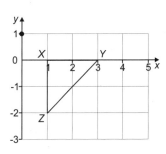

Exercise 11.2C

1   The point *A* is at (3, 1). Find its position after it
    has been rotated about the origin through
    a   90° anticlockwise   **b**   180°
    c   90° clockwise

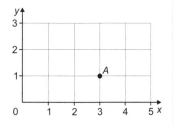

2   Copy the diagram, and rotate the triangle
    through 90° about (0, 3). Write down the
    coordinates of the new vertices.

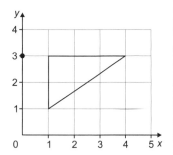

3   Copy the diagram, and rotate the triangle
    through 180° about (0, 1). Write down the
    coordinates of the new vertices.

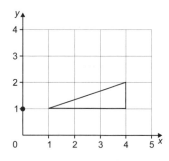

4   A triangle has vertices at (2, 1), (4, 2) and (3, 4). Plot the triangle, and rotate it
    through 90° about (1, 1). Write down the coordinates of the new vertices.

5   A rectangle has vertices at (2, 3), (2, 4), (5, 4) and (5, 3). Plot the rectangle,
    and rotate it through 90° clockwise about (1, 2). Write down the coordinates
    of the new vertices.

6   Plot the triangle with vertices at (1, 1), (3, 5) and (6, 2). Rotate the triangle
    through 80° about (0, 1). Write down the coordinates of the new vertices.

7   Plot the quadrilateral with vertices at (0, 3), (1, 5), (4, 4) and (6, 1). Rotate the
    quadrilateral through 50° clockwise about (1, 1). Write down the coordinates
    of the new vertices.

Finding the centre and angle of rotation

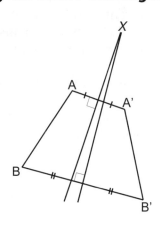

Suppose a shape has been rotated. Then each point and its image are the same distance from the centre of rotation.

To find the centre, take a point A and its image A'. Find the perpendicular bisector of AA'. Repeat, for another point B.
The centre of rotation is at the intersection X of the two perpendicular bisectors.

You can check using tracing paper. Trace the original shape on to the paper. Turn the paper about the centre of rotation. The original shape should move on to the image.

EXAMPLE 6

In the diagram, ABC has been rotated to $A'B'C'$. Find the centre of rotation.

Solution

A is at $(0, 4)$, and A' is at $(4, 4)$. The perpendicular bisector of AA' is the vertical line $x = 2$.
B is at $(2, 4)$, and B' is at $(4, 2)$. The perpendicular bisector of BB' is the sloping line $y = x$.
These lines meet at $(2, 2)$.
The centre of rotation is $(2, 2)$

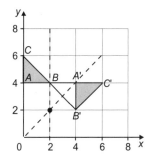

Exercise 11.2D

1 In the diagram, PQR has been rotated to $P'Q'R'$.
   Trace the diagram and find the centre of rotation.

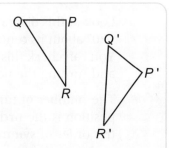

2 In the diagram, ABC has been rotated to $A'B'C'$.
   Find the centre of rotation, and give its
   coordinates.

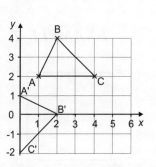

3 A triangle has vertices at (1, 1), (3, 1) and (3, 2). It is rotated to the triangle with vertices (1, 3), (–1, 3) and (–1, 2). Find the centre and angle of rotation.

4 A rectangle has vertices at (1, 1), (2, 1), (2, –1) and (1, –1). It is rotated to the rectangle with vertices at (0, 0), (0, –1), (–2, –1) and (–2, 0). Find the centre and angle of rotation.

5 The triangle of question **3** is rotated to the triangle with vertices at (1, –1), (1, 1) and (0, 1). Find the centre and angle of rotation.

6 The rectangle of question **4** is rotated to the rectangle with vertices at (4, 1), (3, 1), (3, 3) and (4, 3). Find the centre and angle of rotation.

7 The rear door of a car can rotate from the closed position *AB* to the open position *CD*. Copy the diagram, and find the centre and angle of rotation.

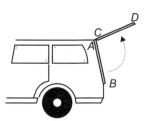

8 This diagram represents the wheels of a bicycle from above. If the rear wheel is rotated to the position of the front wheel, find the centre of rotation. (This is the centre of the circle along which the bicycle is turning.)

11.3

Look at this diagram. It is unchanged if it is rotated through 120° about its centre. The shape has **rotational symmetry**. You can check this by copying the shape on to tracing paper, and turning the paper through 120°.

The number of turns to get the shape back to its original position is the **order of symmetry**. For the shape above, the order of symmetry is 3.

EXAMPLE 7

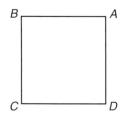

Find the order of symmetry of a square.

Solution

Let the square be *ABCD*. After turning through 90°, *A* is at *B*, *B* is at *C*, *C* is at *D* and *D* is at *A*. Repeat this rotation to a total of 4 turns, and *A* is back to *A*, and so on.

The order of symmetry is 4.

Exercise 11.3A

1 Find the order of symmetry of these shapes.
   a a rectangle   b a parallelogram   c an equilateral triangle
   d a regular pentagon   e a regular hexagon

2 Which of the shapes below has rotational symmetry? Give the order of symmetry for those that do have symmetry.
   a   b   c

3 Complete the shapes below so that they have rotational symmetry of the order given.
   a   b

 order 4   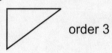 order 3

4 Plot points at (1, 1), (1, 6), (5, 9) and (5, 4). Join the points. What is the order of rotational symmetry of this shape?

5 Plot points at (1, 1), (4, 5), (0, 8) and (−3, 4). Join the points. What is the order of rotational symmetry of this shape?

6 Write out the digits 0 to 9. Which of them has rotational symmetry? Which has line symmetry?

7 Write out the letters A to Z. Which of them has rotational symmetry? Which has line symmetry?

Rotational symmetry of solids

A solid can also have rotational symmetry. A solid can be rotated about a line, called an **axis**. If the solid occupies the same space after a rotation, then it has rotational symmetry. The order of symmetry is the number of turns to return it to its original position.

EXAMPLE 8

A pyramid has a square base and a vertex above the centre of the base. How many axes of symmetry does the pyramid have? What is its order of symmetry?

Solution

Consider the line through the vertex and the centre of the base. If the pyramid is rotated through 90° about this line, then it occupies the same space.

There is one axis of symmetry.

The order of symmetry is 4.

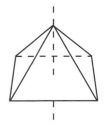

Exercise 11.3B

1   The diagram shows a cube *ABCDEFGH*. Find the order of rotational symmetry about axes which go
    a   through the centres of *ABCD* and *EFGH*
    b   through the centres of *AB* and *GH*
    c   along *AG*.

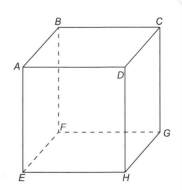

2   This diagram shows a cuboid with sides 3 cm, 4 cm and 5 cm. How many axes of symmetry does it have? What is the order for each axis of symmetry?

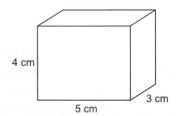

3   The diagram shows a cuboid with sides 3 cm, 3 cm and 5 cm. How many axes of symmetry does it have? What is the order for each axis of symmetry?

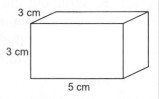

4   How many axes of symmetry are there for a regular tetrahedron? For each axis give the order of symmetry.

5   A prism has a cross-section which is an equilateral triangle. How many axes of symmetry does it have? For each axis give the order of symmetry.

6   How many axes of symmetry are there for
    a   a cone   b   a hemisphere.

7   Describe the axes of symmetry of the Earth.

Summary

● A rotation turns shapes through a fixed angle. If no sense or direction is given, the angle is anticlockwise.

- In a rotation one point remains fixed. This point is the centre of rotation.
- To find the centre of rotation, find the intersection of two perpendicular bisectors of lines that each join a point to its image.
- If a shape is unchanged after rotation, it has rotational symmetry. The order of symmetry is the number of turns to return the shape to its original position.

Activity 11

1   A pattern is made from a simple shape repeated and transformed in different ways. It can be shown that there are 17 basic types of pattern. Below are three types of pattern. Try to find as many others as you can.

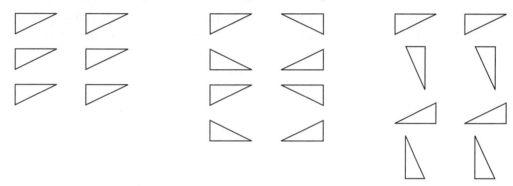

2   What happens when a reflection is repeated? Draw a simple shape, and reflect it twice in two mirror lines. Take the cases where
(a)   the mirror lines are parallel
(b)   the mirror lines are perpendicular.
Try for some other pairs of mirror lines. What can you say?

Progress exercise 11

1   Rotate the W shape through 30° clockwise.

2   A number 6 is rotated through 180°. What number is it now?
3   Copy the shape and rotate it through 90° anticlockwise.

4   Plot a triangle with vertices at (–1, 2), (1, 3) and (2, 2). Rotate the triangle about (2, 2) through 90°.

5 Rotate the triangle of question **4** about (0, 1) through 180°.

6 What is the order of rotational symmetry of a regular octagon?

7 Complete the shape so that it has rotational symmetry of order 4.

8 The cross-section of a prism is an isosceles triangle which is not equilateral. How many axes of symmetry does it have?

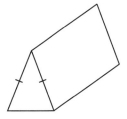

Puzzles 11

1 Draw a shape which has line symmetry but no rotational symmetry.

2 Draw a shape which has rotational symmetry but no line symmetry.

3 What is the order of symmetry of a circle?

4 The diagram shows two equal squares. Describe three different transformations which will take the left square to the right square.

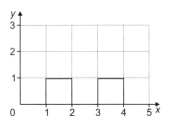

5 1961 was the last year with rotational symmetry. When will be the next year with rotational symmetry?

12

Congruence

This unit uses
- Translations, rotations and reflections
- Equal angles
- Construction of triangles

12.1 Transformations

After a translation, rotation or reflection, a figure has not altered its size or shape. It has only changed its position. The figure before the transformation and the figure after the transformation would fit exactly on top of each other.

Exercise 12.1A

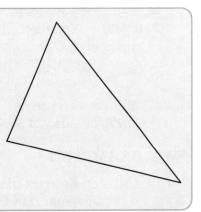

1 Copy this triangle and translate it by the methods of Unit 5. Cut one triangle out, and show that it fits exactly on top of the other.
2 Rotate the triangle of question **1** by the methods of Unit 11. Cut one triangle out, and show that it fits exactly on top of the other.
3 Reflect the triangle of question **1** by the methods of Unit 4. Cut one triangle out, and show that it fits exactly on top of the other.

If two figures, say *ABC* and *PQR*, have exactly the same shape and size, they are **congruent** to each other. In Exercise 12.1A you found that

If *ABC* is translated to *PQR*, then *ABC* is congruent to *PQR*.
If *ABC* is rotated to *PQR*, then *ABC* is congruent to *PQR*.
If *ABC* is reflected to *PQR*, then *ABC* is congruent to *PQR*.

Direct and opposite congruence

Perhaps you noticed a difference between **3**, and **1** and **2**. With a translation or a rotation, you can place the first triangle directly on top of the other. With a reflection, you must turn the triangle over before placing it on top of the other. If you don't need to turn the triangle over, then the triangles have **direct** congruence. If you do need to turn the triangle over, then the triangles have **opposite** congruence.

So a triangle and its image after translation or rotation have direct congruence. A triangle and its image after reflection have opposite congruence.

If two triangles are directly congruent, then both are lettered clockwise or both anticlockwise. If they have opposite congruence, then one triangle is lettered clockwise and the other is lettered anticlockwise. The diagram shows a pair of triangles with direct congruence and a pair of triangles with opposite congruence.

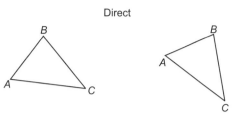

For the top pair, the letters *ABC* go clockwise round both triangles. For the bottom pair, the letters are anticlockwise for the left triangle and clockwise for the right triangle.

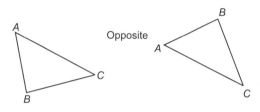

If two triangles *ABC* and *PQR* are congruent, then we write

$$ABC \equiv PQR$$

If $ABC \equiv PQR$, then all the sides of *ABC* are equal to the sides of *PQR*, and all the angles of *ABC* are equal to the angles of *PQR*.

$$AB = PQ \qquad BC = QR \qquad CA = RP$$
$$\angle A = \angle P \qquad \angle B = \angle Q \qquad \angle C = \angle R$$

The sides and angles are equal in the order given. It is *not* true that $\triangle ABC \equiv \triangle QPR$, because $\angle A \neq \angle Q$.

EXAMPLE 1

ABC is an isosceles triangle, with $AB = AC$. Join *A* to the midpoint *D* of *BC*. Write down a pair of congruent triangles.

Solution
The left triangle *ABD* is reflected in *AD* to the right triangle *ACD*. Notice that *B* is reflected to *C*, and *A* and *D* stay fixed.

$$\triangle ABD \equiv \triangle ACD$$

(*Note* We must write the triangles in the correct order. It is not true that $\triangle ABD \equiv \triangle CDA$, as $AB \neq CD$.)
The triangles are reflections of each other. Hence the congruence is opposite.

> **N O T E**
> When you state that two triangles are congruent, you must give the letters in the correct order.

Exercise 12.1B

1. Which of the triangles below are congruent to each other? In each case state whether it is direct or opposite congruence.

   a   **b** 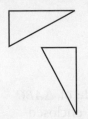   **c**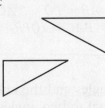

2. Which of the triangles below are congruent to each other? State whether the congruence is direct or opposite.

   a   **b**   **c**   **d** **e**

   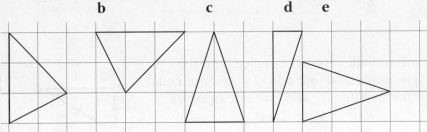

3. $ABCD$ is a kite, with $AB = AD$ and $CB = CD$. Join the diagonal AC. Write down a pair of congruent triangles.

4. $PQRS$ is a rhombus. Join the diagonals PR and QS at X. Write down four triangles which are congruent to each other.

5. $ABCDE$ is a regular pentagon, and X is its centre. Join X to the vertices. Write down five triangles which are congruent to each other.

6. Draw a circle, and let AB be a chord. Let O be the centre of the circle, and let M be the midpoint of AB. Find two triangles which are congruent to each other.

7. Draw a circle, and let AB and BC be chords of equal length. Let O be the centre of the circle. Find two triangles which are congruent to each other.

12.2 Conditions for congruence

Two triangles $\triangle ABC$ and $\triangle PQR$ are congruent if any of the following sets of conditions hold.

SSS

The sides of $\triangle ABC$ are equal to the sides of $\triangle PQR$.

$$AB = PQ \qquad BC = QR \qquad CA = RP$$

SAS

Two sides and the enclosed angle of △*ABC*
are equal to two sides and the enclosed
angle of △*PQR*.

$$AB = PQ \qquad AC = PR$$
$$\angle BAC = \angle QPR$$

ASA

Two angles and the enclosed side of △*ABC*
are equal to two angles and the enclosed
side of △*PQR*.

$$AB = PQ \qquad \angle ABC = \angle PQR$$
$$\angle BAC = \angle QPR$$

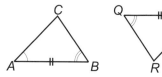

RHS

Both triangles are right-angled, and the
hypotenuse and one side of △*ABC* are equal
to the hypotenuse and one side of △*PQR*.

$$\angle BAC = \angle QPR = 90° \qquad BC = QR$$
$$AB = PQ$$

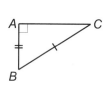

When you show that two triangles are
congruent, always give the reason, by
writing SSS, SAS, ASA or RHS.

 ## EXAMPLE 2

ABCD is a parallelogram. Join the diagonal *AC*.
Find a pair of congruent triangles. Is the
congruence direct or opposite?

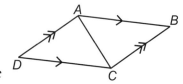

Solution
Opposite sides of a parallelogram are equal. Hence

$$AB = CD$$
$$CB = AD$$

AC is common to both triangles.

Hence △*ABC* is congruent to △*CDA*   (SSS)
(*Note* The order of the letters is important. It is not true that △*ABC* is congruent to
△*DCA*, as *CA* ≠ *BC*.)
Both *ABC* and *CDA* are written clockwise, so the congruence is direct.

EXAMPLE 3

ABCDE is a regular pentagon. Join *AC* and *AD*. Show that △*ABC* ≡ △*AED*.

Solution

Because *ABCDE* is regular,

$$AB = AE$$

$$BC = ED$$

$$\angle ABC = \angle AED.$$

Hence $\triangle ABC \equiv \triangle AED$ (SAS)

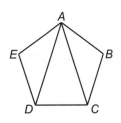

Exercise 12.2

1 Which of the pairs of triangles below are congruent to each other? In each case give the reason for the congruence.

a   **b**   **c**

2 $\triangle ABC$ is isosceles, with $AB = AC$. Drop a perpendicular from A to D on BC. Show that $\triangle ADB \equiv \triangle ADC$.

3 *ABCD* is a kite, with $AB = AD$ and $CB = CD$. Join AC. Show that $\triangle ACB \equiv \triangle ACD$.

4 *ABCDEF* is a regular hexagon. Join AC and AE. Show that $\triangle ABC \equiv \triangle AFE$.

5 The diagram shows two lines AB and CD which meet at X. AC is equal and parallel to BD. Show that $\triangle AXC \equiv \triangle BXD$.

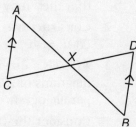

6 In the diagram two lines AB and CD meet at X. $AX = XD$ and $CX = XB$. Show that $\triangle AXC \equiv \triangle DXB$.

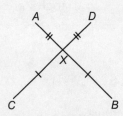

7 Two lines AB and PQ meet at X. $AX = XB$ and $PX = XQ$. Show that $\triangle AXP \equiv \triangle BXQ$. Find another pair of congruent triangles.

8 *ABCD* is a kite, with $AB = AD$ and $CB = CD$. Let AC and BD cross at X. Use question **3** to show that $\angle BAX = \angle DAX$. Hence show that $\triangle BAX \equiv \triangle DAX$. Find another pair of congruent triangles.

9 *ABCD* is a quadrilateral for which $AB = CD$ and $\angle ABC = \angle DCB$. Show that $\triangle ABC \equiv \triangle DCB$.

10 For the quadrilateral of question **9**, let the diagonals AC and DB meet at X. Show that $\angle BAX = \angle CDX$. Hence show that $\triangle AXB \equiv \triangle DXC$.

There are rules for constructing a triangle. See Unit 12 of Book 1. These rules exactly match the conditions for congruence of a triangle.

SSS If you know three sides of a triangle, then you can construct it.

SAS If you know two sides and the enclosed angle of a triangle, then you can construct it.

ASA If you know two angles and the enclosed side of a triangle, then you can construct it.

RHS If you know the hypotenuse and another side of a right-angled triangle, then by Pythagoras' theorem you can find the third side. Hence you can construct the triangle (SSS).

Recall that if you know two sides of a triangle and an angle *not* enclosed, then there may be more than one possible triangle. Similarly, SSA is not a condition for congruence.

Exercise 12.3

1 Suppose there are two triangles *ABC* and *PQR*, for which $AB = PQ = 7$ cm, $BC = QR = 6$ cm, and $\angle BAC = \angle QPR = 60°$. Draw $\triangle ABC$ and $\triangle PQR$, and show that they may not be congruent to each other.

2 Construct two different triangles for which $AB = 5$ cm, $BC = 4$ cm and $\angle BAC = 40°$.

3 *ABCD* is a quadrilateral for which *AB* is parallel to *CD* and $AD = BC$. Draw two diagrams of *ABCD*, one of which is a parallelogram and the other one is not a parallelogram.

Consider the triangles $\triangle ADC$ and $\triangle BCD$. Show that in one diagram the triangles are congruent, and in the other they are not congruent.

12.4 Congruence to prove theorems

You can use congruent triangles to prove theorems. For example, there is a theorem which states that the base angles of an isosceles triangle are equal. In the next example we prove this theorem, by cutting the triangle into two congruent triangles.

EXAMPLE 4

$\triangle ABC$ is isosceles, with $AB = AC$. Show that $\angle B = \angle C$. (Base angles of an isosceles triangle are equal.)

Solution

Join A to the midpoint D of BC. (As in Example 1.)

$AB = AC$ (Given)
$BD = CD$ (By construction)
AD is common

Hence $\triangle ADB \equiv \triangle ADC$ (SSS)
Hence $\angle B = \angle C$

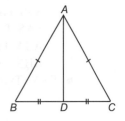

> **N O T E**
> Always give the reason when you say that two triangles are congruent.

Exercise 12.4

1. $ABCDE$ is a regular pentagon. Show that $\triangle ABC \equiv \triangle AED$, and hence show that $AC = AD$.

2. $ABCD$ is a quadrilateral, and the diagonals AC and BD bisect each other at X. (So $AX = CX$ and $BX = DX$.) Show that $\angle XAB = \angle XCD$ and $\angle XBC = \angle XDA$. Show that $ABCD$ is a parallelogram.

3. $ABCD$ is a rhombus. The diagonals AC and BD meet at X. Show that $\triangle XAB \equiv \triangle XAD$. Show that $\angle AXB = 90°$. (Diagonals of a rhombus are perpendicular.)

4. O is the centre of the circle. OX is perpendicular to the chord AB. Show that $AX = BX$.

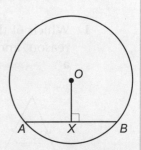

5. ABC is isosceles, with $AB = AC$. D and E are points on AB and AC, with $AD = AE$. Show that $DC = EB$.

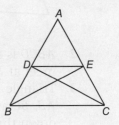

Summary

- After a translation, rotation or reflection, a figure has the same shape and size. Two figures with the same shape and size are congruent.
- Figures which are translations or rotations of each other have direct congruence, and figures which are reflections of each other have opposite congruence.

- The conditions for congruence of two triangles are
  - SSS Three sides equal
  - SAS Two sides and the included angle equal
  - ASA Two angles and the included side equal
  - RHS Both triangles right-angled, hypotenuse and one other side equal
- SSA (Two sides and an angle not included) is not a condition for congruence.

Activity 12

Recall from Activity 8 of Book 1 that a tessellation is a covering of a surface with identical shapes. The shapes are *congruent* to each other. Is the congruence direct or opposite?

1 Cut out several congruent right-angled triangles. It is best to use paper in which one side is different from the other. Show that there are tessellations with these triangles so that
   (a) all the triangles are directly congruent to each other
   (b) neighbouring triangles are oppositely congruent to each other.

2 Cut out several scalene triangles. You can tessellate with these triangles. Are the triangles directly or oppositely congruent?

Progress exercise 12

1 Which of the pairs of triangles below are congruent? In each case give the reason, and state whether the congruence is direct or opposite.

a

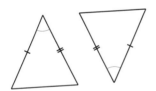

b

c

2 *ABCD* is a kite, for which $AB = AD$ and $CB = CD$. The diagonals *AC* and *BD* meet at *X*. Write down three pairs of congruent triangles.

3 Triangle *ABC* is equilateral. *D*, *E* and *F* are points on *AB*, *BC* and *CA* for which $AD = BE = CF$. Write down three triangles which are congruent to each other.
   What sort of triangle is $\triangle DEF$?

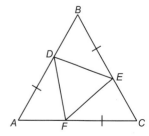

4 In the diagram O is the centre of the circle. The tangents from T touch the circle at A and B. Show that $TA = TB$.

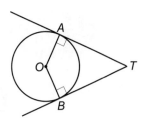

Puzzles 12

1 For triangles ABC and PQR, $AB = PQ$, $BC = QR$, $\angle BAC = \angle QPR$ and BC is longer than AB. Show by construction that $\triangle ABC \equiv \triangle PQR$.

2 $ABCD$ and $PQRS$ are quadrilaterals with equal sides, that is, $AB = PQ$, $BC = QR$, $CD = RS$ and $DA = SP$. Is $ABCD$ congruent to $PQRS$? (This would be condition SSSS for congruence of quadrilaterals.)

3 $ABCD$ and $PQRS$ are quadrilaterals with equal angles and one equal side, that is, $AB = PQ$, $\angle A = \angle P$, $\angle B = \angle Q$, $\angle C = \angle R$ and $\angle D = \angle S$. Is $ABCD$ congruent to $PQRS$? (This would be condition AAAAS for congruence of quadrilaterals.)

13

Inequalities

This unit uses
- Solving linear equations
- Coordinates
- The equation of a straight line

13.1 Simple linear inequalities

The statement $x < 5$ says that x is *less* than 5.

The statement $x + 4 < 10$ says if you add 4 to x the answer must be less than 10. In other words, x must be less than 6 $(x < 6)$.

So, if $x + 4 < 10$
$$x < 10 - 4 \qquad \text{Subtracting 4 from both sides}$$
$$x < 6$$

This is like solving the equation $x + 4 = 10$.

Here is another example. Solve:

$$4x < 16$$
$$x < \tfrac{16}{4} \qquad \text{divide each side by 4}$$
So $x < 4$

In general, the rules for solving inequalities are the same as for solving equations except for multiplying or dividing by a *negative* number.

The statement $2°C < 5°C$ is true

but if you multiply each side by –1:

$-2°C < -5°C$ is false, because $-5°C$ is colder than $-2°C$.

The inequality sign is *reversed*.
We have the following rules:

> **R U L E S**
> 1. **You can add or subtract the same quantity on each side of an inequality, and it remains true.**
> 2. **You can multiply or divide each side of an inequality by a positive number and it remains true.**
> 3. **When you multiply or divide each side of an inequality by a negative number, it only remains true if you reverse the direction of the inequality.**

EXAMPLE 1

Solve the following inequalities.

(a) $2x + 1 < 9$ (b) $3x + 2 < x + 11$ (c) $x - 5 < 4x + 1$

(d) $\frac{1}{4}x - 3 < \frac{1}{4}(2x - 1)$

Solution

(a) $2x + 1 < 9$

$\qquad\qquad 2x < 9 - 1 \qquad$ Subtracting 1

$\qquad\qquad\quad x < \frac{8}{2} \qquad\qquad$ Dividing by 2

$\qquad$ Hence $x < 4$

(b) $3x + 2 < x + 11$

$\qquad\quad 3x - x < 11 - 2 \qquad\qquad$ Subtracting x and 2

$\qquad\qquad 2x < 9$

$\qquad$ So $x < \frac{9}{2}$, that is, $x < 4.5$

(c) *Method A*

$\qquad\quad x - 5 < 4x + 1$

$\qquad\quad x - 4x < 1 + 5$

$\qquad\quad -3x < 6$

$\qquad$ Divide each side by -3 and *reverse* the inequality

$\qquad\qquad x > \frac{6}{-3}$

$\qquad$ So $x > -2$

Method B

$\qquad\quad x - 5 < 4x + 1$

$\qquad\quad -5 - 1 < 4x - x$

$\qquad\qquad -6 < 3x$

$\qquad\qquad -2 < x.$

> **NOTE**
> Try to keep the x terms positive.

$\qquad$ Clearly $x > -2$ is exactly the same as $-2 < x$. The second method does not involve reversing the inequality sign.

(d) $\qquad\qquad \frac{1}{4}x - 3 < \frac{1}{4}(2x - 1)$

$\qquad\qquad\quad \frac{1}{4}x - 3 < \frac{1}{2}x - \frac{1}{4} \qquad$ Removing the bracket

$\qquad$ Multiply each side of the equation by 4 to remove the fractions

$\qquad 4 \times \frac{1}{4}x - 4 \times 3 < 4 \times \frac{1}{2}x - 4 \times \frac{1}{4}$

$\qquad\qquad\quad x - 12 < 2x - 1$

$\qquad\qquad -12 + 1 < 2x - x$

$\qquad\qquad\qquad -11 < x$

$\qquad$ So $x > -11$

As well as the symbols $<$ and $>$, you can also use the inequality and equal signs combined $\geq$ and $\leq$. The statement $x \geq 5$ means that x is either greater than 5 or equal to 5. The rules for manipulating $\leq$ and $\geq$ are the same as for $<$ and $>$.

EXAMPLE 2

(a) Solve the inequality $4x + 3 \leq 7x - 14$

(b) Hence find the smallest integer that is a solution of the inequality
$$4x + 3 \leq 7x - 14.$$

Solution

(a) $4x + 3 \leq 7x - 14$

$3 + 14 \leq 7x - 4x$

$17 \leq 3x$

$x \geq \dfrac{17}{3}$

So $x \geq 5\frac{2}{3}$

(b) x is a whole number. The smallest whole number that is greater than or equal to $5\frac{2}{3}$ is 6.
Hence, the answer is $x = 6$

Exercise 13.1

State whether the following are true or false:

1. $-4 < 5$ 2. $\frac{1}{4} > 0.25$ 3. $\frac{1}{4} \geq 0.25$ 4. $-3 < -8$
5. $2 > -4$ 6. $\frac{3}{4} < 0.75$ 7. $-8 \leq 1$ 8. $(0.1)^2 < 0.1$
9. If $x^2 < 4$ then $x < 2$ 10. $x^2 > x^3$ if $0 < x < 1$

Solve the following inequalities.

11. $x - 5 > 3$ 12. $3x + 4 \leq 2$ 13. $\frac{1}{2}x + 1 < 5$
14. $0.1x - 5 > 4$ 15. $5 - x \geq 2$ 16. $7 - 2x < 11$
17. $x + 1 < 2x + 4$ 18. $3x - 1 < 2x - 5$ 19. $3x + 7 < 7x + 9$
20. $1 - 2x \geq x - 3$ 21. $\frac{1}{2} - 2x < 3x - 1$ 22. $2(x + 3) - 3(x - 1) \leq 12$
23. $\dfrac{2x + 8}{-3} < 20$ 24. $\frac{1}{2}x - 4 \geq 3 - \frac{2}{3}x$ 25. $-4x - 5 \geq 5x - 7$

26. Find the largest integers that satisfy the following inequalities.
    a. $4x + 7 \leq 15$ b. $3x + 5 \leq 2$
    c. $4x < -8$ d. $6x - 3 < 4x - 3$
    e. $2x + 7 \leq 9 - x$ f. $13 + x \geq 4x + 7$
    g. $\frac{1}{2}x + 5 > 2x + 1$ h. $3x - 2 < \frac{1}{3}x + 5$

27. Find the smallest integers that satisfy the following inequalities.
    a. $3 + x > 1$ b. $3x + 5 \geq 1$
    c. $2x + 3 > 5 - x$ d. $6x + 1 \geq x - 8$

13.2 The number line

It is sometimes useful to represent inequalities on a number line. If an endpoint is not included, mark it with an empty circle. If an endpoint is included, mark it with a solid circle.

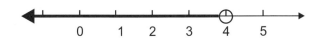

If $x < 4$, you mark the line to the *left* of 4. An empty circle at 4 indicates that 4 is *not* included.

If $-2 < x \leq 1$, then -2 will have an empty circle around it but 1 will have a solid circle.

A statement such as $-2 < x \leq 1$ is called a **compound** inequality, because it is made up of two inequalities, $x > -2$, and $x \leq 1$.

You must be careful when combining inequalities not to end up with an impossible statement:

> If $3 \leq x$ and $x \leq -1$, don't write this as $3 \leq x \leq -1$. This is actually saying that 3 is smaller than -1, which is not true.

EXAMPLE 3

Solve the compound inequality $11 \leq 2x - 1 < 15$. Represent your answers on a number line.

Solution

Add 1 to each part of the inequality

$$11 + 1 \leq 2x < 15 + 1$$

$$12 \leq 2x < 16$$

$$6 \leq x < 8 \qquad \text{Dividing by 2}$$

The line can now be drawn.

Exercise 13.2

1 Write the following pairs of simple inequalities as a single compound inequality, when it is possible.
   a $x > 4$ and $x \leq 6$ b $x \leq 3$ and $x > -2$ c $5 \geq x$ and $x > 7$
   d $x \leq 0.5$ and $x > 0$ e $x + 1 > 3$ and $x \leq 8$
2 Illustrate the following compound inequalities on a number line.
   a $3 < x \leq 5$ b $6 > x > 3.5$ c $-6 \leq x \leq -1$
   d $2\frac{3}{4} \leq x < 4$ e $-2\frac{1}{2} \leq x \leq 3$

Solve the following compound inequalities and represent the answer on a number line.

3 $5 \leq 3x - 1 < 15$ 4 $11 < 2x + 3 \leq 17$ 5 $3 \leq 4x - 3 \leq 7$
6 $1 < \frac{1}{2}x - 5 < 3$ 7 $5 \leq \frac{2}{5}x + 1 < 7$ 8 $-1 < 3 - x < 5$
9 $-5 \leq 4 - 3x \leq -2$ 10 $7 \leq 3 - 2x < 15$

If you are given two or more inequalities that have to be true at the same time, they are called simultaneous inequalities. They can be solved by algebra or by the number line.

EXAMPLE 4

Find the whole numbers that satisfy both inequalities $x < 5$ and $2x \geq 1$.

Solution

$2x \geq 1$ means that $x \geq \frac{1}{2}$

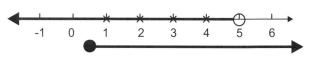

The diagram shows both inequalities marked on the number line. You can see clearly where the two overlap. We only require whole numbers, and these have been marked with a cross.

So $x = 1, 2, 3, 4$

EXAMPLE 5

Solve the inequalities $3x - 1 \leq 8$ and $3 - 2x < 1$. Represent the solution on the number line.

Solution

$$3x - 1 \leq 8, \text{ so } 3x \leq 8 + 1 \; (= 9), \text{ hence } x \leq 3$$
$$3 - 2x < 1, \text{ so } 3 - 1 < 2x, \text{ that is, } 2 < 2x, \text{ hence } 1 < x.$$

These combine to $1 < x \leq 3$. The answer is shown in the diagram.

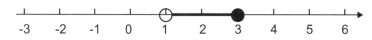

Exercise 13.3

Solve the following pairs of simultaneous inequalities, and show your answer on a number line.

1. $x + 7 > 5$ and $2x - 3 \leq 5$ 2. $x + 10 > 3$ and $x - 5 < 2$
3. $2x + 3 \geq 1$ and $3x - 1 \leq 5$ 4. $\frac{1}{2}x + 1 > 4$ and $\frac{1}{4}x - 3 \leq 1$
5. $\frac{1}{2}x - 3 \leq 1$ and $3 - 4x < x + 8$ 6. $2x - 3 \leq 18$ and $5x \geq 2$
7. $2x + 1 < 4x + 5 \leq 3x + 12$ 8. $x - 7 < 2x + 1 < x + 9$
9. $\frac{1}{2}x + 1 \leq x + 2 < \frac{1}{4}x + 5$ 10. $2x - 3 < 5x + 1 \leq 3x + 9$

13.4 Regions

The inequalities $1 \leq x \leq 4$ and $2 \leq y \leq 4$ can be represented on a two-dimensional coordinate grid.

If you look at the first diagram you will see that the region represented is a rectangle. The method of shading inside the region often leads to a lack of clarity if you want to mark points inside the region. We will use the convention of shading *outside* the region so that it looks like the second diagram.

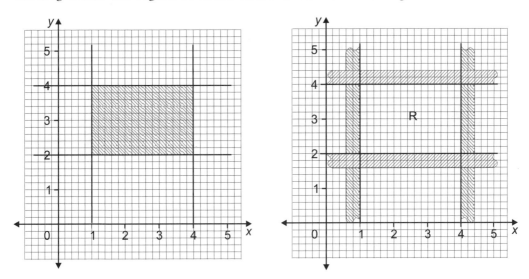

The region can now also be clearly labelled, in this case region R. For this region, the boundary lines are part of the region because the $\leq$ symbol has been used. The following example shows you what to do if the boundary line is not to be included.

EXAMPLE 6

Draw a diagram to identify the region P, defined by $1 < x < 4$ and $-2 \leq y < 1$.

Solution
The lines $x = 1$, $x = 4$, and $y = 1$, are *not* included in the region. For this reason, they are drawn with *dotted* lines. The line $y = -2$ is drawn with a solid line.

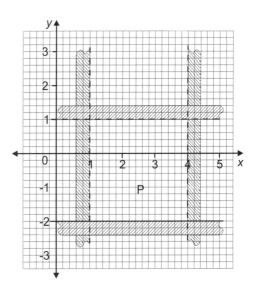

The regions we have looked at so far, have been enclosed on all sides by a boundary. This is not always the case. Sometimes the region partly extends to infinity. Study the following example.

EXAMPLE 7

Show on a diagram, the region
R, defined by $x \geq 3$ and $y > 1$.

Solution
You can see that the region
only has boundary lines on
two sides. The region extends
to infinity in the other
directions. This is another good
reason why it is best to shade
outside the region.

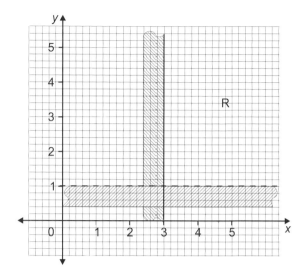

In some cases you are given the region and you have to write down the
inequalities that define it.

EXAMPLE 8

Write down inequalities that
define the region Q shown in
the diagram.

Solution
The line $x = 2$ is *not* included
The line $x = -1$ *is* included
The inequality for x is $-1 \leq x < 2$

The line $y = 2$ is *not* included
The line $y = -1$ *is* included
The inequality for y is
$-1 \leq y < 2$

The region Q is defined by:
$-1 \leq x < 2 \; ; -1 \leq y < 2$

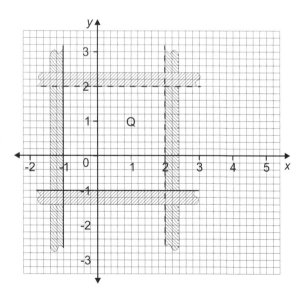

The examples so far have had boundary lines parallel to the axes. We will now
look at sloping boundary lines. Look back at the work you did in Unit 1.

EXAMPLE 9

Draw the region T defined by the inequalities $y < 2x + 1$, $y \geq -2$ and $2x + 3y \leq 12$.

Solution

The line $y = 2x + 1$ is shown below.

$y < 2x + 1$ means that y is *less* than (that is, below) the line $y = 2x + 1$, and so we shade out above the line as shown in the diagram.

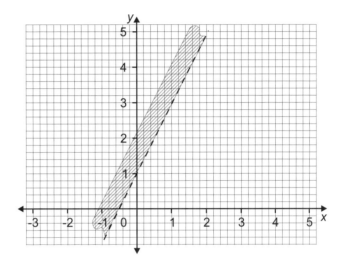

The line $2x + 3y = 12$ is shown next. $2x + 3y \leq 12$ means that $2x + 3y$ is less than or equal to 12. It is below or on the line. We shade out above the line as shown in the diagram.

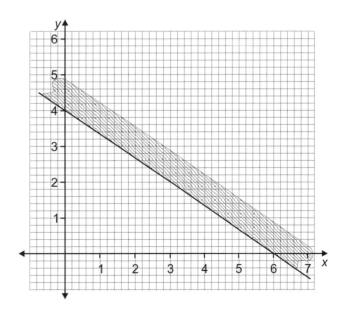

We also know that the region is above or on the line $y = -2$ ($y \geq -2$). If you combine all of these regions together, the region T will look like the one shown below.

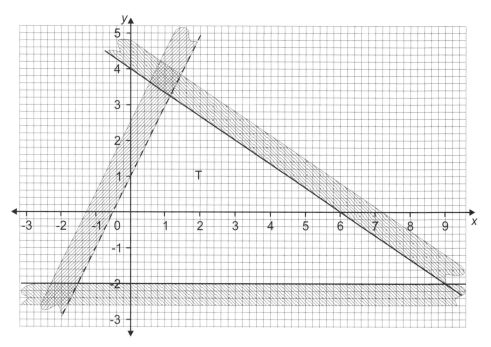

Exercise 13.4

Shade the following regions on squared or graph paper.

1 $x \geq -2$ **2** $y > -1$ **3** $2 < x < 4$

4 $-1 \leq x \leq 3$ and $0 \leq y < 3$

5 Look at the region shown. Write down the inequalities that describe this region.

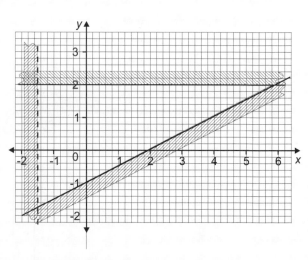

Represent the following regions on a square grid or on graph paper.

6 $x \geq 1$, $y > -2$ and $x + y \leq 7$

7 $x \leq 6$, $y + x > 0$ and $y < 3$

8 $y \geq 3x - 2$, $x \geq -2$ and $y \leq 4$

9 Write down the inequalities that describe the region shown in this diagram.

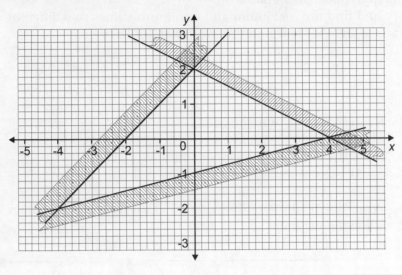

Summary

- Inequalities can be rearranged like equations, but if you multiply or divide by a negative number the inequality sign is reversed.
- Do not write down inequalities that have wrong statements in them such as $4 \geq x \leq 6$, or $-2 > x > 4$.
- Shade the unwanted region when you are finding a region using inequalities.

Activity 13

Maximum and minimum values

On squared paper draw as accurately as you can, the region defined by $x \geq 1$, $y \geq 1$ and $3y + 2x \leq 24$ as shown in the diagram. Mark with a cross all the points in the region where the coordinates are integers.
(Remember to include the boundaries.)

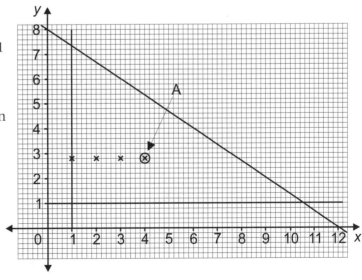

At the point $A(4, 3)$ we find that $x + y = 7$. Now work out $x + y$ at all the other points in the region. What is the largest value of $x + y$ (its maximum)? What is the smallest value (its minimum)?

Try and find the maximum and minimum values of a different expression, such as $3x + 2y$. You will find this work helpful later on.

1 Represent on a number line:
   a $x \leq 3$ **b** $-1 < x < 4$ **c** $5 \leq x < 8$

2 Solve the simultaneous inequalities:
   a $3x - 2 < 8$ and $2x > 5$
   b $2x + 7 \leq 5x - 3$ and $2x - 3 \leq x + 11$

3 Write down compound inequalities that describe the values of x in the following diagrams.

   a   **b**

4 Solve the inequalities:
   a $3x + 5 < 2(x - 6)$ **b** $3 - 7x \leq x + 7$
   c $\frac{1}{3}(2x - 3) \leq 3x - 7$

5 Draw a diagram and shade outside the region R represented by
   a $x \geq -1$, $y < 3$ and $x + y \geq -3$
   b $y \leq x + 6$, $x \leq 4$ and $y > -2$

6 Write down inequalities that describe the region shown.

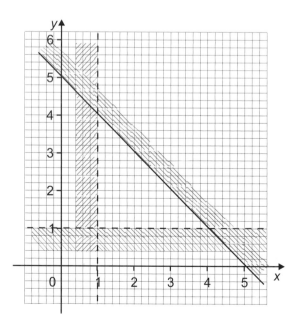

7 Find the integers n for which $2n + 1 \leq 3n - 6 \leq n + 14$.

1 How many points are there with whole numbers as coordinates in the region defined by $x \geq -3, y \geq -1$ and $x + y \leq 8$?

2 Find the greatest value of $x + y$, given that x and y are integers, in the region defined by $x \geq -3, y < 2$ and $x + 2y + 4 \geq 0$.

3 What is wrong with the following argument?

Half a loaf is better than nothing
Nothing is better than heaven
Therefore half a loaf is better than heaven.

4 What is wrong with the following argument?

No cat has two tails
A cat has one more tail than no cat
Therefore a cat has three tails.

14

The tangent ratio

This unit uses

- Similar triangles, with sides in a constant ratio
- Tables to find tangents and inverse tangents

14.1 Definition of tangent

Onyango wants to find the height of this tall, straight tree. How can he find it?

- Cut it down and measure it.
- Climb to the top with a rope, and measure the length of the rope.
- Measure the length to the base of the tree. Measure the angle from the ground to the top of the tree. Make a scale diagram of the tree and the ground.

The third method is safest! How does it work?

The line to the top of the tree makes an angle with the horizontal. This angle is the **angle of elevation**. Onyango measures this angle as 35°. He measures the distance to the base of the tree as 10 m.

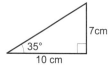

In his diagram, the length along the ground is 10 cm, and he measures the height of the tree as 7 cm.

There are two triangles: the triangle formed by the real tree and the triangle formed by the tree in the diagram.

These triangles are different sizes. But they have the same shape. The *ratio* between corresponding lengths is the same.

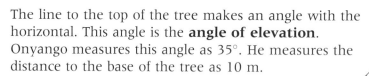

$$\frac{\text{height of real tree}}{\text{length along real ground}} = \frac{\text{height of tree in diagram}}{\text{length along ground in diagram}}$$

$$\frac{\text{height of real tree}}{10 \text{ m}} = \frac{7 \text{ cm}}{10 \text{ cm}} = 0.7$$

Hence the height of the tree is 0.7 × 10 m, which is 7 m.

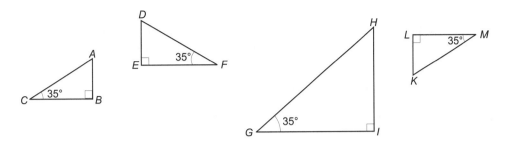

The diagram shows several right-angled triangles, each of which has one angle of 35°. The triangles have different sizes (length of sides), but the same shape (angles). For all the triangles, the ratio between the two sides next to the right angle is the same. It is about 0.7.

$$\frac{AB}{BC} = \frac{DE}{EF} = \frac{HI}{IG} = \frac{KL}{LM} = 0.7$$

The ratio is determined by the angle of 35°. The ratio is the **tangent** of the angle of 35°.

Tangent is shortened to **tan**.

$$\tan 35° = 0.7$$

You can find the approximate values of tangents by measurement.

Exercise 14.1

Draw a line AB of length 10 cm. Draw a perpendicular at B. At A, construct angles of 10°, 20°, 30° and so on. The lines meet the perpendicular at C_1, C_2, C_3 as shown in the diagram.

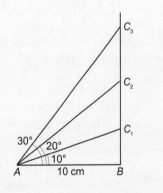

For each angle, measure BC_1, BC_2, BC_3 and so on, and divide it by 10. This is the approximate tangent of the angle. Fill in the table below.

angle	tangent
10°	
20°	
30°	
40°	
50°	
60°	

The method of Exercise 14.1 is very slow and inaccurate. To find the tan of an angle, you do not need to make a drawing. To find the tan of an angle, you use tables.

In the tables at the back of the book find the page of natural tangents. Look down the left hand column. Next to 35 you find the value of tan 35°.

$$\tan 35° = 0.7002$$

This value is very close to 0.7.

Fractions of a degree are measured in minutes or in decimal. There are 60 minutes (60′) in 1 degree. So for example $36' = \frac{36}{60}° = \frac{3}{5}° = 0.6°$.

Note also that $0.05 = \frac{1}{20}$. Hence $0.05° = \frac{1}{20}° = 3'$.

To find the tangent of 24° 40′, find the row for 24°. This begins with .4452. Go across to the number in the row which is headed 36′ and 0°.6. The entry is 4578.

Degrees	0′	6′	12′	18′	24′	30′	36′	42′	48′	54′	Mean differences				
	0°.0	0°.1	0°.2	0°.3	0°.4	0°.5	0°.6	0°.7	0°.8	0°.9	1	2	3	4	5
23	.4245	4265	4286	4307	4327	4348	4369	4390	4411	4431	3	7	10	14	17
24	.4452	4473	4494	4515	4536	4557	4578	4599	4621	4642	4	7	11	14	18

The difference between 40′ and 36′ is 4′. In the 4 column of the mean differences you find 14. Add this to 4578.

$$4578 + 14 = 4592$$

Hence tan 24° 40′ = 0.4592.

EXAMPLE 1

Alice stands 200 m from the base of a tall building. The angle of elevation of the top of the building is 24°. What is the height of the building?

Solution
The ratio of the height to the length along the ground is the tangent of 24°.

$$\tan 24° = \frac{\text{height}}{200}$$

From tables find that tan 24° = 0.4452. Multiply this by 200.

$$\text{height} = 200 \times 0.4452 = 89.04$$

The height of the building is 89 m.

Exercise 14.2

1   Use tables to find these.
   a tan 72°   **b** tan 38°   **c** tan 27.4°
   d tan 22° 12′   **e** tan 41° 13′   **f** tan 55° 29′

2 In Exercise 14.1 you found the values of tan 10°, tan 20° and so on by measurement. Check these values using tables. How accurate were you?

3 Point *A* is 20 m from the base of a tall tree.
The angle of elevation of the top is 43°.
Find the height of the tree.

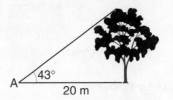

4 The diagram shows a tall building. The angle of elevation of the top from point *X* is 32° 48′. The point *X* is 400 m from the base of the building. Find the height of the building.

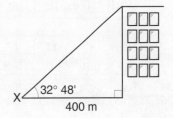

5 A boat is 100 m from the base of a cliff. From the boat, the angle of elevation of the top of the cliff is 28° 32′. Find the height of the cliff.

6 A triangle has a right angle at *A*. The angle *B* is 26° and *AB* = 4 cm. Find *AC*.

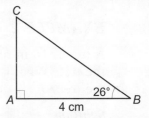

7 Find the lengths marked by letters in these triangles.

a

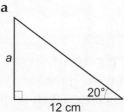

b

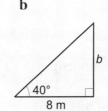

c

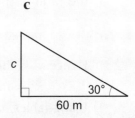

8 A flagstaff is on top of a building. 80 m from the base of the building, the angle of elevation of the top of the flagstaff is 38°, and the angle of elevation of the top of the building is 32°. How tall is the flagstaff?

14.3 Finding the angle

The tangent function works from the angle to the ratio. The **inverse tangent** function works from the ratio to the angle. This function is written as **tan⁻¹**.

$$\tan 35° = 0.7$$

Hence $35° = \tan^{-1} 0.7$

In the diagram, the building is 146 m high, and the distance to the base of the building is 200 m. If the angle of elevation is $x°$, then

$$\tan x° = \frac{146}{200} = 0.73$$

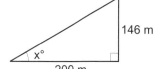

146 m

200 m

Hence $x° = \tan^{-1}0.73$. You can use tables to find $x°$, as follows.

Using tables

With tables, find the value just below 0.73. This is 0.7292, at $36° \ 6'$.

Degrees	0' 0°.0	6' 0°.1	12' 0°.2	18' 0°.3	24' 0°.4	30' 0°.5	36' 0°.6	42' 0°.7	48' 0°.8	54' 0°.9	Mean differences				
											1	2	3	4	5
35	.7002	7028	7054	7080	7107	7133	7159	7186	7212	7239	4	9	13	18	22
36	.7265	7292	7319	7346	7373	7400	7427	7454	7481	7508	5	9	14	18	23

We need 0.0008 to reach 0.73. In the mean differences, the closest is 9, under 2'.

$$\tan^{-1}0.73 = 36° \ 6' + 2' = 36° \ 8'.$$

EXAMPLE 2

A tree is 15 m high. Silas stands 10 m from the base of the tree. What is the angle of elevation of the top of the tree?

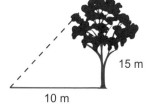

15 m

10 m

Solution
Let the angle of elevation be $x°$. The tangent of $x°$ is the ratio of the sides.

$$\tan x° = \frac{15}{10} = 1.5$$

Hence $x°$ is the inverse tangent of 1.5

$$x° = \tan^{-1}1.5$$

Using tables, $\tan^{-1}1.5 = 56° \ 19'$.
The angle of elevation is $56° \ 19'$.

NOTE
When finding the ratio, use the tan function. When finding the angle, use the $\tan^{-1}$ function.

Exercise 14.3A

1 Use tables to find these.
   a $\tan^{-1}0.8481$ b $\tan^{-1}1.514$ c $\tan^{-1}0.3169$
   d $\tan^{-1}0.4$ e $\tan^{-1}1.2$ f $\tan^{-1}0.5731$
2 A wall is 3 m high. From a point 6 m from the base of the wall, what is the angle of elevation of the top of the wall?

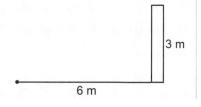

3 m

6 m

3 A boat is 400 m from the base of a cliff. The cliff is 50 m high. What is the angle of elevation of the top of the cliff?

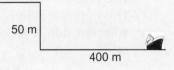

50 m

400 m

4 A beam leans against a wall. The foot of the beam is 1.6 m from the base of the wall, and the beam reaches 1.2 m up the wall. What is the angle between the beam and the ground?

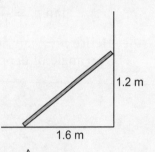

1.2 m

1.6 m

5 In △ABC, ∠ABC = 90°, AB = 14 cm and CB = 20 cm. Find ∠BCA.

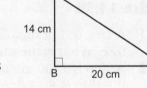

A

14 cm

B   20 cm   C

6 Find the angles marked by letters in the triangles below.

a

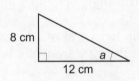

8 cm

a

12 cm

b

16 m

B

10 m

c

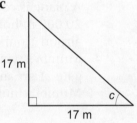

17 m

17 m

c

Angle of depression

In the diagram on the right, A is on top of a tower and B is on the ground. When B looks up at A, the angle of elevation is the angle between the line AB and the horizontal. When A looks down at B, the **angle of depression** is also the angle between the line AB and the horizontal.

A

angle of depression

angle of elevation

B

In both cases, the angle is between AB and the *horizontal*. The angles are the same.

EXAMPLE 3

Kariuki is on the top of a 200 m cliff, looking down at a boat which is 1000 m out to sea. What is the angle of depression of the boat from the top of the cliff?

Solution

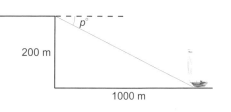

The angle is marked $p°$ in the diagram. The opposite side is 200 m, and the adjacent side is 1000 m. Use the tangent ratio.

$$\tan p° = \frac{200}{1000} = 0.2$$

Hence $p° = \tan^{-1} 0.2$. From tables, this is $11° \ 19'$. The angle of depression is $11° \ 19'$.

> **NOTE**
> The angles of elevation and of depression are measured to the horizontal, not the vertical.

Exercise 14.3B

1 A tree is 5 m high. The point X is on the ground, 20 m from the base of the tree. What is the angle of depression of X from the top of the tree?

2 A ship is 1500 m out to sea. From the top of a cliff, the angle of depression of the ship is 8°. What is the height of the cliff?

3 A plane is coming in to land at Jomo Kenyatta airport. It is 5000 m high, and 20 000 m horizontally from the airport. What is the angle of depression of the airport from the plane?

4 Mumbi's window is 15 m above the ground. From her window, she can see a gate at an angle of depression of 27°. How far is the gate from the base of Mumbi's building?

Summary

- The angle of elevation of a high object is the angle between the horizontal and a line to the top of the object.
- The tangent (tan) of the angle of elevation gives the ratio of the height of the object to its horizontal distance.
- You can find tangents from tables.
- The inverse tangent function ($\tan^{-1}$) gives the angle of elevation from the ratio of height to horizontal distance.

Activity 14

You can measure angles of elevation and depression using a **clinometer**. You may have made one last year. If not, look at page 184 of Book 1 to see how to make one.

Use your clinometer to measure the angles of elevation of buildings, trees, flagstaffs and so on. Use the tangent ratio to find their heights.

1 Use tables to find tan 34° 32′.
2 Use tables to find tan⁻¹ 1.225.
3 A man stands 40 m from the base of a tree. The
angle of elevation of the top of the tree is 38°. If
the man's eyes are 1.5 m above the ground,
what is the height of the tree?

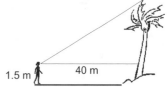

4 A straight tree trunk leans against a wall. The base of the trunk is 2 m from the
base of the wall, and the top of the trunk is 8 m high. What is the angle
between the trunk and the wall?
5 Hamid wants to find the width of a straight river. He
stands directly opposite a tree on the other side. He then
walks 20 m along the river, and the line from him to
the tree now makes 82° with the bank. How wide is
the river?

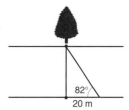

1 Suppose A and B are complementary angles, that is $A + B = 90°$. What is the
relationship between tan A and tan B?
2 In $\triangle PQR$, $\angle QPR = 90°$, $QR = 40$ cm and $QP = 32$ cm. Find $\angle PQR$.
3 A tree is on the other side of a river. Martha wants to know how high it is. She
measures the angle of elevation of the top of the tree as 28°. She then walks
10 m towards the tree, and finds that the angle of elevation of the top is now
34°. How high is the tree?

15

Sine and cosine ratios

This unit uses
- The definition of the tangent of an angle
- Tables to find tangents
- Tables to find inverse tangents

15.1

In Unit 14 you met the tangent ratio of the sides of a
right-angled triangle. This is the ratio of the sides next
to the right angle. There are two other ratios, which
involve the hypotenuse of the right-angled triangle.
These ratios are sine and cosine.

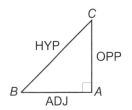

To define these functions we must name the sides of a right-angled triangle.
In triangle ABC, $\angle A = 90°$. We define the ratios of the triangle in terms of the
angle at B.

Hypotenuse or *HYP*   The longest side of the triangle, BC.
Opposite or *OPP*   The side of the triangle opposite B, AC.
Adjacent or *ADJ*   The side of the triangle next to B, BA.

There are three basic ratios between these sides. Already we have met tangent
(tan). The other two are sine (sin) and cosine (cos).

$$\sin \angle B = \frac{\text{opp}}{\text{hyp}}$$

$$\cos \angle B = \frac{\text{adj}}{\text{hyp}}$$

$$\tan \angle B = \frac{\text{opp}}{\text{adj}}$$

At the beginning of Unit 14, Onyango measured the angle of elevation of the top
of the tree as $35°$, and the distance to its base as 10 m. He wanted to know the
height of the tree.
The height of the tree is the OPP side.
The distance to the base is the ADJ side.
The tan function links OPP and ADJ.

$$\tan 35° = \frac{\text{opp}}{\text{adj}} = \frac{\text{height}}{10}$$

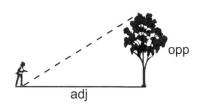

EXAMPLE 1

In triangle XYZ, $X = 90°$, $YZ = 5$ cm, $XY = 4$ cm and $XZ = 3$ cm. Find the sin, cos and tan of $\angle Y$.

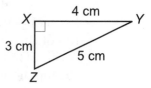

Solution

This triangle is not in the same position as the one we used to define the ratios at the start of this unit. So first label the sides of the triangle to avoid confusion.

The side farthest from X is YZ. This is the Hypotenuse, 5 cm.
The side opposite Y is XZ. This is the Opposite, 3 cm.
The side next to Y is XY. This is the Adjacent, 4 cm.

Now write down the ratios.

$$\sin \angle Y = \frac{\text{opp}}{\text{hyp}} = \frac{3}{5} = 0.6$$

$$\cos \angle Y = \frac{\text{adj}}{\text{hyp}} = \frac{4}{5} = 0.8$$

$$\tan \angle Y = \frac{\text{opp}}{\text{adj}} = \frac{3}{4} = 0.75$$

The sin, cos and tan of $\angle Y$ are 0.6, 0.8 and 0.75

Exercise 15.1

1 The diagram shows a triangle LMN.
   $\angle L = 90°$, $MN = 50$ cm, $LM = 14$ cm
   and $LN = 48$ cm.
   Find the sin, cos and tan of $\angle M$.

2 In $\triangle ABC$, $\angle B = 90°$, $AC = 34$ cm, $BC = 16$ cm and
   $AB = 30$ cm. Write down the sin, cos and tan of $\angle C$.

3 The diagram shows a beam leaning against a wall.
   The length of the beam is 3 m, the base of the beam is
   1.8 m from the base of the wall and the beam reaches
   2.4 m up the wall. Write down the sin, cos and tan of
   the angle between the beam and the ground.

4 The diagram shows a tall mast secured by a rope.
   The rope is 20 m long, the mast is 16 m high and
   the distance between the foot of the rope and the
   foot of the mast is 12 m. Find the sin, cos and tan
   of the angle $x°$ between the rope and the ground.

5 Chemwada walks in a straight line for 100m. He
   ends up 60 m North and 80 m East of his starting
   point. His bearing (the angle between his journey
   and North) is $x°$. Find the sin, cos and tan of $x°$.

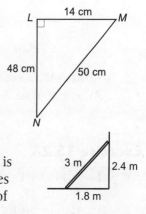

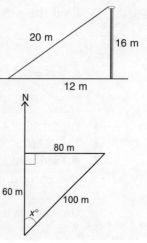

6 Nafula stands 40 m from the base of a 9 m high building. The distance from her feet to the top of the building is 41 m. If $x°$ is the angle of elevation of the top of the building from her feet, find the sin, cos and tan of $x°$.

7 A cliff is 31 m high. A ship is 480 m from the base of the cliff, and 481 m from the top of the cliff. If x is the angle of depression of the ship from the top of the cliff, find the sin, cos and tan of $x°$.

15.2 Use of sine

In Unit 14 we had examples of using the tangent ratio. Now we have examples of using the sine ratio.

You can use tables to find values of sines. The method is the same as for tangents.

EXAMPLE 2

In triangle ABC, $\angle A = 90°$, $\angle B = 43°$ and $BC = 4$ m. Find AC.

Solution

Here BC is the hypotenuse of the triangle, and AC is the opposite side.

$$\sin 43° = \frac{\text{opp}}{\text{hyp}} = \frac{AC}{4}$$

From tables find that $\sin 43° = 0.6820$

$$0.6820 = \frac{AC}{4}$$

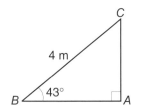

Hence $AC = 0.6820 \times 4 = 2.728$

AC is equal to 2.73 m (correct to 3 significant figures).

Exercise 15.2A

1 Find the values of these.

   a $\sin 38°$ **b** $\sin 43° \, 30'$ **c** $\sin 21° \, 21'$

   d $\sin 28.8°$ **e** $\sin 64.15°$ **f** $\sin 53.75°$

2 Find the sides marked with letters in these diagrams.

   a   **b**   **c**

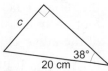

3 In $\triangle ABC$, $\angle A = 90°$, $B = 72°$ and $BC = 20$ cm. Find AC.

4 In $\triangle LMN$, $\angle M = 90°$, $L = 29° \, 34'$ and $LN = 10$ m. Find MN.

5 A ladder of length 4 m leans against a wall. The angle between the ladder and the ground is 78°. How high up the wall does the ladder reach?

6 A stick of length 2 m is held at 27° to the vertical. How long is the shadow of the stick when the sun is directly overhead?

7 I walk 10 m along a plank which is at 9° to horizontal. How far have I risen?

8 The angle of elevation of the top of a tree is 22°. The distance to the top of the tree is 80 m. How high is the tree?

9 A ship is out to sea. The angle of elevation of a cliff is 13°, and the distance to the top of the cliff is 1000 m. Find the height of the cliff.

Finding the angle

The sine function is the ratio of the opposite side to the hypotenuse. The function gives the ratio in terms of the angle.

You can reverse the function. If you know this ratio, then you can find the angle. The function which does this is **inverse sine**, written **$\sin^{-1}$**.

$\sin 30° = 0.5.$
Hence $30° = \sin^{-1} 0.5$

You can use tables to find $\sin^{-1}$, in the same way as for $\tan^{-1}$.

EXAMPLE 3

In the triangle ABC, $A = 90°$, $BC = 20$ cm and $AC = 7$ cm. Find $\angle B$.

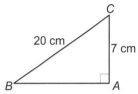

Solution

Here BC is the hypotenuse and AC is the opposite side.

$$\sin \angle B = \frac{\text{opp}}{\text{hyp}} = \frac{7}{20} = 0.35$$

So $\angle B = \sin^{-1} 0.35$
Using tables, $\sin^{-1} 0.35 = 20° \ 29'$.
$\angle B$ is equal to $20° \ 29'$.

> **N O T E**
> If you know an angle and want to find a side, then use sin, cos or tan. If you know two sides and want to find an angle, then use $\sin^{-1}$, $\cos^{-1}$ or $\tan^{-1}$.

Exercise 15.2B

1 Use tables to find these.
  a $\sin^{-1} 0.3$ **b** $\sin^{-1} 0.255$ **c** $\sin^{-1} 0.7336$

2 Find the angles marked by letters in these triangles.

  a   **b**   **c**

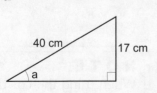 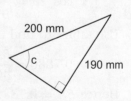

3 In $\triangle ABC$, $\angle A = 90°$, $AB = 10$ cm and $CA = 7$ cm. Find $\angle B$.

4 In $\triangle LMN$, $\angle M = 90°$, $LN = 12$ m and $MN = 7.5$ m. Find $\angle L$.

5 A girder of length 5 m leans against a wall, reaching 4.5 m up it. Find the angle between the girder and the ground.

6 A straight path slopes uphill. After walking 80 m along the path, Atieno has risen 10 m. What is the angle of slope of the path?

7 Juma stands 40 m from the base of a building. The distance to the top of the building is 64 m. What is the angle of elevation of the top of the building?

8 The diagonal of a rectangle is 20 cm. The shorter side of the rectangle is 8 cm. Find the angle between the diagonal and the longer side.

15.3

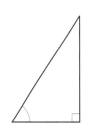

You can use tables to find values of cosines. There is a slight difference from sines or tangents.

Look at these two triangles, in which the HYP side is the same length. In the second triangle, the marked angle is *greater* but the ADJ side is *smaller*. As the angle increases, the adjacent side decreases. Hence the cosine of the angle decreases. ($\cos = \dfrac{\text{adj}}{\text{hyp}}$)

So cosine is a *decreasing* function. So *subtract* the number in the difference column.

For example, to find cos 24° 45′, find the entry for 24° 42′ to be 9085. In the 3 column of the differences there is 4. Subtract 4 from 9085, obtaining 9081.

So cos 24° 45′ = 0.9081

EXAMPLE 4

In triangle ABC, $\angle A = 90°$, $\angle B = 38°$ and $BC = 40$ cm. Find AB.

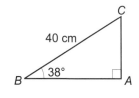

Solution

Here BC is the hypotenuse of the triangle, and AB is the adjacent side.

$$\cos \angle B = \frac{\text{adj}}{\text{hyp}} = \frac{BA}{40}$$

Use tables to find that cos 38° = 0.7880

$$0.7880 = \frac{BA}{40}$$

Hence $BA = 0.7880 \times 40 = 31.52$
BA is equal to 31.5 cm
(correct to 3 significant figures).

> **N O T E**
> When using the cos tables, *subtract* the number in the differences column, as you did when using reciprocal tables.

Exercise 15.3A

1 Find the values of these.
   a cos 59° 54′   **b** cos 27° 13′   **c** cos 33° 56′
   d cos 43.2°   **e** cos 62.65°   **f** cos 28.05°
2 Find the sides marked by letters in these diagrams.

   a 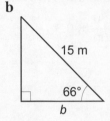   **b**   **c**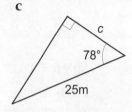

3 In △ABC, ∠A = 90°, ∠B = 58° and BC = 8 cm. Find AB.
4 In △LMN, ∠M = 90°, ∠N = 62° 8′ and LN = 8 cm. Find NM.
5 A ladder of length 2.5 m leans against a wall, making an angle 65° with the ground. Find the distance from the base of the ladder to the base of the wall.
6 A flagstaff is secured by a straight rope which is 20 m long. The angle between the rope and the flagstaff is 81°. How tall is the flagstaff?
7 A straight path slopes at 14° to the horizontal. If I walk 500 m along the path, how far have I gone horizontally?
8 The diagonal of a rectangle is 30 cm long. The angle between the diagonal and the longer side is 38°. Find the length of the longer side.
9 A 2 m pole is placed in the ground, at 22° to the vertical. How high is the top of the pole above the ground?
10 Wanjiki looks up at the top of a building. The angle of elevation of the top is 32.5°, and the distance to the top is 80 m. What is the distance to the base of the building?

Finding the angle

The ratio of adjacent to hypotenuse is the cosine of an angle. If you know this ratio, then you can find the angle. The function which does this is **inverse cosine**, written **cos⁻¹**.

$$\cos 60° = 0.5$$
$$\text{Hence } 60° = \cos^{-1} 0.5$$

You can use tables to find cos⁻¹. There is a slight difference from sin⁻¹ and tan⁻¹. Cosine is a decreasing function. So look in the tables for the value which is just *above* the required value. Then look in the differences.
For example, find cos⁻¹ 0.67. The value just above this is 0.6704, for cos 47° 54′. This value is 0.0004 too high. Look in the mean differences, to find 4 in the 2 column. So *add* 2′ to 47° 54′.

$$\cos^{-1} 0.67 = 47° 56′$$

EXAMPLE 5

In the triangle ABC, $\angle A = 90°$, $BC = 500$ mm
and $AB = 150$ mm. Find $\angle B$.

Solution

Here BC is the hypotenuse and AB is the adjacent side.

$$\cos B = \frac{\text{adj}}{\text{hyp}} = \frac{150}{500} = 0.3$$

So $\angle B = \cos^{-1} 0.3$.

Using tables, $\cos^{-1} 0.3 = 72° \, 32'$.

$\angle B$ is equal to $72° \, 32'$.

Exercise 15.3B

1 Find these.

    a $\cos^{-1} 0.4$ **b** $\cos^{-1} 0.1284$ **c** $\cos^{-1} \frac{2}{3}$

2 Find the angles marked by letters in these triangles.

    a   **b**   **c**

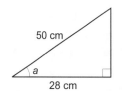

3 In $\triangle ABC$, $\angle A = 90°$, $AC = 6$ m and $BC = 8$ m. Find $\angle C$.

4 In $\triangle LMN$, $\angle M = 90°$, $LN = 50$ cm and $MN = 34$ cm. Find $\angle N$.

5 The diagonal of a rectangle is 16 cm, and the shorter side is 7 cm. Find the angle between the diagonal and the shorter side.

6 A tall building was originally 80 m high. But it began to lean, so that it is now only 76 m high. What is the angle between the building and the vertical?

7 Munyiri walks 100 m along a straight path, travelling 92 m horizontally. What is the angle of slope of the path?

8 A spear of length 2 m leans against a wall, reaching 1.7 m up it. What is the angle between the spear and the wall?

15.4 Bearings

In Unit 18 of Book 1 we showed how to describe a direction as a **bearing**. The bearing of a direction is the angle it makes with North, in a clockwise direction. Trigonometry (using the relations between the sides and angles of triangles) is very useful for navigation. If you know the distance and bearing of a journey, then you can find how far North and how far East it is.

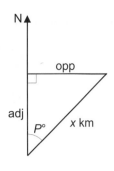

N

opp

adj

P°

x km

Suppose you have travelled x km, along a bearing of $P°$. In the diagram, the hypotenuse is x km, the north part of the journey is the ADJ and the East part of the journey is the OPP. Hence

East part of journey $= \sin P° \times x$ km
North part of journey $= \cos P° \times x$ km

EXAMPLE 6

A ship sails 150 km on a bearing of 145°. How far East has the ship gone?

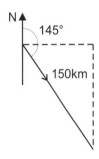

N

145°

150km

Solution

The diagram shows the journey. The direction makes 145° with North. Hence the angle it makes with East is

$$145° - 90° = 55°$$

In the triangle of the diagram, the journey is the HYP and the East distance is the ADJ. Use the cosine ratio.

$$\cos 55° = \frac{\text{adj}}{\text{hyp}} = \frac{\text{East distance}}{150 \text{ km}}$$

From tables find that cos 55° is 0.5736. Hence the East distance is

$$0.5736 \times 150 \text{ km} = 86.04 \text{ km}$$

The ship has travelled 86 km East.

> **NOTE**
> Measure a bearing from North, and clockwise.

Exercise 15.4

1. In Example 6, find how far South the ship has travelled.
2. A ship travels 200 km on a bearing of 048°. Find how far North and how far East it has travelled.
3. A plane flies 1000 km on a bearing of 340°. Find how far North and how far West it has travelled.
4. A plane flies 400 km on a bearing of 230°. Find how far South and how far West it has travelled.
5. A ship sails so that it is 40 km North and 25 km East of its starting point. What is the bearing on which it has sailed?
6. A plane flies for 200 km roughly North East, ending 130 km North of its starting point. What is the bearing on which it has flown?
7. Njoroge walks 20 km North and 16 km West. On what bearing should he walk to get back to his starting point?

8 A plane flies for 100 km on a bearing of 030°, then for 200 km on a bearing of 075°.

    a How far North has it gone?

    b How far East has it gone

    c What is its bearing from its starting point?

9 A ship sails for 500 km on a bearing of 120°, then for 800 km on a bearing of 350°.

    a How far North has it gone?

    b How far East has it gone?

    c What is its bearing from its starting point?

Summary

- The three sides of a right-angled triangle are the Hypotenuse, Opposite and Adjacent. The three main ratios are

$$\sin \angle B = \frac{\text{opp}}{\text{hyp}}$$

$$\cos \angle B = \frac{\text{adj}}{\text{hyp}}$$

$$\tan \angle B = \frac{\text{opp}}{\text{adj}}$$

- The functions $\sin^{-1}$, $\cos^{-1}$ and $\tan^{-1}$ give the angle in terms of the ratio.
- If you know the bearing of a journey, then you can use sine and cosine to find the East and North distance travelled.

Activity 15

You can make your own sine or cosine table using graph paper.

Draw a quarter circle of radius 10 cm. Draw radii making 10°, 20°, 30° and so on with the x-axis. Find the x-coordinate of the endpoint of each radius, and divide by 10. This gives the cosine of the angle. Similarly the y-coordinate divided by 10 gives the sine of the angle.

How could you extend the diagram to get the sine or cosine of angles greater than 90°?

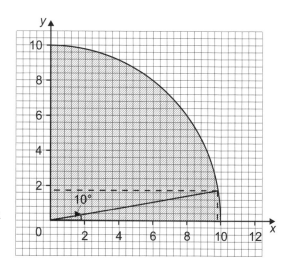

1 Find these.
   a sin 48° 32′   **b** sin⁻¹0.467   **c** cos 62°   **d** cos⁻¹0.43

2 Evaluate the sides of these triangles marked by letters.

a

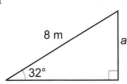

b

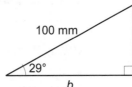

3 Evaluate the angles of these triangles marked by letters.

a

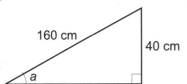

b

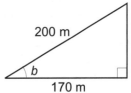

4 In △ABC, ∠A = 90°, BC = 15 cm and AC = 9 cm. Find ∠C.

5 In △PQR, ∠Q = 90°, PR = 40 m and ∠P = 38°. Find QR.

6 A road slopes at 8° to the horizontal. If a car is driven 100 m along the road, how much has it risen by?

7 A roof is 5 m long. The ridge is 1 m higher than the gutter. What is the angle of slope of the roof?

8 I walk 20 km on a bearing of 200°. How far South and West am I from my starting point?

1 Which of the following can you find? Why?
   a sin⁻¹1.7   **b** cos⁻¹1.7   **c** tan⁻¹1.7

2 Suppose A and B are complementary (A + B = 90°). What is the relationship between sin A and cos B? Why?

3 If you look at the tables, you will see that sin 30° is *exactly* 0.5. Why?

4 A ship sails for 200 m, ending up 70 m East of its starting point. What are the two possible bearings along which it has sailed?

16

Circle theorems

This unit uses
- The words connected with circles
- The words connected with angles

A circle consists of all the points a fixed distance from a fixed point. The following list gives the words connected with the circle.

- **Centre**. The fixed point at the middle of the circle.
- **Radius**. The fixed distance from the centre to points on the circle.

- **Chord**. The straight line joining two points *A* and *B* on the circle.
- **Arc**. The part of the circle between *A* and *B*.
- **Major/minor arc**. The longer arc between *A* and *B* is the major arc, and the shorter arc is the minor arc.

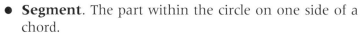

- **Segment**. The part within the circle on one side of a chord.
- **Major/minor segment**. The larger of the two segments is the major segment, and the smaller segment is the minor segment.

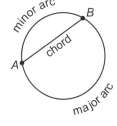

- **Diameter**. A straight line through the centre of the circle
- **Semicircle**. The half of a circle cut off by a diameter.

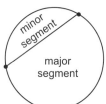

- **Sector**. The region within a circle between two radii.

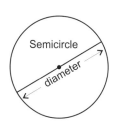

Suppose *AB* is a chord, and *C* is another point on the circle. The angle ∠*ACB* is **subtended** by the chord *AB*.

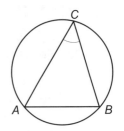

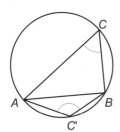

Notice that *AB* subtends two angles, one on the major arc and one on the minor arc. The angle in the minor arc is obtuse, and the angle in the major arc is acute.

There are several facts about circles. They are called **circle theorems**.

16.1 Angle at centre

Theorem 1

The angle subtended by a chord at the centre is twice the angle subtended at the circumference.

In the diagram, *AB* is a chord, *O* is the centre and *C* is on the circumference. The theorem states that
∠*AOB* = 2 × ∠*ACB*.

Proof
Extend *CO* to *F* as shown. Let ∠*CAO* = *x* and ∠*CBO* = *y*.
Both triangles *AOC* and *BOC* are isosceles, hence ∠*ACO* = *x* and ∠*BCO* = *y*.
Now ∠*AOF* = 2*x* and ∠*BOF* = 2*y*, as they are the exterior angles of the triangles.
So ∠*AOB* = 2*x* + 2*y*, and ∠*ACB* = *x* + *y*.
Hence ∠*AOB* = 2 × ∠*ACB*, as required.

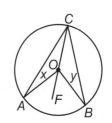

Note   In this proof we took *C* in the major segment. The theorem still holds if *C* is in the minor segment. In this case the *reflex* angle *AOB* is twice ∠*ACB*.

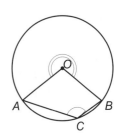

The theorem also holds if the lines of the diagram cross each other, as shown.

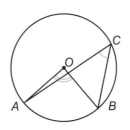

EXAMPLE 1

In the diagram O is the centre of the circle. Find the angle $\angle OAB$.

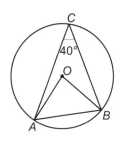

Solution

$\angle AOB$ is the angle at the centre, and $\angle ACB$ is the angle at the circumference.

From the theorem, $\angle AOB = 2 \times \angle ACB$
$$= 2 \times 40° = 80°.$$

OAB is an isosceles triangle, hence $\angle OAB = \angle OBA$

$\angle OAB = \frac{1}{2} \times (180° - 80°) = \frac{1}{2} \times 100°.$

$\angle OAB = 50°.$

> **N O T E**
> Always state the reasons for your steps.

Exercise 16.1

1 Verify the theorem by construction. Draw a circle with centre O, and take a chord AB. Take a point C on the circumference. Show by measurement that $\angle AOB = 2 \times \angle ACB$.

2 Find the angles marked by letters in these diagrams. In each case O is the centre of the circle.

a
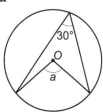

b
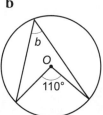

c
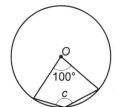

3 The diagram is not to scale. If $x = 48°$ find y.

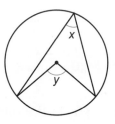

4 The diagram is not to scale. If $a = 108°$ find b.

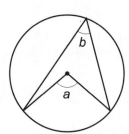

5 O is the centre of the circle. $\angle CAO = 44°$ and $\angle CBO = 32°$. Find $\angle AOB$.

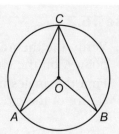

6 AB is a chord of a circle with centre O. C is a point on the other side of the circle. If $\angle OAB = 65°$ find $\angle ACB$.

7 In the diagram, O is the centre of the circle and $OA = OB = AB$. Find $\angle ACB$.

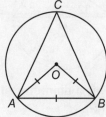

8 $ABCDE$ is a regular pentagon inscribed in a circle. Calculate $\angle ADB$.

9 Triangle ABC is inscribed in a circle of centre O. If $\angle AOB = 130°$ and $\angle BOC = 145°$ find the angles of triangle ABC.

16.2   Angle in a semicircle

Theorem 2

The angle subtended by a diameter in a semicircle is 90.

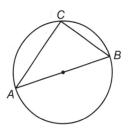

Proof
Let O be the centre of the circle. From Theorem 1, the angle at the centre is twice the angle on the circumference.
Hence $\angle AOB = 2 \times \angle ACB$.
AOB is a straight line. Hence $\angle AOB = 180°$.
So $180° = 2 \times \angle ACB$. Hence $\angle ACB = 90°$.

EXAMPLE 2

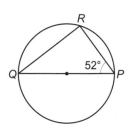

PQ is a diameter of a circle, and R a point on the circumference. $\angle QPR = 52°$.
Find $\angle PQR$.

Solution
$\angle PRQ = 90°$, as it is the angle in a semicircle. Hence
$\angle PQR = 180° - 90° - 52° = 38°$.
$\angle PQR = 38°$

> **N O T E**
> Always state the reasons for your steps.

Exercise 16.2

1 Verify the theorem by construction. Draw a circle with diameter *AB*. Take a
point *C* on the circumference. By measurement, check that ∠*ACB* = 90°.

2 Find the angles marked by letters in these diagrams. In each case *O* is the
centre of the circle.

    a   **b**   **c**

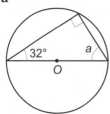 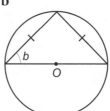 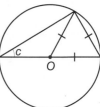

3 *MN* is a diameter of a circle, and *L* is a point on the circle. If ∠*MNL* = 35° find
∠*NML*.

4 *AB* and *CD* are diameters of a circle. Show that *ACBD* is a rectangle.

5 *AB* is a diameter of a circle radius 10 cm, and *C* is a point on the
circumference. If *CB* = 12 cm find *CA*. (Remember Pythagoras)

6 *AB* is a diameter of a circle radius 16 cm, and *C* is a point on the
circumference. If *CB* = 7 cm find ∠*CAB*. (Remember trigonometry)

7 *AB* is a diameter of a circle radius 40 cm, and *C* is a point on the
circumference. If ∠*CBA* = 62° then find *CA*.

8 In the following *XY* is the diameter of a circle and *Z* is a point on the
circumference.

    a If *XY* = 60 mm and *YZ* = 48 mm find *XZ*.

    b If *XY* = 20 cm and ∠*XYZ* = 40° find *XZ*.

    c If *XY* = 4 cm and *XZ* = 3 cm find ∠*ZXY*.

    d If *ZX* = 12 cm and *ZY* = 10cm find the radius of the circle.

16.3 Angles in the same segment

Theorem 3

Angles in the same segment are equal.
If *AB* is a chord, and *C* and *D* are in the
same segment, then ∠*ACB* = ∠*ADB*.

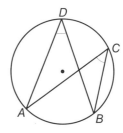

Proof
This follows directly from Theorem 1. If *O* is the centre of the circle, then
∠*AOB* = 2 × ∠*ACB* = 2 × ∠*ADB*. It follows that ∠*ACB* = ∠*ADB*.

Exercise 16.3

1 Verify the theorem by construction. Draw a circle, and a chord AB. Take points C_1, C_2, C_3 and C_4 on the circle, in the same segment. By measurement show that $\angle AC_1B = \angle AC_2B = \angle AC_3B = \angle AC_4B$.

2 Find the angles marked by letters in these diagrams.

a 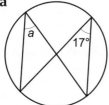 b 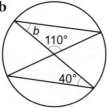 c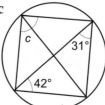

3 In these diagrams, fill in all the angles.

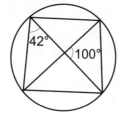

4 The diagram is not to scale.
   a If $\angle ABD = 33°$ and $\angle BDC = 41°$ find $\angle CXD$.
   b If $\angle AXD = 66°$ and $\angle DBC = 45°$ find $\angle BDA$.

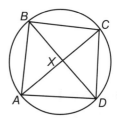

5 In this diagram AB is parallel to CD. If $\angle CBA = 38°$ find $\angle AXC$.

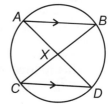

6 In the diagram $\angle EAB = 22°$ and $\angle AED = 36°$. Find $\angle BCE$.

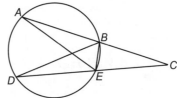

7 Show that the triangles ABX and DCX have the same angles.

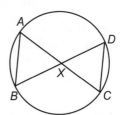

8 *A, B, C* and *D* are points on a circle, lettered clockwise. $\angle ABD = 47°$ and $\angle ADB = 52°$. Find $\angle DCB$.

9 *W, X, Y* and *Z* are points on a circle, lettered clockwise. *XZ* and *WY* meet at *Q*. $\angle XWY = 25°$ and $\angle WQX = 102°$. Find $\angle WYZ$.

16.4

A quadrilateral is called **cyclic** if it is inscribed in a circle (all its vertices are on the circle).

Theorem 4

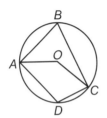

Opposite angles of a cyclic quadrilateral are supplementary (add up to 180°).
If *ABCD* are the points of the quadrilateral, then $\angle ABC + \angle ADC = 180°$.
Proof
This follows directly from Theorem 1. If *O* is the centre of the circle, then $\angle ABC = \frac{1}{2} \times \angle AOC$. Also
$\angle ADC = \frac{1}{2} \times (\text{reflex } \angle AOC)$

So $\angle ABC + \angle ADC = \frac{1}{2}(\angle AOC + \text{reflex } \angle AOC) = \frac{1}{2} \times 360° = 180°$, as required.

Theorem 5

The exterior angle of a cyclic quadrilateral is equal to the opposite angle.
In the diagram, $\angle DAB = \angle BCE$.

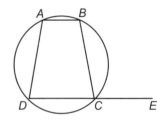

Proof
This follows directly from Theorem 4.
$$\begin{aligned}\angle BCE &= 180° - \angle BCD &&\text{(angles in a straight line)}\\ &= 180° - (180° - \angle DAB) &&\text{(angles in a cyclic quadrilateral)}\\ &= \angle DAB\end{aligned}$$

EXAMPLE 3

In the diagram *O* is the centre of the circle.
If $\angle AOC = 110°$ find $\angle ADC$.

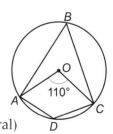

Solution
$$\begin{aligned}\angle ABC &= \tfrac{1}{2}\angle AOC &&\text{(angle at centre)}\\ &= 55°\\ \angle ADC &= 180° - \angle ABC &&\text{(opposite angles of a cyclic quadrilateral)}\\ &= 180° - 55°\end{aligned}$$
Hence $\angle ADC = 125°$

Exercise 16.4

1 Verify the theorems by construction. Draw a circle, and label points A, B, C and D on the circumference. Show by measurement that
∠ABC + ∠ADC = 180°.
Extend DC to E. Show by measurement that ∠DAB = ∠BCE.

2 Find the angles marked with letters in these diagrams.

a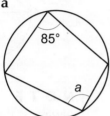

b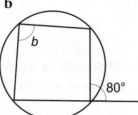

c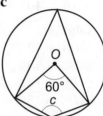

3 Fill in the angles in these diagrams.

a

b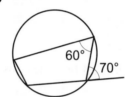

4 ACF and BDE are straight lines.
∠BAC = 100°. Find ∠CFE. What can you say about the lines AB and FE?

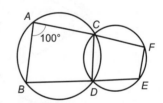

5 In this diagram ∠ABC = 70° and ∠BCD = 120°. Find ∠CED.

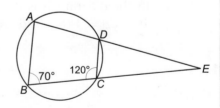

6 ABCD is a cyclic quadrilateral. If ∠BCD = 72° find ∠DAB.

7 PQRS is a cyclic quadrilateral. If ∠PQR = 112° find ∠PSR.

8 ABCD is a cyclic quadrilateral. AB and DC meet at E outside the circle. If ∠DAB = 82° and ∠EBC = 77° find ∠BEC.

9 WXYZ is a cyclic quadrilateral. WX and ZY meet at T outside the circle. ∠XTY = 22° and ∠YXT = 67°. Find ∠ZWX and ∠WZY.

16.5

In the previous examples and exercises you have known which theorem to use. Sometimes you must decide which theorem to use. In some problems you use more than one theorem.

EXAMPLE 4

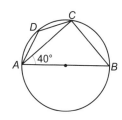

AB is a diameter.
$\angle CAB = 40°$. Find $\angle ADC$.

Solution

$\angle ACB = 90°$	(angle in a semicircle)
$\angle ABC = 50°$	(angle sum of a triangle)
$\angle ADC = 180° - 50°$	(angles of a cyclic quadrilateral)
$\angle ADC = 130°$	

N O T E
Always state the reasons for your step

Exercise 16.5

1 Find the angles marked by letters in these diagrams. The centre of a circle is labelled O.

a

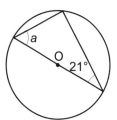

b

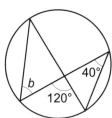

2 In the diagram O is the centre of the circle. If $\angle ACB = 148°$, find $\angle AOB$.

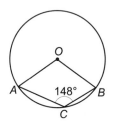

3 In this diagram $AB = AC$. Show that $\angle ADX = \angle ADB$.

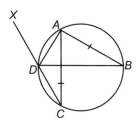

4 AB is perpendicular to CD. The centre of the circle is O. If $\angle AOC = 116°$ find $\angle BOD$.

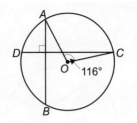

5 In this diagram $ABCD$ is a parallelogram. AB cuts the circle at E. Show that triangle CBE is isosceles.

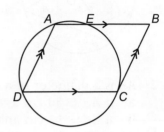

6 $ABCD$ is a cyclic parallelogram. What else can you say about $ABCD$?

7 $ABCD$ is a kite, with $AB = AD$ and $CB = CD$. If $ABCD$ is cyclic find $\angle ABC$.

Summary

- Suppose AB is a chord of a circle, O is the centre and C a point on the circumference. Then $\angle AOB = 2 \times \angle ACB$.
- Suppose AB is a diameter of a circle and C is a point on the circumference. Then $\angle ACB = 90°$.
- Suppose AB is a chord of a circle and C and D are points on the circumference in the same segment. Then $\angle ACB = \angle ADB$.
- A cyclic quadrilateral has all its vertices on a circle.
- Suppose $ABCD$ is a cyclic quadrilateral. Then $\angle DAB + \angle DCB = 180°$.

Activities 16

A cyclic quadrilateral is inside a circle. If a quadrilateral is outside a circle and all its sides touch the circle, then the circle is called an **inscribed circle**, as shown in the diagram.

Draw a circle, and draw a quadrilateral outside it. Measure the sides of the quadrilateral. Do you notice anything? Try with some other circles.

Try to prove any result you may have found.

1 Find the angles in these diagrams. O denotes the centre of the circle.

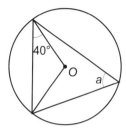 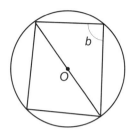 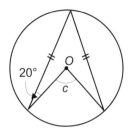

2 *AB* is a diameter of a circle, and *C* is a point on the circumference.
   a If *AB* = 50 cm and *CB* = 14 cm find *CA*.
   b If *CB* = 12 cm and *CA* = 16 cm find ∠*CAB*.

3 *ABCDEFGHI* is a regular nonagon inscribed in a circle. Find ∠*AGB*.

4 *ABC* is an acute-angled triangle inscribed in a circle. Points *P*, *Q* and *R* are on the minor arcs of *AB*, *BC* and *CA* respectively. Show that

$$∠APB + ∠BQC + ∠CRA = 360°$$

5 The diagram is not to scale.
   a If *a* = 140° find *b*, *c* and *d*.
   b If *b* = 80° find *a*, *c* and *d*.
   c If *c* = 35° find *a*, *b* and *d*.
   d If *d* = 130° find *a*, *b* and *c*.
   e If *a* = *d* find *a*, *b* and *c*.

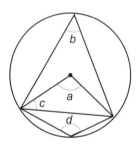

1 A ladder leans against a wall. The ladder slowly slides down the wall. What path does the centre of the ladder follow?

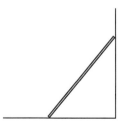

2 After the proof of Theorem 1 we stated that it holds even if the angle at the centre is obtuse (see diagram). Prove the theorem in this case.

3 After the proof of Theorem 1 we stated that it holds even if the lines cross (see diagram). Prove the theorem in this case.

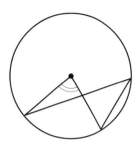

4 Draw an acute-angled triangle *ABC*. Construct, using ruler and compasses only, the point *X* in the triangle for which $\angle AXB = \angle BXC = \angle CXA$.
(This point is called the *Euler* centre of the triangle. It is the point for which $XA + XB + XC$ is as small as possible.)

5 Mark two points *A* and *B* on paper. Draw the path of a point *P* which moves so that $\angle APB = 90°$.

17 Areas

This unit uses
- The formulae for area
- Trigonometry
- The angles of polygons

17.1

If a triangle has base b and height h, then its area is given by

$$\frac{1}{2}bh$$

In many cases we do not know the base and the height. We can find the area of the triangle from other formulae.

(i) The formula $\frac{1}{2}ab \sin C$

Label the angles of the triangle as A, B and C. Label the sides of the triangle as a, b and c, so that side a is opposite angle A, side b is opposite angle B, and side c is opposite angle C.
Suppose we know two adjacent sides of the triangle, a and b, and that we know the angle between them C. Then the area of the triangle is

$$\frac{1}{2}ab \sin C$$

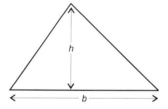

Proof
From the diagram, b is the base of the triangle. Drop a perpendicular from B to AC. Let the foot of the perpendicular be D. Then

$$\sin C = \frac{BD}{BC} = \frac{BD}{a}$$

Hence $BD = a \times \sin C$.

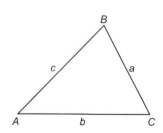

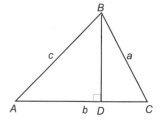

But BD is the height of the triangle. Substitute in the area formula $\frac{1}{2}bh$.

$$\text{Area} = \frac{1}{2}b \times a \times \sin C$$
$$= \frac{1}{2}ab \sin C$$

Note   This formula is in terms of a, b and C. There are also formulae in terms of b, c and A, and in terms of c, a and B. The area is given by any of these formulae

$$\frac{1}{2}ab \sin C \qquad 1\frac{1}{2}bc \sin A \qquad \frac{1}{2}ca \sin B$$

> RULE
>
> **In general, the area is half the product of two sides and the sine of the angle between them.**

EXAMPLE 1

Find the area of this triangle.

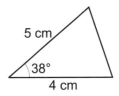

Solution
The adjacent sides are 5 cm and 4 cm, and the angle is 38°. Use the formula

$$\text{Area} = \frac{1}{2} \times 5 \times 4 \times \sin 38°$$
$$= 10 \times 0.6157 \qquad \text{(Using tables)}$$
$$= 6.157$$

The area is 6.16 cm^2.

EXAMPLE 2

Two sides of a triangle are 5 cm and 6 cm. The area of the triangle is 12 cm^2. Find the angle enclosed between the sides.

Solution
    Let the angle be x. From the formula, the area of a triangle is

$$\frac{1}{2} \times 5 \times 6 \times \sin x.$$

Hence $15 \sin x = 12$

$\sin x = 12 \div 15 = 0.8$.

From tables find that $\sin^{-1} 0.8 = 53°8'$

The angle is $53°8'$

Exercise 17.1A

1 Find the area of these triangles. Give your answers correct to 3 significant figures.

a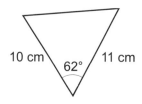

b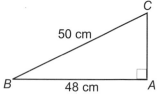

2 In triangle PQR, $\angle QPR = 53°$, $PQ = 6$ cm and $RP = 7$ cm. Find the area of the triangle.

3 In triangle LMN, $LM = 2$ m, $LN = 3$ m and $\angle MLN = 68°$. Find the area of the triangle.

4 The diagram shows a right-angled triangle, with $\angle A = 90°$, $BC = 50$ cm and $AB = 48$ cm.

Find the area of the triangle in these two ways, and check that the answers are the same.

   a Use Pythagoras' theorem to find AC, then use the formula $\frac{1}{2}bh$.

   b Use trigonometry to find $\angle B$, then use the formula $\frac{1}{2}ac \sin B$.

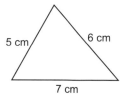

5 The area of $\triangle ABC$ is 8 m². $BC = 3$ m and $\angle ABC = 52°$. Find AB.

6 The area of $\triangle XYZ$ is 20 cm². $XY = 10$ cm and $\angle XYZ = 77°$. Find YZ.

7 The area of $\triangle PQR$ is 1.2 km². $QR = 2$ km and $\angle QRP = 81°$. Find RP.

8 In triangle ABC, $AB = 10$ cm and $BC = 16$ cm. The area of the triangle is 60 cm². Find $\angle ABC$.

9 In triangle PQR, $QR = 0.4$ m and $RP = 0.2$ m. The area of the triangle is 0.025 m². Find $\angle QRP$.

(ii) The formula $\sqrt{s(s-a)(s-b)(s-c)}$

Suppose, as above, that the three sides of the triangle are a, b and c. Let s be half the sum of the sides, that is $s = \frac{1}{2}(a+b+c)$, so s is half the perimeter of the triangle. Then the area is given by

$$\sqrt{s(s-a)(s-b)(s-c)}$$

EXAMPLE 3

The sides of a triangle are 5 cm, 6 cm and 7 cm.
Find its area.

Solution

Find s, and then use the formula.

$$s = \frac{1}{2}(5 + 6 + 7) = \frac{1}{2} \times 18 = 9$$

$$
\begin{aligned}
Area &= \sqrt{s(s-a)(s-b)(s-c)} \\
&= \sqrt{9(9-5)(9-6)(9-7)} \\
&= \sqrt{9 \times 4 \times 3 \times 2} \\
&= \sqrt{216} \\
&= 14.70 \qquad \text{(Using tables)}
\end{aligned}
$$

The area is 14.7 cm².

Exercise 17.1B

1 Find the areas of these triangles.

   a

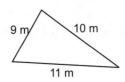

   b

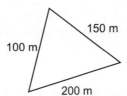

2 In $\triangle ABC$, $AB = 6$ cm, $BC = 8$ cm and $CA = 12$ cm. Find the area of the triangle.

3 In $\triangle PQR$, $PQ = 2$ m, $QR = 3$ m and $RP = 4$ m. Find the area of the triangle.

4 Find the area of a triangle ABC with $AB = 7$ cm, $BC = 8$ cm and $CA = 9$ cm. Use the formula $\frac{1}{2}bh$ to find the length of the perpendicular from A to BC.

5 A triangle has sides 10 cm, 13 cm and 15 cm. Find the length of the shortest perpendicular from a vertex to the opposite side.

6 Suppose ABC is an equilateral triangle of side 10 cm. Then each angle is equal to 60°. Find the area of the triangle using the two formulae
   a $\frac{1}{2}ab \sin C$, putting $a = b = 10$ cm and $C = 60°$
   b $\sqrt{s(s-a)(s-b)(s-c)}$, putting $a = b = c = 10$ cm and $s = 15$ cm.
   Are your answers the same?

7 Look again at question 4 of Exercise 17.1A. You know the three sides of the triangle. Use the formula $\sqrt{s(s-a)(s-b)(s-c)}$ to find its area. Is the answer the same as by the other two methods?

8 A triangular plot of land has sides 80 m, 100 m and 140 m. Find the area of the plot in
   a square metres   b hectares.

Note

Compare this section of this unit with the conditions for congruence in Unit 12, and the construction of triangles in Unit 12 of Book 1. You can find the area of a triangle if you know the following.

SSS (three sides). Use the formula $\sqrt{s(s-a)(s-b)(s-c)}$.
SAS (two sides and the enclosed angle). Use the formula $\frac{1}{2}ab\sin C$.
RHS (right-angle, hypotenuse, side) Use Pythagoras' theorem to find the third side, then use the formula $\frac{1}{2}bh$.

The fourth condition is ASA (two angles and the enclosed side). This is more complicated. See question **2** of the puzzles at the end of this unit.

Exercise 17.1C

Find the areas of the triangles described below.
1 $AB = 8$ cm, $AC = 7$ cm, $\angle BAC = 90°$.
2 $PQ = 5$ m, $QR = 7$ m, $PR = 8$ m.
3 $XY = 40$ m, $YZ = 30$ m, $\angle XYZ = 38°$.

17.2

The area of a polygon can be found by cutting it up into triangles.

EXAMPLE 4

A regular octagon is inscribed in a circle of radius 5 cm.
Find the area of the octagon.

Solution
Cut the octagon into 8 triangles, as shown. For each triangle, the angle at the centre of the circle is $360° \div 8$, giving $45°$. So the area of each triangle is

$$\frac{1}{2} \times 5 \times 5 \times \sin 45°$$

So the total area is

$$8 \times \frac{1}{2} \times 5 \times 5 \times \sin 45°$$

$$= 100 \times \sin 45°$$
$$= 100 \times 0.7071 \qquad \text{(Using tables)}$$

The area is 70.7 cm².

EXAMPLE 5

Find the area of a regular octagon of side 4 cm.

Solution
Divide the octagon into 8 triangles. Divide one of these triangles in half, as shown. The angle $\angle AOB = 45°$, hence $\angle AOD = 22\frac{1}{2}°$, and $\angle DAO = 67\frac{1}{2}°$.

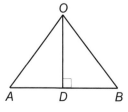

$$OD = 2 \times \tan 67\frac{1}{2}°$$

So the area of the triangle OAB is

$$\tfrac{1}{2} \times 4 \times 2 \times \tan 67\tfrac{1}{2}^{\circ} = 4 \times \tan 67\tfrac{1}{2}^{\circ}$$

The total area of the octagon is

$$8 \times 4 \times \tan 67\tfrac{1}{2}^{\circ}$$
$$= 32 \times \tan 67\tfrac{1}{2}^{\circ}$$
$$= 77.23$$

The area of the octagon is 77 cm^2

Working:

Number	Log
32	1.5051
tan 67.5	0.3827
77.23	1.8878

EXAMPLE 6

Find the area of the quadrilateral shown.

Solution
The quadrilateral is split into two triangles. For each
triangle, use the formula

$$\sqrt{s(s-a)(s-b)(s-c)}.$$

For the left hand triangle, $s = \tfrac{1}{2}(5 + 6 + 7) = 9$
Hence the area is

$$\sqrt{9 \times 4 \times 3 \times 2} = \sqrt{216} = 14.70$$

For the right hand triangle, $s = \tfrac{1}{2}(7 + 8 + 9) = 12$
Hence the area is

$$\sqrt{12 \times 5 \times 4 \times 3} = \sqrt{720} = 26.83$$

Add these, obtaining 41.53
The area is 41.53 cm^2.

Exercise 17.2

1 A regular pentagon is inscribed in a circle of radius 10 cm. Find the area of
the pentagon.
2 Find the area of a regular pentagon of side 4 cm.
3 Find the area of a regular decagon (10 sides) inscribed in a circle of
radius 5 cm.
4 Find the area of a regular decagon of side 20 cm.
5 Find the area of this trapezium.

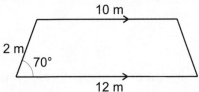

6 A rhombus has sides of length 12 cm, and one angle is 65°. Find the area of
the rhombus.

7 A parallelogram has sides of length 4 cm and 7 cm, and one angle is 47°. Find the area of the parallelogram.

8 Find the areas of these quadrilaterals.

a

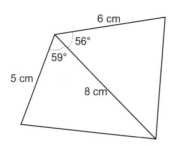

b

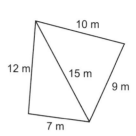

9 A quadrilateral $ABCD$ has $AB = 6$ cm, $BC = 8$ cm, $CD = 10$ cm, $DA = 11$ cm and $CA = 7$ cm. Find the area of the quadrilateral.

17.3

The surface area of a pyramid is the sum of the base area and the area of the triangular sides. Sometimes you need to use Pythagoras' theorem to find the area of the sides. The following example shows the method.

EXAMPLE 7

A pyramid has a square base of side 10 cm and height 15 cm. Find the surface area of the pyramid.

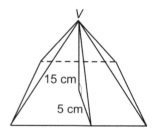

Solution
The area of the base is 10×10 cm², giving 100 cm².
Take a line from the vertex V to the middle of one of the sides of the base. The vertical rise of this line is 15 cm.
The horizontal run of this line is $\frac{1}{2} \times 10 = 5$ cm.
Hence the length of the line is $\sqrt{15^2 + 5^2} = \sqrt{225 + 25} = \sqrt{250}$ cm
So the area of each triangle is $\frac{1}{2} \times 10 \times \sqrt{250}$ cm² $= 5\sqrt{250}$ cm²
The total area is $100 + 4 \times 5\sqrt{250}$ cm²
$$= 100 + 20\sqrt{250}$$
$$= 100 + 316.2$$
The area is 416 cm².

Exercise 17.3

1 A pyramid has a square base of side 20 cm and height 5 cm. Find its total surface area.

2 A pyramid has a square base of side 10 cm and height 12 cm. Find the surface area of its triangular faces.

3 A pyramid has a rectangular base which is 40 cm by 60 cm. Its vertex is 20 cm above the centre of the base. Find the total surface area of the pyramid.

4 The base of a pyramid is a right-angled triangle with sides 3 cm, 4 cm and 5 cm. The vertex of the pyramid is 10 cm vertically above the right-angle. Find the total surface area of the pyramid.

5 The Great Pyramid in Egypt, built almost 5000 years ago, has a square base of side 230 m and height 147 m. Find the area of its triangular faces.

Summary

- Label a triangle so that side a is opposite angle A, and so on.
- The area of a triangle is $\frac{1}{2}ab \sin C$ or $\frac{1}{2} ac \sin B$ or $\frac{1}{2} bc \sin A$.
- Let $s = \frac{1}{2}(a + b + c)$. The area of a triangle is $\sqrt{s(s - a)(s - b)(s - c)}$.
- Find the area of a polygon by cutting it into triangles.
- The surface area of a pyramid is the sum of the base and the triangular sides.

Activity 17

If you draw a regular polygon with a large number of sides, then it looks like a circle. So the area of this polygon is close to that of a circle, πr^2.

Take a regular polygon with 100 sides. Find its area in these cases:

a The polygon is drawn inside a circle of radius 1.

b The polygon is drawn outside a circle of radius 1.

Explain your results.

Progress exercise 17

1 Find the areas of these triangles.

a

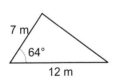

b

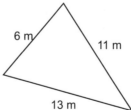

2 A regular dodecagon (12 sides) is inscribed in a circle of radius 10 cm. Find the area of the dodecagon.

3 Find the area of a regular dodecagon of side 4 cm.

4 Find the areas of these quadrilaterals.

a

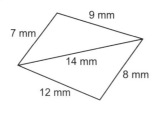

b

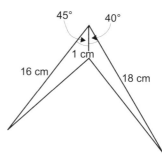

5 A pyramid has a rectangular base of sides 10 cm and 12 cm. Its vertex is 15 cm above the centre of the base. Find the area of the triangular faces of the pyramid.

6 The base of a pyramid is a regular hexagon of side 10 cm. Its vertex is 20 cm above the centre of the base. Find the total surface area of the pyramid.

1 This chapter has introduced two formulae for the area of a triangle, $\frac{1}{2}ab \sin C$ and $\sqrt{s(s-a)(s-b)(s-c)}$. By putting these equal to each other, find a formula for sin C in terms of a, b, c and s.

Consider the right-angled triangle with sides 3, 4 and 5. Find the sine of the smallest angle using the formula you have found. Does it agree with that found by trigonometry?

2 ASA (two angles and the enclosed side) is a condition for congruence of triangles. Hence if you know ASA then you must be able to find the area of the triangle. Suppose $\angle A = 56°$, $\angle B = 66°$ and $AB = 8$ cm.
   a What is C?
   b Drop a perpendicular from A to D on BC. Find AD.
   c Find AC.
   d Use the formula $\frac{1}{2}bc \sin A$ to find the area of triangle ABC.

3 In triangle PQR, $PQ = 10$ cm, $\angle P = 68°$ and $\angle Q = 61°$. Use the method in question **2** to find the area of $\triangle PQR$.

4 Three formulae for the area of a triangle are $\frac{1}{2}ab \sin C$, $\frac{1}{2}bc \sin A$ and $\frac{1}{2}ca \sin B$. These expressions are equal. Prove the following formula

$$\frac{\sin A}{a} = \frac{\sin B}{b} = \frac{\sin C}{c}$$

This is known as the **sine rule**. You will meet it next year.

5 In $\triangle ABC$, $AB = 6$ cm, $BC = 7$ cm and $CA = 13$ cm. Use the formula $\sqrt{s(s-a)(s-b)(s-c)}$ to find the area of the triangle. Explain the answer.

18

Measurement of solids

This unit uses
- The areas of simple shapes
- The names of solids
- The volumes of simple solids

18.1 Pyramids and cones

This diagram shows a cuboid, a cylinder, a pyramid and a cone.

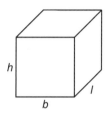  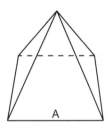 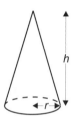

The cuboid and the cylinder are examples of prisms.
The volume of a cuboid is given by

$$V = lbh$$

The volume of a cylinder is given by

$$V = \pi r^2 h$$

For both of these solids, the volume is given by

$$V = Ah, \text{ where } A \text{ is the area of cross-section.}$$

Now look at the pyramid and the cone. The pyramid tapers to a point from a base, which is usually a rectangle.
The cone tapers to a point from a base, which is a circle.
For both these solids, the volume is a third that of the corresponding prism with the same base. The volume of a pyramid is a third that of the corresponding cuboid.

$$V = \tfrac{1}{3}Ah$$

The volume of a cone is a third that of the corresponding cylinder.

$$V = \tfrac{1}{3}\pi r^2 h$$

You may have done Activity 21, **2** in Book 1, in which you made three equal pyramids which fitted together to make a cube. It follows that the volume of each of these pyramids is a third the volume of the cube.

EXAMPLE 1

A cone has base radius 4 cm and height 9 cm. Find its volume.

Solution

Use the formula, putting $r = 4$ and $h = 9$.

$$V = \frac{1}{3}\pi \times 4^2 \times 9$$

$$= 48 \times \pi \quad \text{Taking } \pi = 3.142, \log \pi = 0.4972$$

$$= 150.9$$

Working:

Number	Log
48	1.6812
π	0.4972
150.9	2.1784

The volume is 151 cm^3.

Exercise 18.1

1 A pyramid is 12 cm high, and its base is a square of side 5 cm. Find its volume.

2 Find the volume of a pyramid which has a rectangular base of sides 20 m and 10 m and height 15 m.

3 The Great Pyramid of Egypt (mentioned in Unit 17) has a square base of side 230 m and a height of 147 m. Find its volume.

4 Find the volume of a cone of height 10 cm and base radius 4 cm.

5 Find the volume of a cone of base radius 2 m and height 3 m.

6 A pyramid has a square base of side 10 cm and volume 500 cm^3. Find its height.

7 A pyramid with a square base has height 12 m and volume 64 m^3. Find the side of the base.

8 A cone has base radius 10 cm and volume 120 cm^3. Find its height.

9 A cone has height 12 cm and volume 50 cm^3. Find its base radius.

10 A cone has volume 250 cm^3.
   a If the base radius is 20 cm find the height.
   b If the height is 10 cm find the base radius.

11 A pyramid with a square base has volume 80 m^3.
   a If the side of the base is 4 m find the height.
   b If the height is 8 m find the side of the base.

18.2 Spheres

A sphere is a round solid, like a ball. If the sphere has radius r, then its volume V is

$$V = \tfrac{4}{3}\pi r^3$$

The surface area A of the sphere is

$$A = 4\pi r^2$$

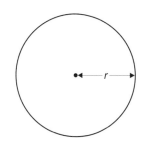

EXAMPLE 2

Find the volume and surface area of a sphere of radius 0.46 m.

Solution

Apply the formulae, putting $r = 0.46$.

$$V = \frac{4}{3}\pi 0.46^3$$

$$= 0.4079$$

The volume is 0.408 m^3.

$$A = 4\pi 0.46^2$$

$$= 2.660$$

The area is 2.66 m^2.

Working:

Number	Log
$\frac{4}{3}$	0.1249
π	0.4972
0.46	$\bar{1}.6628$
0.46^3	$\bar{2}.9884$
0.4079	$\bar{1}.6105$

Working:

Number	Log
4	0.6021
π	0.4972
0.46	$\bar{1}.6628$
0.46^2	$\bar{1}.3256$
2.660	0.4249

Exercise 18.2

1 A sphere has radius 6 cm. Find its volume and surface area.
2 A sphere has diameter 1.3 m. Find its volume and surface area.
3 Find the volume of a hemisphere of radius 10 cm. Find the total area of the curved and the flat surfaces.
4 Find the total surface area of a hemisphere of radius 4 m.
5 Find a formula for the total surface area of a hemisphere of radius r.
6 A sphere has surface area 64π cm^2. Find its radius.
7 A sphere has volume 0.44 m^3. Find its radius.
8 A sphere has surface area 200 cm^2. Find its volume.
9 A sphere has volume 33 m^3. Find its surface area.
10 A sphere has radius 12 cm.
   a Find its volume.   b Find its surface area.
11 A sphere has surface area 48 cm^2.
   a Find its radius.   b Find its volume.
12 A sphere has volume 1240 m^3.
   a Find its radius.   b Find its surface area.

18.3 Surface area of cones

The height, h, of a cone is its *perpendicular* height. It is not the length of the slanting edge. The length of the slanting edge, l, is given by Pythagoras' theorem.

$$l = \sqrt{r^2 + h^2}$$

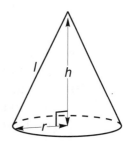

Imagine cutting along the side of the cone and unfolding. You would get a sector of a circle. The radius of this circle is l, and the arc length is the circumference of the cone base, $2\pi r$. Hence the area of the curved side, which is the area of this sector, is the area of the circle, πl^2, reduced in the ratio $\dfrac{2\pi r}{2\pi l}$, which is $\dfrac{r}{l}$.

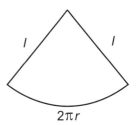

Area of curved side $= \pi l^2 \times \dfrac{r}{l} = \pi r l$

So the total area of the cone is
$$\pi r^2 + \pi r l = \pi r (r + l)$$

EXAMPLE 3

A cone has base radius 4 cm and height 3 cm. Find its curved surface area.

Solution

The slant height l is given by
$$l = \sqrt{4^2 + 3^2} = \sqrt{16 + 9} = \sqrt{25} = 5$$

Now use the formula.

$$\begin{aligned} \text{Area} &= \pi \times 4 \times (4 + 5) \\ &= \pi \times 36 \\ &= 113.1 \end{aligned}$$

The curved area of the cone is 113 cm^2.

Exercise 18.3

1. Find the surface area of a cone with base radius 5 cm and height 12 cm.
2. Find the surface area of a cone with base radius 7 m and height 24 m.
3. The base radius of a cone is 6 cm and its surface area is 160π cm^2. Find its slant height, and hence find its height.
4. The base radius of a cone is 10 m, and its surface area is 800 m^2. Find its height.
5. A cone has base radius 4 cm and volume 150 cm^3. Find its height, and hence find its surface area.
6. A cone has base radius 20 cm and surface area 6000 cm^2. Find its volume.
7. A cone has base radius 10 cm and height 12 cm.
   a. Find its volume.　　b. Find its total surface area.
8. A cone has base radius 5 m and volume 25 m^3.
   a. Find its height.　　b. Find its total surface area.
9. A cone has height 12 cm and volume 80 cm^3.
   a. Find its base radius.　　b. Find its total surface area.
10. A cone has base radius 20 cm and total surface area 3000 cm^2.
    a. Find its slant height.　　b. Find its height.
    c. Find its volume.

18.4 Combinations of shapes

Some solids are formed by combining simpler solids. To find the total volume, add the volumes of the simpler solids.

EXAMPLE 4

The solid shown is a cone on top of a cylinder. Find the total volume.

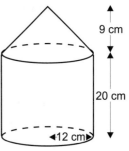

Solution

For the cylinder, the volume is $\pi r^2 h$, where $r = 12$ cm and $h = 20$ cm.

For the cone, the volume is $\frac{1}{3}\pi r^2 h$, where $r = 12$ cm and $h = 9$ cm.

$$\text{Volume} = \pi \times 12^2 \times 20 + \frac{1}{3}\pi \times 12^2 \times 9$$

$$= \pi 144(20 + 3) \qquad \text{(Factorising by } \pi 12^2)$$

$$= \pi 144 \times 23$$

$$= 10\ 400$$

The volume is 10 400 cm³.

Sometimes it is easier to subtract one volume from another.

EXAMPLE 5

A hollow rubber ball has inside radius 5 cm and outside radius 6 cm. Find the volume of the rubber.

Solution

Subtract the volume of the hollow from the volume of the whole ball.

Volume of whole ball $= \frac{4}{3}\pi 6^3$

Volume of hollow $= \frac{4}{3}\pi 5^3$

$$\text{Volume of rubber} = \frac{4}{3}\pi 6^3 - \frac{4}{3}\pi 5^3$$

$$= \frac{4}{3}\pi(216 - 125) \qquad \text{(Factorising by } \frac{4}{3}\pi)$$

$$= \frac{4}{3}\pi 91$$

$$= 381.2$$

The volume of rubber is 381 cm³.

Exercise 18.4A

1 A pencil is a cylinder 12 cm long and with base
radius 1 cm. It is sharpened, so that the end is a
cone of height 2 cm. Find the volume of the
pencil.

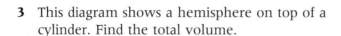

2 The diagram shows a pyramid on top of a cube.
Find the total volume.

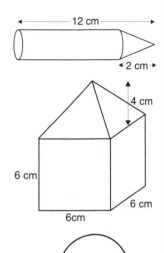

3 This diagram shows a hemisphere on top of a
cylinder. Find the total volume.

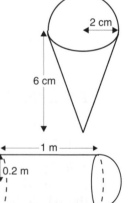

4 An ice-cream consists of a hemisphere on top of a cone.
Find its volume.

5 A heating boiler is in the form of a cylinder with
hemispheres at each end. Find its volume.

6 A hollow ball has outside radius 11 cm and inside radius 10 cm. Find the
volume of rubber in the ball.

7 A hollow cylinder has external height 9 cm and external radius 5 cm. It is
made of material 1 cm thick. Find the volume of material used to make it.

8 The diagram shows a solid cylinder with a hemisphere
scooped out at one end. Find its volume.

9 The diagram shows a hemispherical bowl. The external radius is 8 cm, and the bowl is made of material 1 cm thick. Find the volume of the material.

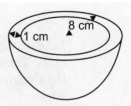

10 A cylinder with base radius 5 cm contains water. A sphere of radius 3 cm is put into the cylinder. The sphere is covered by water, and the water does not overflow. How much has the water risen by?

EXAMPLE 6

Find the surface area of the solid of Example 4.

Solution
We want the curved surface area of the cone, the curved surface area of the cylinder, and *one* circle at the base of the cylinder.

$$\text{Slant height of cone} = \sqrt{12^2 + 9^2} = \sqrt{144 + 81} = \sqrt{225} = 15$$
$$\text{Curved surface area of cone} = \pi \times 12 \times 15$$
$$\text{Curved surface area of cylinder} = 2\pi \times 12 \times 20$$
$$\text{Area of circle} = \pi \times 12^2$$

$$\text{Total surface area} = \pi \times 180 + \pi \times 480 + \pi \times 144$$
$$= \pi(180 + 480 + 144)$$
$$= \pi \times 804 = 2526$$

The surface area is 2526 cm².

Exercise 18.4B

1 Find the surface area of the pencil of question **1** of Exercise 18.4A.
2 Find the surface area of the shape of question **2** of Exercise 18.4A.
3 Find the surface area of the shape of question **3** of Exercise 18.4A.
4 Find the surface area of the ice-cream of question **4** of Exercise 18.4A.
5 Find the surface area of the boiler of question **5** of Exercise 18.4A.
6 Find the surface area of the bowl of question **9** of Exercise 18.4A.

Summary

- The volume of a cone or a pyramid is $\frac{1}{3}$ the base area times the height.
- The volume of a sphere is $\frac{4}{3}\pi r^3$. The surface area of a sphere is $4\pi r^2$.
- The slant height of a cone is $l = \sqrt{r^2 + h^2}$. The curved surface area of a cone is $\pi r l$.

1 Take a strip of paper, twist it once and then join its ends. The result should look like the diagram. How many surfaces does it have? How many edges does it have? (This shape is called a **Moebius strip**.)

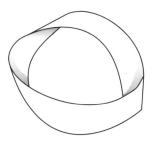

2 Much of the food we eat comes in packages. Most packages are cuboids, but some packages are prisms or pyramids. Some milk cartons are tetrahedra. Find one of these packages, and calculate its volume by the methods of this chapter. Is your answer the same as the volume written on the carton?

1 Find the volume of
   a a pyramid with a square base of side 8 cm and height 6 cm
   b a cone with base radius 7 cm and height 4 cm.
2 A sphere has radius 3 cm. Find its volume and surface area.
3 A sphere has volume 18 cm^3. Find its radius and surface area.
4 Find the surface area of the cone of question **1b**.
5 The diagram shows a cylinder with a cone cut out of it. Find its volume.

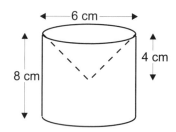

6 Find the surface area of the solid of question **5**.

1 The curved surface of a cone is made from a sector of 216° from a circle of radius 5 cm. Find the base radius and height of the cone.
2 What angle and radius of sector do you need for a cone with base radius 5 cm and height 13 cm?
3 A cylinder of base radius 4 cm contains water to a depth of 5 cm. A tall solid cylinder of base radius 2 cm is placed vertically in the first cylinder. The second cylinder is not immersed, and the water does not overflow. By how much does the water rise?

4 The diagram shows two cylinders, which have the same volume.
The heights of the cylinders are in the ratio 1 : 5.
What is the ratio of their base radii?

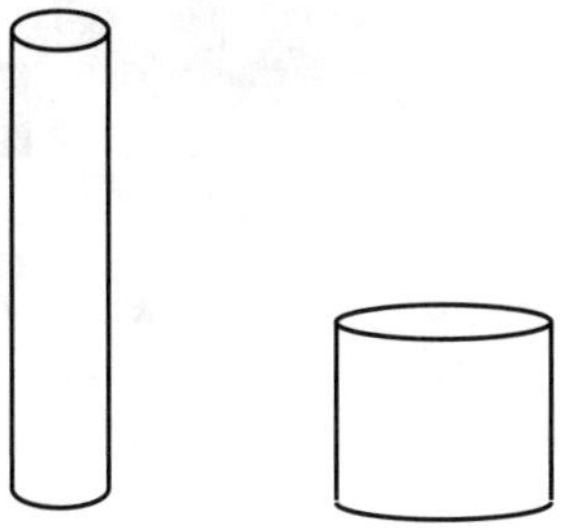

5 A cone has base radius *r*. What is its least possible surface area?

19 Enlargement and similarity

This unit uses
- Drawing instruments
- Fractions and ratios
- Geometry of parallel lines

19.1 Enlargement

When a figure (the **object**) is changed into a different figure (the **image**) it has been transformed. The mathematical rule to carry out the change is a **transformation**. So far you have looked at translations, reflections and rotations, which all change the position of a figure without altering its size. This unit deals with enlargement, which alters the size of the object as well as its position.

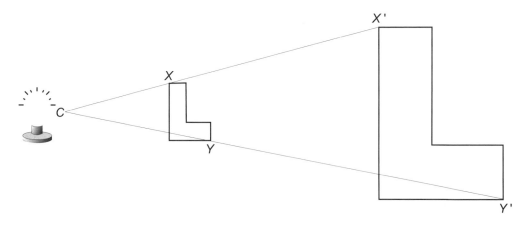

In this diagram, the object is enlarged on to a screen by a light placed at C (called the **centre of enlargement**). The lengths of the image are all three times the lengths of the corresponding sides of the object. We say that the **linear scale factor** of the enlargement is 3. Looking at individual light rays

$$CX' = 3 \times CX$$

Similarly,

$$CY' = 3 \times CY.$$

For any line from the centre of enlargement, the distance to the image point is 3 times the distance to the object point.

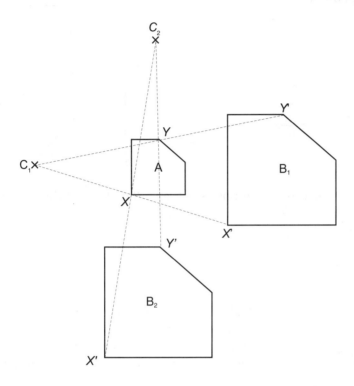

In this diagram an object **A** is enlarged by a scale factor 2 using two different centres of enlargement, C_1 and C_2. The images, **B**$_1$ and **B**$_2$, are then the same size and shape but in different positions. The following exercise shows how to construct the diagram.

Exercise 19.1A

1   Make a copy of object A in the diagram above with the points C_1 and C_2. Draw a faint line from C_1 to a point X on a corner of object **A**. Extend this line to X', where $C_1X' = 2 \times C_1X$. Repeat, with all the corners of **A**. This gives the first image, **B**$_1$.

2   Repeat question **1**, using C_2 as the centre of enlargement to give the second image, **B**$_2$.

3   Measure two sides on shapes **B**$_1$ and **B**$_2$ and check that they are 2 (the scale factor) times the corresponding lengths on **A**.

If an enlargement from point C sends point X to point X', CXX' is a straight line. Similarly if point Y is sent to Y', then CYY' is a straight line. To find the centre of enlargement, find the intersection of XX' and YY' (extended).

EXAMPLE 1

Make a copy of this diagram and
find the position of the centre of
enlargement. What is the scale
factor of the enlargement?

Solution

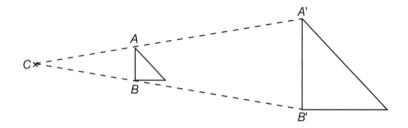

Join any two pairs of corresponding points AA' and BB'. Extend these lines until
they meet at C. This is the centre of enlargement.

Measure CA as 3 cm and CA' as 8 cm.

The scale factor is $\dfrac{CA'}{CA} = \dfrac{8}{3} = 2\frac{2}{3}$.

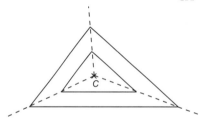

If the centre of enlargement is inside the
shape, the effect is as shown in this diagram.
Here the triangle has been enlarged by a scale
factor of 2 about the centre of enlargement C.

Exercise 19.1B

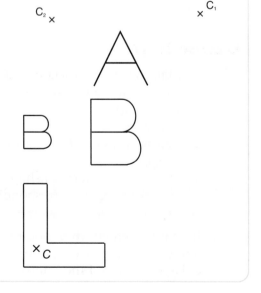

1 Make a copy of this diagram and
    enlarge the letter A
    a by a scale factor of 2 centre C_1
    b by a scale factor of 1.5 centre C_2.

2 Make a copy of the diagram. Find
    the centre of enlargement and the
    linear scale factor of the enlargement.

3 Make a copy of this diagram. Enlarge
    the L shape by a scale factor of 2.5
    with C as the centre of enlargement.

If the linear scale factor is less than 1, then the image will be smaller than the object. Even though the shape gets smaller, it is still called an enlargement.

Exercise 19.2

1 Make a copy of $\triangle FGH$ and the centre C. Find point F' so that $CF' = \frac{1}{4}CF$. Repeat with G and H.

Check that $F'G' = \frac{1}{4}FG$.

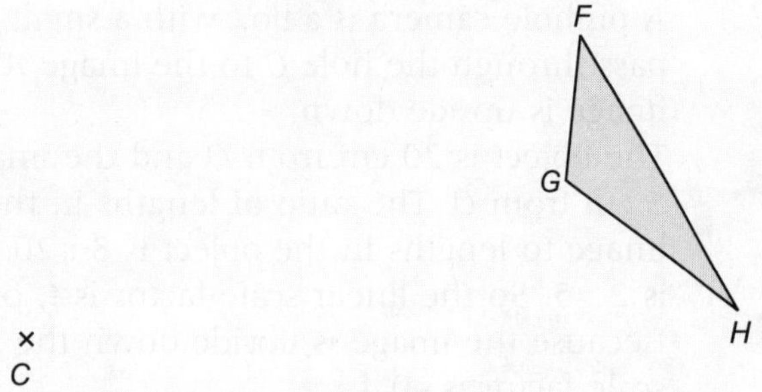

$\times$
C

2 The lower L shape has been enlarged to the upper L shape. Make a copy of the diagram and find the centre of enlargement. What is the scale factor of the enlargement?

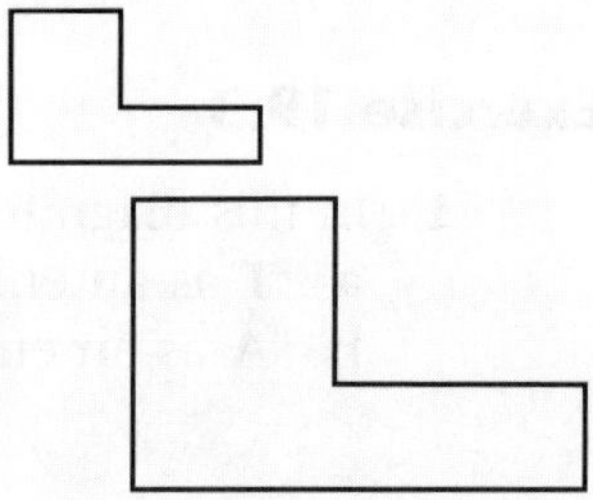

3 Copy the diagram on to squared paper. Enlarge the shape
   a by scale factor $\frac{1}{3}$, from centre X
   b by scale factor $\frac{1}{2}$, from centre Y.

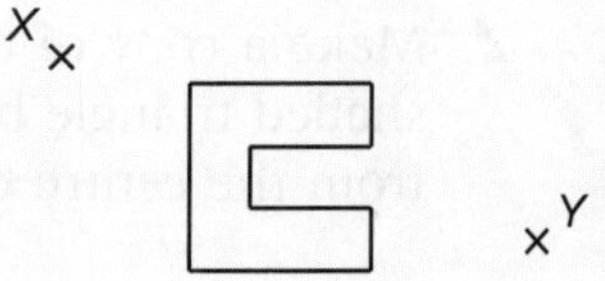

X
$\times$

$\times Y$

4 In this diagram, show that shape P is not an enlargement of shape Q.

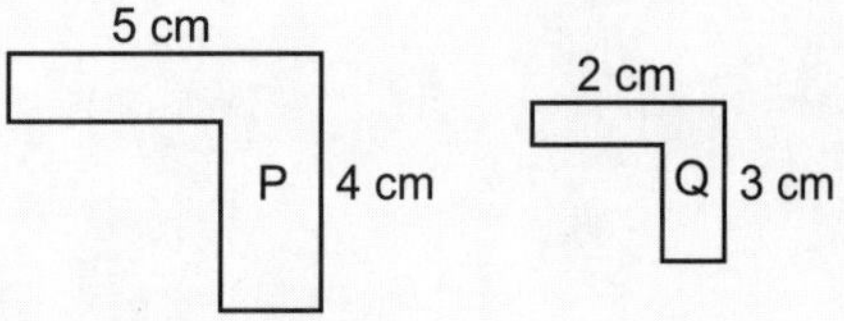

5 A photograph of a house shows a window that measures 2.8 cm by 1.2 cm. If the photograph is enlarged by a scale factor of $\frac{4}{5}$, what are the measurements of the window in the new photograph?

5 cm

2 cm

P | 4 cm

Q | 3 cm

6 Make a copy of this diagram. On the same diagram enlarge $\triangle ABC$ by factors of $\frac{1}{2}$ and $1\frac{1}{2}$, using O as the centre of enlargement.

A

$\times$
O

C

B

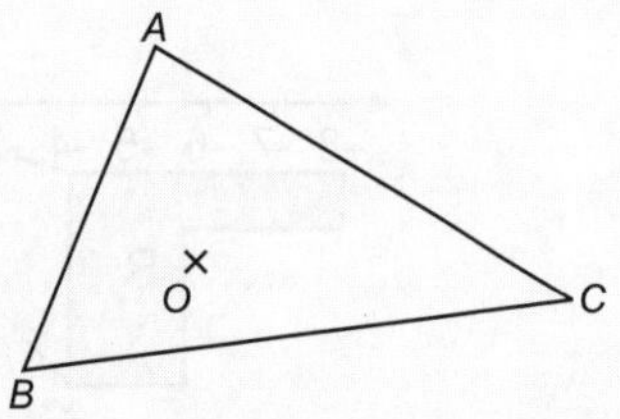

This diagram shows a simple pinhole camera.

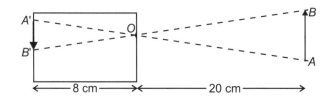

A pinhole camera is a box with a small hole at one end. Rays from the object *AB* pass through the hole *O* to the image *A'B'* at the back of the box. Notice that the image is upside down.

The object is 20 cm from *O* and the image is 8 cm from *O*. The ratio of lengths in the image to lengths in the object is 8 : 20, which is 2 : 5. So the linear scale factor is $\frac{2}{5}$, or 0.4. Because the image is upside down the linear scale factor is −0.4.

> **NOTE**
> When the centre of enlargement is between the object and the image, the scale factor is negative.

Exercise 19.3

1   In this diagram, what is the scale factor of
    a   **T** as an enlargement of **A**
    b   **A** as an enlargement of **T**?

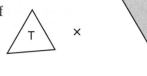

2   Make a copy of the diagram. Enlarge the shaded triangle by a scale factor of −2 from the centre of enlargement at *O*.

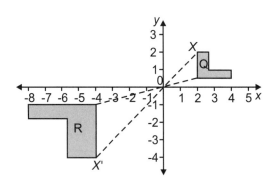

Often it is easier to use coordinates for an enlargement, since it is easier to place points. In the diagram **R** is an enlargement of **Q**, centre (0, 0) and scale factor −2. *X* has coordinates (2, 2). The image of *X* is twice the distance from (0, 0) in the opposite direction. This is done by multiplying the coordinates by −2. So *X'* has coordinates (−4, −4).

EXAMPLE 2

Enlarge the shape shown by
a a scale factor of 1.5 about (0, 2)
b a scale factor of –2 about (1, 1).

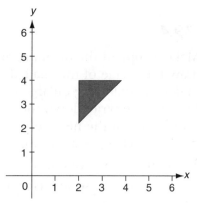

Solution

a For each vertex, find its displacement from the centre. Multiply this displacement by 1.5. Then measure the new displacement from the centre. This gives the new point. It helps to set out the working as below.

Point	Displacement from (0, 2)	New displacement	New point
(2, 2)	2 right	3 right	(3, 2)
(2, 4)	2 right, 2 up	3 right, 3 up	(3, 5)
(4, 4)	4 right, 2 up	6 right, 3 up	(6, 5)

The new triangle is shown.

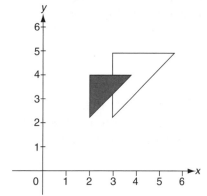

b Here the scale factor is negative. So reverse the direction of the displacement, i.e. convert 'right' to 'left', and 'up' to 'down'.

Point	Displacement from (1, 1)	New displacement	New point
(2, 2)	1 right, 1 up	2 left, 2 down	(–1, –1)
(2, 4)	1 right, 3 up	2 left, 6 down	(–1, –5)
(4, 4)	3 right, 3 up	6 left, 6 down	(–5, –5)

The new triangle is shown.

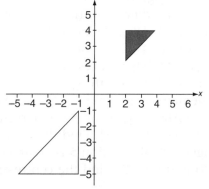

Exercise 19.4

1 Make a copy of the diagram, and draw the image of the shaded shape under the following enlargements. In each case write down the coordinates of the new vertices.

   a   centre (1, 0), scale factor 2

   b   centre (1, 3), scale factor $\frac{1}{2}$

   c   centre (2, 2), scale factor 3

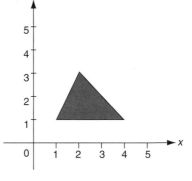

2 Make a copy of the diagram, and draw the image of the shaded shape under the following enlargements. In each case write down the coordinates of the new vertices.

   a   centre (0, 2), scale factor –2

   b   centre (1, 2), scale factor –1

   c   centre (–2, 0), scale factor $-\frac{1}{2}$.

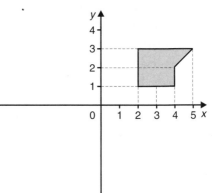

3 Referring to the diagram, find the centre and scale factor of the enlargement of the upper shape to the lower shape.

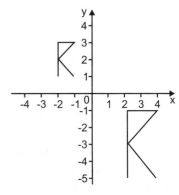

4 Plot the quadrilateral with point $A(0, 0)$, $B(1, 1)$, $C(0, 3)$ and $D(–1, 1)$. Find the image of the quadrilateral under these enlargements. In each case state the coordinates of the image of A.

   a   centre (3, 1), scale factor 2

   b   centre (0, 4), scale factor $-\frac{1}{2}$

5 Triangle ABC has vertices at (1, 1), (3, 1) and (3, 2). Triangle $A'B'C'$ has vertices at (1, 0), (5, 0) and (5, 2). Find the centre and scale factor of the enlargement which takes $\triangle ABC$ to $\triangle A'B'C'$.

6 Triangle ABC of question **5** is enlarged to the triangle with vertices at (2.5, 2), (3.5, 2) and (3.5, 2.5). Find the centre and scale factor of the enlargement.

7 Triangle ABC of question **5** is enlarged to the triangle with vertices at (–2, 4), (–6, 4) and (–6, 2). Find the centre and scale factor of the enlargement.

Two shapes are similar if one is
congruent to an enlargement of the
other. In the diagram, $\triangle A'B'C'$ is an
enlargement of $\triangle ABC$ and hence
$\triangle A'B'C'$ is similar to $\triangle ABC$.
When writing down similar shapes
the order of the letters is important

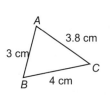
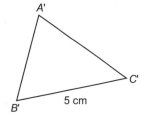

(as it is with congruent triangles). So $\triangle A'B'C'$ is not similar to $\triangle BAC$. When two
shapes are similar, angles in the same positions are equal. So

$$\angle BAC = \angle B'A'C'$$
$$\angle ABC = \angle A'B'C'$$
$$\angle BCA = \angle B'C'A'$$

The ratios of corresponding sides of similar figures are equal. Hence

$$\frac{A'B'}{AB} = \frac{A'C'}{AC} = \frac{B'C'}{BC}$$

For the example above $\dfrac{B'C'}{BC} = \dfrac{5}{4}$, so the scale factor is $\frac{5}{4}$, or 1.25

So $\dfrac{A'B'}{3} = \dfrac{5}{4}$, giving $A'B' = \dfrac{15}{4} = 3.75$ cm.

Similarly $\dfrac{A'C'}{3.8} = 1.25$, giving $A'C' = 3.8 \times 1.25 = 4.75$ cm.

R U L E
**You can show that two shapes are similar, by showing that they have
the same angles, or that the ratios of corresponding sides are the
same.**

EXAMPLE 3

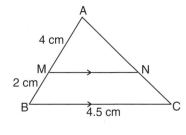

In $\triangle ABC$, M is on AB with $AM = 4$ cm and $MB = 2$ cm.
N is on AC, and MN is parallel to BC.
(a) Show that $\triangle AMN$ is similar to $\triangle ABC$.
(b) If $BC = 4.5$ cm find MN.

Solution
(a) $\angle AMN = \angle ABC$ (corresponding angles)
     $\angle ANM = \angle ACB$ (corresponding angles)
     $\angle MAN = \angle BAC$ (same angle)

Hence the angles of $\triangle ABC$ are the same as the angles in $\triangle AMN$. It follows that
$\triangle ABC$ and $\triangle AMN$ are similar.

(b) From (a), it follows that

$$\frac{AM}{AB} = \frac{MN}{BC}$$

$$\frac{4}{6} = \frac{MN}{4.5}$$

Therefore $MN = \frac{2}{3} \times 4.5 = 3$ cm.

EXAMPLE 4

From the diagram, write down a pair of similar triangles. Hence find the length of DE.

Solution
Notice that $\dfrac{CD}{CB} = \dfrac{9}{6} = 1.5$ and $\dfrac{CE}{CA} = \dfrac{12}{8} = 1.5$. Hence

$\triangle CDE$ is an enlargement of $\triangle CBA$, with centre C and linear scale factor -1.5. It follows that $\triangle CDE$ is similar to $\triangle CBA$.

The ratio of DE to BA must also be 1.5.

$DE = 1.5 \times BA = 1.5 \times 7 = 10.5$ cm.

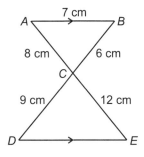

Exercise 19.5

1   From the diagram write down two similar triangles. Hence find the length of RT.

2   Show that $\triangle BDC$ is similar to $\triangle ABC$.

3   In diagram, show that $\triangle ABC$ and $\triangle EDC$ are similar. Hence find
    a CD **b** AB

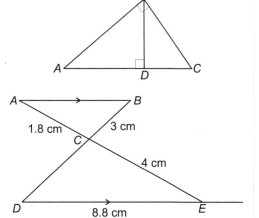

4   $ABCD$ is a cyclic quadrilateral. The diagonals AC and BD meet at X inside the circle. Use a result of Unit 16 to show that $\triangle ABX$ is similar to $\triangle DCX$. If $AX = 5$ cm, $XC = 4$ cm and $XB = 8$ cm find XD.

5 *ABCD* is a cyclic quadrilateral. The chords *AB* and *DC* meet at *X* outside the circle. Use a result of Unit 16 to show that $\triangle ADX$ is similar to $\triangle CBX$.
If *AX* = 30 m, *XD* = 25 m and *XC* = 15 m find *XB*.

6 Four rectangles have vertices as given below. Plot the rectangles, and state, with reasons, which pairs are similar.

    Rectangle 1: (1, 1) (3, 1) (3, 2) (1, 2)
    Rectangle 2: (4, 2) (6, 2) (6, 5) (4, 5)
    Rectangle 3: (−4, 2) (−2, 2) (−2, 6) (−4, 6)
    Rectangle 4: (0, 4) (1.5, 4) (1.5, 5) (0, 5)

7 Which of the following statements are true?
a All squares are similar to each other.
b All rectangles are similar to each other.
c All pentagons are similar to each other
d All regular pentagons are similar to each other.

Summary

- An enlargement is given by a scale factor and a centre. All distances from the centre are multiplied by the scale factor.
- If the scale factor is between 0 and 1 the shape gets smaller.
- If the scale factor is negative, the shape is inverted.
- If a shape is enlarged to another, the two shapes are similar. The scale factor is the ratio between pairs of corresponding sides.
- When stating that two shapes are similar, the order of lettering is important.

Activity 19

Squares can be fitted together to make a similar shape, as shown below.

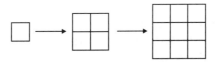

L shapes can also be fitted together to make similar shapes.

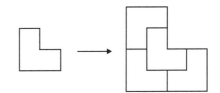

So can *certain* trapezia.

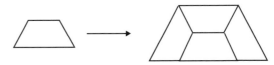

Investigate shapes that can be joined together to make similar shapes.

1   Copy the diagram on a grid. Enlarge the
    shape by a scale factor of 1.5 with A as
    the centre of enlargement.

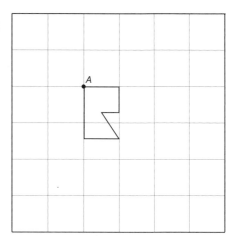

2   **A** is an enlargement of the shaded shape. What are
    the coordinates of the centre of enlargement, and
    what is the scale factor?

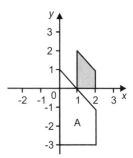

3   Triangle **A** is an enlargement
    of triangle **B**. State the scale
    factor of the enlargement,
    and find x and y.

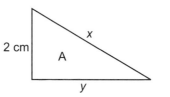

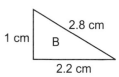

4   Make a copy of the diagram. If $\triangle P'Q'R'$ is an
    enlargement of $\triangle PQR$, find the centre of
    enlargement and the scale factor.

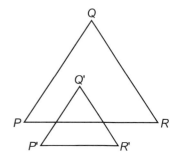

5 Make a copy of the diagram. Make an enlargement of the rhombus, with centre O and scale factor 2.2. Write down the length of the image of the side AB.

6 A rectangle is 6 cm by 2 cm. What are the lengths of the sides of this rectangle, after an enlargement
    a of scale factor −2   **b** of scale factor −0.4?

7 Calculate the lengths of SR and UO.

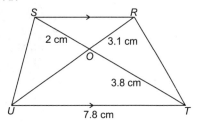

8 These two triangles are similar. Find x and y.

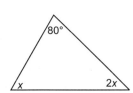
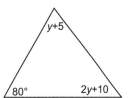

Puzzles 19

1 a Show that $\triangle ABC$ is similar to $\triangle BDC$.
    b Show that

$$\frac{x}{a} = \frac{a}{b} \quad \text{and} \quad \frac{b-x}{c} = \frac{c}{b}$$

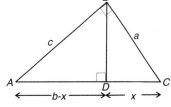

Hence prove Pythagoras' theorem,
that $b^2 = a^2 + c^2$.

2 A rectangle $ABCD$ is enlarged by scale factor 2 from D, to $A'B'C'D'$, The result is enlarged by scale factor $\frac{1}{3}$ from D'. What single transformation is equivalent to the two combined enlargements?

3 What other transformation is equivalent to an enlargement of scale factor −1?

20 Area and volume ratio

20.1

Look at the diagram. It shows a square **A**, 1 cm by 1 cm, and a larger square **B**, 4 cm by 4 cm. The scale factor of the enlargement from **A** to **B** is 1 : 4.

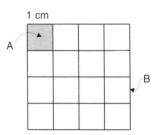

If you look at the *area* of **A** and the area of **B**, they are 1 cm^2 and 16 cm^2 respectively. The area ratio for the enlargement from **A** to **B** is therefore 1 : 16 and *not* 1 : 4. This is because area occupies *two* dimensions in space.

The linear scale factor = 1 : 4
The area scale factor = $1^2 : 4^2 = 1 : 16$

The scale factor of the enlargement shown below is 1 : 2.5

The area of **A** is 4 cm^2
The area of **B** is 25 cm^2

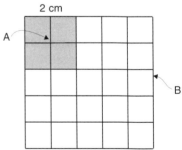

The ratio of the areas is equal to

$$4 : 25 = 1 : 6.25$$

But $6.25 = 2.5^2$
Hence the ratio of the areas = $1^2 : 2.5^2$

Since the ratio 1 : 2.5 = 2 : 5 and the ratio of the areas is 4 : 25, we have the result summarised in the rule:

> R U L E
>
> **If the linear scale factor of an enlargement is $a : b$, then the area scale factor of the enlargement is $a^2 : b^2$.**

EXAMPLE 1

The diagram shows two similar
triangles *ABC* and *PQR*. If the area
of the larger triangle is 12 cm², find
the area of the smaller triangle.

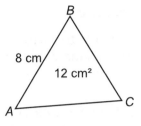
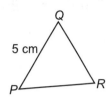

Solution
The linear scale factor = 8 : 5
The area scale factor = $8^2 : 5^2 = 64 : 25$

$$= 1 : \frac{25}{64}$$

The area of the smaller triangle = $12 \times \frac{25}{64}$

$$= 3 \times \frac{25}{16} = \frac{75}{16}$$

$$= 4\frac{11}{16} \text{ cm}^2$$

Exercise 20.1A

1 The diagram shows two similar
   triangles *RTU* and ABC. If the
   area of the smaller triangle is
   5 cm², find the area of the larger
   triangle.

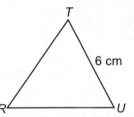
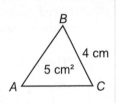

2 A plan of a room has area 250 cm². Find the area of the room if the plan is to
   a scale of 1 : 20.

3 Two regular pentagons have sides of length 6 cm and 9 cm. What is the ratio
   of the areas of the pentagons? Simplify your answer.

4 Two circles have radii 2 cm and 3 cm respectively. What is the ratio of their
   areas?

5 A photograph has area 80 cm². It is enlarged by a linear scale factor of 1 : 4.
   What is the area of the enlarged photograph?

6 A photocopy of a picture is an enlargement of the original by a scale factor of
   1 : 1.5. If the area of the enlargement is 90 cm², what is the area of the
   original?

7 The sides of a triangle are increased by a factor of 1.6. If the area of the
   triangle was 25 m², what is it after the increase?

8 A certain television screen has area 500 cm² and a diagonal of length 32 cm.
   The next largest size of screen is the same shape, but with diagonal 40 cm.
   What is the area of the next size of screen?

9 Soup cans are made in two sizes. The cans are the same shape, but one has
   height 8 cm and the other 10 cm. If the surface area of the larger can is
   480 cm², what is the surface area of the smaller can?

10 Each of a set of four tables has the same shape, but their heights are 50 cm,
    60 cm, 70 cm and 80 cm. The area of the top of the second smallest is
    900 cm². What are the areas of the tops of the other tables?

Finding the linear scale factor

If you know the area scale factor, then since the operation of taking the square root is the reverse of square, we have the rule:

> **R U L E**
>
> **If the area scale factor of an enlargement is $m : n$, then the linear scale factor of the enlargement is $\sqrt{m} : \sqrt{n}$**

The next example shows how to use this rule. You will need tables of square roots.

EXAMPLE 2

A circle has radius 8 cm. What is the radius of a circle with twice the area?

Solution
Since all circles are similar:
Area scale factor $= 1 : 2$
Linear scale factor $= \sqrt{1} : \sqrt{2}$
$\qquad\qquad\qquad = 1 : 1.414$
The radius of the larger circle $= 8 \times 1.414$ cm
$\qquad\qquad\qquad\qquad\qquad = 11.3$ cm (3 sig figs)

> **N O T E**
> All circles are similar.

Sometimes, questions about enlargements use percentages. They can be tackled using the idea of a multiplier.

EXAMPLE 3

The sides of a rectangle are increased by 20%. Find the percentage increase in the area of the rectangle.

Solution
An increase of 20% is the same as using a multiplying factor of 1.20.
Hence, the linear scale factor $= 1 : 1.20$
The area scale factor $\qquad = 1 : 1.20^2$
$\qquad\qquad\qquad\qquad\quad = 1 : 1.44$
A multiplier of 1.44 corresponds to an increase of 44%.
Hence the area is increased by 44%.

Exercise 20.1B

1   A photograph is enlarged so that its area increases from 20 cm^2 to 51.2 cm^2. Find the scale factor of the enlargement.

2   The labels on two sizes of bottle are similar rectangles. The areas of the labels are in the ratio 16 : 25. Find the measurements of the smaller label, if the larger label measures 5.5 cm by 3.5 cm.

3   Paper is made in sizes A1, A2, A3 etc. The shapes are similar. The area of A3 paper is twice the area of A4 paper. If A4 paper measures 210 mm by 300 mm, find the dimensions of A3 paper.

4   A5 paper has half the area of A4 paper (see the previous question). What are the dimensions of A4 paper?

5   Two similar rectangles have areas 80 cm² and 60 cm². The length of the smaller rectangle is 12 cm. What is the length of the larger rectangle?

6   Two circles have areas in the ratio 2:3. If the radius of the smaller circle is 1.8 cm what is the radius of the larger circle?

7   A balloon is inflated so that its diameter is increased by 15%. Find the percentage increase in the surface area. (Assume the balloon is a sphere.)

8   The sides of a standard size television screen are 10% greater than the sides of an economy screen. If the economy screen has area 800 cm², what is the area of the standard screen?

9   A national park is enlarged, so that its lengths increase by 5%. If the area used to be 100 km², what is the new area?

10   The area of a circular lake increased by 20%. What is the percentage increase in its radius?

11   A new version of football has a pitch whose area is 40% less than the standard size. Assuming that the pitches have the same shape, what is the percentage decrease in the length of the pitch?

12   A photograph is enlarged so that its area increases by 80%. Find the percentage increase in its sides.

20.2   Changing units

The diagram shows a 1 cm square, divided into mm. There are 10 mm in 1 cm, but notice there are 10×10, i.e. 100, mm² in 1 cm².

1 cm $= 10$ mm. But 1 cm² $= 100$ mm².

Similarly, there are 100^2 cm² in 1 m².

1 m $= 100$ cm. But 1 m² $= 10\ 000$ cm²

In general, to convert area units, square the factor for length units.

EXAMPLE 4

A scale model of a car is made. The length of the model is 40 cm, the length of the actual car is 4 metres. If the area of the actual car door is 1.5 m² what is the area of the model car door in cm²?

Solution
The linear scale factor is 40 cm to 4 m

$$= 40 \text{ cm to } 400 \text{ cm}$$

$$= 1 : 10$$

Hence the area scale factor $= 1^2 : 10^2 = 1 : 100$
The area of the real door $= 1.5$ m^2
The area of the model door $= 1.5 \div 100$
$= 0.015$ m^2
To change m^2 into cm^2 needs the fact that 1 m $= 100$ cm
So 1 m$^2 = 1$ m $\times 1$ m $= 100$ cm $\times 100$ cm
$= 10\,000$ cm^2
The area of the car door $= 0.015 \times 10\,000$
$= 150$ cm^2

Maps

When a map is drawn, it is a reduction in size of the land it represents. It can be thought of as a similar shape. Since the map is very small compared to the real thing, large numbers are involved. Often a map will be drawn using a scale of 1 : 50 000. However, you can make the working easier by using methods similar to those in the next example.

EXAMPLE 5

A map is drawn to a scale of 1 : 20 000. Find the area in km^2 of a lake which has an area of 15 cm^2 on the map.

Solution
The linear scale factor $= 1 : 20\,000$
This means that 1 cm represents 20 000 cm.
To convert cm to km you divide by 100 000
Hence 1 cm represents 20 000 $\div$ 100 000 $= 0.2$ km.
The ratio is 1 cm : 0.2 km
The area scale factor is 1^2cm$^2 : 0.2^2$km^2
1cm$^2 : 0.04$km^2
Hence an area of 15 cm^2 represents $15 \times 0.04 = 0.6$ km^2

Exercise 20.2

1 A diagram of a house shows the floor as an area of 200 cm^2. If the scale of the map is 1 : 80 find the area of the real floor. Give your answer in m^2.
2 A model of a sailing ship is in the scale 1 : 200. The area of the real sails is 480 m^2. Find the area of the sails of the model. Give your answer in cm^2.
3 A map is drawn to a scale of 1 : 50 000. Find the values on the map of
   a the length of a 20 km railway line in cm
   b the area of a 25 km^2 lake in cm^2.
4 A map has been drawn to a scale of 1 : n. If an area of forest known to be 400 km^2 is represented by an area of 25 cm^2 on the map, find the value of n.
5 A map is drawn to a scale of 1 : 50 000. How would you convert cm^2 on the map into km^2?
6 A map is drawn to a scale of 1 : 40 000. Find the area of a region in km^2 if it covers an approximate rectangle measuring 15 cm by 12 cm on the map.

The diagram shows a cube which has been enlarged by a scale factor 3. There are 27 cubes in the larger one, and so the volume ratio $= 1 : 27$
$$= 1^3 : 3^3$$
This is because a cube occupies *three* dimensions in space, and so there is a linear $1 : 3$ enlargement in three directions.

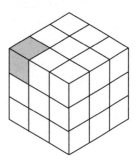

We can state in the same way as for areas the following:

> **RULE**
>
> **If a shape is enlarged by a linear scale factor of $m : n$, the volumes are enlarged in the ratio $m^3 : n^3$.**
> **If the volume ratio of similar figures is $a : b$, then the linear scale factor is $\sqrt[3]{a} : \sqrt[3]{b}$**

You will need to look back at how to find roots (page 96). Answers are usually given to 3 significant figures when they do not come out as whole numbers.
Note The mass of an object is proportional to its volume. So if two solids are similar in the ratio $a : b$, then their masses are in the ratio $a^3 : b^3$.

EXAMPLE 6

Two spanners are similar in the ratio $2 : 3$. The mass of the smaller spanner is 0.16 kg. What is the mass of the larger spanner?

Solution
The ratio of the volumes, and hence of the masses, is $2^3 : 3^3$. This is $8 : 27$.
Multiply 0.16 by $\frac{27}{8}$.
$$0.16 \times \frac{27}{8} = 0.54$$
The mass of the larger spanner is 0.54 kg

EXAMPLE 7

Two spheres have surface areas in the ratio $9 : 25$. Find the ratio of their volumes.

Solution
The area scale factor $= 9 : 25$
The linear scale factor $= \sqrt{9} : \sqrt{25}$
$\qquad\qquad\qquad\quad = 3 : 5$
The volume ratio $\qquad = 3^3 : 5^3$
$\qquad\qquad\qquad\quad = 27 : 125$

> **NOTE**
> All spheres are similar.

EXAMPLE 8

Two similar bottles contain 3 litres and 2 litres of a soft drink. If the height of the larger bottle is 25 cm, what is the height of the smaller bottle?

Solution

The volumes are in the ratio 2 : 3, which is 1 : 1.5.
The linear scale factor is $1 : \sqrt[3]{1.5}$.
The height of the smaller bottle is $25 \div \sqrt[3]{1.5}$
The height is 21.8 cm

Number	Log
25	1.3979
1.5	0.1791
$\sqrt[3]{1.5}$	0.0587 ($\div$ by 3)
21.84	1.3392

EXAMPLE 9

A weather balloon is inflated by 25%. What is the percentage increase in the surface area of the balloon?

Solution

If the volume *increases* by 25%, this is the same as using a volume multiplier of 1.25.

The volume ratio $= 1 : 1.25$
The linear scale factor $= 1 : \sqrt[3]{1.25}$
$\qquad\qquad\qquad\quad = 1 : 1.077$
The area scale factor $= 1 : 1.077^2$
$\qquad\qquad\qquad\quad = 1 : 1.16$

If the area is multiplied by 1.16, then the percentage increase is 16%.

Exercise 20.3

1 Two packets of sugar are similar, with their sides in the ratio 4 : 5. If the smaller packet contains 800 cm³ of sugar, what does the larger packet contain?

2 Two bottles of juice are similar, with their heights in the ratio 3 : 4. If the larger bottle contains 1.2 litres of juice, what does the smaller bottle contain?

3 Two solid spheres have radii in the ratio 1 : 3. If the volume of the smaller sphere is 21 cm³ find the volume of the larger sphere.

4 The sides of a 'Super' packet of butter are 1.5 times the sides of a 'Standard' packet. If the 'Standard' packet contains 200 cm³ find how much the 'Super' packet contains.

5 Two spheres have volumes in the ratio 1 : 2. Find the ratio between their radii.

6 Two bottles of oil contain 2 litres and 1.5 litres. The bottles are similar. If the height of the larger bottle is 20 cm find the height of the smaller bottle.

7 Two similar cans of soup contain 800 cm³ and 1000 cm³. If the radius of the smaller can is 3 cm find the radius of the larger can.

8 Two spheres have volumes 8 cm³ and 27 cm³. What is the ratio of the surface areas of the spheres?

9 The corresponding sides of two similar bricks are 15 cm and 20 cm. What is the ratio of their volumes? Simplify your answers.

10 Two similar metal bars are made from the same material. If the lengths of the bars are 8 cm and 12 cm, find the ratio of their masses. If the mass of the smaller bar is 160 g, what is the mass of the larger bar?

11 The volumes of two similar cans are 80 cm³ and 200 cm³. Find **a** the ratio of the heights **b** the ratio of the surface areas of the cans.

12 A spherical balloon is inflated so that its radius increases by 20%. If the volume was 400 cm³, what is it after the increase?

13 A mango grew so that all its dimensions increased by 10%. If its volume was 100 cm³ before the increase, what was it after the increase?

14 A balloon is inflated by 20%. What is the percentage increase in the surface area?

20.4 Frustum of a cone

If the top part of a cone A is removed by a plane cut parallel to the base, the remaining bottom part B is called a **frustum** of a cone.

The ideas of similar figures and enlargements can be used with frustums.

The part cut off is similar to the original cone.

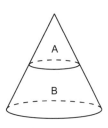
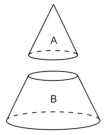

EXAMPLE 10

A cone, of base radius 8 cm and slanting edge length 20 cm, is cut half way along the edge by a plane parallel to the base. What is the radius of the top of the frustum formed?

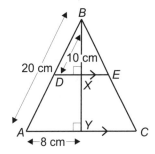

Solution
Triangle *BXD* is similar to triangle *BYA*.

So $\dfrac{DX}{8} = \dfrac{10}{20}$, hence $DX = \dfrac{10 \times 8}{20} = 4$ cm

The radius of the top of the frustum is 4 cm.

EXAMPLE 11

A frustum is made from a cone of height 10 cm. If the radius of the top is 4 cm, and the radius of the bottom is 5 cm, what is the height of the frustum? What is the ratio of the curved surface area of the frustum to that of the cone?

Solution

Let the height of the frustum be h cm. Then the height of the cone removed is $10 - h$ cm.

Using similar triangles $\dfrac{10 - h}{10} = \dfrac{4}{5}$

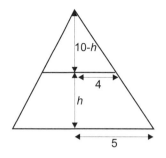

So
$$50 - 5h = 40$$
$$10 = 5h$$
$$h = 2$$

The height of the frustum is 2 cm.

The linear scale factor for the removed cone to the complete cone
$$= 4 : 5$$

The ratio of the curved surface areas of the two cones
$$= 16 : 25$$

The ratio of curved surface area of the frustum to the complete cone
$$= 25 - 16 : 25$$
$$= 9 : 25$$

Exercise 20.4

1 A cone is cut by a plane parallel to the base halfway up. The original cone had volume 80 cm³ and curved surface area 100 cm².
   a What is the volume of the cone cut off?
   b What is the volume of the remaining frustum?
   c What is the curved surface area of the cone cut off?
   d What is the curved surface area of the remaining frustum?

2 A frustum is made by cutting the top 5 cm from a cone of height 20 cm. The base radius of the original cone is 8 cm.
   a What is the top radius of the frustum?
   b What is the ratio between the volumes of the original cone and the frustum?
   c What is the ratio between the curved surface areas of the original cone and the frustum?

3 A lampshade is in the shape of a frustum of a cone with measurements as shown in the diagram. What would be the height of the cone for which the frustum is the lower part?

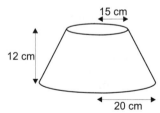

4 A solid frustum is made from a cone. The height of the frustum is 10 cm, the top radius is 20 cm and the bottom radius is 30 cm.
   a Find the height of the cone
   b The original cone had mass 100 kg. What is the mass of the frustum?

5 A block of wood is in the shape of a frustum, with height 8 cm, top radius 3 cm and bottom radius 5 cm.
  a Find the height of the cone of which the frustum is the lower part.
  b The block has mass 300 grams. What would be the mass of the original cone?

6 A cone of slanting edge 30 cm and base radius 10 cm is cut parallel to the base one third of the way from the base along the slanting edge.
Find
  a the height of the frustum made
  b the ratio of the volume of the cone removed to the volume of the complete cone.

7 How would you cut a cone with a plane parallel to the base, so that the resulting two parts had the same volume?

Summary

- If a shape is enlarged by a scale factor k, areas will be enlarged by a scale factor k^2 and volumes by a scale factor k^3.
- Map scales can sometimes be worked with, as a ratio of different units.

Activity 20

Tiles
Floor tiles measure $\frac{1}{2}$ m by $\frac{1}{2}$ m. What is the *minimum* number of tiles that are needed to cover a floor that measures
(a) 10 m by 8 m
(b) $7\frac{1}{2}$ m by $6\frac{1}{2}$ m
(c) 8.6 m by 7.8 m
(d) x m by y m.

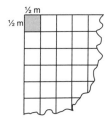

Progress exercise 20

1 A square with an area of 8.6 cm² is enlarged by a scale factor 5. What is the area of the enlarged square?
2 Two circles have diameters 5 cm and 8 cm. What is the ratio of their areas?
3 A football of radius 15 cm is deflated by 20% of its volume. What is the new radius of the ball?
4 A map is drawn to a scale of 1 : 30 000. The winding river appears to be about 15 cm long. What is its length in km?
5 Tiles measuring 0.75 m by 0.75 m are laid on a large floor measuring 30 m by $22\frac{1}{2}$ m. No tiles are broken. How many tiles are needed?

6 Two similar containers have volumes in the ratio 5 : 8. Find the ratios of the surface areas of the containers.

7 A balloon has a volume of 150 cm³. It is inflated on two occasions and each time its radius is increased by 10%. What is the final volume of the balloon?

1 A cone of slant height 20 cm is cut into two pieces by a plane one third of the distance from the base along the slant edge and parallel to the base. Show that the volume of the cone and the frustum formed are in the ratio 8 : 19.

2 A cylinder is altered in size by increasing the radius by 40%, and reducing the height by 20%. If the volume of the cylinder is originally 100 cm³, what will be the volume of the altered cylinder?

3 In the diagram, *B* divides *AC* in the ratio 2 : 1. Find the ratio of the area of triangle *ABE* to the area of the parallelogram *EBFD*.

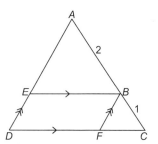

21 Solving right-angled triangles

This unit uses
- The three trigonometrical ratios
- Pythagoras' theorem
- Tables for trigonometrical functions and logarithms

21.1 Use of sine, cosine and tangent ratios

In Units 14 and 15 you used the trigonometric ratios sine, cosine and tangent. Often it is hard to decide which to use.

If you know one side and one angle (other than the right angle) of a right-angled triangle, then you can find the other sides.

If you know two sides of a right-angled triangle, then you can find the angles.

In both cases you use a ratio: sine, cosine or tangent. Follow these steps to make sure you use the correct ratio.

- Label the right-angle of the triangle.

- The side farthest from the right angle is the hypotenuse. Label this HYP.

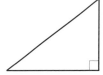

- There is an angle that you know, or want to know. Mark this angle.

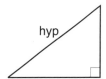

- The side farthest from the angle is the opposite side. Label this OPP.

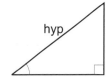

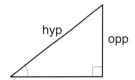

- The side next to the angle is the adjacent side. Label this ADJ.

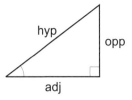

If you are finding a side, you know one other side. If you are finding an angle, you know two sides. In both cases, you are interested in two sides. Write down the correct ratio, according to the list below.

- If the sides are OPP and HYP, write down the formula for sin.
- If the sides are ADJ and HYP, write down the formula for cos.
- If the sides are OPP and ADJ, write down the formula for tan.

Now find the unknown side or unknown angle, by the methods so far.

EXAMPLE 1

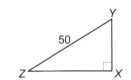

In the triangle XYZ, $X = 90°$, $YZ = 50$ and $Y = 63°12'$. Find YX.

Solution

Follow the steps carefully. The right angle is already marked, at X. The side farthest from X is YZ. Label this HYP.

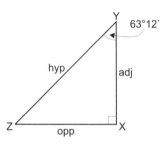

The other angle we know is at Y, so label this $63°12'$. The side farthest from Y is the opposite side, XZ. Label this OPP.

The side next to Y is the adjacent side, YX. Label this ADJ.

This diagram shows the triangle with all the sides labelled.

We *know* the HYP side, and we *want to know* the ADJ side. The formula which connects HYP and ADJ is cos. Write down the formula for cos.

$$\cos 63°12' = \frac{\text{adj}}{\text{hyp}} = \frac{YX}{50}$$

From tables, $\cos 63° 12' = 0.4509$

$$0.4509 = \frac{YX}{50}$$

Hence $YX = 50 \times 0.4509 = 22.545$
$YX = 22.5$ (correct to 3 significant figures).

EXAMPLE 2

A radio mast is held vertical by two ropes, which are 40 m long. These ropes make $37°$ with the ground. How tall is the mast?

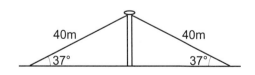

Solution

The mast is vertical, so it makes $90°$ with the ground. Mark in the right-angle. Farthest from this is the rope, so mark this length with HYP.

The angle of 37° is between the rope and the ground. Mark in this angle.
Farthest from this angle is the mast, so mark this with OPP.
The distance between the base of the
mast and the base of the rope is the ADJ.
The diagram shows the triangle with all
the sides labelled.

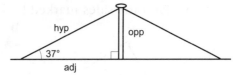

We know the HYP and we want to know the OPP. The ratio which connects HYP
and OPP is sin. Write down the sin formula.

$$\sin 37° = \frac{\text{opp}}{\text{hyp}} = \frac{\text{opp}}{40}$$

By tables find that, sin 37° = 0.6018.

$$0.6018 = \frac{\text{opp}}{40}$$

Multiply by 40, to obtain OPP = 40 × 0.6018 = 24.07.
The height of the mast is 24.1 m (correct to 3 significant figures).

EXAMPLE 3

A vertical cliff is 60 m high. A boat is on a lake, 200 m from the base of the cliff.
What is the angle of elevation of the top of the cliff from the boat?

Solution

The cliff makes 90° with the water. Mark this angle as a right angle. Mark the side
opposite with HYP.
We want to find the angle of elevation, which is the angle between the line from
the boat to the cliff and the horizontal. Mark this angle as $P°$.
The side farthest from $P°$ is the cliff. Mark this as OPP. The side next to $P°$ is the
distance from the boat to the base of the cliff. Mark this as ADJ.
This diagram shows the triangle with all the sides
labelled.

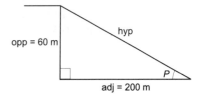

We know OPP and ADJ. The ratio connecting these sides is tan. Write down the
tan formula.

$$\tan P° = \frac{\text{opp}}{\text{adj}} = \frac{60}{200} = 0.3$$

Hence $P° = \tan^{-1} 0.3$. Using tables, $\tan^{-1} 0.3 = 16°42'$.
The angle of elevation is $16°42'$.

> **NOTE**
> Make sure that you use the correct ratio. If you are not sure which to use,
> then label the sides with HYP, OPP and ADJ.

Exercise 21.1

1   Find the sides marked by letters in these triangles.

a 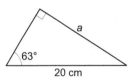   **b** 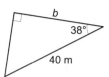   **c**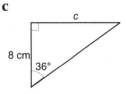

2   Find the angles marked by letters in these triangles.

a 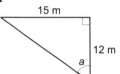   **b** 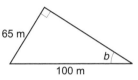   **c**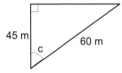

3   Triangle ABC is right-angled at B. In each of the following cases find the side or angle.
a $AB = 4$ cm and $BC = 6$ cm. Find $\angle BAC$.
b $AC = 8$ cm and $\angle BCA = 53°$. Find BC.
c $AC = 10$ cm and $CB = 7$ cm. Find $\angle BAC$.
d $AB = 40$ m and $\angle BAC = 29°$. Find CB.

4   A rectangle is 10 cm by 8 cm. What is the angle between the diagonal and the longer side?

5   The neck of a giraffe is 2 m long, and its shoulders are 2.5 m above the ground. If the neck is at 22° to the vertical, how high above the ground can it reach?

6   A beam of length 1.6 m leans against a wall, reaching 1.2 m up the wall. What is the angle between the beam and the ground?

7   I travel 80 km on a bearing of 058°. How far North have I gone?

21.2

If you use tables for these problems, then the calculations can be complicated. At the end of this book there are three sets of tables, giving the logarithms of the sine, cosine and tangent functions. If you use these tables, then the calculation is quicker. You can look up the logarithm of a sine in one operation, instead of having to find the sine first and then its logarithm.

EXAMPLE 4

Suppose you want to find a side AB, where

$$\sin 27°24' = \frac{AB}{32.49}$$

Solution

$AB = 32.49 \times \sin 27°24'$. Look up the logarithm of 32.49. Look up 27°24′ in the log sin table. Then add, and look up the antilog. The calculation is set out below.

Number	Log
32.49	1.5117
sin 27°24′	$\bar{1}$.6629
14.95	1.1746

Hence $AB = 14.95$

EXAMPLE 5

You want to find an angle $x°$, where

$$\tan x° = \frac{97.2}{54.8}$$

Use logarithms to divide 97.2 by 54.8, leaving the answer as a logarithm. Look up this logarithm in the log tan table. This gives the angle directly. The calculations are below.

Number	Log
97.2	1.9877
54.8	1.7388
	0.2489

Use the log tan table to find the angle corresponding to 0.2489. This is 60°35′. The angle is 60°35′.

Exercise 21.2

In this exercise use the log sine, log cosine and log tangent tables.

1 Find the lengths marked by letters in the triangles below.

   a   **b**   **c**

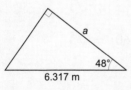
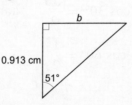
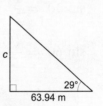

2 Find the angles marked by letters in the triangles below.

   a   **b**   **c**

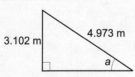
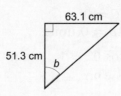
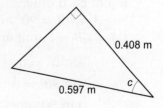

3 Evaluate these expressions.

a $\dfrac{7.321 \times \cos 54°}{\sin 63°}$ **b** $\dfrac{\tan 58°}{61.22 \times \cos 52°}$

c $\sin^{-1}\left(\dfrac{0.562 \times \sin 51°}{0.6733}\right)$ **d** $\cos^{-1}\left(\dfrac{4.553^2}{\sqrt{884.5}}\right)$

21.3 Special angles

There are special angles, for which we do not need the tables.

45°

The diagram shows an isosceles right-angled triangle.
$\angle A = 90°$, $AB = AC = 1$ unit.
It follows that $BC = \sqrt{1^2 + 1^2} = \sqrt{2}$ units (Pythagoras'
theorem), and that $\angle B = \angle C = 45°$. Hence

$$\sin 45° = \frac{1}{\sqrt{2}} \quad \cos 45° = \frac{1}{\sqrt{2}} \quad \tan 45° = 1$$

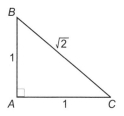

60° and 30°

The diagram shows an equilateral triangle of side 2 units.
Drop a perpendicular from A to the midpoint D of BC.
Then $BD = 1$ unit.
It follows that
$AD = \sqrt{2^2 - 1^2} = \sqrt{3}$ units, $\angle B = 60°$ and $\angle DAB = 30°$.

$$\sin 30° = \frac{1}{2} \quad \cos 30° = \frac{\sqrt{3}}{2} \quad \tan 30° = \frac{1}{\sqrt{3}}$$

$$\sin 60° = \frac{\sqrt{3}}{2} \quad \cos 60° = \frac{1}{2} \quad \tan 60° = \sqrt{3}$$

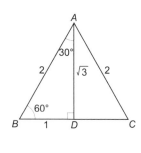

0° and 90°

The diagram shows a triangle in which two sides
are getting closer together. Eventually they lie on
top of each other.
So $\angle A = \angle B = 90°$ and $\angle C = 0°$.
$CA = CB = 1$ unit and $AB = 0$ units.

$$\sin 0° = 0 \quad \cos 0° = 1 \quad \tan 0° = 0$$

$$\sin 90° = 1 \quad \cos 90° = 0$$

$\tan 90°$ does not exist, as you cannot divide by 0.

Exercise 21.3

Write up the results above by completing the table below.

	0°	30°	45°	60°	90°
sin					
cos					
tan					

This table should be learned by heart

21.4 Relationships between the ratios

You know three trigonometric ratios: sin, cos and tan. But if you know one of them, then you can find the other two.

There are several important equations linking sin, cos and tan, which are true for all angles.

(a) $\tan x = \dfrac{\sin x}{\cos x}$

(b) $\cos^2 x + \sin^2 x = 1$ (Note that $\cos^2 x$ means $(\cos x)^2$, and so on.)

(c) $\sin x = \cos(90° - x)$ and $\cos x = \sin(90° - x)$

Proof

(a) Use the definitions of sin and cos.

$$\frac{\sin x}{\cos x} = \frac{\frac{\text{opp}}{\text{hyp}}}{\frac{\text{adj}}{\text{hyp}}} = \frac{\text{opp}}{\text{adj}} \quad \text{(cancelling hyp)}$$

Notice that this is the definition of tan. Hence

$$\tan x = \frac{\sin x}{\cos x}$$

(b) In the diagram the hypotenuse is 1 unit.
Hence the adjacent side is $1 \times \cos x$, and the opposite side is $\sin x$. Now use Pythagoras' theorem

$$(\cos x)^2 + (\sin x)^2 = 1$$

That is, $\cos^2 x + \sin^2 x = 1$

(c) In this diagram, a is the opposite side for angle x and the adjacent side for angle $90° - x$. For both angles, b is the hypotenuse. Hence
$$\sin x = \tfrac{a}{b} = \cos(90° - x)$$

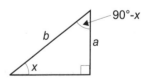

EXAMPLE 6

If $\sin x = \frac{7}{25}$ find $\cos x$ and $\tan x$.

Solution
The opposite side is 7 and the hypotenuse is 25.
By Pythagoras' theorem, the third side, the adjacent, is $\sqrt{25^2 - 7^2} = 24$.
Hence $\cos x = \frac{24}{25}$ and $\tan x = \frac{7}{24}$.

EXAMPLE 7

Find x if $\sin x = \cos 43°$.

Solution

We know that $\cos 43° = \sin (90°- 43°)$

$$= \sin 47°$$

$x = 47°$

Exercise 21.4

1   If $\sin x = \frac{4}{5}$, find $\cos x$ and $\tan x$.
2   If $\cos x = \frac{5}{13}$, find $\sin x$ and $\tan x$.
3   If $\tan x = \frac{16}{30}$, find $\sin x$ and $\cos x$.
4   If $\sin x = 0.3$, find $\cos x$ and $\tan x$, giving your answer correct to 3 significant figures.
5   If $\cos x = 0.4$, find $\sin x$ and $\tan x$, giving your answer correct to 3 significant figures.
6   If $\tan x = 1.2$, find $\sin x$ and $\cos x$, giving your answer correct to 3 significant figures.
7   Solve these equations
   a $\sin x = \cos 77°$ **b** $\cos y = \sin 51°$
8   If $\cos x = 5k$ and $\sin x = 6k$, find k. Hence find x.
9   Suppose $\sin x = 2 \times \cos x$. Find $\tan x$, and hence find x.
10   Solve the equation $\sin y = \frac{1}{2} \cos y$.
11   If $3 \sin x = 5 \cos x$ find x.
12   Suppose $\tan x = 2 \sin x$, and $x \neq 0°$. Find $\cos x$, and hence find x.
13   Solve the equation $\tan x = 3 \sin x$, given that $x \neq 0°$.
14   Solve the equation $\sin x = \cos (x + 30°)$.
15   Solve the equation $\cos x = \sin 2x$.

Summary

- To find out which of sin, cos or tan to use, label the sides of the right-angled triangle.
- The use of log sin, log cos or log tan tables shortens calculations.
- The sin, cos and tan of $0°$, $30°$, $45°$, $60°$ and $90°$ can by found without using tables.
- There are important equations linking sin, cos and tan.

$$\tan x = \frac{\sin x}{\cos x} \qquad \cos^2 x + \sin^2 x = 1$$

$$\sin x = \cos (90° - x) \qquad \cos x = \sin (90° - x)$$

Trigonometry is over 2000 years old. It was developed by a Greek mathematician and astronomer called Hipparchus.

The first trigonometric ratio was the **chord** ratio. It is the ratio of the chord in a circle to the radius. The diagram shows a circle with radius r. The chord of the angle of the sector is written crd x.

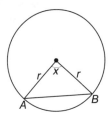

$$\text{crd } x = \frac{AB}{r}$$

1 Find (a) crd $60°$ (b) crd $120°$.
2 Find a rule giving crd x in terms of the sine ratio.
3 Find a rule giving sin x in terms of the crd ratio.

Progress exercise 21

1 Find the sides and angles marked by letters in these triangles.

   a   **b**   **c**   **d**

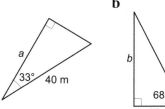

2 Evaluate these expressions.

   a $\dfrac{6.336 \times \cos 33°}{\sin 47°}$ **b** $\tan^{-1}\left(\dfrac{81.44}{32.49}\right)$

3 Without referring to page 224, write down the values of
   a $\sin 30°$ **b** $\cos 45°$ **c** $\tan 0°$

4 Suppose $\cos x = \frac{4}{5}$. Without using tables, find the values of sin x and tan x.

5 Find z, if $\cos z = \sin 27°$.

6 Solve these equations.
   a $2 \times \sin x = 3 \times \cos x$ **b** $\sin (x + 10°) = \cos (x - 30°)$

7 Find m, if $\cos x = 2m$ and $\sin x = 3m$.

Puzzles 21

1 Without using tables, simplify the expression
     $\cos 42° \sin 48° + \sin 42° \cos 48°$.

2 Show that
$$\frac{1}{\cos^2 x} = 1 + \tan^2 x \qquad \frac{1}{\sin^2 x} = 1 + \frac{1}{\tan^2 x}$$

3 Solve the equation $\tan x = \dfrac{4}{\tan x}$.

4 Solve the equation $\tan x = 3 \cos x$.

Consolidation exercises

1 A straight path up a hillside is 200 m long. It rises 25 m.
   a Find the horizontal distance of the path.
   b Find the gradient of the path.
2 Find the gradient of the line joining the following pairs of points.
   a (2, 4) and (5, 7)
   b (−2, 3) and (5, 6)
   c (4, −1) and (−4, 15)
3 The line joining (1, 1) and (2, k) has gradient 5. Find k.
4 Find the gradients and intercepts of these lines.
   a $y = 7x - 2$
   b $3y + 2x = 24$
5 Find the equations of these lines:
   a with gradient 3 and through (2, −3)
   b through the points (3, 6) and (1, 8).
6 A new town is founded. 10 years later its population is 50 000, and 5 years after that its population is 58 000. Let the population be P and the time after founding be t years. Assuming there is a linear relationship between P and t, find an equation giving P in terms of t.
7 Find the equations of these lines:
   a parallel to $y = 3x + 2$ and through (−1, 4)
   b perpendicular to $y = 2x - 1$ and through (4, 2)
   c perpendicular to $3y + 2x = 1$ and through (1, −2).
8 Find the distance between these pairs of points.
   a (1, 3) and (6, 8)
   b (−2, 7) and (3, −2)
9 The vertices of a quadrilateral are at (4, 3), (14, 23), (28, 21) and (26, 7).
   a Show that the quadrilateral is a kite.
   b Show that the quadrilateral is not a rhombus.
   c Show that the diagonals of the quadrilateral are perpendicular.
10 Find the midpoint of the line joining (3, 7) and (−1, −9).
11 Find the equation of the perpendicular bisector of the line joining (3, 10) and (5, −2)

12 A circle has centre (4, 7) and radius 10. Which of the following points lie on the circle?

   a (10, −1)   **b** (10, 11)   **c** (−6, 7)   **d** (6, 8)

13 The table below gives the ages of 40 people in a village gathering. Put the data into a frequency table.

2	15	29	17	7	39	22	47	41	44
40	5	3	33	20	15	12	7	33	5
6	2	12	33	29	49	58	48	26	4
17	14	20	19	3	7	22	52	31	6

14 The sales of cassettes over five days are given below. Using a round symbol to represent 100 cassettes, draw a pictogram for the data.

Day	Mon	Tue	Wed	Thu	Fri
Sales	250	300	275	315	375

15 The pupils in a class were asked how many brothers or sisters they had. The results are below. Illustrate the information in a bar chart.

Number	0	1	2	3	4	5
Frequency	10	13	7	4	1	1

16 Illustrate the information of question **15** in a pie chart.

17 Every day Mwihaka records the time she has to wait for a bus. The results for 40 days are below.

Time (minutes)	0–4	5–9	10–14	15–20
Frequency	15	12	8	5

Show these figures

   a in a histogram   **b** in a frequency polygon.

18 Draw the lines of symmetry of the shapes below.

19 *ABCD* is a kite but not a rhombus. How many lines of symmetry does it have?

20 Draw a hexagon with exactly two lines of symmetry.

21 Find the equation of the line of symmetry of the quadrilateral in question **9**.

22 Make a copy of this diagram, and reflect the shape in the dotted line.

23 Complete this shape so that both dotted lines are lines of symmetry.

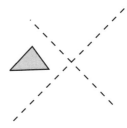

24 Plot the triangle with vertices at (2, 3), (8, 7) and (7, 2). Find the equation of the line of symmetry of the triangle.

25 On graph paper, draw the lines $x = 3$, $y = -2$ and $y = x$.
   a Reflect (2, 7) in the line $x = 3$.
   b Reflect (1, 4) in the line $y = -2$.
   c Reflect (−1, 3) in the line $y = x$.

26 The point (4, 3) is reflected to (7, 3). What is the equation of the mirror line?

27 The point (5, 1) is reflected to (2, 4). What is the equation of the mirror line?

28 *ABCDE* is a regular pentagon. Show that *BD = EC*.

29 A pyramid has a square base, and its vertex is directly above the centre of the square. How many planes of symmetry does the pyramid have?

30 A displacement moves points 3 units left and 2 units up. Write this displacement as a column vector.

31 Find the magnitude of the vector in question **30**.

32 Let $\mathbf{u} = \begin{pmatrix} 4 \\ 7 \end{pmatrix}$ and $\mathbf{v} = \begin{pmatrix} 5 \\ -2 \end{pmatrix}$. Find:

   (i) $3\mathbf{u}$ (ii) $\mathbf{u} + \mathbf{v}$ (iii) $3\mathbf{u} - 2\mathbf{v}$

33 Let *A* be at (3, 7), *B* at (5, 8) and *C* at (9, *k*).

   (i)   Find $\mathbf{AB}$ (ii)   If $\mathbf{AD} = \begin{pmatrix} 7 \\ 1 \end{pmatrix}$ find the coordinates of *D*.

   (iii)   If *A*, *B* and *C* are collinear find *k*.

1 Find the mean of these numbers.
   32   38   41   44   49   50   50   52

2 Use your result for question **1** to find the mean of these numbers.
   0.1232   0.1238   0.1241   0.1244
   0.1249   0.1250   0.1250   0.1252

3 Find the median of the numbers in question **1**.

4 A class contains 12 girls and 18 boys. In a test, the mean of the girls' marks was 42, and the mean for the boys was 40. Find the average for the class as a whole.

5 The table below gives the number of phone calls received in a day by Mrs Mbone over a 20-day period.

Number	0	1	2	3	4	5
Frequency	8	4	4	2	1	1

   a Write down the mode.   **b** Find the mean.   **c** Find the median.

6 The table below gives the number of letters received in a day by a business, over a 60-day period.

Number	0–19	20–39	40–59	60–79	80–100
Frequency	5	16	27	8	4

  a Write down the modal group.   **b** Estimate the mean.
  c Estimate the median.

7 Evaluate these.
  a 5^3 **b** 6^2 **c** $\left(\frac{1}{2}\right)^3$ **d** $(-3)^2$

8 Simplify these expressions.

  a $5^3 \times 5^8$ **b** $x^3 \times x^7$ **c** $2^y \times 2^{3y}$
  d $7^{11} \div 7^5$ **e** $y^8 \div y^3$ **f** $5^{3a} \div 5^a$
  g $(x^3)^5$ **h** $(3y)^3$ **i** $\frac{a^6 \times a^7}{a^3}$
  j $2^x \times 8^{x+1}$ **k** $49^{a+2} \div 7^{a+1}$ **l** $\frac{5^x \times 125^{2x}}{25^{x+2}}$

9 Evaluate these.

  a 17^0 **b** 5^{-1} **c** $64^{\frac{1}{2}}$
  d $27^{\frac{2}{3}}$ **e** $\left(\frac{1}{4}\right)^{-3}$ **f** $16^{-\frac{3}{4}}$

10 Simplify these expressions.
  a $x^4 \div x^{-5}$ **b** $(2m^{-3})^2$ **c** $\sqrt{\left(\frac{2x^3}{8x}\right)}$ **d** $\frac{m^6 n^{-2}}{m^{-3} n^5}$

11 Write these numbers in standard form.
  a 483 000 000   **b** 0.000 002 341

12 Write out these numbers in full.
  a 7.2×10^6 **b** 3.03×10^{-5}

13 Evaluate these expressions, giving your answers in standard form.
  a $3.1 \times 10^7 \times 2 \times 10^3$ **b** $(6.3 \times 10^9) \div (3 \times 10^4)$
  c $4.3 \times 10^{-5} \times 2 \times 10^{-8}$ **d** $(8.2 \times 10^6) \div (2 \times 10^{-3})$
  e $6.2 \times 10^5 \times 2 \times 10^4$ **f** $(2 \times 10^{15}) \div (5 \times 10^9)$
  g $4 \times 10^7 \times 3 \times 10^{-12}$ **h** $(6 \times 10^{-3}) \div (8 \times 10^6)$
  i $3.7 \times 10^8 + 2.1 \times 10^8$ **j** $4.3 \times 10^7 + 6.3 \times 10^6$
  k $5 \times 10^9 - 4 \times 10^8$ **l** $8.3 \times 10^{-7} + 7.2 \times 10^{-8}$

14 A space ship travels at 5.2×10^9 metres per second. How long will it take to cover a distance of 2×10^{19} m?

15 The weight of an empty train is 4.3×10^5 kg. Its cargo weighs 8.1×10^4 kg. What is the total weight of the loaded train?

16 Find these.
  a $\log_4 16$ **b** $\log_3\left(\frac{1}{9}\right)$ **c** $\log_8 2$

17 Use logarithms to evaluate these. Give your answers correct to three significant figures.
  a 3.284×1.226 **b** $8.664 \div 3.292$ **c** $\sqrt[7]{7.734}$
  d 65.33×12.42 **e** $584.4 \div 21.54$ **f** 2.321^{10}
  g 0.3341×0.0219 **h** $0.042\,83 \div 0.000\,1459$ **i** $\sqrt[8]{0.2429}$

18 The surface area of a sphere of radius r is $4\pi r^2$. Find the surface area of a sphere with radius 45.23 cm.

19 If a sum of m shillings is invested for t years at $r\%$ compound interest, it will increase to $m(1 + r/100)^t$. Find the amount that 54 360 sh will increase to after five years at 8.5% compound interest.

20 Expand these expressions, and simplify if possible.

    a $(x + 7)(x - 3)$ **b** $(2a + 3)(3b - 4)$ **c** $(4x - 3)(3x - 5)$

    d $(x - 9)^2$ **e** $(3x + 7)^2$ **f** $(2x - 3)(2x + 3)$

21 Factorise these expressions.

    a $x^2 + 10x + 9$ **b** $x^2 - 8x - 20$ **c** $25x^2 - 9y^2$

    d $3x^2 - 4x - 4$ **e** $5x^2 - 12x + 4$

22 Solve these equations.

    a $x^2 - 9x + 8 = 0$ **b** $x^2 + 6x - 27 = 0$ **c** $2x^2 - 7x + 6 = 0$

    d $x^2 = 5x + 24$ **e** $x + \frac{24}{x} = 11$

23 The length of a rectangle is 4 cm greater than the width. The area is 117 cm². Find the width.

24 Akinyi buys several cabbages at x shillings each, spending 200 shillings. Next day the price is $(x + 5)$ shillings each, and for the same amount of money she can buy 2 fewer cabbages. How many cabbages did she buy on the first day?

25 Find the quadratic equations with roots

    a 3 and 7   **b** –2 and –4   **c** $\frac{1}{3}$ and 6

Consolidation exercise 3 (covers units 11–15)

1 Copy this diagram and rotate the shape through 60° about X.

2 The needle of a compass is pointing due East. The needle rotates through 135°. What direction is it pointing at now?

3 Copy this diagram and rotate the triangle through 90° clockwise about (1, 2).

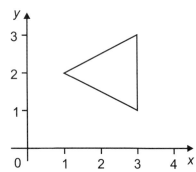

4 Copy this diagram and rotate the triangle through 90° anticlockwise about (2, 1).

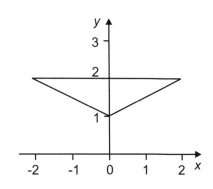

5 Copy this diagram. Find the centre of the rotation which has taken one shape to the other.

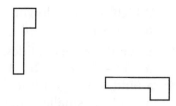

6 The triangle with vertices at (–1, 2), (–2, 2) and (–1, 4) is rotated to the triangle with vertices at (1, 2), (1, 3) and (3, 2). Plot these triangles and find the centre and angle of rotation.

7 What is the order of symmetry of a regular heptagon (7 sides)?

8 Some Chinese characters are shown. For each character, give its order of rotational symmetry.

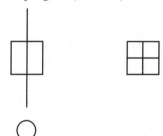

9 Complete the shape so that it has rotational symmetry of order 3.

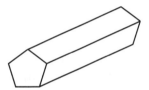

10 A prism has a cross-section which is a regular pentagon. How many axes of symmetry does it have? For each axis give the order of rotational symmetry.

11 Which of the pairs of triangles below are congruent to each other? For each congruent pair, state whether it is direct or opposite congruence.

a   **b**   **c**

12 For each of the congruent pairs of question **11**, give the reason for the congruence.

13 *ABCDEF* is a regular hexagon, with centre at *X*. Write down six triangles which are congruent to each other.

14 *ABCD* is an isosceles trapezium, with *AB* parallel to *CD* and *AD* = *BC*. Sketch *ABCD*, and draw the diagonals *AC* and *BD*. State, with reasons, which pairs of triangles are congruent to each other.

15 Triangles *ABC* and *LMN* are such that *AB* = *LM* = 5 cm, *BC* = *MN* = 4 cm and ∠*BAC* = ∠*MLN* = 30°. Show by construction that the triangles may not be congruent.

16 *ABCD* is a kite, with *AB* = *AD* and *CB* = *CD*. Show, using congruence, that ∠*ABC* = ∠*ADC*.

17 Which of the following are true?

    a $-5 > 1$ **b** $-8 \le -5$ **c** $1\frac{1}{2} > \frac{3}{2}$ **d** $1\frac{1}{2} \ge 1.5$

18 Solve these inequalities.

    a $5x - 2 > 8$ **b** $3x - 7 \le x - 9$ **c** $\frac{1}{2}x + 4 \ge 13 - \frac{1}{4}x$

19 **a** Find the largest integer satisfying $7x - 3 < 30$.

    b Find the smallest integer satisfying $2x + 8 \ge 11$.

20 Illustrate the following inequalities on a number line.

    a $-2 \le x < 3$ **b** $-3 < x \le 1$

21 Solve the following pairs of inequalities and show your answers on a number line.

    a $x + 1 \le 3x - 1 < 2x + 7$ **b** $\frac{1}{4}x - 1 < \frac{1}{2}x + 1 \le \frac{1}{3}x + 4$

22 Sketch the region defined by the inequalities $y \ge 1, y < 3x - 1, y \le 8 - x$.

23 Use tables to find

    a $\tan 62°$ **b** $\tan 38.4°$ **c** $\tan 42°25'$

24 70 m from the base of a tall building, the angle of elevation of the top is $53°$. Find the height of the building.

25 Find the sides marked by letters in these triangles.

    a   **b**   **c**

 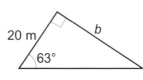 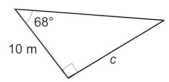

26 Use tables to find

    a $\tan^{-1} 1.3$ **b** $\tan^{1} 0.475$

27 Find the angles marked by letters in these triangles.

    a   **b**

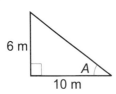 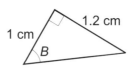

28 A matatu is 3 m high, and Juma's eyes are 1.5 m above his feet. When standing on the top of the matatu, he sees a point on the ground which is 10 m horizontally from him. What is the angle of depression of the point?

29 In $\triangle ABC$, $AB = 34$ cm, $BC = 30$ cm and $CA = 16$ cm.

    a Show that $\triangle ABC$ is right angled at C.

    b Find the sine, cosine and tangent of $\angle BAC$.

30 Use tables to find the following.

    a $\sin 43.2°$ **b** $\cos 64°30'$ **c** $\sin 27°27'$ **d** $\cos 12°50'$

31 Find the lengths marked by letters in these triangles.

    a   **b**

 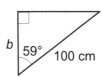

32 In $\triangle XYZ$, $\angle X = 90°$, $\angle Y = 37°$ and $YZ = 8$ cm. Find XY and XZ.

33 A tree is 12 m tall. After a storm it leans at 14° to the vertical. Find the height of the top of the tree above the ground.

34 Use tables to find these.
   a $\sin^{-1}0.532$ **b** $\cos^{-1}0.4921$ **c** $\cos^{-1}0.1744$

35 Find the angles marked by letters in these triangles.

 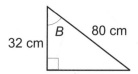

36 In $\triangle PQR$, $\angle Q = 90°$, $PR = 20$ cm and $PQ = 13$ cm. Find $\angle P$ and $\angle R$.

37 The diagonal of a television screen is 50 cm, and the longer side is 38 cm. Find the angle between the diagonal and the longer side.

38 A plane flies 400 km on a bearing of 110°. How far East and South is it from the starting point?

39 A plane flies so that it is 60 km South and 48 km West of its starting point. On what bearing has it been flying?

Consolidation exercise 4 (covers units 16–21)

1 Find the angles marked by letters in these diagrams. In each case give your reasons.

a   **b**   **c**   **d**

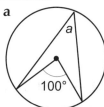 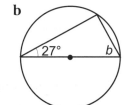 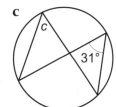 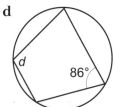

2 AB is a chord of a circle centre O. C is on the circle on the other side of the centre from AB. If $\angle AOB = 67°$ find $\angle ACB$.

3 AB is a diameter of a circle centre O. C is a point on the circle.
   a If $\angle CAB = 39°$ find $\angle CBA$.
   b If $AB = 7$ cm and $AC = 4$ cm find BC.
   c If $AC = 8$ cm and $BC = 9$ cm find $\angle BAC$.

4 Find the angles marked by letters in these diagrams. In each case give your reasons.

a   **b**

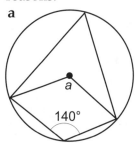 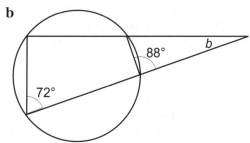

5 *AB* and *CD* are parallel chords of a circle. *AC* and *BD* meet at *X* inside the circle. Show that △*AXB* is isosceles.

6 *AB* and *CD* are parallel chords of a circle. *AC* and *BD* meet at *X* outside the circle. Show that △*AXB* is isosceles.

7 Find the areas of these triangles.

a
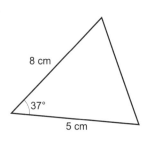

b
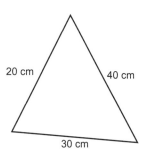

8 A triangle has sides *AB* = 6 cm, *BC* = 7 cm and *CA* = 8 cm.
a Find the area of the triangle.
b Find the length of the perpendicular from *B* to *CA*.

9 Find the area of this quadrilateral.

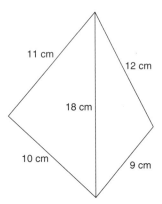

10 A regular octagon is inscribed in a circle of radius 2 m. Find the area of the octagon.

11 A pyramid has a rectangular base which is 50 m by 40 m. The vertex of the pyramid is 30 m above the centre of the base. Find the total surface area of the triangular sides of the pyramid.

12 Find the volumes of the following.
a A pyramid, with a square base of side 10 cm and height 12 cm.
b A cone of height 2 m and base radius 1.5 m.
c A sphere of radius 6 cm.

13 A pyramid has a square base. The height of the pyramid is 20 cm and its volume is 960 cm^3. Find the side of the base.

14 A cone has height 3 cm and volume 14 cm^3. Find the radius of the base.

15 A sphere has volume 8 cm^3. Find its radius.

16 Find the surface area of the sphere of question **15**.

17 A sphere has surface area 12 cm^2. Find its volume.

18 A cone has base 16 cm and height 30 cm.
a Find the slant height of the cone.
b Find the curved surface area of the cone.

19 The base radius of a cone is 12 cm, and its curved surface area is 240π cm^2. Find:
  a the slant height of the cone
  b the height of the cone
  c the volume of the cone.

20 The diagram shows a cylinder with equal cones at each end. The radius of the cylinder is 8 cm, the height of the cylinder is 12 cm and the total height of the solid is 18 cm. Find:
  a the volume of the solid
  b the surface area of the solid.

21 A hollow ball is made from rubber 0.4 cm thick. The external radius of the ball is 6 cm. Find the volume of the rubber.

22 Make a copy of this diagram and enlarge the shape:
  a by factor 2 about A
  b by factor $\frac{1}{2}$ about B
  c by factor -2 about C.

23 Plot the triangle with vertices at $(-2, 2)$ $(0, 1)$ and $(1, 3)$. Enlarge the triangle:
  a by factor 2 about $(-1, 1)$
  b by factor $\frac{1}{2}$ about $(3, 1)$
  c by factor -1 about $(-1, 4)$.

24 The triangle with vertices at $(1, 1)$, $(1, 4)$ and $(4, 4)$ is enlarged to the triangle with vertices at $(-1, 1)$, $(-1, 2)$ and $(0, 2)$. Plot the two triangles, and find the scale factor and centre of the enlargement.

25 In the diagram AB is parallel to CD.
  a Show that $\triangle ABX$ is similar to $\triangle CDX$
  b If $AB = 8$ cm find CD.
  c If $XC = 9$ cm find XA.

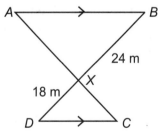

26 Two circles have radii in the ratio $5 : 6$. If the area of the smaller circle is 100 m^2 find the area of the larger circle.

27 Two rectangles are similar, and their areas are 40 cm^2 and 50 cm^2. If the length of the larger rectangle is 9 cm find the length of the smaller rectangle.

28 A map is in the scale $1 : 200\,000$. A lake on the map has area 3 cm^2. What is the area of the real lake? Give your answer in km^2.

29 Two solid cubes are made out of the same material. They have sides 4 cm and 3 cm. If the mass of the larger cube is 800 grams find the mass of the smaller cube.

30 The volume of a sphere is increased by 72.8%. What is the percentage increase in
    a the radius   **b** the surface area.

31 A frustum is made from a solid cone. The frustum is 20 cm high, its bottom radius is 60 cm and its top radius is 20 cm.
    a Find the height of the original cone.
    b The original cone had mass 200 kg. What is the mass of the frustum?
    c Find the ratio of the curved surface area of the frustum to the curved surface area of the cone.

32 Find the lengths marked by letters in these triangles.

a   **b**   **c**

33 Find the angles marked by letters in these triangles.

a   **b**   **c**

34 Write down the values of these.
    a $\sin 30°$ **b** $\tan 60°$ **c** $\cos 45°$

35 In $\triangle ABC$, $\angle A = 90°$, $BC = 20$ cm and $AC = 10$ cm. Without using tables find $\angle B$.

36 If $\sin x = 0.4$, find $\cos x$ and $\tan x$.

37 Solve the equation $\sin x = 3 \cos x$.

38 Solve the equation $\sin 2x = \cos 3x$.

Answers

Exercise 1.1A
1 $\frac{2}{75}$ **2** $\frac{3}{4}$ **3** 10 m **4** 40 m **5** 4

Exercise 1.1B
1 a 4 **b** $\frac{5}{3}$ **c** 3 **d** 1 **e** 3 **f** $\frac{1}{2}$
g −1 **h** $-\frac{2}{5}$ **i** 2 **j** 0
3 7 **4** −2 **5** 2 **6** 0 **7** −1 **8** −6

Exercise 1.2A
a 2 **b** 2 **c** 2 **d** 2

Exercise 1.2B
1 y-values: −2, 1, 4, 7, 10, 13 **2 a** 3 **b** 3 **c** 3 **d** 3 **e** 3

Exercise 1.2C
1 a 4 **b** −3 **c** $\frac{2}{3}$ **d** 2.5 **e** $\frac{2}{3}$ **f** $\frac{5}{3}$
g −1 **h** $-\frac{2}{3}$ **i** 0.2 **j** $-\frac{2}{3}$ **k** $\frac{8}{15}$ **l** $-\frac{9}{20}$
2 a $\frac{1}{2}$ **b** 2 **c** −3 **3** 6 **4** −20 **5** $\frac{1}{2}$
6 $\frac{1}{2}$ **7** 1 **8** $-\frac{3}{7}$

Exercise 1.2D
1 a 5 **b** −3 **c** $\frac{2}{3}$ **d** $-\frac{3}{8}$ **e** 1.5 **f** $\frac{1}{3}$
g −3 **h** 2.5 **i** $-\frac{2}{3}$ **j** 14
2 7 **3** $1\frac{1}{3}$ **4** 1 **5** −4.5 **6** −3
7 a 2 **b** $\frac{2}{5}$ **c** $-\frac{1}{2}$ **d** 6 **e** 1.75 **f** $\frac{8}{3}$
8 −2 **9** 1.5 **10** $-\frac{2}{3}$

Exercise 1.3
1 a $y = 2x - 4$ **b** $y = -\frac{3}{4}x + 2$ **c** $y = 3x - 7$ **d** $y = -2x + 7$
2 a $y = 2x - 1$ **b** $y = -4x + 17$ **c** $y = 2x - 1$ **d** $y = -x + 7$
e $y = 2x + 4$ **f** $y = \frac{1}{4}x + \frac{1}{2}$ **g** $y = 3x - 1.1$ **h** $y = 6x - 383$
3 a $y = \frac{1}{2}x + 1$ **b** $y = 2x + 4$ **c** $y = -3x + 4$

Exercise 1.4
1 $t = 0.1e - 100$ **a** 250 dollars **b** 7000 dollars
2 $l = 0.8w + 16$ **a** 25.6 cm **b** 17.5 kg
3 $b = 2.5u + 1250$ **a** sh 2125 **b** 500
4 $s = 100p - 500$ **a** 14 500 **b** 90
5 $C = 30t + 120\,000$ **a** sh 165 000 **b** 3000
6 $N = -14p + 2900$ **a** 1080 **b** sh 120

Exercise 2.1A
1 a,f & g, b & e   **2** –6   **6** a, d   **7** 16   **8** 8   **9** 7   **10** 3

Exercise 2.1B
1 a & c, a & g, b & d, e & c, e & g, f & d, h & c, h & g
2 a $y = -\frac{1}{2}x + 9$ **b** $y = -\frac{1}{3}x + 1\frac{1}{3}$ **c** $y = 2x - 1$ **d** $y = \frac{4}{3}x + 5$
3 3   **4** –6   **5** –4   **6** 8
7 9   **8** $y = -x + 9$; (4, 5)   **9** $y = -\frac{1}{2}x - \frac{1}{2}$ **10** (1.9, 6.7)

Exercise 2.2
1 a 5   **b** 10   **c** $\sqrt{53}$ **d** $\sqrt{125}$ **3** $\frac{1}{2}$, –2   **5** c
6 (22, 20), (9, –19), (2, –20)   **7** no   **8** no   **9** 4   **10** $\sqrt{41}$

Exercise 2.3
1 a (4,5)   **b** (3,2)   **c** (3.5, 5.5)   **d** (1, –1)   **e** (–2.5, –1.5)
f (–1, 1)   **2 a** $y = x - 1$ **b** $y = -3x + 10$ **c** $y = \frac{3}{5}x + 2\frac{3}{5}$
d $y = -1\frac{1}{2}x + 1$ **3 b** $y = 2x - 1$ **4 b** (6,5)

Exercise 3.3
1 a 10   **b** 98   **2 a** 375   **b** 2150   **3 a** 55   **b** 260
4 a 17   **b** 55

Exercise 3.6
6 a 20   **b** 14   **8 a** 300   **b** 35

Exercise 4.1C
3 0   **4 a** 2   **b** 1   **5 a** 5   **b** 6
8 $x = 5$ **9** $x = 4.5$, $y = 3.5$, $y = x - 1$, $y = -x + 8$
10 $y = -\frac{1}{3}x + 6\frac{1}{3}$, $y = 3x - 2$ **11 a** 1, $y = x + 1$ **b** 1, $x = 2$
c 4, $y = \frac{1}{2}x - 4.5$, $y = -2x + 3$, $y = 3x - 12$, $y = -\frac{1}{3}x - 2$ **d** 0

Exercise 4.2B
1 (4, 2)   **2** (–2, 7)   **3** (7, –1)   **4** (2, –1)   **5** (5, 1)   **6** (2, –8)
7 (4, –2)   **8** (–2, –1)   **9** $x = 5$ **10** $x = 2$ **11** $y = -2$ **12** $y = 1$

Exercise 4.2C
1 (2, 3), (1, 4), (5, 2), (6, 1), (3, 0), (0, 2); (b, a)
2 (0, –2), (–3, 0), (1, –2), (–2, –3), (–2, 3), (–1, 2); (–b, –a)
3 $y = x$ **4** $y = -x$ **5** $y = \pm x$ **6** $x = 0, y = 0$

Exercise 4.4
1 3   **2** 4   **3** 5   **4** 9   **6 a** 4   **b** 2   **c** 7

Exercise 5.1
1 temperature, time, income are scalars
2 (i) $\binom{2}{3}$ (ii) $\binom{-4}{-5}$ **3** $\mathbf{DA} = \binom{-5}{0}$ **4** (i) $\binom{-3}{1}$ (ii) $\binom{-3}{-2}$ (iii) $\binom{-3}{0}$
5 (i) $\binom{2}{3}$ (ii) $\binom{5}{-3}$ (iii) $\binom{-7}{0}$ **6** (5, 11), (7, –3), (2, 17), (–4, 7)

Exercise 5.2
1 (i) $\binom{4}{2}$ (ii) $\binom{5}{-1}$ (iii) $\binom{-1}{3}$ (iv) $\binom{-5}{8}$
2 (i) $\binom{1}{7}$ (ii) $\binom{-5}{-1}$ (iii) $\binom{6}{-9}$ (iv) $\binom{9}{29}$

3 (i) $\begin{pmatrix} 12 \\ -1 \end{pmatrix}$ (ii) $\begin{pmatrix} -6.5 \\ 6 \end{pmatrix}$ (iii) $\begin{pmatrix} -\frac{7}{8} \\ \frac{3}{4} \end{pmatrix}$

5 $k = 3, m = 10$ **6** $x = 3, y = 5$

7 (i) **2a**   (ii) **2a – b**   (iii) **3a**   (iv) **3a + 2b**   (v) **4a + 4b**   (vi) **–3a + 2b**

Exercise 5.3

1 (i) **a & b, f & d**   (ii) (i) plus **a & c, b & c**

2 (i) **BE, CD**   (ii) **AB** etc   (iii) **CE**

Exercise 5.4

2 $\begin{pmatrix} 2 \\ 2 \end{pmatrix}, \begin{pmatrix} 4 \\ 0 \end{pmatrix}, \begin{pmatrix} 1 \\ -1 \end{pmatrix}, \begin{pmatrix} -3 \\ 2 \end{pmatrix}, \begin{pmatrix} -3 \\ -2 \end{pmatrix}$ **3** $\begin{pmatrix} 6 \\ -4 \end{pmatrix}$ **4** (i) $\begin{pmatrix} -3 \\ -10 \end{pmatrix}$ (ii) $\begin{pmatrix} 3 \\ 10 \end{pmatrix}$

5 $\begin{pmatrix} 2 \\ 0 \end{pmatrix}$ **6** $\begin{pmatrix} 7 \\ 10 \end{pmatrix}$

Exercise 5.5

1 13   **2** 5   **3** 9.43   **4** 10   **5** 13.6

6 24   **7** $53\frac{1}{3}$ **8** 8.25   **9** 6.32

Exercise 5.6

1 1:3   **2** 1:2   **3** 4   **4** (ii) 5, 10, 15

Exercise 5.7

1 (i) (4.5, 6.5)   (ii) (8, 1.5)   **2** $m = 8, n = -7$ **3** (–5, 7)

4 (i) (5, 3), (9, 5)

Exercise 5.8

2 (4, –5), (10, –4)   **3** (6,5), (2, –7), (1, 1)

4 (i) $\begin{pmatrix} 3 \\ 5 \end{pmatrix}$ (ii) $\begin{pmatrix} -5 \\ 11 \end{pmatrix}$ (iii) $\begin{pmatrix} -2 \\ -7 \end{pmatrix}$ **5** (5, –2)   **6** (–6, 4)

7 $\begin{pmatrix} 3 \\ -5 \end{pmatrix}$ **8** $\begin{pmatrix} -1 \\ 5 \end{pmatrix}$ **9** (–7, 4.5)

Exercise 6.2

1 a $12\frac{7}{8}$ **b** $37\frac{3}{4}$ **c** 4.925   **d** $1\frac{2}{7}$ **e** $3.6x$ **f** $2w + 6$

2 25.5   **a** 225.5   **b** 51   **c** 74.5   **3** 38.7°   **4** 11.37

5 15.2   **6** 36 km\h

Exercise 6.3

1 a 6   **b** 7.5   **c** 23   **2** 14.8 s   **3** 23.8°   **4** 76.5

Exercise 6.4

1 a 5   **b** 3   **c** 5, 12   **2** 1   **3** 1

Exercise 6.5

1 22.10   **2 a** 7   **b** 7.5   **c** 7.775

3 a 7.21   **b** 7   **c** 7   **4** 2.85   **5** 1.99   **6** 2.85

Exercise 6.6

1 12.75, 12.9   **2** 10–14   **a** 8.4 cm   **b** 9.5 cm

3 a 0.6–0.7   **b** 0.431 s   **c** 0.41 s

4 a 70–79   **b** $80\frac{7}{8}°$ **c** 80.3°

5 a 220–229 s   **b** 218.8 s   **c** 219.4 s

6 a 70–79   **b** 70.8 kg   **c** 71.2 kg

Exercise 7.1

1 8   **2** 64   **3** 49   **4** 32   **5** 3^3 **6** 9^4

7 8^7 **8** $15 \times 15 \times 15$ **9** $x \times x \times x \times x \times x$ **10** $y \times y \times y \times y \times y \times y$

11 10^{100} **12 a** $\frac{1}{8}$ **b** $\frac{1}{9}$ **c** $\frac{27}{64}$ **d** $\frac{9}{4}$

13 a 10^2 **b** 10^3 **c** 10^6 **14** 10^5, 10^7

Exercise 7.2A
1 3^{13} **2** 4^9 **3** x^{11} **4** y^{11} **5** 2^{x+y} **6** 3^{n+m}

7 2^{16} **8** x^{12} **9** 3^6 **10** x^6 **11** 2^{7x} **12** 5^{4y+1}

13 2^{3x-2} **14** 3^{5+x} **15** x^{a+b} **16** y^{5-k} **17** 10^{12}

Exercise 7.2B
1 5^7 **2** 2^5 **3** 7^7 **4** 8^4 **5** 2^{x-y} **6** 3^{n-m}

7 x^4 **8** y^7 **9** 6^{2x} **10** 7^{3n} **11** x^{3n} **12** z^{3m}

13 y^{10} **14** x^4 **15** 2^{x+y-z} **16** z^{10} **17** 2^{x+2} **18** 3^{2x-5}

19 5^{4-x} **20** 7^{7-3x} **21** 3^{6a-1}

Exercise 7.2C
1 2^{15} **2** 5^9 **3** 10^8 **4** x^{18} **5** y^{24} **6** 2^{xy}

7 3^{mn} **8** 5^{3x} **9** 2^{14} **10** 3^{30} **11** 2^{19} **12** 3^7

13 2^{11} **14** 3^6 **15** 2^{16} **16** 3^{17} **17** 2^8 **18** 5^2

19 7^5 **20** 2^{14} **21** 2^{10} **22** 10^8 **23** 3^5 **24** 2^{11}

Exercise 7.3
1 1 **2** 1 **3** 1 **4** $\frac{1}{5}$ **5** $\frac{1}{4}$ **6** $\frac{1}{16}$

7 9 **8** 64 **9** $\frac{9}{4}$ **10** $\frac{64}{27}$ **11** $\frac{4}{5}$ **12** $\frac{3}{4}$

13 2^{-2} **14** 3^{-8} **15** 3^{12} **16** 2^{-12} **17** 2^2 **18** 3^{-4}

19 2^{-3x} **20** 3^{-a}

Exercise 7.4
1 7 **2** 3 **3** 10 **4** 10 **5** $\frac{1}{2}$ **6** $\frac{1}{3}$

7 0.1 **8** 0.5 **9** $\frac{2}{3}$ **10** 2 **11** 3 **12** 2

13 a $7^{\frac{1}{2}}$ **b** $(\frac{1}{3})^{\frac{1}{2}}$ **c** $2^{\frac{1}{3}}$ **d** $8^{\frac{1}{5}}$

Exercise 7.5
1 8 **2** 8 **3** 243 **4** 25 **5** 4^{-3} **6** 7^{-8}

7 12^{-10} **8** 3^{-10} **9** x^2 **10** x^2 **11** x^2 **12** x^6

13 2^{11} **14** 3^{12} **15** 1 **16** $27a^3b^3$ **17** $16x^{12}$ **18** $\frac{1}{27}x^{-9}y^{-6}$

19 $2x^{-2}$ **20** $2y^2$ **21** $\frac{1}{6}x^4$ **22** $a^5b^7c^9$ **23** a^3b^2 **24** $x^{\frac{1}{16}}y^{-\frac{1}{4}}$

25 x^2 **26** $\frac{x}{y}$ **27** $2a^{-1}$ **28** $x^{\frac{5}{6}}$ **29** $a^{3\frac{1}{4}}$ **30** $x^{\frac{1}{6}}$

Exercise 8.1
1 a 8×10^5 **b** 4×10^6 **c** 5×10^7 **d** 1.2×10^5 **e** 4.35×10^7

f 1.2346×10^{11} **g** 5×10^6 **h** 6.3×10^5

2 a 300 000 **b** 47 000 000 **c** 1 270 000

3 5.8×11^{11} m² **4** 6×10^9 **5** 7.3×10^7 km² **6** 3×10^8 m/s

7 10^{12} **8 a** 5×10^8 **b** 5.01×10^{14} **c** 4.73×10^6

9 Betelgeuse **10** Pacific **11** Jupiter

Exercise 8.2
1 a 7×10^{-7} **b** 4×10^{-8} **c** 9×10^{-4} **d** 3.2×10^{-5}

e 1.532×10^{-3} **f** 4.3×10^{-8} **g** 1×10^{-3} **h** 5×10^{-6}

i 7×10^{-9} **2 a** 0.000 4 **b** 0.000 036 **c** 0.000 001 29

3 2.8×10^{-8} m **4** 3×10^{-19} m **5** 10^{-12}

6 a 5×10^{-7} **b** 5.2×10^{-3} **c** 4.3×10^{-4} **d** 7.03×10^{-5}

7 carbon

Exercise 8.3

1 2.8×10^8	**2** 6.9×10^{13}	**3** 7.5×10^{14}	**4** 3.2×10^{18}
5 1.2×10^{10}	**6** 3.6×10^3	**7** 4×10^3	**8** 2×10^6
9 6.2×10^{-14}	**10** 9.6×10^{-2}	**11** 1.2×10^{-6}	**12** 6.4×10^7
13 2×10^{13}	**14** 1.1×10^{-3}	**15** 5×10^5	**16** 3.1×10^6
17 2.8×10^8	**18** 8.8×10^{-10}	**19** 6×10^1	**20** 2.4×10^{-1}
21 8.4×10^{20} m	**22** 5.1×10^8 kg	**23** 4.5×10^7 sh	**24** 8.5×10^{15} kg
25 6×10^{13} kg			

Exercise 8.4

1 4.7×10^9	**2** 7.3×10^7	**3** 1.1×10^{11}	**4** 1.26×10^{10}
5 1.081×10^7	**6** 9.9×10^{-7}	**7** 2.8×10^{-5}	**8** 1.74×10^{-6}
9 2.3×10^{10}	**10** 6.6×10^{40}	**11** 3.4×10^{14}	**12** 3.4×10^{-6}
13 1.8×10^{-9}	**14** 2.2×10^{-12}	**15** 1.72×10^{-10}	**16** 2.4×10^{13}
17 1.2×10^{12}	**18** 4.8×10^{16}	**19** 1.44×10^{20}	**20** 4×10^3
21 7.5×10^5	**22** 6×10^{-5}	**23** 7×10^{-13}	**24** 4.2×10^{-6}
25 2.8×10^{-12}	**26** 8.75×10^{-17}	**27** 3×10^{-11}	**28** 1.08×10^8
29 1.86×10^{-6}	**30** 7.5×10^9	**31** 1.4×10^{14} km	**32** 9×10^{48}
33 6×10^{-9} kg			

Exercise 8.5A

1 7×10^7	**2** 8×10^5	**3** 1.3×10^8	**4** 1.17×10^9
5 1.4×10^{-2}	**6** 1.07×10^{-8}	**7** 2×10^7	**8** 1×10^9
9 5×10^{-9}	**10** 2×10^{-6}	**11** 5.5×10^7 kg	
12 a 2.6×10^8 km	**b** 4×10^7 km	**13 a** 1.59×10^7	**b** 7×10^5

Exercise 8.5B

1 5.4×10^9	**2** 6.8×10^7	**3** 3.8×10^9	**4** 7.32×10^7
5 6.9×10^{-7}	**6** 5×10^{-10}	**7** 4.4×10^8	**8** 1.92×10^{-3}
9 5×10^7	**10** 2×10^{-9}		

11 a 3.89×10^7 km^2 **b** 2.11×10^7 km^2

12 a 2.08×10^8 km   **b** 9.2×10^7 km

13 a 3×10^{-27} kg   **b** 3.6×10^{-27} kg

Exercise 9.1

1 2	**2** 4	**3** 1	**4** 0	**5** 2	**6** 4
7 3	**8** 3	**9** −1	**10** −2	**11** −1	**12** −3
13 $\frac{1}{2}$	**14** $\frac{1}{3}$	**15** $\frac{1}{3}$	**16** $\frac{1}{2}$	**17** $\frac{1}{2}$	**18** $-\frac{1}{2}$
19 2.5	**20** 1.7				

Exercise 9.2

1 a 0.954   **b** 0.176   **c** 0.699   **2 a** 1.748   **b** −0.058   **c** 1.146

3 a 2   **b** 2   **c** −3   **d** k

Exercise 9.3

1 7.566	**2** 7.478	**3** 8.143	**4** 5.601	**5** 8.68	**6** 7.597
7 2.206	**8** 1.504	**9** 2.375	**10** 2.559	**11** 6.112	**12** 1.494
13 1.49	**14** 1.271	**15** 1.552	**16** 1.719	**17** 9.419	**18** 5.868
19 a 2.072	**b** 2.072				

Exercise 9.4A

1 a 1.7215   **b** 2.098   **c** 3.8051   **2 a** 27.76   **b** 280.7   **c** 231 600

3 a 847.2   **b** 2917   **c** 23 370 000   **d** 152 500   **e** 4 074 000

f 2 772 000   **g** 24.03   **h** 160.7   **i** 2.828   **j** 209   **k** 11.26

l 408.7   **m** 49 200 000   **n** 5.387   **o** 204 200

Exercise 9.4B

1 a $\bar{2}.6821$ **b** $\bar{1}.1855$ **c** $\bar{4}.5734$ **2 a** 0.035 79   **b** 0.2925   **c** 0.003 567
3 a 0.001 317   **b** 0.031 86   **c** 0.8913   **d** 0.024 63   **e** 0.000 027 54
  f 11.3   **g** 2.334   **h** 0.004 413   **i** 105.8   **j** 6897   **k** 14.85
  l 0.8217   **m** 0.000 3206   **n** 0.5371   **o** 0.2135
4 6.725 cm^2 **5** 0.1988 m^3 **6** 1059 cm^3 **7** 2.027
8 0.000 098 72

Exercise 10.1

1 a $x^2 + 5x + 6$ **b** $x^2 + 9x + 20$ **c** $x^2 + 13x + 42$ **d** $y^2 + y - 12$
  e $a^2 - 2a - 24$ **f** $b^2 + 5b - 24$ **g** $x^2 - 13x + 36$ **h** $x^2 - 12x + 32$
  i $x^2 - 9x + 18$
2 a $pm + pn + qm + qn$ **b** $ac - ad + bc - bd$ **c** $wy - wz + xy - xz$
  d $jm - jn - km + kn$ **e** $ab - 2a + 3b - 6$ **f** $xy - 3x - 7y + 21$
  g $ab - 9a - 7b + 63$ **h** $wz + 3w + 5z + 15$ **i** $mn + 6m - 4n - 24$
3 a $6x^2 + 13x + 6$ **b** $3y^2 + 19y + 20$ **c** $10z^2 + 11z - 6$
  d $6a^2 - 19a + 10$ **e** $7b^2 - 51b + 14$ **f** $12x^2 - 23x + 5$
  g $8x^2 + 2x - 15$ **h** $10a^2 + 26a + 12$ **i** $6k^2 - 23k + 7$

Exercise 10.2

1 a $x^2 + 2xy + y^2$ **b** $m^2 + 2mn + n^2$ **c** $a^2 + 8a + 16$
  d $b^2 + 6b + 9$ **e** $c^2 + 18c + 81$ **f** $w^2 + w + \frac{1}{4}$
  g $9x^2 + 12x + 4$ **h** $25y^2 + 30y + 9$ **i** $4a^2 + 12ab + 9b^2$
  j $9x^2 + 30xy + 25y^2$ **k** $4m^2 + 28mn + 49n^2$ **l** $25z^2 + 40zw + 16w^2$
2 a $x^2 - 2xy + y^2$ **b** $m^2 - 2mn + n^2$ **c** $x^2 - 10x + 25$
  d $k^2 - 6k + 9$ **e** $a^2 - 14a + 49$ **f** $b^2 - \frac{2}{3}b + \frac{1}{9}$
  g $4x^2 - 20x + 25$ **h** $9a^2 - 24a + 16$ **i** $49y^2 - 28y + 4$
  j $4a^2 - 12ab + 9b^2$ **k** $16x^2 - 40xy + 25y^2$ **l** $4r^2 - 28rt + 49t^2$
3 a $x^2 - y^2$ **b** $m^2 - n^2$ **c** $x^2 - 25$
  d $k^2 - 16$ **e** $y^2 - \frac{1}{4}$ **f** $4a^2 - 9b^2$
  g $25m^2 - 9n^2$ **h** $2x^2 - 8$ **i** $3b^2 - 75$
  j $16k^2 - \frac{1}{4}$

Exercise 10.3A

  1 a 2, 4   **b** 2, 3   **c** 2, 5   **d** 4, 15
  2 $(x + 2)(x + 3)$ **3** $(x + 3)(x + 4)$ **4** $(x + 2)(x + 4)$
  5 $(x + 4)(x + 6)$ **6** $(x + 1)(x + 3)$ **7** $(x + 1)(x + 7)$
  8 $(x + 2)(x + 5)$ **9** $(x + 3)(x + 5)$ **10** $(x + 4)(x + 15)$
11 $(x + 1)(x + 10)$ **12** $(x + 2)(x + 14)$ **13** $(x + 3)(x + 14)$
14 $(x + 2)^2$ **15** $(x + 3)^2$ **16** $(x + 7)^2$
17 $(x + 10)^2$ **18** $(x + 8)^2$ **19** $(x + \frac{1}{2})^2$

Exercise 10.3B

  1 $(x - 3)(x - 4)$ **2** $(x - 4)(x - 5)$ **3** $(x - 1)(x - 4)$
  4 $(x - 3)(x - 7)$ **5** $(x - 4)(x - 6)$ **6** $(x - 5)(x - 12)$
  7 $(x - 2)(x - 8)$ **8** $(x - 2)(x - 13)$ **9** $(x - 4)(x - 9)$
10 $(x - 1)^2$ **11** $(x - 4)^2$ **12** $(x - 5)^2$
13 $(x - 7)^2$ **14** $(x - 6)^2$ **15** $(x - \frac{1}{3})^2$

Exercise 10.3C

  1 $(x + 5)(x - 1)$ **2** $(x - 5)(x + 4)$ **3** $(x - 6)(x + 2)$
  4 $(x + 6)(x - 4)$ **5** $(x - 7)(x + 6)$ **6** $(x + 1)(x - 7)$
  7 $(x + 4)(x - 3)$ **8** $(x - 3)(x + 1)$ **9** $(x + 10)(x - 6)$
10 $(2x - y)(2x + y)$ **11** $(3a - 4b)(3a + 4b)$ **12** $(7x + 1)(7x - 1)$

Exercise 10.3D

1 $(x-2)(x-5)$ **2** $(x+9)(x-4)$ **3** $(x+5)(x+6)$
4 $(x-8)(x+7)$ **5** $(x+25)(x-1)$ **6** $(x-30)(x+2)$
7 $(x-3)(x-21)$ **8** $(x+15)(x-3)$ **9** $(x+2)(x+16)$
10 $(x-7)(x+4)$ **11** $(x-9)(x+4)$ **12** $(x+13)(x-2)$

Exercise 10.4

1 $(x+2)(2x+1)$ **2** $(2x+1)(3x-2)$ **3** $(x+3)(2x-1)$
4 $(x+1)(5x+4)$ **5** $(x+1)(6x+5)$ **6** $(x+6)(6x-1)$
7 $(x-4)(3x+2)$ **8** $(x-3)(3x+2)$ **9** $(2x-1)^2$
10 $(x+3)(5x-2)$ **11** $(2x+1)(4x-3)$ **12** $(x-2)(7x-2)$

Exercise 10.5A

1 3, 4 **2** 2, 3 **3** 4, 15 **4** −1, −5 **5** −5, −6 **6** −5, 3
7 6, −1 **8** 8, −5 **9** −6, 2 **10** 5, 10 **11** 5, −11 **12** 13,−10

Exercise 10.5B

1 $1, \frac{2}{3}$ **2** $-\frac{1}{2}, 1\frac{1}{2}$ **3** $3, -\frac{4}{3}$ **4** $\frac{2}{3}, \frac{3}{2}$ **5** $3, -\frac{5}{2}$ **6** $\frac{1}{2}, \frac{2}{3}$
7 $-\frac{1}{4}, -\frac{2}{3}$ **8** $3, -\frac{2}{7}$ **9** $\frac{2}{3}, -\frac{5}{4}$ **10** $3, \frac{2}{5}$ **11** $\frac{2}{5}, -\frac{3}{2}$ **12** $-2, -\frac{2}{9}$

Exercise 10.5C

1 −2, 7 **2** 2, 4 **3** 4, 5 **4** $3, -\frac{9}{2}$ **5** $2, \frac{19}{3}$ **6** $-3, \frac{19}{6}$
7 5, −12 **8** −2, 9 **9** $2, -\frac{7}{2}$ **10** 1, 3 **11** −2, 4 **12** 5, −12
13 $3, -\frac{1}{2}$ **14** 3, −4 **15** −2, 3 **16** 1, 8 **17** $5, -\frac{9}{5}$ **18** 1, 12

Exercise 10.5D

1 10 cm **2** 7 **3** 5, 12 **4** 3, 8 **5** 5, 7 **6** 8 or 12
7 4 **8** 6 **9** 2 s, 4 s **10** 5 **11** −6 **12** 12 sh
13 38 **14** 6 **15** 140

Exercise 10.6

1 $x^2 - 7x + 12 = 0$ **2** $x^2 - 7x + 10 = 0$ **3** $x^2 + 8x + 7 = 0$
4 $x^2 + 11x + 30 = 0$ **5** $x^2 + 3x - 18 = 0$ **6** $x^2 - x - 20 = 0$
7 $x^2 - 16 = 0$ **8** $8x^2 - 6x + 1 = 0$ **9** $10x^2 - 101x + 10 = 0$
10 $9x^2 + 18x - 7 = 0$ **11** $16x^2 + 16x + 3 = 0$ **12** $64x^2 - 352x + 459$

Exercise 11.1

4 90° **5** W **6** d

Exercise 11.2A

2 5 o'clock **3** 270° **4** 3.45 **5 a** 210° **b** 17.5°
6 88° **7** 132

Exercise 11.2B

1 (2, 2), (2, 4), (−1, 2) **2** (−1, 1), (1, −1), (−3, −1)
3 (0, 3), (0, −1), (2, −1) **4** (1, 2), (1, −1), (−3, 2), (−3, −1)
5 (1, 5), (1, 8), (3, 5), (3, 8), (5, 5) **6** (1, 1), (−1.1, 3.9), (3.3, 4.4)
7 (0, 1), (0.7, 3.7), (4.6, −1)

Exercise 11.2C

1 a (−1, 3) **b** (−3, −1) **c** (1, −3) **2** (0, 4), (0, 7), (2, 4)
3 (−1, 1), (−4, 1), (−4, 0) **4** (1, 2), (0, 4), (−2, 3)
5 (2, 1), (3, 1), (3, −2), (2, −2) **6** (0.2, 2.0), (−3.4, 4.6), (−0.1, 6.1)
7 (1.9, 3.1), (4.1, 3.6), (5.2, 0.7), (4.2, −2.8)

Exercise 11.2D
2 (0, 2) **3** (1, 2), 180° **4** (0, 1), 90° clockwise **5** (2,0), 90° clockwise
6 (2, 1), 180°

Exercise 11.3A
1 a 2 **b** 0 **c** 3 **d** 5 **e** 6 **2 b** 3 **3** 2 **4** 2 **5** 4

Exercise 11.3B
1 a 4 **b** 2 **c** 3 **2** 3; 2 for each **3** 3; 2 with 2, 1 with 4
4 4; 3 for each **5** 4; 1 with 3, 3 with 2
6 a 1 **b** 1

Exercise 12.1B
1 a opposite **b** direct **c** opposite
2 a and **b**, **c** and **e** **3** *ACB, ACD* **4** *XPQ, XPS, XRQ, XRS*
5 *XAB, XBC, XCD, XDE, XEA* **6** *OMA, OMB* **7** *OBA, OBC*

Exercise 12.2
1 a SAS **c** ASA **7** *AXQ, BXP* **8** *BCX, DCX*

Exercise 13.1
1, 3, 5, 7, 8, 9, 10 true **11** $x > 8$ **12** $x \leq -\frac{2}{3}$ **13** $x < 8$
14 $x > 90$ **15** $x \leq 3$ **16** $x > -2$ **17** $x > -3$
18 $x < -4$ **19** $x > -\frac{1}{2}$ **20** $x \leq 1\frac{1}{3}$ **21** $x > 0.3$
22 $x \geq -3$ **23** $x > -34$ **24** $x \geq 6$ **25** $x \leq \frac{2}{9}$
26 a 2 **b** −1 **c** −3 **d** −1 **e** 0 **f** 2
  g 2 **h** 2 **27 a** −1 **b** −1 **c** 0 **d** −1

Exercise 13.2
1 a $4 < x \leq 6$ **b** $-2 < x \leq 3$ **c** not possible **d** $0 < x \leq 0.5$
  e $2 < x \leq 8$ **3** $2 \leq x < 5\frac{1}{3}$ **4** $4 < x \leq 7$ **5** $1\frac{1}{2} \leq x \leq 2\frac{1}{2}$
6 $12 < x < 16$ **7** $10 \leq x < 15$ **8** $-2 < x < 4$ **9** $2 \leq x \leq 3$
10 $-6 < x \leq -2$

Exercise 13.3
1 $-2 < x \leq 4$ **2** $-7 < x < 7$ **3** $-1 \leq x \leq 2$ **4** $6 < x \leq 16$
5 $-1 < x \leq 8$ **6** $\frac{2}{5} \leq x \leq 10\frac{1}{2}$ **7** $-2 < x \leq 7$ **8** $-8 < x < 8$
9 $-2 \leq x < 4$ **10** $-1\frac{1}{3} < x \leq 4$

Exercise 13.4
5 $y \leq 2, x > -1.5, y \geq \frac{1}{2}x - 1$ **9** $y \leq x + 2, y \geq \frac{1}{4}x - 1, y \leq 2 - \frac{1}{2}x$

Exercise 14.2
1 a 3.078 **b** 0.7813 **c** 0.5184 **d** 0.4081 **e** 0.8759 **f** 1.455
3 18.7 m **4** 248 m **5** 54.4 m
6 1.95 cm **7 a** 4.37 cm **b** 6.71 m **c** 34.6 m
8 14.4 m

Exercise 14.3A
1 a 40.3° **b** 56.55° **c** 17° 35′ **d** 21.8° **e** 50.2° **f** 29° 41′
2 26° 34′ **3** 7° 7′ **4** 36° 52′
5 35° **6 a** 33.7° **b** 58° **c** 45°

Exercise 14.3B
1 14° 3′ **2** 211 m **3** 14° 3′ **4** 7.64 m

246 Answers

Exercise 15.1

1 $\frac{24}{25}, \frac{7}{25}, \frac{24}{7}$ 2 $\frac{15}{17}, \frac{8}{17}, \frac{15}{8}$ 3 $\frac{4}{5}, \frac{3}{5}, \frac{4}{3}$ 4 $\frac{4}{5}, \frac{3}{5}, \frac{4}{3}$

5 $\frac{4}{5}, \frac{3}{5}, \frac{4}{3}$ 6 $\frac{9}{41}, \frac{40}{41}, \frac{9}{40}$ 7 $\frac{31}{481}, \frac{480}{481}, \frac{31}{480}$

Exercise 15.2A

1 a 0.6157 b 0.6884 c 0.3641 d 0.4818 e 0.9007 f 0.8064
2 a 6.81 cm b 63.0 m c 12.3cm
3 19.0 cm 4 4.93 m 5 3.91 m 6 0.908 m
7 1.56 m 8 30 m 9 225 m

Exercise 15.2B

1 a 17° 28′ b 14° 46′ c 47° 12′ 2 a 25.15° b 17° 28′ c 71.8°
3 44° 26′ 4 38° 41′ 5 64.15° 6 7° 10′ 7 38° 41′ 8 23° 35′

Exercise 15.3A

1 a 0.5015 b 0.8893 c 0.8297 d 0.7290 e 0.4594 f 0.8825
2 a 14.1 cm b 6.1 m c 5.20 3 4.24 cm 4 3.74 cm
5 1.06 m 6 3.13 m 7 485 m 8 23.6 cm
9 1.85 m 10 67.5 m

Exercise 15.3B

1 a 66° 25′ b 82° 37′ c 48° 11′ 2 a 55° 57′ b 36° 52′ c 48° 11′
3 41.4° 4 47.15° 5 64.05° 6 18.2°
7 23° 4′ 8 31° 47′

Exercise 15.4

1 123 km 2 134 km, 149 km 3 940 km, 342 km
4 219 km, 306 km 5 32° 6 49.45° 7 141° 20′
8 a 138 km b 243 km c 62.4° 9 a 538 km b 294 km c 029°

Exercise 16.1

2 a 60° b 55° c 130° 3 96° 4 54° 5 152°
6 25° 7 30° 8 36° 9 65°, 72.5°, 42.5°

Exercise 16.2

2 a 58° b 45° c 30° 3 55° 5 16 cm 6 13°
7 70.6 cm 8 a 36 cm b 12.9 cm c 41.4° d 7.8 cm

Exercise 16.3

2 a 17° b 30° c 73° 4 a 106° b 69° 5 76°
6 14 ° 8 99° 9 53°

Exercise 16.4

2 a 95° b 80° c 150° 4 80°. Parallel 5 50°
6 108° 7 68° 8 21° 9 91°, 67°

Exercise 16.5

1 a 69° b 80° 2 64° 4 64° 6 rectangle 7 90°

Exercise 17.1A

1 a 48.6 cm² b 3090 m² 2 16.8 cm² 3 2.78 cm²
4 336 cm² 5 6.77 m 6 4.11 cm 7 1.21 km
8 48.6° 9 38.7°

Exercise 17.1B
1 a 42.4 m²   **b** 7260 m²   **2** 21.3 cm²   **3** 2.9 m²
4 28.6 cm²; 6.71 cm   **5** 8.54 cm   **6** 43.3 cm²
8 a 3920 m²   **b** 0.392 ha

Exercise 17.1C
1 28 cm²   **2** 17.3 m²   **3** 369 m²

Exercise 17.2
1 238 cm²   **2** 27.5 cm²   **3** 73.5 cm²   **4** 3080 cm²
5 20.7 m²   **6** 131 cm²   **7** 20.5 cm²
8 a 37cm²   **b** 85 cm²   **9** 55 cm²

Exercise 17.3
1 847 cm²   **2** 260 cm²   **3** 5540 cm²   **4** 67 cm²
5 86 000 cm²

Exercise 18.1
1 100 cm³   **2** 1000 m³   **3** 2 590 000   **4** 168 cm³
5 12.6 m²   **6** 15 cm   **7** 4 m   **8** 1.15 cm
9 2.00 cm   **10 a** 0.597 cm   **b** 4.89 cm   **11 a** 15 m   **b** 5.48 m

Exercise 18.2
1 905 cm³, 452 cm²   **2** 1.15 m³, 5.31 m²   **3** 2090 cm³, 942 cm²
4 151 m²   **5** $3\pi r^2$ **6** 4 cm   **7** 0.472 m
8 266 cm³   **9** 49.8 m²   **10 a** 7240 cm³   **b** 1810 cm²
11 a 1.95 cm   **b** 31.3 cm³   **12 a** 6.66 m   **b** 558 m²

Exercise 18.3
1 283 cm²   **2** 704 m²   **3** $20\frac{2}{3}$ cm, 19.8 cm   **4** 11.8 m
5 28.1 cm, 407 cm²   **6** 30 500 cm³   **7 a** 1260 cm³   **b** 805 cm²
8 a 0.955 m   **b** 158 m²   **9 a** 2.52 cm   **b** 117 cm²
10 a 27.7 cm   **b** 19.2 cm   **c** 8060 cm³

Exercise 18.4A
1 39.8 cm³   **2** 264 cm³   **3** 283 cm³   **4** 41.9 cm³
5 0.159 m³   **6** 1390 cm³   **7** 355 cm³   **8** 4190 cm³
9 354 cm³   **10** 1.44 cm

Exercise 18.4B
1 85.6 cm²   **2** 223 cm²   **3** 236 cm²   **4** 64.9 cm²
5 176 m²   **6** 757 cm²

Exercise 19.2
5 2.24 cm by 0.96 cm

Exercise 19.3
1 a $-\frac{1}{2}$ **b** –2

Exercise 19.4
1 a (1,2), (3, 6), (7, 2)   **b** (1, 2), (1.5, 3), (2.5, 2)   **c** (–1, –1), (2, 5), (8, –1)
2 a (–4, 4), (–4, 0), (–10, 0), (–8, 2), (–8, 4)
   b (0, 3), (0, 1), (–3, 1), (–2, 2), (–2, 3)
   c (–4, –0.5), (–4, –1.5), (–5.5, –1.5), (–5, –1), (–5, –0,5)
3 (–6, 7). 2   **4 a** (–3, –1), (–5, 1), (–3, 7), (–1, 1)
   b (0, 6), (0.5, 5.5), (0, 4.5), (–0.5, 5.5)   **5** (1, 2), 2   **6** (4, 3), $\frac{1}{2}$ **7** (0, 2), –2

Exercise 19.5

1 *PQR, PST*, 0.75 cm **3 a** $6\frac{2}{3}$ cm **b** 3.96 cm **4** 2.5 cm
5 12.5 m **6** 1 & 3, 2 & 4 **7 a & d**

Exercise 20.1A

1 11.25 cm^2 **2** 100 000 cm^2 **3** 4 : 9 **4** 4 : 9 **5** 1280 cm^2
6 40 cm^2 **7** 64 m^2 **8** 781.25 cm^2 **9** 307.2 cm^2
10 625 cm^2, 1225 cm^2, 1600 cm^2

Exercise 20.1B

1 1.6 **2** 4.4 cm by 2.8 cm **3** 297 mm by 424 mm
4 148 mm by 212 mm **5** 13.9 cm **6** 2.20 cm
7 32.35% **8** 968 cm^2 **9** 110.25 km^2 **10** 9.5%
11 22.5% **12** 34%

Exercise 20.2

1 128 m^2 **2** 120 cm^2 **3 a** 40 cm **b** 100 cm^2
4 1 : 400 000 **5** ÷ by 4 **6** 28.8 km^2

Exercise 20.3

1 1562.5 cm^3 **2** 0.506 25 litres **3** 567 cm^3 **4** 675 cm^3
5 1 : 1.26 **6** 18.2 cm **7** 3.23 cm **8** 4 : 9
9 27 : 64 **10** 8 : 27, 540 g **11 a** 1 : 1.36 **b** 1 : 1.84
12 691.2 cm^3 **13** 133.1 cm^3 **14** 44%

Exercise 20.4

1 a 10 cm^3 **b** 70 cm^3 **c** 25 cm^2 **d** 75 cm^2
2 a 2 cm **b** 64 : 63 **c** 16 : 15 **3** 48 cm
4 a 30 cm **b** 70.4 kg **5 a** 20 cm **b** 383 g
6 a 9.43 cm **b** 8 : 27 **7** $\sqrt[3]{0.5}$ from base

Exercise 21.1

1 a 17.8 cm **b** 31.5 **c** 5.81 cm
2 a 51.35° **b** 40.5° **c** 41.4°
3 a 56° 19′ **b** 4.81 cm **c** 44.4° **d** 22.2 m **4** 38° 40′ **5** 4.35 m
6 48.6° **7** 42.4 km

Exercise 21.2

1 a 4.23 cm **b** 1.127 cm **c** 73.11 m
2 a 38.6° **b** 50° 53′ **c** 46° 53′
3 a 4.83 **b** 0.0425 **c** 40° 26′ **d** 45.8°

Exercise 21.4

1 $\frac{3}{5}, \frac{4}{3}$ **2** $\frac{12}{13}, \frac{12}{5}$ **3** $\frac{8}{17}, \frac{15}{17}$
4 0.954, 0.314 **5** 0.917, 2.29 **6** 0.768, 0.640
7 a 13° **b** 39° **8** $\sqrt{\frac{1}{61}}$, 50.2° **9** 2, 63.4° **10** 26.6°
11 59° **12** $\frac{1}{2}$, 60° **13** 70.5° **14** 30° **15** 30°

SQUARES

	0	1	2	3	4	5	6	7	8	9	Mean differences								
											1	2	3	4	5	6	7	8	9
1.0	1.000	1.020	1.040	1.061	1.082	1.103	1.124	1.145	1.166	1.188	2	4	6	8	10	13	15	17	19
1.1	1.210	1.232	1.254	1.277	1.300	1.323	1.346	1.369	1.392	1.416	2	5	7	9	11	14	16	18	21
1.2	1.440	1.464	1.488	1.513	1.538	1.563	1.588	1.613	1.638	1.664	2	5	7	10	12	15	17	20	22
1.3	1.690	1.716	1.742	1.769	1.796	1.823	1.850	1.877	1.904	1.932	3	5	8	11	13	16	19	22	24
1.4	1.960	1.988	2.016	2.045	2.074	2.103	2.132	2.161	2.190	2.220	3	6	9	12	14	17	20	23	26
1.5	2.250	2.280	2.310	2.341	2.372	2.403	2.434	2.465	2.496	2.528	3	6	9	12	15	19	22	25	28
1.6	2.560	2.592	2.624	2.657	2.690	2.723	2.756	2.789	2.822	2.856	3	7	10	13	16	20	23	26	30
1.7	2.890	2.924	2.958	2.993	3.028	3.063	3.098	3.133	3.168	3.204	3	7	10	14	17	21	24	28	31
1.8	3.240	3.276	3.312	3.349	3.386	3.423	3.460	3.497	3.534	3.572	4	7	11	15	18	22	26	30	33
1.9	3.610	3.648	3.686	3.725	3.764	3.803	3.842	3.881	3.920	3.960	4	8	12	16	19	23	27	31	35
2.0	4.000	4.040	4.080	4.121	4.162	4.203	4.244	4.285	4.326	4.368	4	8	12	16	20	25	29	33	37
2.1	4.410	4.452	4.494	4.537	4.580	4.623	4.666	4.709	4.752	4.796	4	9	13	17	21	26	30	34	39
2.2	4.840	4.884	4.928	4.973	5.018	5.063	5.108	5.153	5.198	5.244	4	9	13	18	22	27	31	36	40
2.3	5.290	5.336	5.382	5.429	5.476	5.523	5.570	5.617	5.664	5.712	5	9	14	19	23	28	33	38	42
2.4	5.760	5.808	5.856	5.905	5.954	6.003	6.052	6.101	6.150	6.200	5	10	15	20	24	29	34	39	44
2.5	6.250	6.300	6.350	6.401	6.452	6.503	6.554	6.605	6.656	6.708	5	10	15	20	25	31	36	41	46
2.6	6.760	6.812	6.864	6.917	6.970	7.023	7.076	7.129	7.182	7.236	5	11	16	21	26	32	37	42	48
2.7	7.290	7.344	7.398	7.453	7.508	7.563	7.618	7.673	7.728	7.784	5	11	16	22	27	33	38	44	49
2.8	7.840	7.896	7.952	8.009	8.066	8.123	8.180	8.237	8.294	8.352	6	11	17	23	28	34	40	46	51
2.9	8.410	8.468	8.526	8.585	8.644	8.703	8.762	8.821	8.880	8.940	6	12	18	24	29	35	41	47	53
3.0	9.000	9.060	9.120	9.181	9.242	9.303	9.364	9.425	9.486	9.548	6	12	18	24	30	37	43	49	55
3.1	9.610	9.672	9.734	9.797	9.860	9.923	9.986				6	13	19	25	31	38	44	50	57
3.1								10.05	10.11	10.18	1	1	2	3	3	4	4	5	6
3.2	10.24	10.30	10.37	10.43	10.50	10.56	10.63	10.69	10.76	10.82	1	1	2	3	3	4	5	5	6
3.3	10.89	10.96	11.02	11.09	11.16	11.22	11.29	11.36	11.42	11.49	1	1	2	3	3	4	5	5	6
3.4	11.56	11.63	11.70	11.76	11.83	11.90	11.97	12.04	12.11	12.18	1	1	2	3	3	4	5	6	6
3.5	12.25	12.32	12.39	12.46	12.53	12.60	12.67	12.74	12.82	12.89	1	1	2	3	4	4	5	6	6
3.6	12.96	13.03	13.10	13.18	13.25	13.32	13.40	13.47	13.54	13.62	1	1	2	3	4	4	5	6	7
3.7	13.69	13.76	13.84	13.91	13.99	14.06	14.14	14.21	14.29	14.36	1	2	2	3	4	5	5	6	7
3.8	14.44	14.52	14.59	14.67	14.75	14.82	14.90	14.98	15.05	15.13	1	2	2	3	4	5	5	6	7
3.9	15.21	15.29	15.37	15.44	15.52	15.60	15.68	15.76	15.84	15.92	1	2	2	3	4	5	6	6	7
4.0	16.00	16.08	16.16	16.24	16.32	16.40	16.48	16.56	16.65	16.73	1	2	2	3	4	5	6	6	7
4.1	16.81	16.89	16.97	17.06	17.14	17.22	17.31	17.39	17.47	17.56	1	2	2	3	4	5	6	7	7
4.2	17.64	17.72	17.81	17.89	17.98	18.06	18.15	18.23	18.32	18.40	1	2	3	3	4	5	6	7	8
4.3	18.49	18.58	18.66	18.75	18.84	18.92	19.01	19.10	19.18	19.27	1	2	3	3	4	5	6	7	8
4.4	19.36	19.45	19.54	19.62	19.71	19.80	19.89	19.98	20.07	20.16	1	2	3	4	4	5	6	7	8
4.5	20.25	20.34	20.43	20.52	20.61	20.70	20.79	20.88	20.98	21.07	1	2	3	4	5	5	6	7	8
4.6	21.16	21.25	21.34	21.44	21.53	21.62	21.72	21.81	21.90	22.00	1	2	3	4	5	6	7	7	8
4.7	22.09	22.18	22.28	22.37	22.47	22.56	22.66	22.75	22.85	22.94	1	2	3	4	5	6	7	8	9
4.8	23.04	23.14	23.23	23.33	23.43	23.52	23.62	23.72	23.81	23.91	1	2	3	4	5	6	7	8	9
4.9	24.01	24.11	24.21	24.30	24.40	24.50	24.60	24.70	24.80	24.90	1	2	3	4	5	6	7	8	9
5.0	25.00	25.10	25.20	25.30	25.40	25.50	25.60	25.70	25.81	25.91	1	2	3	4	5	6	7	8	9
5.1	26.01	26.11	26.21	26.32	26.42	26.52	26.63	26.73	26.83	26.94	1	2	3	4	5	6	7	8	9
5.2	27.04	27.14	27.25	27.35	27.46	27.56	27.67	27.77	27.88	27.98	1	2	3	4	5	6	7	8	9
5.3	28.09	28.20	28.30	28.41	28.52	28.62	28.73	28.84	28.94	29.05	1	2	3	4	5	6	7	9	10
5.4	29.16	29.27	29.38	29.48	29.59	29.70	29.81	29.92	30.03	30.14	1	2	3	4	5	7	8	9	10

SQUARES

	0	1	2	3	4	5	6	7	8	9	Mean differences								
											1	2	3	4	5	6	7	8	9
5.5	30.25	30.36	30.47	30.58	30.69	30.80	30.91	31.02	31.14	31.25	1	2	3	4	6	7	8	9	10
5.6	31.36	31.47	31.58	31.70	31.81	31.92	32.04	32.15	32.26	32.38	1	2	3	5	6	7	8	9	10
5.7	32.49	32.60	32.72	32.83	32.95	33.06	33.18	33.29	33.41	33.52	1	2	3	5	6	7	8	9	10
5.8	33.64	33.76	33.87	33.99	34.11	34.22	34.34	34.46	34.57	34.69	1	2	4	5	6	7	8	9	11
5.9	34.81	34.93	35.05	35.16	35.28	35.40	35.52	35.64	35.76	35.88	1	2	4	5	6	7	8	10	11
6.0	36.00	36.12	36.24	36.36	36.48	36.60	36.72	36.84	36.97	37.09	1	2	4	5	6	7	9	10	11
6.1	37.21	37.33	37.45	37.58	37.70	37.82	37.95	38.07	38.19	38.32	1	2	4	5	6	7	9	10	11
6.2	38.44	38.56	38.69	38.81	38.94	39.06	39.19	39.31	39.44	39.56	1	3	4	5	6	8	9	10	11
6.3	39.69	39.82	39.94	40.07	40.20	40.32	40.45	40.58	40.70	40.83	1	3	4	5	6	8	9	10	11
6.4	40.96	41.09	41.22	41.34	41.47	41.60	41.73	41.86	41.99	42.12	1	3	4	5	6	8	9	10	12
6.5	42.25	42.38	42.51	42.64	42.77	42.90	43.03	43.16	43.30	43.43	1	3	4	5	7	8	9	10	12
6.6	43.56	43.69	43.82	43.96	44.09	44.22	44.36	44.49	44.62	44.76	1	3	4	5	7	8	9	11	12
6.7	44.89	45.02	45.16	45.29	45.43	45.56	45.70	45.83	45.97	46.10	1	3	4	5	7	8	9	11	12
6.8	46.24	46.38	46.51	46.65	46.79	46.92	47.06	47.20	47.33	47.47	1	3	4	5	7	8	10	11	12
6.9	47.61	47.75	47.89	48.02	48.16	48.30	48.44	48.58	48.72	48.86	1	3	4	6	7	8	10	11	13
7.0	49.00	49.14	49.28	49.42	49.56	49.70	49.84	49.98	50.13	50.27	1	3	4	6	7	8	10	11	13
7.1	50.41	50.55	50.69	50.84	50.98	51.12	51.27	51.41	51.55	51.70	1	3	4	6	7	9	10	11	13
7.2	51.84	51.98	52.13	52.27	52.42	52.56	52.71	52.85	53.00	53.14	1	3	4	6	7	9	10	12	13
7.3	53.29	53.44	53.58	53.73	53.88	54.02	54.17	54.32	54.46	54.61	1	3	4	6	7	9	10	12	13
7.4	54.76	54.91	55.06	55.20	55.35	55.50	55.65	55.80	55.95	56.10	1	3	4	6	7	9	10	12	13
7.5	56.25	56.40	56.55	56.70	56.85	57.00	57.15	57.30	57.46	57.61	2	3	5	6	8	9	11	12	14
7.6	57.76	57.91	58.06	58.22	58.37	58.52	58.68	58.83	58.98	59.14	2	3	5	6	8	9	11	12	14
7.7	59.29	59.44	59.60	59.75	59.91	60.06	60.22	60.37	60.53	60.68	2	3	5	6	8	9	11	12	14
7.8	60.84	61.00	61.15	61.31	61.47	61.62	61.78	61.94	62.09	62.25	2	3	5	6	8	9	11	13	14
7.9	62.41	62.57	62.73	62.88	63.04	63.20	63.36	63.52	63.68	63.84	2	3	5	6	8	10	11	13	14
8.0	64.00	64.16	64.32	64.48	64.64	64.80	64.96	65.12	65.29	65.45	2	3	5	6	8	10	11	13	14
8.1	65.61	65.77	65.93	66.10	66.26	66.42	66.59	66.75	66.91	67.08	2	3	5	7	8	10	11	13	15
8.2	67.24	67.40	67.57	67.73	67.90	68.06	68.23	68.39	68.56	68.72	2	3	5	7	8	10	12	13	15
8.3	68.89	69.06	69.22	69.39	69.56	69.72	69.89	70.06	70.22	70.39	2	3	5	7	8	10	12	13	15
8.4	70.56	70.73	70.90	71.06	71.23	71.40	71.57	71.74	71.91	72.08	2	3	5	7	8	10	12	14	15
8.5	72.25	72.42	72.59	72.76	72.93	73.10	73.27	73.44	73.62	73.79	2	3	5	7	9	10	12	14	15
8.6	73.96	74.13	74.30	74.48	74.65	74.82	75.00	75.17	75.34	75.52	2	3	5	7	9	10	12	14	16
8.7	75.69	75.86	76.04	76.21	76.39	76.56	76.74	76.91	77.09	77.26	2	4	5	7	9	10	12	14	16
8.8	77.44	77.62	77.79	77.97	78.15	78.32	78.50	78.68	78.85	79.03	2	4	5	7	9	11	12	14	16
8.9	79.21	79.39	79.57	79.74	79.92	80.10	80.28	80.46	80.64	80.82	2	4	5	7	9	11	13	14	16
9.0	81.00	81.18	81.36	81.54	81.72	81.90	82.08	82.26	82.45	82.63	2	4	5	7	9	11	13	14	16
9.1	82.81	82.99	83.17	83.36	83.54	83.72	83.91	84.09	84.27	84.46	2	4	5	7	9	11	13	15	16
9.2	84.64	84.82	85.01	85.19	85.38	85.56	85.75	85.93	86.12	86.30	2	4	6	7	9	11	13	15	17
9.3	86.49	86.68	86.86	87.05	87.24	87.42	87.61	87.80	87.98	88.17	2	4	6	7	9	11	13	15	17
9.4	88.36	88.55	88.74	88.92	89.11	89.30	89.49	89.68	89.87	90.06	2	4	6	8	9	11	13	15	17
9.5	90.25	90.44	90.63	90.82	91.01	91.20	91.39	91.58	91.78	91.97	2	4	6	8	10	11	13	15	17
9.6	92.16	92.35	92.54	92.74	92.93	93.12	93.32	93.51	93.70	93.90	2	4	6	8	10	12	14	15	17
9.7	94.09	94.28	94.48	94.67	94.87	95.06	95.26	95.45	95.65	95.84	2	4	6	8	10	12	14	16	18
9.8	96.04	96.24	96.43	96.63	96.83	97.02	97.22	97.42	97.61	97.81	2	4	6	8	10	12	14	16	18
9.9	98.01	98.21	98.41	98.60	98.80	99.00	99.20	99.40	99.60	99.80	2	4	6	8	10	12	14	16	18

RECIPROCALS

	0	1	2	3	4	5	6	7	8	9	Mean differences								
											1	2	3	4	5	6	7	8	9
1.0	1.0000	0.9901	0.9804	0.9709	0.9615	0.9524	0.9434	0.9346	0.9259	0.9174									
1.1	0.9091	0.9009	0.8929	0.8850	0.8772	0.8696	0.8621	0.8547	0.8475	0.8403									
1.2	0.8333	0.8264	0.8197	0.8130	0.8065	0.8000	0.7937	0.7874	0.7812	0.7752									
1.3	0.7692	0.7634	0.7576	0.7519	0.7463	0.7407	0.7353	0.7299	0.7246	0.7194									
1.4	0.7143	0.7092	0.7042	0.6993	0.6944	0.6897	0.6849	0.6803	0.6757	0.6711	5	10	14	19	24	29	33	38	43
1.5	0.6667	0.6623	0.6579	0.6536	0.6494	0.6452	0.6410	0.6369	0.6329	0.6289	4	8	13	17	21	25	29	33	38
1.6	0.6250	0.6211	0.6173	0.6135	0.6098	0.6061	0.6024	0.5988	0.5952	0.5917	4	7	11	15	18	22	26	29	33
1.7	0.5882	0.5848	0.5814	0.5780	0.5747	0.5714	0.5682	0.5650	0.5618	0.5587	3	6	10	13	16	20	23	26	29
1.8	0.5556	0.5525	0.5495	0.5464	0.5435	0.5405	0.5376	0.5348	0.5319	0.5291	3	6	9	12	15	17	20	23	26
1.9	0.5263	0.5236	0.5208	0.5181	0.5155	0.5128	0.5102	0.5076	0.5051	0.5025	3	5	8	11	13	16	18	21	24
2.0	0.5000	0.4975	0.4950	0.4926	0.4902	0.4878	0.4854	0.4831	0.4808	0.4785	2	5	7	10	12	14	17	19	21
2.1	0.4762	0.4739	0.4717	0.4695	0.4673	0.4651	0.4630	0.4608	0.4587	0.4566	2	4	7	9	11	13	15	17	20
2.2	0.4545	0.4525	0.4505	0.4484	0.4464	0.4444	0.4425	0.4405	0.4386	0.4367	2	4	6	8	10	12	14	16	18
2.3	0.4348	0.4329	0.4310	0.4292	0.4274	0.4255	0.4237	0.4219	0.4202	0.4184	2	4	5	7	9	11	13	14	16
2.4	0.4167	0.4149	0.4132	0.4115	0.4098	0.4082	0.4065	0.4049	0.4032	0.4016	2	3	5	7	8	10	12	13	15
2.5	0.4000	0.3984	0.3968	0.3953	0.3937	0.3922	0.3906	0.3891	0.3876	0.3861	2	3	5	6	8	9	11	12	14
2.6	0.3846	0.3831	0.3817	0.3802	0.3788	0.3774	0.3759	0.3745	0.3731	0.3717	1	3	4	6	7	8	10	11	13
2.7	0.3704	0.3690	0.3676	0.3663	0.3650	0.3636	0.3623	0.3610	0.3597	0.3584	1	3	4	5	7	8	9	11	12
2.8	0.3571	0.3559	0.3546	0.3534	0.3521	0.3509	0.3497	0.3484	0.3472	0.3460	1	2	4	5	6	7	9	10	11
2.9	0.3448	0.3436	0.3425	0.3413	0.3401	0.3390	0.3378	0.3367	0.3356	0.3344	1	2	3	5	6	7	8	9	10
3.0	0.3333	0.3322	0.3311	0.3300	0.3289	0.3279	0.3268	0.3257	0.3247	0.3236	1	2	3	4	5	6	7	9	10
3.1	0.3226	0.3215	0.3205	0.3195	0.3185	0.3175	0.3165	0.3155	0.3145	0.3135	1	2	3	4	5	6	7	8	9
3.2	0.3125	0.3115	0.3106	0.3096	0.3086	0.3077	0.3067	0.3058	0.3049	0.3040	1	2	3	4	5	6	7	8	9
3.3	0.3030	0.3021	0.3012	0.3003	0.2994	0.2985	0.2976	0.2967	0.2959	0.2950	1	2	3	4	4	5	6	7	8
3.4	0.2941	0.2933	0.2924	0.2915	0.2907	0.2899	0.2890	0.2882	0.2874	0.2865	1	2	3	3	4	5	6	7	8
3.5	0.2857	0.2849	0.2841	0.2833	0.2825	0.2817	0.2809	0.2801	0.2793	0.2786	1	2	2	3	4	5	6	6	7
3.6	0.2778	0.2770	0.2762	0.2755	0.2747	0.2740	0.2732	0.2725	0.2717	0.2710	1	2	2	3	4	5	5	6	7
3.7	0.2703	0.2695	0.2688	0.2681	0.2674	0.2667	0.2660	0.2653	0.2646	0.2639	1	1	2	3	4	4	5	6	6
3.8	0.2632	0.2625	0.2618	0.2611	0.2604	0.2597	0.2591	0.2584	0.2577	0.2571	1	1	2	3	3	4	5	5	6
3.9	0.2564	0.2558	0.2551	0.2545	0.2538	0.2532	0.2525	0.2519	0.2513	0.2506	1	1	2	3	3	4	4	5	6
4.0	0.2500	0.2494	0.2488	0.2481	0.2475	0.2469	0.2463	0.2457	0.2451	0.2445	1	1	2	2	3	4	4	5	6
4.1	0.2439	0.2433	0.2427	0.2421	0.2415	0.2410	0.2404	0.2398	0.2392	0.2387	1	1	2	2	3	3	4	5	5
4.2	0.2381	0.2375	0.2370	0.2364	0.2358	0.2353	0.2347	0.2342	0.2336	0.2331	1	1	2	2	3	3	4	4	5
4.3	0.2326	0.2320	0.2315	0.2309	0.2304	0.2299	0.2294	0.2288	0.2283	0.2278	1	1	2	2	3	3	4	4	5
4.4	0.2273	0.2268	0.2262	0.2257	0.2252	0.2247	0.2242	0.2237	0.2232	0.2227	1	1	2	2	3	3	4	4	5
4.5	0.2222	0.2217	0.2212	0.2208	0.2203	0.2198	0.2193	0.2188	0.2183	0.2179	0	1	1	2	2	3	3	4	4
4.6	0.2174	0.2169	0.2165	0.2160	0.2155	0.2151	0.2146	0.2141	0.2137	0.2132	0	1	1	2	2	3	3	4	4
4.7	0.2128	0.2123	0.2119	0.2114	0.2110	0.2105	0.2101	0.2096	0.2092	0.2088	0	1	1	2	2	3	3	4	4
4.8	0.2083	0.2079	0.2075	0.2070	0.2066	0.2062	0.2058	0.2053	0.2049	0.2045	0	1	1	2	2	3	3	3	4
4.9	0.2041	0.2037	0.2033	0.2028	0.2024	0.2020	0.2016	0.2012	0.2008	0.2004	0	1	1	2	2	2	3	3	4
5.0	0.2000	0.1996	0.1992	0.1988	0.1984	0.1980	0.1976	0.1972	0.1969	0.1965	0	1	1	2	2	2	3	3	4
5.1	0.1961	0.1957	0.1953	0.1949	0.1946	0.1942	0.1938	0.1934	0.1931	0.1927	0	1	1	2	2	2	3	3	3
5.2	0.1923	0.1919	0.1916	0.1912	0.1908	0.1905	0.1901	0.1898	0.1894	0.1890	0	1	1	1	2	2	3	3	3
5.3	0.1887	0.1883	0.1880	0.1876	0.1873	0.1869	0.1866	0.1862	0.1859	0.1855	0	1	1	1	2	2	2	3	3
5.4	0.1852	0.1848	0.1845	0.1842	0.1838	0.1835	0.1832	0.1828	0.1825	0.1821	0	1	1	1	2	2	2	3	3

Numbers in difference columns to be subtracted, not added.

RECIPROCALS

	0	1	2	3	4	5	6	7	8	9	Mean differences								
											1	2	3	4	5	6	7	8	9
5.5	0.1818	0.1815	0.1812	0.1808	0.1805	0.1802	0.1799	0.1795	0.1792	0.1789	0	1	1	1	2	2	2	3	3
5.6	0.1786	0.1783	0.1779	0.1776	0.1773	0.1770	0.1767	0.1764	0.1761	0.1757	0	1	1	1	2	2	2	3	3
5.7	0.1754	0.1751	0.1748	0.1745	0.1742	0.1739	0.1736	0.1733	0.1730	0.1727	0	1	1	1	2	2	2	2	3
5.8	0.1724	0.1721	0.1718	0.1715	0.1712	0.1709	0.1706	0.1704	0.1701	0.1698	0	1	1	1	1	2	2	2	3
5.9	0.1695	0.1692	0.1689	0.1686	0.1684	0.1681	0.1678	0.1675	0.1672	0.1669	0	1	1	1	1	2	2	2	3
6.0	0.1667	0.1664	0.1661	0.1658	0.1656	0.1653	0.1650	0.1647	0.1645	0.1642	0	1	1	1	1	2	2	2	2
6.1	0.1639	0.1637	0.1634	0.1631	0.1629	0.1626	0.1623	0.1621	0.1618	0.1616	0	1	1	1	1	2	2	2	2
6.2	0.1613	0.1610	0.1608	0.1605	0.1603	0.1600	0.1597	0.1595	0.1592	0.1590	0	1	1	1	1	2	2	2	2
6.3	0.1587	0.1585	0.1582	0.1580	0.1577	0.1575	0.1572	0.1570	0.1567	0.1565	0	0	1	1	1	1	2	2	2
6.4	0.1563	0.1560	0.1558	0.1555	0.1553	0.1550	0.1548	0.1546	0.1543	0.1541	0	0	1	1	1	1	2	2	2
6.5	0.1538	0.1536	0.1534	0.1531	0.1529	0.1527	0.1524	0.1522	0.1520	0.1517	0	0	1	1	1	1	2	2	2
6.6	0.1515	0.1513	0.1511	0.1508	0.1506	0.1504	0.1502	0.1499	0.1497	0.1495	0	0	1	1	1	1	2	2	2
6.7	0.1493	0.1490	0.1488	0.1486	0.1484	0.1481	0.1479	0.1477	0.1475	0.1473	0	0	1	1	1	1	2	2	2
6.8	0.1471	0.1468	0.1466	0.1464	0.1462	0.1460	0.1458	0.1456	0.1453	0.1451	0	0	1	1	1	1	1	2	2
6.9	0.1449	0.1447	0.1445	0.1443	0.1441	0.1439	0.1437	0.1435	0.1433	0.1431	0	0	1	1	1	1	1	2	2
7.0	0.1429	0.1427	0.1425	0.1422	0.1420	0.1418	0.1416	0.1414	0.1412	0.1410	0	0	1	1	1	1	1	2	2
7.1	0.1408	0.1406	0.1404	0.1403	0.1401	0.1399	0.1397	0.1395	0.1393	0.1391	0	0	1	1	1	1	1	2	2
7.2	0.1389	0.1387	0.1385	0.1383	0.1381	0.1379	0.1377	0.1376	0.1374	0.1372	0	0	1	1	1	1	1	2	2
7.3	0.1370	0.1368	0.1366	0.1364	0.1362	0.1361	0.1359	0.1357	0.1355	0.1353	0	0	1	1	1	1	1	1	2
7.4	0.1351	0.1350	0.1348	0.1346	0.1344	0.1342	0.1340	0.1339	0.1337	0.1335	0	0	1	1	1	1	1	1	2
7.5	0.1333	0.1332	0.1330	0.1328	0.1326	0.1325	0.1323	0.1321	0.1319	0.1318	0	0	1	1	1	1	1	1	2
7.6	0.1316	0.1314	0.1312	0.1311	0.1309	0.1307	0.1305	0.1304	0.1302	0.1300	0	0	1	1	1	1	1	1	2
7.7	0.1299	0.1297	0.1295	0.1294	0.1292	0.1290	0.1289	0.1287	0.1285	0.1284	0	0	1	1	1	1	1	1	2
7.8	0.1282	0.1280	0.1279	0.1277	0.1276	0.1274	0.1272	0.1271	0.1269	0.1267	0	0	0	1	1	1	1	1	1
7.9	0.1266	0.1264	0.1263	0.1261	0.1259	0.1258	0.1256	0.1255	0.1253	0.1252	0	0	0	1	1	1	1	1	1
8.0	0.1250	0.1248	0.1247	0.1245	0.1244	0.1242	0.1241	0.1239	0.1238	0.1236	0	0	0	1	1	1	1	1	1
8.1	0.1235	0.1233	0.1232	0.1230	0.1229	0.1227	0.1225	0.1224	0.1222	0.1221	0	0	0	1	1	1	1	1	1
8.2	0.1220	0.1218	0.1217	0.1215	0.1214	0.1212	0.1211	0.1209	0.1208	0.1206	0	0	0	1	1	1	1	1	1
8.3	0.1205	0.1203	0.1202	0.1200	0.1199	0.1198	0.1196	0.1195	0.1193	0.1192	0	0	0	1	1	1	1	1	1
8.4	0.1190	0.1189	0.1188	0.1186	0.1185	0.1183	0.1182	0.1181	0.1179	0.1178	0	0	0	1	1	1	1	1	1
8.5	0.1176	0.1175	0.1174	0.1172	0.1171	0.1170	0.1168	0.1167	0.1166	0.1164	0	0	0	1	1	1	1	1	1
8.6	0.1163	0.1161	0.1160	0.1159	0.1157	0.1156	0.1155	0.1153	0.1152	0.1151	0	0	0	1	1	1	1	1	1
8.7	0.1149	0.1148	0.1147	0.1145	0.1144	0.1143	0.1142	0.1140	0.1139	0.1138	0	0	0	1	1	1	1	1	1
8.8	0.1136	0.1135	0.1134	0.1133	0.1131	0.1130	0.1129	0.1127	0.1126	0.1125	0	0	0	1	1	1	1	1	1
8.9	0.1124	0.1122	0.1121	0.1120	0.1119	0.1117	0.1116	0.1115	0.1114	0.1112	0	0	0	0	1	1	1	1	1
9.0	0.1111	0.1110	0.1109	0.1107	0.1106	0.1105	0.1104	0.1103	0.1101	0.1100	0	0	0	0	1	1	1	1	1
9.1	0.1099	0.1098	0.1096	0.1095	0.1094	0.1093	0.1092	0.1091	0.1089	0.1088	0	0	0	0	1	1	1	1	1
9.2	0.1087	0.1086	0.1085	0.1083	0.1082	0.1081	0.1080	0.1079	0.1078	0.1076	0	0	0	0	1	1	1	1	1
9.3	0.1075	0.1074	0.1073	0.1072	0.1071	0.1070	0.1068	0.1067	0.1066	0.1065	0	0	0	0	1	1	1	1	1
9.4	0.1064	0.1063	0.1062	0.1060	0.1059	0.1058	0.1057	0.1056	0.1055	0.1054	0	1	0	0	1	1	1	1	1
9.5	0.1053	0.1052	0.1050	0.1049	0.1048	0.1047	0.1046	0.1045	0.1044	0.1043	0	0	0	0	1	1	1	1	1
9.6	0.1042	0.1041	0.1040	0.1038	0.1037	0.1036	0.1035	0.1034	0.1033	0.1032	0	0	0	0	1	1	1	1	1
9.7	0.1031	0.1030	0.1029	0.1028	0.1027	0.1026	0.1025	0.1024	0.1022	0.1021	0	0	0	0	1	1	1	1	1
9.8	0.1020	0.1019	0.1018	0.1017	0.1016	0.1015	0.1014	0.1013	0.1012	0.1011	0	0	0	0	1	1	1	1	1
9.9	0.1010	0.1009	0.1008	0.1007	0.1006	0.1005	0.1004	0.1003	0.1002	0.1001	0	0	0	0	1	1	1	1	1

Numbers in difference columns to be subtracted, not added.

	0	1	2	3	4	5	6	7	8	9	Mean differences								
											1	2	3	4	5	6	7	8	9
1.0	1.000	1.005	1.010	1.015	1.020	1.025	1.030	1.034	1.039	1.044	0	1	1	2	2	3	3	4	4
1.1	1.049	1.054	1.058	1.063	1.068	1.072	1.077	1.082	1.086	1.091	0	1	1	2	2	3	3	4	4
1.2	1.095	1.100	1.105	1.109	1.114	1.118	1.122	1.127	1.131	1.136	0	1	1	2	2	3	3	4	4
1.3	1.140	1.145	1.149	1.153	1.158	1.162	1.166	1.170	1.175	1.179	0	1	1	2	2	3	3	3	4
1.4	1.183	1.187	1.192	1.196	1.200	1.204	1.208	1.212	1.217	1.221	0	1	1	2	2	2	3	3	4
1.5	1.225	1.229	1.233	1.237	1.241	1.245	1.249	1.253	1.257	1.261	0	1	1	2	2	2	3	3	4
1.6	1.265	1.269	1.273	1.277	1.281	1.285	1.288	1.292	1.296	1.300	0	1	1	2	2	2	3	3	3
1.7	1.304	1.308	1.311	1.315	1.319	1.323	1.327	1.330	1.334	1.338	0	1	1	2	2	2	3	3	3
1.8	1.342	1.345	1.349	1.353	1.356	1.360	1.364	1.367	1.371	1.375	0	1	1	1	2	2	3	3	3
1.9	1.378	1.382	1.386	1.389	1.393	1.396	1.400	1.404	1.407	1.411	0	1	1	1	2	2	3	3	3
2.0	1.414	1.418	1.421	1.425	1.428	1.432	1.435	1.439	1.442	1.446	0	1	1	1	2	2	2	3	3
2.1	1.449	1.453	1.456	1.459	1.463	1.466	1.470	1.473	1.476	1.480	0	1	1	1	2	2	2	3	3
2.2	1.483	1.487	1.490	1.493	1.497	1.500	1.503	1.507	1.510	1.513	0	1	1	1	2	2	2	3	3
2.3	1.517	1.520	1.523	1.526	1.530	1.533	1.536	1.539	1.543	1.546	0	1	1	1	2	2	2	3	3
2.4	1.549	1.552	1.556	1.559	1.562	1.565	1.568	1.572	1.575	1.578	0	1	1	1	2	2	2	3	3
2.5	1.581	1.584	1.587	1.591	1.594	1.597	1.600	1.603	1.606	1.609	0	1	1	1	2	2	2	3	3
2.6	1.612	1.616	1.619	1.622	1.625	1.628	1.631	1.634	1.637	1.640	0	1	1	1	2	2	2	2	3
2.7	1.643	1.646	1.649	1.652	1.655	1.658	1.661	1.664	1.667	1.670	0	1	1	1	2	2	2	2	3
2.8	1.673	1.676	1.679	1.682	1.685	1.688	1.691	1.694	1.697	1.700	0	1	1	1	1	2	2	2	3
2.9	1.703	1.706	1.709	1.712	1.715	1.718	1.720	1.723	1.726	1.729	0	1	1	1	1	2	2	2	3
3.0	1.732	1.735	1.738	1.741	1.744	1.746	1.749	1.752	1.755	1.758	0	1	1	1	1	2	2	2	3
3.1	1.761	1.764	1.766	1.769	1.772	1.775	1.778	1.780	1.783	1.786	0	1	1	1	1	2	2	2	3
3.2	1.789	1.792	1.794	1.797	1.800	1.803	1.806	1.808	1.811	1.814	0	1	1	1	1	2	2	2	2
3.3	1.817	1.819	1.822	1.825	1.828	1.830	1.833	1.836	1.838	1.841	0	1	1	1	1	2	2	2	2
3.4	1.844	1.847	1.849	1.852	1.855	1.857	1.860	1.863	1.865	1.868	0	1	1	1	1	2	2	2	2
3.5	1.871	1.873	1.876	1.879	1.881	1.884	1.887	1.889	1.892	1.895	0	1	1	1	1	2	2	2	2
3.6	1.897	1.900	1.903	1.905	1.908	1.910	1.913	1.916	1.918	1.921	0	1	1	1	1	2	2	2	2
3.7	1.924	1.926	1.929	1.931	1.934	1.936	1.939	1.942	1.944	1.947	0	1	1	1	1	2	2	2	2
3.8	1.949	1.952	1.954	1.957	1.960	1.962	1.965	1.967	1.970	1.972	0	1	1	1	1	2	2	2	2
3.9	1.975	1.977	1.980	1.982	1.985	1.987	1.990	1.992	1.995	1.997	0	1	1	1	1	2	2	2	2
4.0	2.000	2.002	2.005	2.007	2.010	2.012	2.015	2.017	2.020	2.022	0	0	1	1	1	1	2	2	2
4.1	2.025	2.027	2.030	2.032	2.035	2.037	2.040	2.042	2.045	2.047	0	0	1	1	1	1	2	2	2
4.2	2.049	2.052	2.054	2.057	2.059	2.062	2.064	2.066	2.069	2.071	0	0	1	1	1	1	2	2	2
4.3	2.074	2.076	2.078	2.081	2.083	2.086	2.088	2.090	2.093	2.095	0	0	1	1	1	1	2	2	2
4.4	2.098	2.100	2.102	2.105	2.107	2.110	2.112	2.114	2.117	2.119	0	0	1	1	1	1	2	2	2
4.5	2.121	2.124	2.126	2.128	2.131	2.133	2.135	2.138	2.140	2.142	0	0	1	1	1	1	2	2	2
4.6	2.145	2.147	2.149	2.152	2.154	2.156	2.159	2.161	2.163	2.166	0	0	1	1	1	1	2	2	2
4.7	2.168	2.170	2.173	2.175	2.177	2.179	2.182	2.184	2.186	2.189	0	0	1	1	1	1	2	2	2
4.8	2.191	2.193	2.195	2.198	2.200	2.202	2.205	2.207	2.209	2.211	0	0	1	1	1	1	2	2	2
4.9	2.214	2.216	2.218	2.220	2.223	2.225	2.227	2.229	2.232	2.234	0	0	1	1	1	1	2	2	2
5.0	2.236	2.238	2.241	2.243	2.245	2.247	2.249	2.252	2.254	2.256	0	0	1	1	1	1	2	2	2
5.1	2.258	2.261	2.263	2.265	2.267	2.269	2.272	2.274	2.276	2.278	0	0	1	1	1	1	2	2	2
5.2	2.280	2.283	2.285	2.287	2.289	2.291	2.293	2.296	2.298	2.300	0	0	1	1	1	1	2	2	2
5.3	2.302	2.304	2.307	2.309	2.311	2.313	2.315	2.317	2.319	2.322	0	0	1	1	1	1	2	2	2
5.4	2.324	2.326	2.328	2.330	2.332	2.335	2.337	2.339	2.341	2.343	0	0	1	1	1	1	1	2	2

	0	1	2	3	4	5	6	7	8	9	Mean differences								
											1	2	3	4	5	6	7	8	9
5.5	2.345	2.347	2.349	2.352	2.354	2.356	2.358	2.360	2.362	2.364	0	0	1	1	1	1	1	2	2
5.6	2.366	2.369	2.371	2.373	2.375	2.377	2.379	2.381	2.383	2.385	0	0	1	1	1	1	1	2	2
5.7	2.387	2.390	2.392	2.394	2.396	2.398	2.400	2.402	2.404	2.406	0	0	1	1	1	1	1	2	2
5.8	2.408	2.410	2.412	2.415	2.417	2.419	2.421	2.423	2.425	2.427	0	0	1	1	1	1	1	2	2
5.9	2.429	2.431	2.433	2.435	2.437	2.439	2.441	2.443	2.445	2.447	0	0	1	1	1	1	1	2	2
6.0	2.449	2.452	2.454	2.456	2.458	2.460	2.462	2.464	2.466	2.468	0	0	1	1	1	1	1	2	2
6.1	2.470	2.472	2.474	2.476	2.478	2.480	2.482	2.484	2.486	2.488	0	0	1	1	1	1	1	2	2
6.2	2.490	2.492	2.494	2.496	2.498	2.500	2.502	2.504	2.506	2.508	0	0	1	1	1	1	1	2	2
6.3	2.510	2.512	2.514	2.516	2.518	2.520	2.522	2.524	2.526	2.528	0	0	1	1	1	1	1	2	2
6.4	2.530	2.532	2.534	2.536	2.538	2.540	2.542	2.544	2.546	2.548	0	0	1	1	1	1	1	2	2
6.5	2.550	2.551	2.553	2.555	2.557	2.559	2.561	2.563	2.565	2.567	0	0	1	1	1	1	1	2	2
6.6	2.569	2.571	2.573	2.575	2.577	2.579	2.581	2.583	2.585	2.587	0	0	1	1	1	1	1	2	2
6.7	2.588	2.590	2.592	2.594	2.596	2.598	2.600	2.602	2.604	2.606	0	0	1	1	1	1	1	2	2
6.8	2.608	2.610	2.612	2.613	2.615	2.617	2.619	2.621	2.623	2.625	0	0	1	1	1	1	1	2	2
6.9	2.627	2.629	2.631	2.632	2.634	2.636	2.638	2.640	2.642	2.644	0	0	1	1	1	1	1	2	2
7.0	2.646	2.648	2.650	2.651	2.653	2.655	2.657	2.659	2.661	2.663	0	0	1	1	1	1	1	2	2
7.1	2.665	2.666	2.668	2.670	2.672	2.674	2.676	2.678	2.680	2.681	0	0	1	1	1	1	1	1	2
7.2	2.683	2.685	2.687	2.689	2.691	2.693	2.694	2.696	2.698	2.700	0	0	1	1	1	1	1	1	2
7.3	2.702	2.704	2.706	2.707	2.709	2.711	2.713	2.715	2.717	2.718	0	0	1	1	1	1	1	1	2
7.4	2.720	2.722	2.724	2.726	2.728	2.729	2.731	2.733	2.735	2.737	0	0	1	1	1	1	1	1	2
7.5	2.739	2.740	2.742	2.744	2.746	2.748	2.750	2.751	2.753	2.755	0	0	1	1	1	1	1	1	2
7.6	2.757	2.759	2.760	2.762	2.764	2.766	2.768	2.769	2.771	2.773	0	0	1	1	1	1	1	1	2
7.7	2.775	2.777	2.778	2.780	2.782	2.784	2.786	2.787	2.789	2.791	0	0	1	1	1	1	1	1	2
7.8	2.793	2.795	2.796	2.798	2.800	2.802	2.804	2.805	2.807	2.809	0	0	1	1	1	1	1	1	2
7.9	2.811	2.812	2.814	2.816	2.818	2.820	2.821	2.823	2.825	2.827	0	0	1	1	1	1	1	1	2
8.0	2.828	2.830	2.832	2.834	2.835	2.837	2.839	2.841	2.843	2.844	0	0	1	1	1	1	1	1	2
8.1	2.846	2.848	2.850	2.851	2.853	2.855	2.857	2.858	2.860	2.862	0	0	1	1	1	1	1	1	2
8.2	2.864	2.865	2.867	2.869	2.871	2.872	2.874	2.876	2.877	2.879	0	0	1	1	1	1	1	1	2
8.3	2.881	2.883	2.884	2.886	2.888	2.890	2.891	2.893	2.895	2.897	0	0	1	1	1	1	1	1	2
8.4	2.898	2.900	2.902	2.903	2.905	2.907	2.909	2.910	2.912	2.914	0	0	1	1	1	1	1	1	2
8.5	2.915	2.917	2.919	2.921	2.922	2.924	2.926	2.927	2.929	2.931	0	0	1	1	1	1	1	1	2
8.6	2.933	2.934	2.936	2.938	2.939	2.941	2.943	2.944	2.946	2.948	0	0	1	1	1	1	1	1	2
8.7	2.950	2.951	2.953	2.955	2.956	2.958	2.960	2.961	2.963	2.965	0	0	1	1	1	1	1	1	2
8.8	2.966	2.968	2.970	2.972	2.973	2.975	2.977	2.978	2.980	2.982	0	0	1	1	1	1	1	1	2
8.9	2.983	2.985	2.987	2.988	2.990	2.992	2.993	2.995	2.997	2.998	0	0	1	1	1	1	1	1	2
9.0	3.000	3.002	3.003	3.005	3.007	3.008	3.010	3.012	3.013	3.015	0	0	0	1	1	1	1	1	1
9.1	3.017	3.018	3.020	3.022	3.023	3.025	3.027	3.028	3.030	3.032	0	0	0	1	1	1	1	1	1
9.2	3.033	3.035	3.036	3.038	3.040	3.041	3.043	3.045	3.046	3.048	0	0	0	1	1	1	1	1	1
9.3	3.050	3.051	3.053	3.055	3.056	3.058	3.059	3.061	3.063	3.064	0	0	0	1	1	1	1	1	1
9.4	3.066	3.068	3.069	3.071	3.072	3.074	3.076	3.077	3.079	3.081	0	0	0	1	1	1	1	1	1
9.5	3.082	3.084	3.085	3.087	3.089	3.090	3.092	3.094	3.095	3.097	0	0	0	1	1	1	1	1	1
9.6	3.098	3.100	3.102	3.103	3.105	3.106	3.108	3.110	3.111	3.113	0	0	0	1	1	1	1	1	1
9.7	3.114	3.116	3.118	3.119	3.121	3.122	3.124	3.126	3.127	3.129	0	0	0	1	1	1	1	1	1
9.8	3.130	3.132	3.134	3.135	3.137	3.138	3.140	3.142	3.143	3.145	0	0	0	1	1	1	1	1	1
9.9	3.146	3.148	3.150	3.151	3.153	3.154	3.156	3.158	3.159	3.161	0	0	0	1	1	1	1	1	1

	0	1	2	3	4	5	6	7	8	9	Mean differences								
											1	2	3	4	5	6	7	8	9
10	3.162	3.178	3.194	3.209	3.225	3.240	3.256	3.271	3.286	3.302	2	3	5	6	8	9	11	12	14
11	3.317	3.332	3.347	3.362	3.376	3.391	3.406	3.421	3.435	3.450	1	3	4	6	7	9	10	12	13
12	3.464	3.479	3.493	3.507	3.521	3.536	3.550	3.564	3.578	3.592	1	3	4	6	7	8	10	11	13
13	3.606	3.619	3.633	3.647	3.661	3.674	3.688	3.701	3.715	3.728	1	3	4	5	7	8	10	11	12
14	3.742	3.755	3.768	3.782	3.795	3.808	3.821	3.834	3.847	3.860	1	3	4	5	7	8	9	11	12
15	3.873	3.886	3.899	3.912	3.924	3.937	3.950	3.962	3.975	3.987	1	3	4	5	6	8	9	10	11
16	4.000	4.012	4.025	4.037	4.050	4.062	4.074	4.087	4.099	4.111	1	2	4	5	6	7	9	10	11
17	4.123	4.135	4.147	4.159	4.171	4.183	4.195	4.207	4.219	4.231	1	2	4	5	6	7	8	10	11
18	4.243	4.254	4.266	4.278	4.290	4.301	4.313	4.324	4.336	4.347	1	2	3	5	6	7	8	9	10
19	4.359	4.370	4.382	4.393	4.405	4.416	4.427	4.438	4.450	4.461	1	2	3	5	6	7	8	9	10
20	4.472	4.483	4.494	4.506	4.517	4.528	4.539	4.550	4.561	4.572	1	2	3	4	6	7	8	9	10
21	4.583	4.593	4.604	4.615	4.626	4.637	4.648	4.658	4.669	4.680	1	2	3	4	5	6	8	9	10
22	4.690	4.701	4.712	4.722	4.733	4.743	4.754	4.764	4.775	4.785	1	2	3	4	5	6	7	8	9
23	4.796	4.806	4.817	4.827	4.837	4.848	4.858	4.868	4.879	4.889	1	2	3	4	5	6	7	8	9
24	4.899	4.909	4.919	4.930	4.940	4.950	4.960	4.970	4.980	4.990	1	2	3	4	5	6	7	8	9
25	5.000	5.010	5.020	5.030	5.040	5.050	5.060	5.070	5.079	5.089	1	2	3	4	5	6	7	8	9
26	5.099	5.109	5.119	5.128	5.138	5.148	5.158	5.167	5.177	5.187	1	2	3	4	5	6	7	8	9
27	5.196	5.206	5.215	5.225	5.235	5.244	5.254	5.263	5.273	5.282	1	2	3	4	5	6	7	8	9
28	5.292	5.301	5.310	5.320	5.329	5.339	5.348	5.357	5.367	5.376	1	2	3	4	5	6	7	7	8
29	5.385	5.394	5.404	5.413	5.422	5.431	5.441	5.450	5.459	5.468	1	2	3	4	5	5	6	7	8
30	5.477	5.486	5.495	5.505	5.514	5.523	5.532	5.541	5.550	5.559	1	2	3	4	4	5	6	7	8
31	5.568	5.577	5.586	5.595	5.604	5.612	5.621	5.630	5.639	5.648	1	2	3	3	4	5	6	7	8
32	5.657	5.666	5.675	5.683	5.692	5.701	5.710	5.718	5.727	5.736	1	2	3	3	4	5	6	7	8
33	5.745	5.753	5.762	5.771	5.779	5.788	5.797	5.805	5.814	5.822	1	2	3	3	4	5	6	7	8
34	5.831	5.840	5.848	5.857	5.865	5.874	5.882	5.891	5.899	5.908	1	2	3	3	4	5	6	7	8
35	5.916	5.925	5.933	5.941	5.950	5.958	5.967	5.975	5.983	5.992	1	2	2	3	4	5	6	7	8
36	6.000	6.008	6.017	6.025	6.033	6.042	6.050	6.058	6.066	6.075	1	2	2	3	4	5	6	7	7
37	6.083	6.091	6.099	6.107	6.116	6.124	6.132	6.140	6.148	6.156	1	2	2	3	4	5	6	7	7
38	6.164	6.173	6.181	6.189	6.197	6.205	6.213	6.221	6.229	6.237	1	2	2	3	4	5	6	6	7
39	6.245	6.253	6.261	6.269	6.277	6.285	6.293	6.301	6.309	6.317	1	2	2	3	4	5	6	6	7
40	6.325	6.332	6.340	6.348	6.356	6.364	6.372	6.380	6.387	6.395	1	2	2	3	4	5	6	6	7
41	6.403	6.411	6.419	6.427	6.434	6.442	6.450	6.458	6.465	6.473	1	2	2	3	4	5	5	6	7
42	6.481	6.488	6.496	6.504	6.512	6.519	6.527	6.535	6.542	6.550	1	2	2	3	4	5	5	6	7
43	6.557	6.565	6.573	6.580	6.588	6.595	6.603	6.611	6.618	6.626	1	2	2	3	4	5	5	6	7
44	6.633	6.641	6.648	6.656	6.663	6.671	6.678	6.686	6.693	6.701	1	1	2	3	4	5	5	6	7
45	6.708	6.716	6.723	6.731	6.738	6.745	6.753	6.760	6.768	6.775	1	1	2	3	4	4	5	6	7
46	6.782	6.790	6.797	6.804	6.812	6.819	6.826	6.834	6.841	6.848	1	1	2	3	4	4	5	6	7
47	6.856	6.863	6.870	6.877	6.885	6.892	6.899	6.907	6.914	6.921	1	1	2	3	4	4	5	6	7
48	6.928	6.935	6.943	6.950	6.957	6.964	6.971	6.979	6.986	6.993	1	1	2	3	4	4	5	6	6
49	7.000	7.007	7.014	7.021	7.029	7.036	7.043	7.050	7.057	7.064	1	1	2	3	4	4	5	6	6
50	7.071	7.078	7.085	7.092	7.099	7.106	7.113	7.120	7.127	7.134	1	1	2	3	4	4	5	6	6
51	7.141	7.148	7.155	7.162	7.169	7.176	7.183	7.190	7.197	7.204	1	1	2	3	4	4	5	6	6
52	7.211	7.218	7.225	7.232	7.239	7.246	7.253	7.259	7.266	7.273	1	1	2	3	3	4	5	6	6
53	7.280	7.287	7.294	7.301	7.308	7.314	7.321	7.328	7.335	7.342	1	1	2	3	3	4	5	5	6
54	7.348	7.355	7.362	7.369	7.376	7.382	7.389	7.396	7.403	7.409	1	1	2	3	3	4	5	5	6

	0	1	2	3	4	5	6	7	8	9	1	2	3	4	5	6	7	8	9
55	7.416	7.423	7.430	7.436	7.443	7.450	7.457	7.463	7.470	7.477	1	1	2	3	3	4	5	5	6
56	7.483	7.490	7.497	7.503	7.510	7.517	7.523	7.530	7.537	7.543	1	1	2	3	3	4	5	5	6
57	7.550	7.556	7.563	7.570	7.576	7.583	7.589	7.596	7.603	7.609	1	1	2	3	3	4	5	5	6
58	7.616	7.622	7.629	7.635	7.642	7.649	7.655	7.662	7.668	7.675	1	1	2	3	3	4	5	5	6
59	7.681	7.688	7.694	7.701	7.707	7.714	7.720	7.727	7.733	7.740	1	1	2	3	3	4	4	5	6
60	7.746	7.752	7.759	7.765	7.772	7.778	7.785	7.791	7.797	7.804	1	1	2	3	3	4	4	5	6
61	7.810	7.817	7.823	7.829	7.836	7.842	7.849	7.855	7.861	7.868	1	1	2	3	3	4	4	5	6
62	7.874	7.880	7.887	7.893	7.899	7.906	7.912	7.918	7.925	7.931	1	1	2	3	3	4	4	5	6
63	7.937	7.944	7.950	7.956	7.962	7.969	7.975	7.981	7.987	7.994	1	1	2	3	3	4	4	5	6
64	8.000	8.006	8.012	8.019	8.025	8.031	8.037	8.044	8.050	8.056	1	1	2	2	3	4	4	5	6
65	8.062	8.068	8.075	8.081	8.087	8.093	8.099	8.106	8.112	8.118	1	1	2	2	3	4	4	5	6
66	8.124	8.130	8.136	8.142	8.149	8.155	8.161	8.167	8.173	8.179	1	1	2	2	3	4	4	5	5
67	8.185	8.191	8.198	8.204	8.210	8.216	8.222	8.228	8.234	8.240	1	1	2	2	3	4	4	5	5
68	8.246	8.252	8.258	8.264	8.270	8.276	8.283	8.289	8.295	8.301	1	1	2	2	3	4	4	5	5
69	8.307	8.313	8.319	8.325	8.331	8.337	8.343	8.349	8.355	8.361	1	1	2	2	3	4	4	5	5
70	8.367	8.373	8.379	8.385	8.390	8.396	8.402	8.408	8.414	8.420	1	1	2	2	3	4	4	5	5
71	8.426	8.432	8.438	8.444	8.450	8.456	8.462	8.468	8.473	8.479	1	1	2	2	3	4	4	5	5
72	8.485	8.491	8.497	8.503	8.509	8.515	8.521	8.526	8.532	8.538	1	1	2	2	3	3	4	5	5
73	8.544	8.550	8.556	8.562	8.567	8.573	8.579	8.585	8.591	8.597	1	1	2	2	3	3	4	5	5
74	8.602	8.608	8.614	8.620	8.626	8.631	8.637	8.643	8.649	8.654	1	1	2	2	3	3	4	5	5
75	8.660	8.666	8.672	8.678	8.683	8.689	8.695	8.701	8.706	8.712	1	1	2	2	3	3	4	5	5
76	8.718	8.724	8.729	8.735	8.741	8.746	8.752	8.758	8.764	8.769	1	1	2	2	3	3	4	5	5
77	8.775	8.781	8.786	8.792	8.798	8.803	8.809	8.815	8.820	8.826	1	1	2	2	3	3	4	4	5
78	8.832	8.837	8.843	8.849	8.854	8.860	8.866	8.871	8.877	8.883	1	1	2	2	3	3	4	4	5
79	8.888	8.894	8.899	8.905	8.911	8.916	8.922	8.927	8.933	8.939	1	1	2	2	3	3	4	4	5
80	8.944	8.950	8.955	8.961	8.967	8.972	8.978	8.983	8.989	8.994	1	1	2	2	3	3	4	4	5
81	9.000	9.006	9.011	9.017	9.022	9.028	9.033	9.039	9.044	9.050	1	1	2	2	3	3	4	4	5
82	9.055	9.061	9.066	9.072	9.077	9.083	9.088	9.094	9.099	9.105	1	1	2	2	3	3	4	4	5
83	9.110	9.116	9.121	9.127	9.132	9.138	9.143	9.149	9.154	9.160	1	1	2	2	3	3	4	4	5
84	9.165	9.171	9.176	9.182	9.187	9.192	9.198	9.203	9.209	9.214	1	1	2	2	3	3	4	4	5
85	9.220	9.225	9.230	9.236	9.241	9.247	9.252	9.257	9.263	9.268	1	1	2	2	3	3	4	4	5
86	9.274	9.279	9.284	9.290	9.295	9.301	9.306	9.311	9.317	9.322	1	1	2	2	3	3	4	4	5
87	9.327	9.333	9.338	9.343	9.349	9.354	9.359	9.365	9.370	9.375	1	1	2	2	3	3	4	4	5
88	9.381	9.386	9.391	9.397	9.402	9.407	9.413	9.418	9.423	9.429	1	1	2	2	3	3	4	4	5
89	9.434	9.439	9.445	9.450	9.455	9.460	9.466	9.471	9.476	9.482	1	1	2	2	3	3	4	4	5
90	9.487	9.492	9.497	9.503	9.508	9.513	9.518	9.524	9.529	9.534	1	1	2	2	3	3	4	4	5
91	9.539	9.545	9.550	9.555	9.560	9.566	9.571	9.576	9.581	9.586	1	1	2	2	3	3	4	4	5
92	9.592	9.597	9.602	9.607	9.612	9.618	9.623	9.628	9.633	9.638	1	1	2	2	3	3	4	4	5
93	9.644	9.649	9.654	9.659	9.664	9.670	9.675	9.680	9.685	9.690	1	1	2	2	3	3	4	4	5
94	9.695	9.701	9.706	9.711	9.716	9.721	9.726	9.731	9.737	9.742	1	1	2	2	3	3	4	4	5
95	9.747	9.752	9.757	9.762	9.767	9.772	9.778	9.783	9.788	9.793	1	1	2	2	3	3	4	4	5
96	9.798	9.803	9.808	9.813	9.818	9.823	9.829	9.834	9.839	9.844	1	1	2	2	3	3	4	4	5
97	9.849	9.854	9.859	9.864	9.869	9.874	9.879	9.884	9.889	9.894	1	1	1	2	3	3	4	4	5
98	9.899	9.905	9.910	9.915	9.920	9.925	9.930	9.935	9.940	9.945	0	1	1	2	2	3	3	4	4
99	9.950	9.955	9.960	9.965	9.970	9.975	9.980	9.985	9.990	9.995	0	1	1	2	2	3	3	4	4

Mean differences: columns 1 2 3 | 4 5 6 | 7 8 9

	0	1	2	3	4	5	6	7	8	9	1 2 3	4 5 6	7 8 9
10	0000	0043	0086	0128	0170	0212	0253	0294	0334	0374	4 9 13 4 8 12	17 21 26 16 20 24	30 34 38 28 32 36
11	0414	0453	0492	0531	0569	0607	0645	0682	0719	0755	4 8 12 4 7 11	15 19 23 15 19 22	27 31 35 26 30 33
12	0792	0828	0864	0899	0934	0969	1004	1038	1072	1106	3 7 11 3 7 10	14 18 21 14 17 20	25 28 32 24 27 31
13	1139	1173	1206	1239	1271	1303	1335	1367	1399	1430	3 7 10 3 7 10	13 16 20 13 16 19	23 26 30 22 25 29
14	1461	1492	1523	1553	1584	1614	1644	1673	1703	1732	3 6 9 3 6 9	12 15 19 12 15 17	22 25 28 20 23 26
15	1761	1790	1818	1847	1875	1903	1931	1959	1987	2014	3 6 9 3 6 8	11 14 17 11 14 17	20 23 26 19 22 24
16	2041	2068	2095	2122	2148	2175	2201	2227	2253	2279	3 5 8 3 5 8	11 14 16 10 13 16	19 22 24 18 21 23
17	2304	2330	2355	2380	2405	2430	2455	2480	2504	2529	3 5 8 2 5 7	10 13 15 10 12 15	18 20 23 17 20 22
18	2553	2577	2601	2625	2648	2672	2695	2718	2742	2765	2 5 7 2 5 7	9 12 14 9 11 14	16 19 21 16 18 21
19	2788	2810	2833	2856	2878	2900	2923	2945	2967	2989	2 4 7 2 4 6	9 11 13 8 11 13	16 18 20 15 17 19
20	3010	3032	3054	3075	3096	3118	3139	3160	3181	3201	2 4 6	8 11 13	15 17 19
21	3222	3243	3263	3284	3304	3324	3345	3365	3385	3404	2 4 6	8 10 12	14 16 18
22	3424	3444	3464	3483	3502	3522	3541	3560	3579	3598	2 4 6	8 10 12	14 15 17
23	3617	3636	3655	3674	3692	3711	3729	3747	3766	3784	2 4 6	7 9 11	13 15 17
24	3802	3820	3838	3856	3874	3892	3909	3927	3945	3962	2 4 5	7 9 11	12 14 16
25	3979	3997	4014	4031	4048	4065	4082	4099	4116	4133	2 3 5	7 9 10	12 14 15
26	4150	4166	4183	4200	4216	4232	4249	4265	4281	4298	2 3 5	7 8 10	11 13 15
27	4314	4330	4346	4362	4378	4393	4409	4425	4440	4456	2 3 5	6 8 9	11 13 14
28	4472	4487	4502	4518	4533	4548	4564	4579	4594	4609	2 3 5	6 8 9	11 12 14
29	4624	4639	4654	4669	4683	4698	4713	4728	4742	4757	1 3 4	6 7 9	10 12 13
30	4771	4786	4800	4814	4829	4843	4857	4871	4886	4900	1 3 4	6 7 9	10 11 13
31	4914	4928	4942	4955	4969	4983	4997	5011	5024	5038	1 3 4	6 7 8	10 11 12
32	5051	5065	5079	5092	5105	5119	5132	5145	5159	5172	1 3 4	5 7 8	9 11 12
33	5185	5198	5211	5224	5237	5250	5263	5276	5289	5302	1 3 4	5 6 8	9 10 12
34	5315	5328	5340	5353	5366	5378	5391	5403	5416	5428	1 3 4	5 6 8	9 10 11
35	5441	5453	5465	5478	5490	5502	5514	5527	5539	5551	1 2 4	5 6 7	9 10 11
36	5563	5575	5587	5599	5611	5623	5635	5647	5658	5670	1 2 4	5 6 7	8 10 11
37	5682	5694	5705	5717	5729	5740	5752	5763	5775	5786	1 2 3	5 6 7	8 9 10
38	5798	5809	5821	5832	5843	5855	5866	5877	5888	5899	1 2 3	5 6 7	8 9 10
39	5911	5922	5933	5944	5955	5966	5977	5988	5999	6010	1 2 3	4 5 7	8 9 10
40	6021	6031	6042	6053	6064	6075	6085	6096	6107	6117	1 2 3	4 5 6	8 9 10
41	6128	6138	6149	6160	6170	6180	6191	6201	6212	6222	1 2 3	4 5 6	7 8 9
42	6232	6243	6253	6263	6274	6284	6294	6304	6314	6325	1 2 3	4 5 6	7 8 9
43	6335	6345	6355	6365	6375	6385	6395	6405	6415	6425	1 2 3	4 5 6	7 8 9
44	6435	6444	6454	6464	6474	6484	6493	6503	6513	6522	1 2 3	4 5 6	7 8 9
45	6532	6542	6551	6561	6571	6580	6590	6599	6609	6618	1 2 3	4 5 6	7 8 9
46	6628	6637	6646	6656	6665	6675	6684	6693	6702	6712	1 2 3	4 5 6	7 7 8
47	6721	6730	6739	6749	6758	6767	6776	6785	6794	6803	1 2 3	4 5 5	6 7 8
48	6812	6821	6830	6839	6848	6857	6866	6875	6884	6893	1 2 3	4 4 5	6 7 8
49	6902	6911	6920	6928	6937	6946	6955	6964	6972	6981	1 2 3	4 4 5	6 7 8

LOGARITHMS

	0	1	2	3	4	5	6	7	8	9	1	2	3	4	5	6	7	8	9
50	6990	6998	7007	7016	7024	7033	7042	7050	7059	7067	1	2	3	3	4	5	6	7	8
51	7076	7084	7093	7101	7110	7118	7126	7135	7143	7152	1	2	3	3	4	5	6	7	8
52	7160	7168	7177	7185	7193	7202	7210	7218	7226	7235	1	2	2	3	4	5	6	7	7
53	7243	7251	7259	7267	7275	7284	7292	7300	7308	7316	1	2	2	3	4	5	6	6	7
54	7324	7332	7340	7348	7356	7364	7372	7380	7388	7396	1	2	2	3	4	5	6	6	7
55	7404	7412	7419	7427	7435	7443	7451	7459	7466	7474	1	2	2	3	4	5	5	6	7
56	7482	7490	7497	7505	7513	7520	7528	7536	7543	7551	1	2	2	3	4	5	5	6	7
57	7559	7566	7574	7582	7589	7597	7604	7612	7619	7627	1	2	2	3	4	5	5	6	7
58	7634	7642	7649	7657	7664	7672	7679	7686	7694	7701	1	1	2	3	4	4	5	6	7
59	7709	7716	7723	7731	7738	7745	7752	7760	7767	7774	1	1	2	3	4	4	5	6	7
60	7782	7789	7796	7803	7810	7818	7825	7832	7839	7846	1	1	2	3	4	4	5	6	6
61	7853	7860	7868	7875	7882	7889	7896	7903	7910	7917	1	1	2	3	4	4	5	6	6
62	7924	7931	7938	7945	7952	7959	7966	7973	7980	7987	1	1	2	3	3	4	5	6	6
63	7993	8000	8007	8014	8021	8028	8035	8041	8048	8055	1	1	2	3	3	4	5	5	6
64	8062	8069	8075	8082	8089	8096	8102	8109	8116	8122	1	1	2	3	3	4	5	5	6
65	8129	8136	8142	8149	8156	8162	8169	8176	8182	8189	1	1	2	3	3	4	5	5	6
66	8195	8202	8209	8215	8222	8228	8235	8241	8248	8254	1	1	2	3	3	4	5	5	6
67	8261	8267	8274	8280	8287	8293	8299	8306	8312	8319	1	1	2	3	3	4	5	5	6
68	8325	8331	8338	8344	8351	8357	8363	8370	8376	8382	1	1	2	3	3	4	4	5	6
69	8388	8395	8401	8407	8414	8420	8426	8432	8439	8445	1	1	2	2	3	4	4	5	6
70	8451	8457	8463	8470	8476	8482	8488	8494	8500	8506	1	1	2	2	3	4	4	5	6
71	8513	8519	8525	8531	8537	8543	8549	8555	8561	8567	1	1	2	2	3	4	4	5	5
72	8573	8579	8585	8591	8597	8603	8609	8615	8621	8627	1	1	2	2	3	4	4	5	5
73	8633	8639	8645	8651	8657	8663	8669	8675	8681	8686	1	1	2	2	3	4	4	5	5
74	8692	8698	8704	8710	8716	8722	8727	8733	8739	8745	1	1	2	2	3	3	4	5	5
75	8751	8756	8762	8768	8774	8779	8785	8791	8797	8802	1	1	2	2	3	3	4	5	5
76	8808	8814	8820	8825	8831	8837	8842	8848	8854	8859	1	1	2	2	3	3	4	5	5
77	8865	8871	8876	8882	8887	8893	8899	8904	8910	8915	1	1	2	2	3	3	4	4	5
78	8921	8927	8932	8938	8943	8949	8954	8960	8965	8971	1	1	2	2	3	3	4	4	5
79	8976	8982	8987	8993	8998	9004	9009	9015	9020	9025	1	1	2	2	3	3	4	4	5
80	9031	9036	9042	9047	9053	9058	9063	9069	9074	9079	1	1	2	2	3	3	4	4	5
81	9085	9090	9096	9101	9106	9112	9117	9122	9128	9133	1	1	2	2	3	3	4	4	5
82	9138	9143	9149	9154	9159	9165	9170	9175	9180	9186	1	1	2	2	3	3	4	4	5
83	9191	9196	9201	9206	9212	9217	9222	9227	9232	9238	1	1	2	2	3	3	4	4	5
84	9243	9248	9253	9258	9263	9269	9274	9279	9284	9289	1	1	2	2	3	3	4	4	5
85	9294	9299	9304	9309	9315	9320	9325	9330	9335	9340	1	1	2	2	3	3	4	4	5
86	9345	9350	9355	9360	9365	9370	9375	9380	9385	9390	1	1	2	2	3	3	4	4	5
87	9395	9400	9405	9410	9415	9420	9425	9430	9435	9440	0	1	1	2	2	3	3	4	4
88	9445	9450	9455	9460	9465	9469	9474	9479	9484	9489	0	1	1	2	2	3	3	4	4
89	9494	9499	9504	9509	9513	9518	9523	9528	9533	9538	0	1	1	2	2	3	3	4	4
90	9542	9547	9552	9557	9562	9566	9571	9576	9581	9586	0	1	1	2	2	3	3	4	4
91	9590	9595	9600	9605	9609	9614	9619	9624	9628	9633	0	1	1	2	2	3	3	4	4
92	9638	9643	9647	9652	9657	9661	9666	9671	9675	9680	0	1	1	2	2	3	3	4	4
93	9685	9689	9694	9699	9703	9708	9713	9717	9722	9727	0	1	1	2	2	3	3	4	4
94	9731	9736	9741	9745	9750	9754	9759	9763	9768	9773	0	1	1	2	2	3	3	4	4
95	9777	9782	9786	9791	9795	9800	9805	9809	9814	9818	0	1	1	2	2	3	3	4	4
96	9823	9827	9832	9836	9841	9845	9850	9854	9859	9863	0	1	1	2	2	3	3	4	4
97	9868	9872	9877	9881	9886	9890	9894	9899	9903	9908	0	1	1	2	2	3	3	4	4
98	9912	9917	9921	9926	9930	9934	9939	9943	9948	9952	0	1	1	2	2	3	3	4	4
99	9956	9961	9965	9969	9974	9978	9983	9987	9991	9996	0	1	1	2	2	3	3	3	4

ANTILOGARITHMS

	0	1	2	3	4	5	6	7	8	9	1 2 3	4 5 6	7 8 9
.00	1000	1002	1005	1007	1009	1012	1014	1016	1019	1021	0 0 1	1 1 1	2 2 2
.01	1023	1026	1028	1030	1033	1035	1038	1040	1042	1045	0 0 1	1 1 1	2 2 2
.02	1047	1050	1052	1054	1057	1059	1062	1064	1067	1069	0 0 1	1 1 1	2 2 2
.03	1072	1074	1076	1079	1081	1084	1086	1089	1091	1094	0 0 1	1 1 1	2 2 2
.04	1096	1099	1102	1104	1107	1109	1112	1114	1117	1119	0 1 1	1 1 2	2 2 2
.05	1122	1125	1127	1130	1132	1135	1138	1140	1143	1146	0 1 1	1 1 2	2 2 2
.06	1148	1151	1153	1156	1159	1161	1164	1167	1169	1172	0 1 1	1 1 2	2 2 2
.07	1175	1178	1180	1183	1186	1189	1191	1194	1197	1199	0 1 1	1 1 2	2 2 2
.08	1202	1205	1208	1211	1213	1216	1219	1222	1225	1227	0 1 1	1 1 2	2 2 3
.09	1230	1233	1236	1239	1242	1245	1247	1250	1253	1256	0 1 1	1 1 2	2 2 3
.10	1259	1262	1265	1268	1271	1274	1276	1279	1282	1285	0 1 1	1 1 2	2 2 3
.11	1288	1291	1294	1297	1300	1303	1306	1309	1312	1315	0 1 1	1 2 2	2 2 3
.12	1318	1321	1324	1327	1330	1334	1337	1340	1343	1346	0 1 1	1 2 2	2 2 3
.13	1349	1352	1355	1358	1361	1365	1368	1371	1374	1377	0 1 1	1 2 2	2 3 3
.14	1380	1384	1387	1390	1393	1396	1400	1403	1406	1409	0 1 1	1 2 2	2 3 3
.15	1413	1416	1419	1422	1426	1429	1432	1435	1439	1442	0 1 1	1 2 2	2 3 3
.16	1445	1449	1452	1455	1459	1462	1466	1469	1472	1476	0 1 1	1 2 2	2 3 3
.17	1479	1483	1486	1489	1493	1496	1500	1503	1507	1510	0 1 1	1 2 2	2 3 3
.18	1514	1517	1521	1524	1528	1531	1535	1538	1542	1545	0 1 1	1 2 2	2 3 3
.19	1549	1552	1556	1560	1563	1567	1570	1574	1578	1581	0 1 1	1 2 2	3 3 3
.20	1585	1589	1592	1596	1600	1603	1607	1611	1614	1618	0 1 1	1 2 2	3 3 3
.21	1622	1626	1629	1633	1637	1641	1644	1648	1652	1656	0 1 1	2 2 2	3 3 3
.22	1660	1663	1667	1671	1675	1679	1683	1687	1690	1694	0 1 1	2 2 2	3 3 3
.23	1698	1702	1706	1710	1714	1718	1722	1726	1730	1734	0 1 1	2 2 2	3 3 4
.24	1738	1742	1746	1750	1754	1758	1762	1766	1770	1774	0 1 1	2 2 2	3 3 4
.25	1778	1782	1786	1791	1795	1799	1803	1807	1811	1816	0 1 1	2 2 2	3 3 4
.26	1820	1824	1828	1832	1837	1841	1845	1849	1854	1858	0 1 1	2 2 3	3 3 4
.27	1862	1866	1871	1875	1879	1884	1888	1892	1897	1901	0 1 1	2 2 3	3 3 4
.28	1905	1910	1914	1919	1923	1928	1932	1936	1941	1945	0 1 1	2 2 3	3 4 4
.29	1950	1954	1959	1963	1968	1972	1977	1982	1986	1991	0 1 1	2 2 3	3 4 4
.30	1995	2000	2004	2009	2014	2018	2023	2028	2032	2037	0 1 1	2 2 3	3 4 4
.31	2042	2046	2051	2056	2061	2065	2070	2075	2080	2084	0 1 1	2 2 3	3 4 4
.32	2089	2094	2099	2104	2109	2113	2118	2123	2128	2133	0 1 1	2 2 3	3 4 4
.33	2138	2143	2148	2153	2158	2163	2168	2173	2178	2183	0 1 1	2 2 3	3 4 4
.34	2188	2193	2198	2203	2208	2213	2218	2223	2228	2234	1 1 2	2 3 3	4 4 5
.35	2239	2244	2249	2254	2259	2265	2270	2275	2280	2286	1 1 2	2 3 3	4 4 5
.36	2291	2296	2301	2307	2312	2317	2323	2328	2333	2339	1 1 2	2 3 3	4 4 5
.37	2344	2350	2355	2360	2366	2371	2377	2382	2388	2393	1 1 2	2 3 3	4 4 5
.38	2399	2404	2410	2415	2421	2427	2432	2438	2443	2449	1 1 2	2 3 3	4 4 5
.39	2455	2460	2466	2472	2477	2483	2489	2495	2500	2506	1 1 2	2 3 3	4 5 5
.40	2512	2518	2523	2529	2535	2541	2547	2553	2559	2564	1 1 2	2 3 4	4 5 5
.41	2570	2576	2582	2588	2594	2600	2606	2612	2618	2624	1 1 2	2 3 4	4 5 5
.42	2630	2636	2642	2649	2655	2661	2667	2673	2679	2685	1 1 2	2 3 4	4 5 6
.43	2692	2698	2704	2710	2716	2723	2729	2735	2742	2748	1 1 2	3 3 4	4 5 6
.44	2754	2761	2767	2773	2780	2786	2793	2799	2805	2812	1 1 2	3 3 4	4 5 6
.45	2818	2825	2831	2838	2844	2851	2858	2864	2871	2877	1 1 2	3 3 4	5 5 6
.46	2884	2891	2897	2904	2911	2917	2924	2931	2938	2944	1 1 2	3 3 4	5 5 6
.47	2951	2958	2965	2972	2979	2985	2992	2999	3006	3013	1 1 2	3 3 4	5 5 6
.48	3020	3027	3034	3041	3048	3055	3062	3069	3076	3083	1 1 2	3 4 4	5 6 6
.49	3090	3097	3105	3112	3119	3126	3133	3141	3148	3155	1 1 2	3 4 4	5 6 6

ANTILOGARITHMS

	0	1	2	3	4	5	6	7	8	9	1	2	3	4	5	6	7	8	9
.50	3162	3170	3177	3184	3192	3199	3206	3214	3221	3228	1	1	2	3	4	4	5	6	7
.51	3236	3243	3251	3258	3266	3273	3281	3289	3296	3304	1	2	2	3	4	5	5	6	7
.52	3311	3319	3327	3334	3342	3350	3357	3365	3373	3381	1	2	2	3	4	5	5	6	7
.53	3388	3396	3404	3412	3420	3428	3436	3443	3451	3459	1	2	2	3	4	5	6	6	7
.54	3467	3475	3483	3491	3499	3508	3516	3524	3532	3540	1	2	2	3	4	5	6	6	7
.55	3548	3556	3565	3573	3581	3589	3597	3606	3614	3622	1	2	2	3	4	5	6	7	7
.56	3631	3639	3648	3656	3664	3673	3681	3690	3698	3707	1	2	3	3	4	5	6	7	8
.57	3715	3724	3733	3741	3750	3758	3767	3776	3784	3793	1	2	3	3	4	5	6	7	8
.58	3802	3811	3819	3828	3837	3846	3855	3864	3873	3882	1	2	3	4	4	5	6	7	8
.59	3890	3899	3908	3917	3926	3936	3945	3954	3963	3972	1	2	3	4	5	5	6	7	8
.60	3981	3990	3999	4009	4018	4027	4036	4046	4055	4064	1	2	3	4	5	6	6	7	8
.61	4074	4083	4093	4102	4111	4121	4130	4140	4150	4159	1	2	3	4	5	6	7	8	9
.62	4169	4178	4188	4198	4207	4217	4227	4236	4246	4256	1	2	3	4	5	6	7	8	9
.63	4266	4276	4285	4295	4305	4315	4325	4335	4345	4355	1	2	3	4	5	6	7	8	9
.64	4365	4375	4385	4395	4406	4416	4426	4436	4446	4457	1	2	3	4	5	6	7	8	9
.65	4467	4477	4487	4498	4508	4519	4529	4539	4550	4560	1	2	3	4	5	6	7	8	9
.66	4571	4581	4592	4603	4613	4624	4634	4645	4656	4667	1	2	3	4	5	6	7	9	10
.67	4677	4688	4699	4710	4721	4732	4742	4753	4764	4775	1	2	3	4	5	7	8	9	10
.68	4786	4797	4808	4819	4831	4842	4853	4864	4875	4887	1	2	3	4	6	7	8	9	10
.69	4898	4909	4920	4932	4943	4955	4966	4977	4989	5000	1	2	3	5	6	7	8	9	10
.70	5012	5023	5035	5047	5058	5070	5082	5093	5105	5117	1	2	4	5	6	7	8	9	11
.71	5129	5140	5152	5164	5176	5188	5200	5212	5224	5236	1	2	4	5	6	7	8	10	11
.72	5248	5260	5272	5284	5297	5309	5321	5333	5346	5358	1	2	4	5	6	7	9	10	11
.73	5370	5383	5395	5408	5420	5433	5445	5458	5470	5483	1	3	4	5	6	8	9	10	11
.74	5495	5508	5521	5534	5546	5559	5572	5585	5598	5610	1	3	4	5	6	8	9	10	12
.75	5623	5636	5649	5662	5675	5689	5702	5715	5728	5741	1	3	4	5	7	8	9	10	12
.76	5754	5768	5781	5794	5808	5821	5834	5848	5861	5875	1	3	4	5	7	8	9	11	12
.77	5888	5902	5916	5929	5943	5957	5970	5984	5998	6012	1	3	4	5	7	8	10	11	12
.78	6026	6039	6053	6067	6081	6095	6109	6124	6138	6152	1	3	4	6	7	8	10	11	13
.79	6166	6180	6194	6209	6223	6237	6252	6266	6281	6295	1	3	4	6	7	9	10	11	13
.80	6310	6324	6339	6353	6368	6383	6397	6412	6427	6442	1	3	4	6	7	9	10	12	13
.81	6457	6471	6486	6501	6516	6531	6546	6561	6577	6592	2	3	5	6	8	9	11	12	14
.82	6607	6622	6637	6653	6668	6683	6699	6714	6730	6745	2	3	5	6	8	9	11	12	14
.83	6761	6776	6792	6808	6823	6839	6855	6871	6887	6902	2	3	5	6	8	9	11	13	14
.84	6918	6934	6950	6966	6982	6998	7015	7031	7047	7063	2	3	5	6	8	10	11	13	15
.85	7079	7096	7112	7129	7145	7161	7178	7194	7211	7228	2	3	5	7	8	10	12	13	15
.86	7244	7261	7278	7295	7311	7328	7345	7362	7379	7396	2	3	5	7	8	10	12	13	15
.87	7413	7430	7447	7464	7482	7499	7516	7534	7551	7568	2	3	5	7	9	10	12	14	16
.88	7586	7603	7621	7638	7656	7674	7691	7709	7727	7745	2	4	5	7	9	11	12	14	16
.89	7762	7780	7798	7816	7834	7852	7870	7889	7907	7925	2	4	5	7	9	11	13	14	16
.90	7943	7962	7980	7998	8017	8035	8054	8072	8091	8110	2	4	6	7	9	11	13	15	17
.91	8128	8147	8166	8185	8204	8222	8241	8260	8279	8299	2	4	6	8	9	11	13	15	17
.92	8318	8337	8356	8375	8395	8414	8433	8453	8472	8492	2	4	6	8	10	12	14	15	17
.93	8511	8531	8551	8570	8590	8610	8630	8650	8670	8690	2	4	6	8	10	12	14	16	18
.94	8710	8730	8750	8770	8790	8810	8831	8851	8872	8892	2	4	6	8	10	12	14	16	18
.95	8913	8933	8954	8974	8995	9016	9036	9057	9078	9099	2	4	6	8	10	12	15	17	19
.96	9120	9141	9162	9183	9204	9226	9247	9268	9290	9311	2	4	6	8	11	13	15	17	19
.97	9333	9354	9376	9397	9419	9441	9462	9484	9506	9528	2	4	7	9	11	13	15	17	20
.98	9550	9572	9594	9616	9638	9661	9683	9705	9727	9750	2	4	7	9	11	13	16	18	20
.99	9772	9795	9817	9840	9863	9886	9908	9931	9954	9977	2	5	7	9	11	14	16	18	20

NATURAL SINES

Degrees	0' 0°.0	6' 0°.1	12' 0°.2	18' 0°.3	24' 0°.4	30' 0°.5	36' 0°.6	42' 0°.7	48' 0°.8	54' 0°.9	1	2	3	4	5
												Mean differences			
0	1.000	1.000	1.000	1.000	1.000	1.000	.9999	9999	9999	9999	0	0	0	0	0
1	.9998	9998	9998	9997	9997	9997	9996	9996	9995	9995	0	0	0	0	0
2	.9994	9993	9993	9992	9991	9990	9990	9989	9988	9987	0	0	0	0	1
3	.9986	9985	9984	9983	9982	9981	9980	9979	9978	9977	0	0	1	1	1
4	.9976	9974	9973	9972	9971	9969	9968	9966	9965	9963	0	0	1	1	1
5	.9962	9960	9959	9957	9956	9954	9952	9951	9949	9947	0	1	1	1	2
6	.9945	9943	9942	9940	9938	9936	9934	9932	9930	9928	0	1	1	1	2
7	.9925	9923	9921	9919	9917	9914	9912	9910	9907	9905	0	1	1	2	2
8	.9903	9900	9898	9895	9893	9890	9888	9885	9882	9880	0	1	1	2	2
9	.9877	9874	9871	9869	9866	9863	9860	9857	9854	9851	0	1	1	2	2
10	.9848	9845	9842	9839	9836	9833	9829	9826	9823	9820	1	1	2	2	3
11	.9816	9813	9810	9806	9803	9799	9796	9792	9789	9785	1	1	2	2	3
12	.9781	9778	9774	9770	9767	9763	9759	9755	9751	9748	1	1	2	3	3
13	.9744	9740	9736	9732	9728	9724	9720	9715	9711	9707	1	1	2	3	3
14	.9703	9699	9694	9690	9686	9681	9677	9673	9668	9664	1	1	2	3	4
15	.9659	9655	9650	9646	9641	9636	9632	9627	9622	9617	1	2	2	3	4
16	.9613	9608	9603	9598	9593	9588	9583	9578	9573	9568	1	2	2	3	4
17	.9563	9558	9553	9548	9542	9537	9532	9527	9521	9516	1	2	3	3	4
18	.9511	9505	9500	9494	9489	9483	9478	9472	9466	9461	1	2	3	4	5
19	.9455	9449	9444	9438	9432	9426	9421	9415	9409	9403	1	2	3	4	5
20	.9397	9391	9385	9379	9373	9367	9361	9354	9348	9342	1	2	3	4	5
21	.9336	9330	9323	9317	9311	9304	9298	9291	9285	9278	1	2	3	4	5
22	.9272	9265	9259	9252	9245	9239	9232	9225	9219	9212	1	2	3	4	6
23	.9205	9198	9191	9184	9178	9171	9164	9157	9150	9143	1	2	3	5	6
24	.9135	9128	9121	9114	9107	9100	9092	9085	9078	9070	1	2	4	5	6
25	.9063	9056	9048	9041	9033	9026	9018	9011	9003	8996	1	3	4	5	6
26	.8988	8980	8973	8965	8957	8949	8942	8934	8926	8918	1	3	4	5	6
27	.8910	8902	8894	8886	8878	8870	8862	8854	8846	8838	1	3	4	5	7
28	.8829	8821	8813	8805	8796	8788	8780	8771	8763	8755	1	3	4	6	7
29	.8746	8738	8729	8721	8712	8704	8695	8686	8678	8669	1	3	4	6	7
30	.8660	8652	8643	8634	8625	8616	8607	8599	8590	8581	1	3	4	6	7
31	.8572	8563	8554	8545	8536	8526	8517	8508	8499	8490	2	3	5	6	8
32	.8480	8471	8462	8453	8443	8434	8425	8415	8406	8396	2	3	5	6	8
33	.8387	8377	8368	8358	8348	8339	8329	8320	8310	8300	2	3	5	6	8
34	.8290	8281	8271	8261	8251	8241	8231	8221	8211	8202	2	3	5	7	8
35	.8192	8181	8171	8161	8151	8141	8131	8121	8111	8100	2	3	5	7	8
36	.8090	8080	8070	8059	8049	8039	8028	8018	8007	7997	2	3	5	7	9
37	.7986	7976	7965	7955	7944	7934	7923	7912	7902	7891	2	4	5	7	9
38	.7880	7869	7859	7848	7837	7826	7815	7804	7793	7782	2	4	5	7	9
39	.7771	7760	7749	7738	7727	7716	7705	7694	7683	7672	2	4	6	7	9
40	.7660	7649	7638	7627	7615	7604	7593	7581	7570	7559	2	4	6	8	9
41	.7547	7536	7524	7513	7501	7490	7478	7466	7455	7443	2	4.	6	8	10
42	.7431	7420	7408	7396	7385	7373	7361	7349	7337	7325	2	4	6	8	10
43	.7314	7302	7290	7278	7266	7254	7242	7230	7218	7206	2	4	6	8	10
44	.7193	7181	7169	7157	7145	7133	7120	7108	7096	7083	2	4	6	8	10

NATURAL SINES

Degrees	0' 0°.0	6' 0°.1	12' 0°.2	18' 0°.3	24' 0°.4	30' 0°.5	36' 0°.6	42' 0°.7	48' 0°.8	54' 0°.9	Mean differences 1	2	3	4	5
45	.7071	7083	7096	7108	7120	7133	7145	7157	7169	7181	2	4	6	8	10
46	.7193	7206	7218	7230	7242	7254	7266	7278	7290	7302	2	4	6	8	10
47	.7314	7325	7337	7349	7361	7373	7385	7396	7408	7420	2	4	6	8	10
48	.7431	7443	7455	7466	7478	7490	7501	7513	7524	7536	2	4	6	8	10
49	.7547	7559	7570	7581	7593	7604	7615	7627	7638	7649	2	4	6	8	9
50	.7660	7672	7683	7694	7705	7716	7727	7738	7749	7760	2	4	6	7	9
51	.7771	7782	7793	7804	7815	7826	7837	7848	7859	7869	2	4	5	7	9
52	.7880	7891	7902	7912	7923	7934	7944	7955	7965	7976	2	4	5	7	9
53	.7986	7997	8007	8018	8028	8039	8049	8059	8070	8080	2	3	5	7	9
54	.8090	8100	8111	8121	8131	8141	8151	8161	8171	8181	2	3	5	7	8
55	.8192	8202	8211	8221	8231	8241	8251	8261	8271	8281	2	3	5	7	8
56	.8290	8300	8310	8320	8329	8339	8348	8358	8368	8377	2	3	5	6	8
57	.8387	8396	8406	8415	8425	8434	8443	8453	8462	8471	2	3	5	6	8
58	.8480	8490	8499	8508	8517	8526	8536	8545	8554	8563	1	3	5	6	8
59	.8572	8581	8590	8599	8607	8616	8625	8634	8643	8652	1	3	4	6	7
60	.8660	8669	8678	8686	8695	8704	8712	8721	8729	8738	1	3	4	6	7
61	.8746	8755	8763	8771	8780	8788	8796	8805	8813	8821	1	3	4	6	7
62	.8829	8838	8846	8854	8862	8870	8878	8886	8894	8902	1	3	4	5	7
63	.8910	8918	8926	8934	8942	8949	8957	8965	8973	8980	1	3	4	5	6
64	.8988	8996	9003	9011	9018	9026	9033	9041	9048	9056	1	3	4	5	6
65	.9063	9070	9078	9085	9092	9100	9107	9114	9121	9128	1	2	4	5	6
66	.9135	9143	9150	9157	9164	9171	9178	9184	9191	9198	1	2	3	5	6
67	.9205	9212	9219	9225	9232	9239	9245	9252	9259	9265	1	2	3	4	6
68	.9272	9278	9285	9291	9298	9304	9311	9317	9323	9330	1	2	3	4	5
69	.9336	9342	9348	9354	9361	9367	9373	9379	9385	9391	1	2	3	4	5
70	.9397	9403	9409	9415	9421	9426	9432	9438	9444	9449	1	2	3	4	5
71	.9455	9461	9466	9472	9478	9483	9489	9494	9500	9505	1	2	3	4	5
72	.9511	9516	9521	9527	9532	9537	9542	9548	9553	9558	1	2	3	3	4
73	.9563	9568	9573	9578	9583	9588	9593	9598	9603	9608	1	2	3	3	4
74	.9613	9617	9622	9627	9632	9636	9641	9646	9650	9655	1	2	2	3	4
75	.9659	9664	9668	9673	9677	9681	9686	9690	9694	9699	1	1	2	3	4
76	.9703	9707	9711	9715	9720	9724	9728	9732	9736	9740	1	1	2	3	3
77	.9744	9748	9751	9755	9759	9763	9767	9770	9774	9778	1	1	2	3	3
78	.9781	9785	9789	9792	9796	9799	9803	9806	9810	9813	1	1	2	2	3
79	.9816	9820	9823	9826	9829	9833	9836	9839	9842	9845	1	1	2	2	3
80	.9848	9851	9854	9857	9860	9863	9866	9869	9871	9874	0	1	1	2	2
81	.9877	9880	9882	9885	9888	9890	9893	9895	9898	9900	0	1	1	2	2
82	.9903	9905	9907	9910	9912	9914	9917	9919	9921	9923	0	1	1	2	2
83	.9925	9928	9930	9932	9934	9936	9938	9940	9942	9943	0	1	1	1	2
84	.9945	9947	9949	9951	9952	9954	9956	9957	9959	9960	0	1	1	1	2
85	.9962	9963	9965	9966	9968	9969	9971	9972	9973	9974	0	0	1	1	1
86	.9976	9977	9978	9979	9980	9981	9982	9983	9984	9985	0	0	1	1	1
87	.9986	9987	9988	9989	9990	9990	9991	9992	9993	9993	0	0	0	1	1
88	.9994	9995	9995	9996	9996	9997	9997	9997	9998	9998	0	0	0	0	0
89	.9998	9999	9999	9999	9999	1.000	1.000	1.000	1.000	1.000	0	0	0	0	0
90	1.000														

NATURAL COSINES

Degrees	0′ 0°.0	6′ 0°.1	12′ 0°.2	18′ 0°.3	24′ 0°.4	30′ 0°.5	36′ 0°.6	42′ 0°.7	48′ 0°.8	54′ 0°.9	Mean differences				
											1	2	3	4	5
0	1.000	1.000	1.000	1.000	1.000	1.000	.9999	9999	9999	9999	0	0	0	0	0
1	.9998	9998	9998	9997	9997	9997	9996	9996	9995	9995	0	0	0	0	0
2	.9994	9993	9993	9992	9991	9990	9990	9989	9988	9987	0	0	0	0	1
3	.9986	9985	9984	9983	9982	9981	9980	9979	9978	9977	0	0	1	1	1
4	.9976	9974	9973	9972	9971	9969	9968	9966	9965	9963	0	0	1	1	1
5	.9962	9960	9959	9957	9956	9954	9952	9951	9949	9947	0	1	1	1	2
6	.9945	9943	9942	9940	9938	9936	9934	9932	9930	9928	0	1	1	1	2
7	.9925	9923	9921	9919	9917	9914	9912	9910	9907	9905	0	1	1	2	2
8	.9903	9900	9898	9895	9893	9890	9888	9885	9882	9880	0	1	1	2	2
9	.9877	9874	9871	9869	9866	9863	9860	9857	9854	9851	0	1	1	2	2
10	.9848	9845	9842	9839	9836	9833	9829	9826	9823	9820	1	1	2	2	3
11	.9816	9813	9810	9806	9803	9799	9796	9792	9789	9785	1	1	2	2	3
12	.9781	9778	9774	9770	9767	9763	9759	9755	9751	9748	1	1	2	3	3
13	.9744	9740	9736	9732	9728	9724	9720	9715	9711	9707	1	1	2	3	3
14	.9703	9699	9694	9690	9686	9681	9677	9673	9668	9664	1	1	2	3	4
15	.9659	9655	9650	9646	9641	9636	9632	9627	9622	9617	1	2	2	3	4
16	.9613	9608	9603	9598	9593	9588	9583	9578	9573	9568	1	2	2	3	4
17	.9563	9558	9553	9548	9542	9537	9532	9527	9521	9516	1	2	3	3	4
18	.9511	9505	9500	9494	9489	9483	9478	9472	9466	9461	1	2	3	4	5
19	.9455	9449	9444	9438	9432	9426	9421	9415	9409	9403	1	2	3	4	5
20	.9397	9391	9385	9379	9373	9367	9361	9354	9348	9342	1	2	3	4	5
21	.9336	9330	9323	9317	9311	9304	9298	9291	9285	9278	1	2	3	4	5
22	.9272	9265	9259	9252	9245	9239	9232	9225	9219	9212	1	2	3	4	6
23	.9205	9198	9191	9184	9178	9171	9164	9157	9150	9143	1	2	3	5	6
24	.9135	9128	9121	9114	9107	9100	9092	9085	9078	9070	1	2	4	5	6
25	.9063	9056	9048	9041	9033	9026	9018	9011	9003	8996	1	3	4	5	6
26	.8988	8980	8973	8965	8957	8949	8942	8934	8926	8918	1	3	4	5	6
27	.8910	8902	8894	8886	8878	8870	8862	8854	8846	8838	1	3	4	5	7
28	.8829	8821	8813	8805	8796	8788	8780	8771	8763	8755	1	3	4	6	7
29	.8746	8738	8729	8721	8712	8704	8695	8686	8678	8669	1	3	4	6	7
30	.8660	8652	8643	8634	8625	8616	8607	8599	8590	8581	1	3	4	6	7
31	.8572	8563	8554	8545	8536	8526	8517	8508	8499	8490	2	3	5	6	8
32	.8480	8471	8462	8453	8443	8434	8425	8415	8406	8396	2	3	5	6	8
33	.8387	8377	8368	8358	8348	8339	8329	8320	8310	8300	2	3	5	6	8
34	.8290	8281	8271	8261	8251	8241	8231	8221	8211	8202	2	3	5	7	8
35	.8192	8181	8171	8161	8151	8141	8131	8121	8111	8100	2	3	5	7	8
36	.8090	8080	8070	8059	8049	8039	8028	8018	8007	7997	2	3	5	7	9
37	.7986	7976	7965	7955	7944	7934	7923	7912	7902	7891	2	4	5	7	9
38	.7880	7869	7859	7848	7837	7826	7815	7804	7793	7782	2	4	5	7	9
39	.7771	7760	7749	7738	7727	7716	7705	7694	7683	7672	2	4	6	7	9
40	.7660	7649	7638	7627	7615	7604	7593	7581	7570	7559	2	4	6	8	9
41	.7547	7536	7524	7513	7501	7490	7478	7466	7455	7443	2	4	6	8	10
42	.7431	7420	7408	7396	7385	7373	7361	7349	7337	7325	2	4	6	8	10
43	.7314	7302	7290	7278	7266	7254	7242	7230	7218	7206	2	4	6	8	10
44	.7193	7181	7169	7157	7145	7133	7120	7108	7096	7083	2	4	6	8	10

Number in difference columns to be subtracted, not added.

NATURAL COSINES

Degrees	0′ 0°.0	6′ 0°.1	12′ 0°.2	18′ 0°.3	24′ 0°.4	30′ 0°.5	36′ 0°.6	42′ 0°.7	48′ 0°.8	54′ 0°.9	Mean differences 1	2	3	4	5
45	.7071	7059	7046	7034	7022	7009	6997	6984	6972	6959	2	4	6	8	10
46	.6947	6934	6921	6909	6896	6884	6871	6858	6845	6833	2	4	6	8	11
47	.6820	6807	6794	6782	6769	6756	6743	6730	6717	6704	2	4	6	9	11
48	.6691	6678	6665	6652	6639	6626	6613	6600	6587	6574	2	4	7	9	11
49	.6561	6547	6534	6521	6508	6494	6481	6468	6455	6441	2	4	7	9	11
50	.6428	6414	6401	6388	6374	6361	6347	6334	6320	6307	2	4	7	9	11
51	.6293	6280	6266	6252	6239	6225	6211	6198	6184	6170	2	5	7	9	11
52	.6157	6143	6129	6115	6101	6088	6074	6060	6046	6032	2	5	7	9	12
53	.6018	6004	5990	5976	5962	5948	5934	5920	5906	5892	2	5	7	9	12
54	.5878	5864	5850	5835	5821	5807	5793	5779	5764	5750	2	5	7	9	12
55	.5736	5721	5707	5693	5678	5664	5650	5635	5621	5606	2	5	7	10	12
56	.5592	5577	5563	5548	5534	5519	5505	5490	5476	5461	2	5	7	10	12
57	.5446	5432	5417	5402	5388	5373	5358	5344	5329	5314	2	5	7	10	12
58	.5299	5284	5270	5255	5240	5225	5210	5195	5180	5165	2	5	7	10	12
59	.5150	5135	5120	5105	5090	5075	5060	5045	5030	5015	3	5	8	10	13
60	.5000	4985	4970	4955	4939	4924	4909	4894	4879	4863	3	5	8	10	13
61	.4848	4833	4818	4802	4787	4772	4756	4741	4726	4710	3	5	8	10	13
62	.4695	4679	4664	4648	4633	4617	4602	4586	4571	4555	3	5	8	10	13
63	.4540	4524	4509	4493	4478	4462	4446	4431	4415	4399	3	5	8	10	13
64	.4384	4368	4352	4337	4321	4305	4289	4274	4258	4242	3	5	8	11	13
65	.4226	4210	4195	4179	4163	4147	4131	4115	4099	4083	3	5	8	11	13
66	.4067	4051	4035	4019	4003	3987	3971	3955	3939	3923	3	5	8	11	14
67	.3907	3891	3875	3859	3843	3827	3811	3795	3778	3762	3	5	8	11	14
68	.3746	3730	3714	3697	3681	3665	3649	3633	3616	3600	3	5	8	11	14
69	.3584	3567	3551	3535	3518	3502	3486	3469	3453	3437	3	5	8	11	14
70	.3420	3404	3387	3371	3355	3338	3322	3305	3289	3272	3	5	8	11	14
71	.3256	3239	3223	3206	3190	3173	3156	3140	3123	3107	3	6	8	11	14
72	.3090	3074	3057	3040	3024	3007	2990	2974	2957	2940	3	6	8	11	14
73	.2924	2907	2890	2874	2857	2840	2823	2807	2790	2773	3	6	8	11	14
74	.2756	2740	2723	2706	2689	2672	2656	2639	2622	2605	3	6	8	11	14
75	.2588	2571	2554	2538	2521	2504	2487	2470	2453	2436	3	6	8	11	14
76	.2419	2402	2385	2368	2351	2334	2317	2300	2284	2267	3	6	8	11	14
77	.2250	2233	2215	2198	2181	2164	2147	2130	2113	2096	3	6	9	11	14
78	.2079	2062	2045	2028	2011	1994	1977	1959	1942	1925	3	6	9	11	14
79	.1908	1891	1874	1857	1840	1822	1805	1788	1771	1754	3	6	9	11	14
80	.1736	1719	1702	1685	1668	1650	1633	1616	1599	1582	3	6	9	12	14
81	.1564	1547	1530	1513	1495	1478	1461	1444	1426	1409	3	6	9	12	14
82	.1392	1374	1357	1340	1323	1305	1288	1271	1253	1236	3	6	9	12	14
83	.1219	1201	1184	1167	1149	1132	1115	1097	1080	1063	3	6	9	12	14
84	.1045	1028	1011	0993	0976	0958	0941	0924	0906	0889	3	6	9	12	14
85	.0872	0854	0837	0819	0802	0785	0767	0750	0732	0715	3	6	9	12	15
86	.0698	0680	0663	0645	0628	0610	0593	0576	0558	0541	3	6	9	12	15
87	.0523	0506	0488	0471	0454	0436	0419	0401	0384	0366	3	6	9	12	15
88	.0349	0332	0314	0297	0279	0262	0244	0227	0209	0192	3	6	9	12	15
89	.0175	0157	0140	0122	0105	0087	0070	0052	0035	0017	3	6	9	12	15
90	.0000														

Number in difference columns to be subtracted, not added.

NATURAL TANGENTS

Degrees	0' 0°.0	6' 0°.1	12' 0°.2	18' 0°.3	24' 0°.4	30' 0°.5	36' 0°.6	42' 0°.7	48' 0°.8	54' 0°.9	Mean differences				
											1	2	3	4	5
0	.0000	0017	0035	0052	0070	0087	0105	0122	0140	0157	3	6	9	12	15
1	.0175	0192	0209	0227	0244	0262	0279	0297	0314	0332	3	6	9	12	15
2	.0349	0367	0384	0402	0419	0437	0454	0472	0489	0507	3	6	9	12	15
3	.0524	0542	0559	0577	0594	0612	0629	0647	0664	0682	3	6	9	12	15
4	.0699	0717	0734	0752	0769	0787	0805	0822	0840	0857	3	6	9	12	15
5	.0875	0892	0910	0928	0945	0963	0981	0998	1016	1033	3	6	9	12	15
6	.1051	1069	1086	1104	1122	1139	1157	1175	1192	1210	3	6	9	12	15
7	.1228	1246	1263	1281	1299	1317	1334	1352	1370	1388	3	6	9	12	15
8	.1405	1423	1441	1459	1477	1495	1512	1530	1548	1566	3	6	9	12	15
9	.1584	1602	1620	1638	1655	1673	1691	1709	1727	1745	3	6	9	12	15
10	.1763	1781	1799	1817	1835	1853	1871	1890	1908	1926	3	6	9	12	15
11	.1944	1962	1980	1998	2016	2035	2053	2071	2089	2107	3	6	9	12	15
12	.2126	2144	2162	2180	2199	2217	2235	2254	2272	2290	3	6	9	12	15
13	.2309	2327	2345	2364	2382	2401	2419	2438	2456	2475	3	6	9	12	15
14	.2493	2512	2530	2549	2568	2586	2605	2623	2642	2661	3	6	9	12	16
15	.2679	2698	2717	2736	2754	2773	2792	2811	2830	2849	3	6	9	13	16
16	.2867	2886	2905	2924	2943	2962	2981	3000	3019	3038	3	6	9	13	16
17	.3057	3076	3096	3115	3134	3153	3172	3191	3211	3230	3	6	10	13	16
18	.3249	3269	3288	3307	3327	3346	3365	3385	3404	3424	3	6	10	13	16
19	.3443	3463	3482	3502	3522	3541	3561	3581	3600	3620	3	7	10	13	16
20	.3640	3659	3679	3699	3719	3739	3759	3779	3799	3819	3	7	10	13	17
21	.3839	3859	3879	3899	3919	3939	3959	3979	4000	4020	3	7	10	13	17
22	.4040	4061	4081	4101	4122	4142	4163	4183	4204	4224	3	7	10	14	17
23	.4245	4265	4286	4307	4327	4348	4369	4390	4411	4431	3	7	10	14	17
24	.4452	4473	4494	4515	4536	4557	4578	4599	4621	4642	4	7	11	14	18
25	.4663	4684	4706	4727	4748	4770	4791	4813	4834	4856	4	7	11	14	18
26	.4877	4899	4921	4942	4964	4986	5008	5029	5051	5073	4	7	11	15	18
27	.5095	5117	5139	5161	5184	5206	5228	5250	5272	5295	4	7	11	15	18
28	.5317	5340	5362	5384	5407	5430	5452	5475	5498	5520	4	8	11	15	19
29	.5543	5566	5589	5612	5635	5658	5681	5704	5727	5750	4	8	12	15	19
30	.5774	5797	5820	5844	5867	5890	5914	5938	5961	5985	4	8	12	16	20
31	.6009	6032	6056	6080	6104	6128	6152	6176	6200	6224	4	8	12	16	20
32	.6249	6273	6297	6322	6346	6371	6395	6420	6445	6469	4	8	12	16	20
33	.6494	6519	6544	6569	6594	6619	6644	6669	6694	6720	4	8	13	17	21
34	.6745	6771	6796	6822	6847	6873	6899	6924	6950	6976	4	9	13	17	21
35	.7002	7028	7054	7080	7107	7133	7159	7186	7212	7239	4	9	13	18	22
36	.7265	7292	7319	7346	7373	7400	7427	7454	7481	7508	5	9	14	18	23
37	.7536	7563	7590	7618	7646	7673	7701	7729	7757	7785	5	9	14	18	23
38	.7813	7841	7869	7898	7926	7954	7983	8012	8040	8069	5	9	14	19	24
39	.8098	8127	8156	8185	8214	8243	8273	8302	8332	8361	5	10	15	20	24
40	.8391	8421	8451	8481	8511	8541	8571	8601	8632	8662	5	10	15	20	25
41	.8693	8724	8754	8785	8816	8847	8878	8910	8941	8972	5	10	16	21	26
42	.9004	9036	9067	9099	9131	9163	9195	9228	9260	9293	5	11	16	21	27
43	.9325	9358	9391	9424	9457	9490	9523	9556	9590	9623	6	11	17	22	28
44	.9657	9691	9725	9759	9793	9827	9861	9896	9930	9965	6	11	17	23	29

NATURAL TANGENTS

Degrees	0' 0°.0	6' 0°.1	12' 0°.2	18' 0°.3	24' 0°.4	30' 0°.5	36' 0°.6	42' 0°.7	48' 0°.8	54' 0°.9	Mean differences				
											1	2	3	4	5
45	1.0000	0035	0070	0105	0141	0176	0212	0247	0283	0319	6	12	18	24	30
46	1.0355	0392	0428	0464	0501	0538	0575	0612	0649	0686	6	12	18	25	31
47	1.0724	0761	0799	0837	0875	0913	0951	0990	1028	1067	6	13	19	25	32
48	1.1106	1145	1184	1224	1263	1303	1343	1383	1423	1463	7	13	20	27	33
49	1.1504	1544	1585	1626	1667	1708	1750	1792	1833	1875	7	14	21	28	34
50	1.1918	1960	2002	2045	2088	2131	2174	2218	2261	2305	7	14	22	29	36
51	1.2349	2393	2437	2482	2527	2572	2617	2662	2708	2753	8	15	23	30	38
52	1.2799	2846	2892	2938	2985	3032	3079	3127	3175	3222	8	16	24	31	39
53	1.3270	3319	3367	3416	3465	3514	3564	3613	3663	3713	8	16	25	33	41
54	1.3764	3814	3865	3916	3968	4019	4071	4124	4176	4229	9	17	26	34	43
55	1.4281	4335	4388	4442	4496	4550	4605	4659	4715	4770	9	18	27	36	45
56	1.4826	4882	4938	4994	5051	5108	5166	5224	5282	5340	10	19	29	38	48
57	1.5399	5458	5517	5577	5637	5697	5757	5818	5880	5941	10	20	30	40	50
58	1.6003	6066	6128	6191	6255	6319	6383	6447	6512	6577	11	21	32	43	53
59	1.6643	6709	6775	6842	6909	6977	7045	7113	7182	7251	11	23	34	45	56
60	1.7321	7391	7461	7532	7603	7675	7747	7820	7893	7966	12	24	36	48	60
61	1.8040	8115	8190	8265	8341	8418	8495	8572	8650	8728	13	26	38	51	64
62	1.8807	8887	8967	9047	9128	9210	9292	9375	9458	9542	14	27	41	55	68
63	1.9626	9711	9797	9883	9970	2.0057	2.0145	2.0233	2.0323	2.0413	15	29	44	58	73
64	2.0503	0594	0686	0778	0872	0965	1060	1155	1251	1348	16	31	47	63	78
65	2.1445	1543	1642	1742	1842	1943	2045	2148	2251	2355	17	34	51	67	85
66	2.2460	2566	2673	2781	2889	2998	3109	3220	3332	3445	18	37	55	73	92
67	2.3559	3673	3789	3906	4023	4142	4262	4383	4504	4627	20	40	60	79	99
68	2.4751	4876	5002	5129	5257	5386	5517	5649	5782	5916	22	43	65	87	108
69	2.6051	6187	6325	6464	6605	6746	6889	7034	7179	7326	24	47	71	95	119
70	2.7475	7625	7776	7929	8083	8239	8397	8556	8716	8878	26	52	78	104	131
71	2.9042	9208	9375	9544	9714	9887	3.0061	3.0237	3.0415	3.0595	29	58	87	116	145
72	3.0777	0961	1146	1334	1524	1716	1910	2106	2305	2506	32	64	96	129	161
73	3.2709	2914	3122	3332	3544	3759	3977	4197	4420	4646	36	72	108	144	180
74	3.4874	5105	5339	5576	5816	6059	6305	6554	6806	7062	41	81	122	163	204
75	3.7321	7583	7848	8118	8391	8667	8947	9232	9520	9812	46	93	139	186	232
76	4.0108	0408	0713	1022	1335	1653	1976	2303	2635	2972	53	107	160	213	267
77	4.3315	3662	4015	4373	4737	5107	5483	5864	6252	6646					
78	4.7046	7453	7867	8288	8716	9152	9594	5.0045	5.0504	5.0970					
79	5.1446	1929	2422	2924	3435	3955	4486	5026	5578	6140					
80	5.6713	7297	7894	8502	9124	9758	6.0405	6.1066	6.1742	6.2432					
81	6.3138	3859	4596	5350	6122	6912	7720	8548	9395	7.0264	Mean differences cease				
82	7.1154	2066	3002	3962	4947	5958	6996	8062	9158	8.0285	to be sufficiently				
83	8.1443	2636	3863	5126	6427	7769	9152	9.0579	9.2052	9.3572	accurate.				
84	9.5144	9.6768	9.845	10.02	10.20	10.39	10.58	10.78	10.99	11.20					
85	11.43	11.66	11.91	12.16	12.43	12.71	13.00	13.30	13.62	13.95					
86	14.31	14.67	15.06	15.46	15.89	16.35	16.83	17.34	17.89	18.46					
87	19.08	19.74	20.45	21.20	22.02	22.90	23.86	24.90	26.03	27.27					
88	28.64	30.14	31.82	33.69	35.80	38.19	40.92	44.07	47.74	52.08					
89	57.29	63.66	71.62	81.85	95.49	114.6	143.2	191.0	286.5	573.0					
90	∞														

LOGARITHMS OF SINES

Degrees	0' 0°.0	6' 0°.1	12' 0°.2	18' 0°.3	24' 0°.4	30' 0°.5	36' 0°.6	42' 0°.7	48' 0°.8	54' 0°.9	1	2	3	4	5
0	−∞	$\bar{3}$.2419	5429	7190	8439	9408	$\bar{2}$.0200	$\bar{2}$.0870	$\bar{2}$.1450	$\bar{2}$.1961					
1	$\bar{2}$.2419	2832	3210	3558	3880	4179	4459	4723	4971	5206					
2	$\bar{2}$.5428	5640	5842	6035	6220	6397	6567	6731	6889	7041					
3	$\bar{2}$.7188	7330	7468	7602	7731	7857	7979	8098	8213	8326					
4	$\bar{2}$.8436	8543	8647	8749	8849	8946	9042	9135	9226	9315	16	32	48	64	80
5	$\bar{2}$.9403	9489	9573	9655	9736	9816	9894	9970	$\bar{1}$.0046	$\bar{1}$.0120	13	26	39	52	65
6	$\bar{1}$.0192	0264	0334	0403	0472	0539	0605	0670	0734	0797	11	22	34	44	55
7	$\bar{1}$.0859	0920	0981	1040	1099	1157	1214	1271	1326	1381	10	19	29	38	48
8	$\bar{1}$.1436	1489	1542	1594	1646	1697	1747	1797	1847	1895	8	17	25	34	42
9	$\bar{1}$.1943	1991	2038	2085	2131	2176	2221	2266	2310	2353	8	15	23	30	38
10	$\bar{1}$.2397	2439	2482	2524	2565	2606	2647	2687	2727	2767	7	14	20	27	34
11	$\bar{1}$.2806	2845	2883	2921	2959	2997	3034	3070	3107	3143	6	12	19	25	31
12	$\bar{1}$.3179	3214	3250	3284	3319	3353	3387	3421	3455	3488	6	11	17	23	28
13	$\bar{1}$.3521	3554	3586	3618	3650	3682	3713	3745	3775	3806	5	11	16	21	26
14	$\bar{1}$.3837	3867	3897	3927	3957	3986	4015	4044	4073	4102	5	10	15	20	24
15	$\bar{1}$.4130	4158	4186	4214	4242	4269	4296	4323	4350	4377	5	9	14	18	23
16	$\bar{1}$.4403	4430	4456	4482	4508	4533	4559	4584	4609	4634	4	9	13	17	21
17	$\bar{1}$.4659	4684	4709	4733	4757	4781	4805	4829	4853	4876	4	8	12	16	20
18	$\bar{1}$.4900	4923	4946	4969	4992	5015	5037	5060	5082	5104	4	8	11	15	19
19	$\bar{1}$.5126	5148	5170	5192	5213	5235	5256	5278	5299	5320	4	7	11	14	18
20	$\bar{1}$.5341	5361	5382	5402	5423	5443	5463	5484	5504	5523	3	7	10	14	17
21	$\bar{1}$.5543	5563	5583	5602	5621	5641	5660	5679	5698	5717	3	6	10	13	16
22	$\bar{1}$.5736	5754	5773	5792	5810	5828	5847	5865	5883	5901	3	6	9	12	15
23	$\bar{1}$.5919	5937	5954	5972	5990	6007	6024	6042	6059	6076	3	6	9	12	15
24	$\bar{1}$.6093	6110	6127	6144	6161	6177	6194	6210	6227	6243	3	6	8	11	14
25	$\bar{1}$.6259	6276	6292	6308	6324	6340	6356	6371	6387	6403	3	5	8	11	13
26	$\bar{1}$.6418	6434	6449	6465	6480	6495	6510	6526	6541	6556	3	5	8	10	13
27	$\bar{1}$.6570	6585	6600	6615	6629	6644	6659	6673	6687	6702	2	5	7	10	12
28	$\bar{1}$.6716	6730	6744	6759	6773	6787	6801	6814	6828	6842	2	5	7	9	12
29	$\bar{1}$.6856	6869	6883	6896	6910	6923	6937	6950	6963	6977	2	4	7	9	11
30	$\bar{1}$.6990	7003	7016	7029	7042	7055	7068	7080	7093	7106	2	4	6	9	11
31	$\bar{1}$.7118	7131	7144	7156	7168	7181	7193	7205	7218	7230	2	4	6	8	10
32	$\bar{1}$.7242	7254	7266	7278	7290	7302	7314	7326	7338	7349	2	4	6	8	10
33	$\bar{1}$.7361	7373	7384	7396	7407	7419	7430	7442	7453	7464	2	4	6	8	10
34	$\bar{1}$.7476	7487	7498	7509	7520	7531	7542	7553	7564	7575	2	4	6	7	9
35	$\bar{1}$.7586	7597	7607	7618	7629	7640	7650	7661	7671	7682	2	4	5	7	9
36	$\bar{1}$.7692	7703	7713	7723	7734	7744	7754	7764	7774	7785	2	3	5	7	9
37	$\bar{1}$.7795	7805	7815	7825	7835	7844	7854	7864	7874	7884	2	3	5	7	8
38	$\bar{1}$.7893	7903	7913	7922	7932	7941	7951	7960	7970	7979	2	3	5	6	8
39	$\bar{1}$.7989	7998	8007	8017	8026	8035	8044	8053	8063	8072	2	3	5	6	8
40	$\bar{1}$.8081	8090	8099	8108	8117	8125	8134	8143	8152	8161	1	3	4	6	7
41	$\bar{1}$.8169	8178	8187	8195	8204	8213	8221	8230	8238	8247	1	3	4	6	7
42	$\bar{1}$.8255	8264	8272	8280	8289	8297	8305	8313	8322	8330	1	3	4	6	7
43	$\bar{1}$.8338	8346	8354	8362	8370	8378	8386	8394	8402	8410	1	3	4	5	7
44	1.8418	8426	8433	8441	8449	8457	8464	8472	8480	8487	1	3	4	5	6

Mean differences span columns 1–5.

LOGARITHMS OF SINES

Degrees	0' 0°.0	6' 0°.1	12' 0°.2	18' 0°.3	24' 0°.4	30' 0°.5	36' 0°.6	42' 0°.7	48' 0°.8	54' 0°.9	Mean differences 1	2	3	4	5
45	$\overline{1}$.8495	8502	8510	8517	8525	8532	8540	8547	8555	8562	1	2	4	5	6
46	$\overline{1}$.8569	8577	8584	8591	8598	8606	8613	8620	8627	8634	1	2	4	5	6
47	$\overline{1}$.8641	8648	8655	8662	8669	8676	8683	8690	8697	8704	1	2	3	5	6
48	$\overline{1}$.8711	8718	8724	8731	8738	8745	8751	8758	8765	8771	1	2	3	4	6
49	$\overline{1}$.8778	8784	8791	8797	8804	8810	8817	8823	8830	8836	1	2	3	4	5
50	$\overline{1}$.8843	8849	8855	8862	8868	8874	8880	8887	8893	8899	1	2	3	4	5
51	$\overline{1}$.8905	8911	8917	8923	8929	8935	8941	8947	8953	8959	1	2	3	4	5
52	$\overline{1}$.8965	8971	8977	8983	8989	8995	9000	9006	9012	9018	1	2	3	4	5
53	$\overline{1}$.9023	9029	9035	9041	9046	9052	9057	9063	9069	9074	1	2	3	4	5
54	$\overline{1}$.9080	9085	9091	9096	9101	9107	9112	9118	9123	9128	1	2	3	4	5
55	$\overline{1}$.9134	9139	9144	9149	9155	9160	9165	9170	9175	9181	1	2	3	3	4
56	$\overline{1}$.9186	9191	9196	9201	9206	9211	9216	9221	9226	9231	1	2	3	3	4
57	$\overline{1}$.9236	9241	9246	9251	9255	9260	9265	9270	9275	9279	1	2	2	3	4
58	$\overline{1}$.9284	9289	9294	9298	9303	9308	9312	9317	9322	9326	1	2	2	3	4
59	$\overline{1}$.9331	9335	9340	9344	9349	9353	9358	9362	9367	9371	1	1	2	3	4
60	$\overline{1}$.9375	9380	9384	9388	9393	9397	9401	9406	9410	9414	1	1	2	3	4
61	$\overline{1}$.9418	9422	9427	9431	9435	9439	9443	9447	9451	9455	1	1	2	3	3
62	$\overline{1}$.9459	9463	9467	9471	9475	9479	9483	9487	9491	9495	1	1	2	3	3
63	$\overline{1}$.9499	9503	9506	9510	9514	9518	9522	9525	9529	9533	1	1	2	3	3
64	$\overline{1}$.9537	9540	9544	9548	9551	9555	9558	9562	9566	9569	1	1	2	2	3
65	$\overline{1}$.9573	9576	9580	9583	9587	9590	9594	9597	9601	9604	1	1	2	2	3
66	$\overline{1}$.9607	9611	9614	9617	9621	9624	9627	9631	9634	9637	1	1	2	2	3
67	$\overline{1}$.9640	9643	9647	9650	9653	9656	9659	9662	9666	9669	1	1	2	2	3
68	$\overline{1}$.9672	9675	9678	9681	9684	9687	9690	9693	9696	9699	0	1	1	2	2
69	$\overline{1}$.9702	9704	9707	9710	9713	9716	9719	9722	9724	9727	0	1	1	2	2
70	$\overline{1}$.9730	9733	9735	9738	9741	9743	9746	9749	9751	9754	0	1	1	2	2
71	$\overline{1}$.9757	9759	9762	9764	9767	9770	9772	9775	9777	9780	0	1	1	2	2
72	$\overline{1}$.9782	9785	9787	9789	9792	9794	9797	9799	9801	9804	0	1	1	2	2
73	$\overline{1}$.9806	9808	9811	9813	9815	9817	9820	9822	9824	9826	0	1	1	2	2
74	$\overline{1}$.9828	9831	9833	9835	9837	9839	9841	9843	9845	9847	0	1	1	1	2
75	$\overline{1}$.9849	9851	9853	9855	9857	9859	9861	9863	9865	9867	0	1	1	1	2
76	$\overline{1}$.9869	9871	9873	9875	9876	9878	9880	9882	9884	9885	0	1	1	1	2
77	$\overline{1}$.9887	9889	9891	9892	9894	9896	9897	9899	9901	9902	0	1	1	1	1
78	$\overline{1}$.9904	9906	9907	9909	9910	9912	9913	9915	9916	9918	0	1	1	1	1
79	$\overline{1}$.9919	9921	9922	9924	9925	9927	9928	9929	9931	9932	0	0	1	1	1
80	$\overline{1}$.9934	9935	9936	9937	9939	9940	9941	9943	9944	9945	0	0	1	1	1
81	$\overline{1}$.9946	9947	9949	9950	9951	9952	9953	9954	9955	9956	0	0	1	1	1
82	$\overline{1}$.9958	9959	9960	9961	9962	9963	9964	9965	9966	9967	0	0	1	1	1
83	$\overline{1}$.9968	9968	9969	9970	9971	9972	9973	9974	9975	9975	0	0	0	1	1
84	$\overline{1}$.9976	9977	9978	9978	9979	9980	9981	9981	9982	9983	0	0	0	0	1
85	$\overline{1}$.9983	9984	9985	9985	9986	9987	9987	9988	9988	9989	0	0	0	0	0
86	$\overline{1}$.9989	9990	9990	9991	9991	9992	9992	9993	9993	9994	0	0	0	0	0
87	$\overline{1}$.9994	9994	9995	9995	9996	9996	9996	9996	9997	9997	0	0	0	0	0
88	$\overline{1}$.9997	9998	9998	9998	9998	9999	9999	9999	9999	9999	0	0	0	0	0
89	$\overline{1}$.9999	9999	0.0000	0000	0000	0000	0000	0000	0000	0000					
90	0.0000														

LOGARITHMS OF COSINES

Degrees	0′ 0°.0	6′ 0°.1	12′ 0°.2	18′ 0°.3	24′ 0°.4	30′ 0°.5	36′ 0°.6	42′ 0°.7	48′ 0°.8	54′ 0°.9	Mean differences				
											1	2	3	4	5
0	0.0000	0000	0000	0000	0000	0000	0000	0000	0000	1̄.9999	0	0	0	0	0
1	1̄.9999	9999	9999	9999	9999	9999	9998	9998	9998	9998	0	0	0	0	0
2	1̄.9997	9997	9997	9996	9996	9996	9996	9995	9995	9994	0	0	0	0	0
3	1̄.9994	9994	9993	9993	9992	9992	9991	9991	9990	9990	0	0	0	0	0
4	1̄.9989	9989	9988	9988	9987	9987	9986	9985	9985	9984	0	0	0	0	0
5	1̄.9983	9983	9982	9981	9981	9980	9979	9978	9978	9977	0	0	0	0	1
6	1̄.9976	9975	9975	9974	9973	9972	9971	9970	9969	9968	0	0	0	1	1
7	1̄.9968	9967	9966	9965	9964	9963	9962	9961	9960	9959	0	0	1	1	1
8	1̄.9958	9956	9955	9954	9953	9952	9951	9950	9949	9947	0	0	1	1	1
9	1̄.9946	9945	9944	9943	9941	9940	9939	9937	9936	9935	0	0	1	1	1
10	1̄.9934	9932	9931	9929	9928	9927	9925	9924	9922	9921	0	0	1	1	1
11	1̄.9919	9918	9916	9915	9913	9912	9910	9909	9907	9906	0	1	1	1	1
12	1̄.9904	9902	9901	9899	9897	9896	9894	9892	9891	9889	0	1	1	1	1
13	1̄.9887	9885	9884	9882	9880	9878	9876	9875	9873	9871	0	1	1	1	2
14	1̄.9869	9867	9865	9863	9861	9859	9857	9855	9853	9851	0	1	1	1	2
15	1̄.9849	9847	9845	9843	9841	9839	9837	9835	9833	9831	0	1	1	1	2
16	1̄.9828	9826	9824	9822	9820	9817	9815	9813	9811	9808	0	1	1	2	2
17	1̄.9806	9804	9801	9799	9797	9794	9792	9789	9787	9785	0	1	1	2	2
18	1̄.9782	9780	9777	9775	9772	9770	9767	9764	9762	9759	0	1	1	2	2
19	1̄.9757	9754	9751	9749	9746	9743	9741	9738	9735	9733	0	1	1	2	2
20	1̄.9730	9727	9724	9722	9719	9716	9713	9710	9707	9704	0	1	1	2	2
21	1̄.9702	9699	9696	9693	9690	9687	9684	9681	9678	9675	0	1	1	2	2
22	1̄.9672	9669	9666	9662	9659	9656	9653	9650	9647	9643	1	1	2	2	3
23	1̄.9640	9637	9634	9631	9627	9624	9621	9617	9614	9611	1	1	2	2	3
24	1̄.9607	9604	9601	9597	9594	9590	9587	9583	9580	9576	1	1	2	2	3
25	1̄.9573	9569	9566	9562	9558	9555	9551	9548	9544	9540	1	1	2	2	3
26	1̄.9537	9533	9529	9525	9522	9518	9514	9510	9506	9503	1	1	2	3	3
27	1̄.9499	9495	9491	9487	9483	9479	9475	9471	9467	9463	1	1	2	3	3
28	1̄.9459	9455	9451	9447	9443	9439	9435	9431	9427	9422	1	1	2	3	3
29	1̄.9418	9414	9410	9406	9401	9397	9393	9388	9384	9380	1	1	2	3	4
30	1̄.9375	9371	9367	9362	9358	9353	9349	9344	9340	9335	1	1	2	3	4
31	1̄.9331	9326	9322	9317	9312	9308	9303	9298	9294	9289	1	2	2	3	4
32	1̄.9284	9279	9275	9270	9265	9260	9255	9251	9246	9241	1	2	2	3	4
33	1̄.9236	9231	9226	9221	9216	9211	9206	9201	9196	9191	1	2	3	3	4
34	1̄.9186	9181	9175	9170	9165	9160	9155	9149	9144	9139	1	2	3	3	4
35	1̄.9134	9128	9123	9118	9112	9107	9101	9096	9091	9085	1	2	3	4	5
36	1̄.9080	9074	9069	9063	9057	9052	9046	9041	9035	9029	1	2	3	4	5
37	1̄.9023	9018	9012	9006	9000	8995	8989	8983	8977	8971	1	2	3	4	5
38	1̄.8965	8959	8953	8947	8941	8935	8929	8923	8917	8911	1	2	3	4	5
39	1̄.8905	8899	8893	8887	8880	8874	8868	8862	8855	8849	1	2	3	4	5
40	1̄.8843	8836	8830	8823	8817	8810	8804	8797	8791	8784	1	2	3	4	5
41	1̄.8778	8771	8765	8758	8751	8745	8738	8731	8724	8718	1	2	3	5	6
42	1̄.8711	8704	8697	8690	8683	8676	8669	8662	8655	8648	1	2	3	5	6
43	1̄.8641	8634	8627	8620	8613	8606	8598	8591	8584	8577	1	2	4	5	6
44	1.8569	8562	8555	8547	8540	8532	8525	8517	8510	8502	1	2	4	5	6

Numbers in difference columns to be subtracted, not added.

LOGARITHMS OF COSINES

Degrees	0' 0°.0	6' 0°.1	12' 0°.2	18' 0°.3	24' 0°.4	30' 0°.5	36' 0°.6	42' 0°.7	48' 0°.8	54' 0°.9	1	2	3	4	5
											Mean differences					
45	1̄.8495	8487	8480	8472	8464	8457	8449	8441	8433	8426	1	3	4	5	6
46	1̄.8418	8410	8402	8394	8386	8378	8370	8362	8354	8346	1	3	4	5	7
47	1̄.8338	8330	8322	8313	8305	8297	8289	8280	8272	8264	1	3	4	6	7
48	1̄.8255	8247	8238	8230	8221	8213	8204	8195	8187	8178	1	3	4	6	7
49	1̄.8169	8161	8152	8143	8134	8125	8117	8108	8099	8090	1	3	4	6	7
50	1̄.8081	8072	8063	8053	8044	8035	8026	8017	8007	7998	2	3	5	6	8
51	1̄.7989	7979	7970	7960	7951	7941	7932	7922	7913	7903	2	3	5	6	8
52	1̄.7893	7884	7874	7864	7854	7844	7835	7825	7815	7805	2	3	5	7	8
53	1̄.7795	7785	7774	7764	7754	7744	7734	7723	7713	7703	2	3	5	7	9
54	1̄.7692	7682	7671	7661	7650	7640	7629	7618	7607	7597	2	4	5	7	9
55	1̄.7586	7575	7564	7553	7542	7531	7520	7509	7498	7487	2	4	6	7	9
56	1̄.7476	7464	7453	7442	7430	7419	7407	7396	7384	7373	2	4	6	8	10
57	1̄.7361	7349	7338	7326	7314	7302	7290	7278	7266	7254	2	4	6	8	10
58	1̄.7242	7230	7218	7205	7193	7181	7168	7156	7144	7131	2	4	6	8	10
59	1̄.7118	7106	7093	7080	7068	7055	7042	7029	7016	7003	2	4	6	9	11
60	1̄.6990	6977	6963	6950	6937	6923	6910	6896	6883	6869	2	4	7	9	11
61	1̄.6856	6842	6828	6814	6801	6787	6773	6759	6744	6730	2	5	7	9	12
62	1̄.6716	6702	6687	6673	6659	6644	6629	6615	6600	6585	2	5	7	10	12
63	1̄.6570	6556	6541	6526	6510	6495	6480	6465	6449	6434	3	5	8	10	13
64	1̄.6418	6403	6387	6371	6356	6340	6324	6308	6292	6276	3	5	8	11	13
65	1̄.6259	6243	6227	6210	6194	6177	6161	6144	6127	6110	3	6	8	11	14
66	1̄.6093	6076	6059	6042	6024	6007	5990	5972	5954	5937	3	6	9	12	15
67	1̄.5919	5901	5883	5865	5847	5828	5810	5792	5773	5754	3	6	9	12	15
68	1̄.5736	5717	5698	5679	5660	5641	5621	5602	5583	5563	3	6	10	13	16
69	1̄.5543	5523	5504	5484	5463	5443	5423	5402	5382	5361	3	7	10	14	17
70	1̄.5341	5320	5299	5278	5256	5235	5213	5192	5170	5148	4	7	11	14	18
71	1̄.5126	5104	5082	5060	5037	5015	4992	4969	4946	4923	4	8	11	15	19
72	1̄.4900	4876	4853	4829	4805	4781	4757	4733	4709	4684	4	8	12	16	20
73	1̄.4659	4634	4609	4584	4559	4533	4508	4482	4456	4430	4	9	13	17	21
74	1̄.4403	4377	4350	4323	4296	4269	4242	4214	4186	4158	5	9	14	18	23
75	1̄.4130	4102	4073	4044	4015	3986	3957	3927	3897	3867	5	10	15	20	24
76	1̄.3837	3806	3775	3745	3713	3682	3650	3618	3586	3554	5	11	16	21	26
77	1̄.3521	3488	3455	3421	3387	3353	3319	3284	3250	3214	6	11	17	23	28
78	1̄.3179	3143	3107	3070	3034	2997	2959	2921	2883	2845	6	12	19	25	31
79	1̄.2806	2767	2727	2687	2647	2606	2565	2524	2482	2439	7	14	20	27	34
80	1̄.2397	2353	2310	2266	2221	2176	2131	2085	2038	1991	8	15	23	30	38
81	1̄.1943	1895	1847	1797	1747	1697	1646	1594	1542	1489	8	17	25	34	42
82	1̄.1436	1381	1326	1271	1214	1157	1099	1040	0981	0920	10	19	29	38	48
83	1̄.0859	0797	0734	0̄670	0̄605	0̄539	0̄472	0403	0̄334	0̄264	11	22	33	44	55
84	1.0192	0120	0046	2̄.9970	2̄.9894	2̄.9816	2̄.9736	2̄.9655	2̄.9573	2̄.9489	13	26	39	52	65
85	2̄.9403	9315	9226	9135	9042	8946	8849	8749	8647	8543	16	32	48	64	80
86	2̄.8436	8326	8213	8098	7979	7857	7731	7602	7468	7330					
87	2̄.7188	7041	6889	6731	6567	6397	6220	6035	5842	5640					
88	2̄.5428	5206	4971	4723	4459	4̄179	3̄880	3̄558	3̄210	2832					
89	2̄.2419	1961	1450	0870	0200	3̄.9408	3̄.8439	3̄.7190	3̄.5429	3̄.2419					
90	—∞														

Numbers in difference columns to be subtracted, not added.

LOGARITHMS OF TANGENTS

Degrees	0′ 0°.0	6′ 0°.1	12′ 0°.2	18′ 0°.3	24′ 0°.4	30′ 0°.5	36′ 0°.6	42′ 0°.7	48′ 0°.8	54′ 0°.9	1	2	3	4	5
0	$-\infty$	$\bar{3}$.2419	$\bar{3}$.5429	$\bar{3}$.7190	$\bar{3}$.8439	$\bar{3}$.9409	$\bar{2}$.0200	$\bar{2}$.0870	$\bar{2}$.1450	$\bar{2}$.1962					
1	$\bar{2}$.2419	2833	3211	3559	3881	4181	4461	4725	4973	5208					
2	$\bar{2}$.5431	5643	5845	6038	6223	6401	6571	6736	6894	7046					
3	$\bar{2}$.7194	7337	7475	7609	7739	7865	7988	8107	8223	8336					
4	$\bar{2}$.8446	8554	8659	8762	8862	8960	9056	9150	9241	9331	16	32	48	64	81
5	$\bar{2}$.9420	9506	9591	9674	9756	9836	9915	9992	$\bar{1}$.0068	$\bar{1}$.0143	13	26	40	53	66
6	$\bar{1}$.0216	0289	0360	0430	0499	0567	0633	0699	0764	0828	11	22	34	45	56
7	$\bar{1}$.0891	0954	1015	1076	1135	1194	1252	1310	1367	1423	10	20	29	39	49
8	$\bar{1}$.1478	1533	1587	1640	1693	1745	1797	1848	1898	1948	9	17	26	35	43
9	$\bar{1}$.1997	2046	2094	2142	2189	2236	2282	2328	2374	2419	8	16	23	31	39
10	$\bar{1}$.2463	2507	2551	2594	2637	2680	2722	2764	2805	2846	7	14	21	28	35
11	$\bar{1}$.2887	2927	2967	3006	3046	3085	3123	3162	3200	3237	6	13	19	26	32
12	$\bar{1}$.3275	3312	3349	3385	3422	3458	3493	3529	3564	3599	6	12	18	24	30
13	$\bar{1}$.3634	3668	3702	3736	3770	3804	3837	3870	3903	3935	6	11	17	22	28
14	$\bar{1}$.3968	4000	4032	4064	4095	4127	4158	4189	4220	4250	5	10	16	21	26
15	$\bar{1}$.4281	4311	4341	4371	4400	4430	4459	4488	4517	4546	5	10	15	20	25
16	$\bar{1}$.4575	4603	4632	4660	4688	4716	4744	4771	4799	4826	5	9	14	19	23
17	$\bar{1}$.4853	4880	4907	4934	4961	4987	5014	5040	5066	5092	4	9	13	18	22
18	$\bar{1}$.5118	5143	5169	5195	5220	5245	5270	5295	5320	5345	4	8	13	17	21
19	$\bar{1}$.5370	5394	5419	5443	5467	5491	5516	5539	5563	5587	4	8	12	16	20
20	$\bar{1}$.5611	5634	5658	5681	5704	5727	5750	5773	5796	5819	4	8	12	15	19
21	$\bar{1}$.5842	5864	5887	5909	5932	5954	5976	5998	6020	6042	4	7	11	15	19
22	$\bar{1}$.6064	6086	6108	6129	6151	6172	6194	6215	6236	6257	4	7	11	14	18
23	$\bar{1}$.6279	6300	6321	6341	6362	6383	6404	6424	6445	6465	3	7	10	14	17
24	$\bar{1}$.6486	6506	6527	6547	6567	6587	6607	6627	6647	6667	3	7	10	13	17
25	$\bar{1}$.6687	6706	6726	6746	6765	6785	6804	6824	6843	6863	3	7	10	13	16
26	$\bar{1}$.6882	6901	6920	6939	6958	6977	6996	7015	7034	7053	3	6	9	13	16
27	$\bar{1}$.7072	7090	7109	7128	7146	7165	7183	7202	7220	7238	3	6	9	12	15
28	$\bar{1}$.7257	7275	7293	7311	7330	7348	7366	7384	7402	7420	3	6	9	12	15
29	$\bar{1}$.7438	7455	7473	7491	7509	7526	7544	7562	7579	7597	3	6	9	12	15
30	$\bar{1}$.7614	7632	7649	7667	7684	7701	7719	7736	7753	7771	3	6	9	12	14
31	$\bar{1}$.7788	7805	7822	7839	7856	7873	7890	7907	7924	7941	3	6	9	11	14
32	$\bar{1}$.7958	7975	7992	8008	8025	8042	8059	8075	8092	8109	3	6	8	11	14
33	$\bar{1}$.8125	8142	8158	8175	8191	8208	8224	8241	8257	8274	3	5	8	11	14
34	$\bar{1}$.8290	8306	8323	8339	8355	8371	8388	8404	8420	8436	3	5	8	11	14
35	$\bar{1}$.8452	8468	8484	8501	8517	8533	8549	8565	8581	8597	3	5	8	11	13
36	$\bar{1}$.8613	8629	8644	8660	8676	8692	8708	8724	8740	8755	3	5	8	11	13
37	$\bar{1}$.8771	8787	8803	8818	8834	8850	8865	8881	8897	8912	3	5	8	10	13
38	$\bar{1}$.8928	8944	8959	8975	8990	9006	9022	9037	9053	9068	3	5	8	10	13
39	$\bar{1}$.9084	9099	9115	9130	9146	9161	9176	9192	9207	9223	3	5	8	10	13
40	$\bar{1}$.9238	9254	9269	9284	9300	9315	9330	9346	9361	9376	3	5	8	10	13
41	$\bar{1}$.9392	9407	9422	9438	9453	9468	9483	9499	9514	9529	3	5	8	10	13
42	$\bar{1}$.9544	9560	9575	9590	9605	9621	9636	9651	9666	9681	3	5	8	10	13
43	$\bar{1}$.9697	9712	9727	9742	9757	9772	9788	9803	9818	9833	3	5	8	10	13
44	$\bar{1}$.9848	9864	9879	9894	9909	9924	9939	9955	9970	9985	3	5	8	10	13

LOGARITHMS OF TANGENTS

Degrees	0' 0°.0	6' 0°.1	12' 0°.2	18' 0°.3	24' 0°.4	30' 0°.5	36' 0°.6	42' 0°.7	48' 0°.8	54' 0°.9	Mean differences 1	2	3	4	5
45	.0001	0015	0030	0045	0061	0076	0091	0106	0121	0136	3	5	8	10	13
46	.0152	0167	0182	0197	0212	0228	0243	0258	0273	0288	3	5	8	10	13
47	.0303	0319	0334	0349	0364	0379	0395	0410	0425	0440	3	5	8	10	13
48	.0456	0471	0486	0501	0517	0532	0547	0562	0578	0593	3	5	8	10	13
49	.0608	0624	0639	0654	0670	0685	0700	0716	0731	0746	3	5	8	10	13
50	.0762	0777	0793	0808	0824	0839	0854	0870	0885	0901	3	5	8	10	13
51	.0916	0932	0947	0963	0978	0994	1010	1025	1041	1056	3	5	8	10	13
52	.1072	1088	1103	1119	1135	1150	1166	1182	1197	1213	3	5	8	10	13
53	.1229	1245	1260	1276	1292	1308	1324	1340	1356	1371	3	5	8	11	13
54	.1387	1403	1419	1435	1451	1467	1483	1499	1516	1532	3	5	8	11	13
55	.1548	1564	1580	1596	1612	1629	1645	1661	1677	1694	3	5	8	11	14
56	.1710	1726	1743	1759	1776	1792	1809	1825	1842	1858	3	5	8	11	14
57	.1875	1891	1908	1925	1941	1958	1975	1992	2008	2025	3	6	8	11	14
58	.2042	2059	2076	2093	2110	2127	2144	2161	2178	2195	3	6	9	11	14
59	.2212	2229	2247	2264	2281	2299	2316	2333	2351	2368	3	6	9	12	14
60	.2386	2403	2421	2438	2456	2474	2491	2509	2527	2545	3	6	9	12	15
61	.2562	2580	2598	2616	2634	2652	2670	2689	2707	2725	3	6	9	12	15
62	.2743	2762	2780	2798	2817	2835	2854	2872	2891	2910	3	6	9	12	15
63	.2928	2947	2966	2985	3004	3023	3042	3061	3080	3099	3	6	9	13	16
64	.3118	3137	3157	3176	3196	3215	3235	3254	3274	3294	3	6	10	13	16
65	.3313	3333	3353	3373	3393	3413	3433	3453	3473	3494	3	7	10	13	17
66	.3514	3535	3555	3576	3596	3617	3638	3659	3679	3700	3	7	10	14	17
67	.3721	3743	3764	3785	3806	3828	3849	3871	3892	3914	4	7	11	14	18
68	.3936	3958	3980	4002	4024	4046	4068	4091	4113	4136	4	7	11	15	19
69	.4158	4181	4204	4227	4250	4273	4296	4319	4342	4366	4	8	12	15	19
70	.4389	4413	4437	4461	4484	4509	4533	4557	4581	4606	4	8	12	16	20
71	.4630	4655	4680	4705	4730	4755	4780	4805	4831	4857	4	8	13	17	21
72	.4882	4908	4934	4960	4986	5013	5039	5066	5093	5120	4	9	13	18	22
73	.5147	5174	5201	5229	5256	5284	5312	5340	5368	5397	5	9	14	19	23
74	.5425	5454	5483	5512	5541	5570	5600	5629	5659	5689	5	10	15	20	25
75	.5719	5750	5780	5811	5842	5873	5905	5936	5968	6000	5	10	16	21	26
76	.6032	6065	6097	6130	6163	6196	6230	6264	6298	6332	6	11	17	22	28
77	.6366	6401	6436	6471	6507	6542	6578	6615	6651	6688	6	12	18	24	30
78	.6725	6763	6800	6838	6877	6915	6954	6994	7033	7073	6	13	19	26	32
79	.7113	7154	7195	7236	7278	7320	7363	7406	7449	7493	7	14	21	28	35
80	.7537	7581	7626	7672	7718	7764	7811	7858	7906	7954	8	16	23	31	39
81	.8003	8052	8102	8152	8203	8255	8307	8360	8413	8467	9	17	26	35	43
82	.8522	8577	8633	8690	8748	8806	8865	8924	8985	9046	10	20	29	39	49
83	.9109	9172	9236	9301	9367	9433	9501	9570	9640	9711	11	22	34	45	56
84	.9784	9857	9932	1.0008	1.0085	1.0164	1.0244	1.0326	1.0409	1.0494	13	26	40	53	66
85	1.0580	0669	0759	0850	0944	1040	1138	1238	1341	1446	16	32	48	64	81
86	1.1554	1664	1777	1893	2012	2135	2261	2391	2525	2663					
87	1.2806	2954	3106	3264	3429	3599	3777	3962	4155	4357					
88	1.4569	4792	5027	5275	5539	5819	6119	6441	6789	7167					
89	1.7581	8038	8550	9130	9800	2.0591	2.1561	2.2810	2.4571	2.7581					